2/02

THE CULTURE OF BUILDING

THE CULTURE OF BUILDING

HOWARD DAVIS

New York   Oxford

Oxford University Press

1999

Oxford University Press

Oxford   New York
Athens   Auckland   Bangkok   Bogotá   Buenos Aires   Calcutta
Cape Town   Chennai   Dar es Salaam   Delhi   Florence   Hong Kong   Istanbul
Karachi   Kuala Lumpur   Madrid   Melbourne   Mexico City   Mumbai
Nairobi   Paris   São Paulo   Singapore   Taipei   Tokyo   Toronto   Warsaw

and associated companies in
Berlin   Ibadan

Published by Oxford University Press, Inc.
198 Madison Avenue, New York, New York 10016

Oxford is a registered trademark of Oxford University Press

Publication of this book was supported by a grant from the
Graham Foundation for Advanced Studies in the Fine Arts.

Library of Congress Cataloging-in-Publication Data
Davis, Howard, 1948–
The culture of building / by Howard Davis.
p.   cm.
Includes bibliographical references and index.
ISBN 0-19-511294-6
1. Building.   2. Corporate culture.
3. Architecture and society.   I. Title.
TH153.D374   1999
720—dc21   98-19051

9 8 7 6 5 4 3 2 1
Printed in Hong Kong
on acid-free paper

To the memory of my father,
member of the New York City building trades

PREFACE

Myoshinji Temple, in Kyoto, is a place that for hundreds of years has harbored many traditional crafts, including carpentry, roof-tile manufacture, gardening, screen painting, plastering, metal work, bell casting, and others. The craftsmen who built it were working—and continue to work—within ancient traditions that embodied discipline and an insistence on perfection. As I write this, I am sitting at the edge of one of the temple's gardens, in a physical world of beauty and peace, an exemplar of one of the great traditions of world architecture.

Outside is modern Japan, and there can be few contrasts in the world that are more extreme. The world outside is one of bright lights, pachinko parlors and convenience stores, businessmen and skyscrapers, buildings trying to be as different from each other as possible. The people who built that world work within contemporary traditions of window manufacture, concrete prefabrication, steel erection, curtain wall assembly, mortgage finance.

A similar contrast exists in some form in most countries of the world, in which there are fundamental differences between traditional and contemporary systems of building production, linked to fundamental differences in the environments they produce. The world of traditional building is not a golden past that must be reattained. But if one believes, as I do, that the modern built environment is to a large extent brutal and alienating, and that traditional environments contained at least elements of human feeling and aesthetic sensibility, one is face-to-face with the question of understanding the past and traditional practice in ways that can shed light on improving the present.

This book was conceived through experiences that helped make me aware of the importance of the social contexts in which building happens, and how those contexts affect the built result. In professional work in different countries, I realized the importance of working in the framework of local systems and local competencies, instead of assuming that my knowledge was necessarily superior. In my travels I saw both the beauty of traditional architecture, and the ways it had been submerged by real cultural and economic forces, transformed into the ubiquitous concrete frame, re-bar, and concrete block buildings that have become the new global vernacular. Through much of this, I was trying to reconcile, in my teaching, the often conflicting needs for the quality of the individual building on the one hand and the improvement of the built world as a whole on the other—all the while listening to the frustrations of students about to enter a professional world in which such conflicts have not been resolved.

This book is an essay about the origins and potentials of contemporary building practice. It depends on cross-cultural comparisons rather than intensive studies of one or two cultures, and one of my intentions is to help break down intellectual barriers that have up until now prevented us from seeing the world of building as a whole. These barriers—between the vernacular and "high-style" architecture, between different cultural traditions, between tradition and innovation, between craftsmanship and technology, between architectural practice and building practice—are artificial creations that do not respect the complex human interactions that guide building activity. Any act of building is connected to all others, and its success depends ultimately upon improving the overall conditions of shared knowledge and human relationships on which the production of the built world depends.

I wrote this book in optimism and hope for the new century, as the quality of buildings and cities is re-emerging as a central responsibility and challenge.

I am grateful to the many people and organizations who have helped me with this book: to the Graham Foundation for Advanced Studies in the Fine Arts for a generous publication grant; the University of Texas at Austin for a summer grant that allowed me to research the ancient lights doctrine in London; to two offices of the University of Oregon—the Humanities Center for appointing me one of its first Humanities Fellows to develop a first draft of the book and the Office of Research and Sponsored Programs for two summer grants that allowed me to explore the building cultures of London and New York in the eighteenth and nineteenth centuries; and to Columbia University, which gave me visiting scholar status in 1996. Two department heads of the Department of Architecture at the University of Oregon, Donald Corner and Michael Utsey, have been generous with research leaves and have allowed me to teach courses on the material in this book.

Discussions with many people have helped me think through the ideas discussed here. David Week and I have had conversations in the four corners of the world about culture and building; Hajo Neis and I have discussed Japanese and German building practice and the question of how innovative ideas are implemented; Tom Kerr has been the most knowledgeable guide to modern Indian cities; John Rowell, Don Corner, Peter Keyes, and Rob Thallon have helped me understand contemporary building and planning practice and housing production. I have valued my connection to the Vernacular Architecture Forum, whose members have broadened the scope of scholarship in the field while maintaining the highest standards of quality.

Several colleagues were generous enough to read and comment on the entire manuscript: Chris Alexander, Greg Brokaw, Jyoti Hosagrahar, Peter Keyes, Hajo Neis, John Rowell, Nick Seemann, Rob Thallon, Glenda Utsey, and David Week. Jenny Young applied a perceptive literary and architectural eye to an edit of the final draft. Members of a graduate seminar at the University of Oregon read an early version and were as frank as they needed to be.

Many other people helped in large and small ways: John Anstey, Rasem Badran, Greg Burgess, Peter Clegg, Christie Coffin, Alvin Comiter, Ken Costigan, Philip Dole, Stephen Duff, Gail Feld, Jerry Finrow, Alan Forrest, Avi Friedman, Bill Gilland, Peter Ho, Joanne Hogarth, Aso Jaff, Ramzi Kawar, David Krawitz, Aaron Lamport, Paul Larson, Ron Lovinger, Andrew Morrogh, Brook Muller, Paul Oliver, Jorn Orum-Nielsen, the office of Patricia and John Patkau, Leland Roth; Dr. Shigemura, Tsutomu; Mimi Sullivan, Seishi Unuma, Ellen Weiss, and two anonymous reviewers for Oxford University Press. Donald Corner and Jenny Young have been the most loyal friends and knowing colleagues.

Graduate student research assistants have been particularly helpful: Linda Babetski, Lewis Chui, Decker Flynn, Stewart Green, Donald Harris, Ken Hutchinson, Ellen Linstead, and Corey Saft. Peter DeMaria drew the axonometrics in chapter 9. Kevin Sauser designed early versions of the page layouts and the simulation drawings of the Islamic city in chapter 9. Adam Sharkey was of great help with the selection of all the illustrations and in the final production of the manuscript. John Paull and Anup Janardhanan did many of the line drawings and diagrams.

Many archives allowed me the use of their collections. Special thanks are due to Mrs. Marie Draper, archivist for the Bedford Estate in London and at Woburn Abbey in Bedfordshire; Mireille Galinou, curator of the prints, paintings, and photographs collection of the Museum of London; Mary Beth Betts, architecture curator of the New-York Historical Society; and Sheila Klos, Architecture and Allied Arts Librarian at the University of Oregon.

My greatest help has come from Christopher Alexander, who wrote things a long time ago that resonated with me and who through his friendship, his own example, and numerous conversations about this book has challenged and inspired me for nearly twenty-five years. His help with the manuscript over the last year was critical in clarifying its intention and form. To a large extent, the book is an outgrowth of ideas that he has put forward and represents an attempt to ask questions about the social frameworks that might make possible the kinds of building processes, and the kinds of buildings that can enhance our lives, that he is working to achieve.

A Note on Language

Despite the fact that women have, over history, often taken a central role in the planning, construction, and use of buildings, before the final decades of the nineteenth century there were very few female architects in England or the United States; before the middle of the twentieth century there were very few female construction workers. The language used in this book reflects those facts. I have used terms like "craftsmen" and "tradesmen," and "he"/"his," referring to architects and building workers at times when they were virtually all men, and I have tried to use such words as "craftsperson," and to shift between female and male gender when such language would help to point up the slowly changing contemporary situation.

Eugene, Oregon   H. D.
October 16, 1998

CONTENTS

THE CULTURE OF BUILDING

INTRODUCTION

Two Billion Buildings

> In succession
> Houses rise and fall, crumble, are extended,
> Are removed, destroyed, restored, or in their place
> Is an open field, or a factory, or a by-pass.
> Old stone to new building, old timber to new fires,
> Old fires to ashes, and ashes to the earth . . .
>
> T. S. Eliot, "East Coker,"
> *Four Quartets*

The Built World

There are between *1 and 2 billion buildings* on the earth.[1] How did they come to be, and how can the knowledge of their origins help us improve buildings in the future?

This book argues that large-scale improvements to the built world do not depend solely on the individual acts of architects and city planners; instead, they depend largely on the gradual transformation of the *building culture*—the coordinated system of knowledge, rules, and procedures that is shared by people who participate in the building activity and that determines the form buildings and cities take.

Only recently has systematic exploration of the nature of the built world begun, along with the beginnings of a general understanding of *just how it comes to be the way it is*. We understand quite a bit about various components of this world, taken individually—about architectural styles, or the prices of building materials, or the history of zoning regulation, or the ways in which building plans have evolved hand in hand with social life, or how the craft economy was replaced by modern manufacturing, or the role building developers play in the emergence of land-use patterns.

What is lacking is a general framework of thought in which all of these things are related—a framework in which *the process of building production* as a

Figure I.1. View from the Empire State Building, 1984. There are over 800,000 buildings in New York City.

whole is understood in terms of the various components that make it up. Such a framework is needed, and not only from an academic point of view. The built world is not in very good shape, and the responsibility for this situation cannot be laid at the hand of any one profession. It is counterproductive to lay blame primarily on architects, or banks, or an uneducated public, or any one sector of society. Architects are right when they say that they are at the mercy of building codes and client committees and have no time to do a good job within available fees. Builders are right when they say that architects leave too much out of drawings. Ordinary citizens are right when they complain about lifeless cities and the lack of affordable housing. Building officials are right when they are strict in their enforcement of codes. Insurance companies are right when they exert pressure on the building codes. Bankers are right when they base their lending decisions on appraisers, who are right in the way they base their appraisals on the current market. Architectural educators are right in their criticisms of the profession, and the profession is right in its criticism of the schools.

Everyone is "right," yet the built environment does not really get better. It satisfies the quantifiable and separate needs of individual institutions, but as many people have pointed out, much of it is fragmented, lacking in humanity, without real depth of feeling.[2] The widespread acknowledgment of these problems makes it critical to look at the history of their cultural and institutional sources. The idea that increased knowledge about the building culture might lead to the improvement of the built world is the central purpose of this book.

Figure I.2. Austin, Texas, 1986

The Culture of Building

The culture of building is the coordinated system of knowledge, rules, procedures, and habits that surrounds the building process in a given place and time.[3]

The building culture is responsible for the character and formation of the *collection of everyday buildings*, in addition to individual, well-known buildings, at a given time and place. This culture is a collective phenomenon: thousands of different buildings are produced through shared processes held together by shared knowledge—of what to build and also of how to build—rather than through individual acts of creation.

Within a building culture, construction is rarely a solitary act, isolated from the material, social, and aesthetic world around it. A building's construction is almost always embedded in a recognizable web of human relationships between many participants: contractors, craftspeople, clients, building users, architects, building officials, bankers, materials suppliers, surveyors, building appraisers, real estate brokers, manufacturers. This web of relationships, in turn, is characterized by the predictable ways people carry out their jobs and the predictable ways they deal with each other.

As in any culture, the actions of members of the building culture are guided by a relatively small number of rule systems and habits of belief and behavior. These define the culture itself. The participants in the building process share common understandings that may be only partly understood by the larger culture outside them. But at the same time, the building culture is a part of the larger world, embedded in it, and the two worlds share ideas,

Figure I.3.
Stone delivery in
Jaisalmer, Rajasthan,
India, 1988

Figure I.4.
New England Medical
Center, Boston, under
construction, 1980

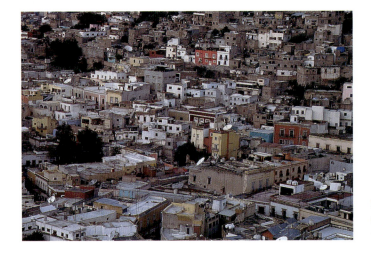

Figure I.5.
Guanajuato, Mexico,
1994

Figure I.6.
Delft, The Netherlands,
1990

Figure I.7.
House construction,
Eugene, Oregon, 1989

Figure I.8.
Sheet-metal
fabrication shop, 1996

business practices, attitudes about buildings and the environment, and forms of education and training.

The product of the building culture is the built world as a whole—the world of houses and warehouses, churches and libraries, schools and factories, barns and shops, the monumental and the everyday, the imported and the vernacular, the famous and the unknown. This world, much larger than the world with which architects usually concern themselves but intimately tied to it, is what makes up people's everyday experience of buildings and towns—and vast quantities of money and resources are used toward its construction.

The Cathedral and the Bicycle Shed

The first step in understanding the source of the 2 billion buildings in the world lies in going beyond the traditional concerns of architectural history, toward a view which recognizes that all buildings have significance and are part of a complex, collective phenomenon.

At the beginning of *An Outline of European Architecture*, Nikolaus Pevsner wrote a sentence that has been widely quoted: "A bicycle shed is a building; Lincoln Cathedral is a piece of architecture."[4] This statement represents an intellectual tradition that until very recently has divided the world of building into two separate parts. Architectural history, a descendant of nineteenth-century German art-historical scholarship, traditionally recognized only certain buildings as worthy of study: buildings built by ruling elites, built to last, and built for religious or spiritual reasons. Churches, town halls, universities and libraries, castles and palaces make up most of the buildings that have been studied by architectural historians.

Yet the vast majority of buildings in the world—the ordinary building fabric of cities and towns, including houses and workshops and minor civic buildings, and virtually all buildings in the countryside apart from churches, castles, villas, and manor houses—have until recently not been considered fit subject for study and are barely covered in the best-known books about architectural history. The bulk of the built world that people see and experience every day is made up of these vernacular buildings, both domestic and public, rather than monuments or buildings designed as extraordinary events in deliberate breaks from tradition.[5]

In fact, "architecture" and "building" are different aspects of the same phenomenon. One characteristic of any building culture is that it links all buildings together—large and small, domestic and public, architect-designed or not—so that from a real point of view, the word vernacular itself loses meaning, and it makes more sense to seek understandings that do not make such distinctions.[6] It is the inherent conservatism of building knowledge and technique, combined with the diffusion of knowledge and technique over time and geographical space, that leads to the continuities and variety in the world of building.

These kinds of understandings have been central to new investigations in both architectural history and vernacular architecture. Scholars in many different schools of thought have seen the importance of the artifact in cultural

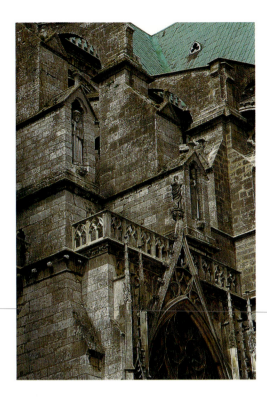

Figure I.9.
Chartres Cathedral, 1997

Figure I.10. Santorini, Greece, 1981. The houses at the top were built after neo-classical styles had been reintroduced following Greek independence in the nine-teenth century.

continuity and recognized the value and depth of traditional forms. These scholars use varying descriptions and models, but they all recognize that the cultural nature of the artifact may be defined by a few attributes of common understanding.

The architect, builder, and author Christopher Alexander sees these attributes in terms of patterns or centers and has stressed archetypal relationships that cut across history and culture. Alexander's formulations explain how the built world may be understood as a continuous structure that includes buildings of different sizes and types, and how this structure is connected to human purposes.[7]

Some architectural theorists, such as Leon and Rob Krier, and Aldo Rossi, saw common attributes in terms of historically repeated configurations or types. This was understood by some architects as a systematic way of understanding connections to the continuity of architectural history and to the physical continuity of the city, both of which were ruptured by several decades of ahistorical modernism, beginning in the 1920s.[8] The theoretical work of N. J. Habraken has dealt with how the form of the built environment, based on repeated configurations and acted on by a variety of agents, changes over time.[9]

Modern scholarship in vernacular architecture emerged from cultural anthropology and cultural geography. It began through attempts to describe the artifacts of a cultural landscape in terms of a systematic classification of buildings and building elements.[10] The folklorist Henry Glassie developed a structuralist approach to building types and thereby helped to connect the field of vernacular architecture to linguistics and anthropology.[11] Scholarship on vernacular building types now stresses both their classification and their social origin—and has shown the ways in which building knowledge spreads throughout and across cultures.

These formulations emerge from different intellectual places. But they speak to similar sorts of continuities in the built world: continuities that link architectural and urban space, the present to the past, and one culture to another. Together, this approach represents a new view of the world: one in which the relationships among things are as important as the classification of things themselves, and one which makes it very difficult to sustain a view of architecture that excludes vernacular, ordinary building from a general understanding.

Ultimately, this understanding goes beyond an understanding of form and social context and includes the process of building itself. The continuities of building form that exist between the vernacular and the nonvernacular (and between one place and another) come about because buildings are built in a world in which most of the various players—craftsmen, building inspectors, architects, masons—do not fundamentally change the way they work because of Pevsner's distinction between "architecture" and "building." They tend to do the same things, although perhaps to different degrees, on different kinds of buildings.

This leads to a different view of Lincoln Cathedral and the bicycle shed. The cathedral may share features with a parish church, for example, for a simple reason: the same people, or people trained in the same craft, worked on them both. These people were doing what they knew how to do, some applying their knowledge to a cathedral, others applying their knowledge to the church. The parish church shares features with a smaller manor house. The manor house shares features with a merchant's house. The merchant's house is similar in some ways to a smaller house, similar to a farm building, and so on, down through history to the bicycle shed. And this continuity points up the importance of *process*—what people know and how they work—as the mechanism through which the building culture operates to produce the built world.

The Process of Building

The idea of the building culture represents a view of the social process that results in the form of the built world. Rather than individual phenomena that result from independent acts of creation, buildings are products of social processes that vary in systematic ways from place to place and over time.

Building is a highly complex process entailing a sequence of discrete steps:

- Making the decision to build in the first place.
- Choosing and developing appropriate building sites.
- Regulating the character and placement of building on these sites.
- Financing the construction.
- Designing the building.
- Producing and supplying materials.
- Constructing the building.
- Regulating the building's construction.
- Occupying, using, and modifying the building.

Of course, in their particulars these steps differ from culture to culture. In Renaissance Europe, much building was financed by private patrons. In modern American culture it is financed by banks. In traditional Chinese culture the site was chosen through principles of *feng shui* (geomancy). In eighteenth-century London, sites were laid out by large landowners who tried to carve as many sites as possible out of a piece of land. In medieval Europe, building activity was regulated by guilds. In modern American culture it is governed by municipal building departments. To some extent, these particulars—and differences among them—define the cultures themselves.

These steps also differ in their relation to each other. In so-called primitive cultures where buildings are built from materials taken from the land around them, the production of materials is the same as the "financing" of the building. In advanced industrial cultures, the production and supply of materials includes prefabrication: steps that partly construct the building before on-site construction begins. In some situations the decision to build comes directly from the conditions of occupancy and use. In others the decision is based on more abstract financial or symbolic need. So the definition of these steps themselves is fluid and may take on different forms in different cultures.

Moreover, in many building cultures today, these steps are initiated and controlled by formal institutions. For example:

- *Making the decision to build:* Developers, pension funds, large corporations
- *Choosing and developing building sites:* Developers, government planning departments, regulatory bodies, banks, title companies, appraisers, environmental groups, soils engineers, lawyers
- *Regulating the placement and character of building:* Zoning bodies, utility districts, neighborhood organizations, lawyers, environmental and other regulatory bodies
- *Finance:* Banks, savings and loan organizations, escrow companies, large private investors, appraisers, community development corporations, accounting firms
- *Design:* Institutional clients, architectural firms, large materials suppliers, civil engineering firms, landscape architects, consultants
- *Materials:* Materials suppliers and manufacturers, producers' and manufacturers' cartels, trade associations, banks, fabrication shops, testing laboratories, truckers, truckers' unions
- *Construction:* Contracting firms, construction management firms, building trades unions, safety regulating bodies, banks, manufacturers and distributors
- *Regulation of construction:* Building code regulating bodies, workplace safety regulating bodies, testing laboratories, insurance companies

Architectural history has tended not to see buildings as the result of such processes. But it is only through understanding process that it is possible to understand "2 billion buildings"—and their character—as clear and coherent phenomena. The tens of thousands of buildings under construction at any time are being created through processes that involve tens of thousands, hundreds of thousands of people who are responsible for different aspects of the overall process. In a particular place, they are acting in coordinated ways according to similar systems of knowledge and rules. In the same way that the study of living things started with taxonomic classification but went on to address biological processes, the emphasis on the artifact as a finished and complete thing can be balanced with an understanding of the process through which the artifact came to be.

Today the question of process is being examined by economic and social historians, who have studied such things as the economic background to building development, the rise of building labor unions, and the relationships between the building trades.[12] One of the major themes of building history is the gradual transformation of craft production, during the eighteenth and nineteenth centuries, into industrial production. This development was accompanied by many other changes in society, including urbanization, the accumulation and concentration of capital, and the growth of professions. While related to vernacular architecture research, building history does not include a strong emphasis on buildings as artifacts with symbolic, cultural meaning, as opposed to objects of production, exchange, and profit.

The understanding of process depends on seeing technology as a human system. The word *technology* is sometimes interpreted to indicate something that is particularly modern. It is seen in opposition to craft processes, seen as dealing with large, impersonal machines or sophisticated engineering. The word is also sometimes connected to a realm of human activity that is at some distance from art, particularly when technology is associated with science.

But of course the word *technology* need not have the connotation of the modern or the unartistic. In its broadest sense, technology refers to the entire means of production and is not limited to tools and machines. No tool or machine can be understood outside the context of the actions of the person who is using both it and the other tools used in conjunction with it. In Japanese building, the transformation of the double bevel chisel to the single bevel chisel allowed for much greater precision in cuts and the simultaneous development of more complex joints.[13] The commercial manufacture of pigment for house paint, which came about with the invention of new machinery, was accompanied by a gradual decline in the ability of American house painters to make their own colors.[14] Technology includes people and tools together and is associated with particular results in construction and detail.[15] In these broad terms, a building culture is itself, in one sense, a technological system—and the development of building cultures over history has gone hand in hand with changes to what we usually understand as technology.

So far the discussion has only laid out the idea of the building culture itself, in terms of the range of artifacts that are considered within it, and the human processes that produce them. But if these ideas are to be useful for positive change in the contemporary world, we need to be able to make judgments based on value. As the built world is the product of building cultures, we need to be able to critically look at building cultures in terms of their effectiveness in making good environments and improving the lives of people who work and dwell in them—and who build them. This leads to the idea of healthy building cultures.

Healthy Building Cultures

In a healthy building culture, buildings of meaning and value are being made by people who are themselves improving their lives through making those buildings. The various parts of the culture reinforce each other and make it stronger, its customs and rules are understandable and make sense, and the culture's stability and its ability to change according to new conditions are in balance.

The Long-Term Value of Buildings and Types

The health of a building culture lies partly in its ability to produce artifacts of long-term human and spiritual value, or to maintain building knowledge that has such value.

By this definition, we have no trouble seeing the building cultures that produced the churches and palazzi of Renaissance Florence, or the religious

Figure I.11. A street in Bath, 1983. The terraced house type is highly adaptable.

buildings of early Ottoman Istanbul, or the squares and crescents of Georgian Bath, Bristol, London, or Edinburgh, as having aspects of good health. Those buildings lasted, have stood the test of time, and continue to be aesthetic paradigms.

With buildings that are in more of a state of change—tents of nomadic peoples, mud buildings in villages that may be in continuous states of slow but steady transformation—the building itself might not have permanence, but the village as a whole might. Although the building may last just a few years, the village may last a lot longer: it is being collectively and continuously produced by the members of the building culture.

Long-term value may also come from the strength of the type or rules of design and the resultant flexibility of the type over time. Examples are courtyard houses, row houses, and many other vernacular configurations that are maintained as culturally shared design ideas even as the buildings themselves change. But in a building culture where the artifact and the type both have transient value, the artifact does not contribute to the health of the culture. This is the case with contemporary building types like "superstores" in American suburbs: these buildings not only drain life out of cities but become obsolete once their original use has reached its end—sometimes a matter of only a few years.

Shared Knowledge: Rules and Rule Systems That Are Understandable and That Make Sense

In a healthy building culture, knowledge is shared among many people, inside and outside the culture, and there is common understanding of build-

Figure I.12.
Traditional log building in
Ukraine, 1991. The product
of shared knowledge.

ings and the way they are built. This is not to say that knowledge is equally
shared or that everyone is equally skilled in designing buildings or building
them—of course the greatest works of architecture depended on specialists
who maintained knowledge and language that other people were not privy to
and who devoted their lives to their work. But even so, such buildings are
approachable—they represent ideas and ways of life that are felt by people,
their designs are familiar, and their construction involves techniques and
processes that people can understand intuitively even if they cannot carry
them out themselves.

Another way of putting this is that knowledge and processes are "transparent"—one can see through them to their intention; they are obvious in
their ability to achieve an accepted purpose. Historic building processes like
timber framing, and the bracing and cutting of joints it entailed, were transparent in this way—anyone could see the effect of the brace and the joint on
the stability of the frame, and although the skill of carpentry itself was
restricted, what carpenters were doing was commonly understood.

This understanding, and the sharing of knowledge that it allows, helps to
maintain individuals' connections with each other and thereby helps the culture itself to maintain its integrity and definition.

Cultural Sustainability

Healthy building cultures have systems of knowledge, design, production,
and exchange that reinforce each other, even as the culture may have interactions with cultures outside it. For example, the building industry and artistic
life may be mutually supportive when the money spent on building helps to

Figure I.13.
Apartment buildings in Striy, Ukraine, 1991. The products of an unsustainable building culture.

regenerate economic and cultural life. Moreover, a building culture that causes another culture to wither is not healthy: witness the Japanese building industry's use of hardwood from Malaysian rain forests for concrete form work—and how this contributes to the destruction of those forests and their cultures.[16] Centralized Soviet control over countries like Ukraine had devastating effects on the building cultures of those cultures, wiping out traditional and useful knowledge.[17] In Papua New Guinea in the late 1970s, all new government housing was based on three prototypes, using technologies of concrete blocks and sheet metal imported from Australia—this in a country with a rich and still-living tradition of wooden buildings.[18] In these cases, none of the changes introduced from outside were a natural evolution of the culture. Neither the culture being exploited nor the culture doing the exploiting could exist without one of them being destroyed.

A Balance between Stability and Change, Tradition and Innovation

A healthy building culture can change even as it is stable enough to provide continuity. It can take care of new needs as they arise, without upheaval; it has the ability to learn from experience and not be destroyed in the process. During the eighteenth century, when a series of building laws gradually reshaped building in London, carpenters and bricklayers were able to easily incorporate these laws into their practice. During the nineteenth century, the introduction of electricity and central heating into buildings was able to be absorbed into a process that included many other trades. The building culture was able to incorporate innovation into its normal practice.

But such gradual incorporation of change may have its limits. By the beginning of the twentieth century, as the number of building trades and laws mushroomed, a fundamental change in the culture divorced architects from direct relationship with craft. And one can only speculate that in large parts of the contemporary building culture, the gradual buildup of well-

Figure I.14.
Old and new in
Amsterdam, 1990.
The balance between
stability and change.

intentioned rules based on the prospect of litigation has become so onerous that a fundamental change will again be necessary.

In more general terms, the idea of tradition as a handing down of attitudes, habits, and rules is integral to the definition and coherence of a culture.[19] Shared traditions allow people to maintain connections to a common past, and therefore to each other. But the concept has a charged meaning, particularly today, when the world is changing so fast. After all, modernism, as it has been defined through the twentieth century, is inherently antitraditional. The idea of "traditional architecture"—particularly traditional vernacular architecture—is sometimes seen as static, locked in the past, and inappropriate to today's society; those who promulgate it are regarded as hopelessly reactionary and conservative.[20] Indeed, if we look at tradition purely in this way, as buildings from the past, such criticisms may be valid. But if tradition is seen not as a blind handing down of habits and objects but as part of a process in which what has come before has the ability to teach, then the concept takes on a more dynamic meaning.[21]

The notion of tradition existing as part of a dynamic process is made even more powerful when we consider the relationship between tradition and innovation. Once again, these are opposite sides of the same coin. Sometimes "tradition" is appropriate for conditions that do not change, or that change slowly enough that habit can still prevail; sometimes innovation is needed for conditions that have changed, so new responses are needed. In a culture that is functioning well, tradition and innovation may each be appropriate responses to particular situations.

Finally, a healthy building culture is not something that is purely instrumental with respect to buildings. It is not like the machines and production system in a factory, which exist only to produce a particular product. Instead, there is a reciprocal relationship between the quality of the product and the increased health of the culture itself: members of the culture are better off for having been a part of it. It generates its own life, and not purely in economic terms: it engenders a sense of self-satisfaction, of increased life, in the architects and builders and other people who are involved in it. William Morris expressed this idea eloquently in an 1885 discussion of labor:

> The chief source of art is man's pleasure in his daily necessary work, which expresses itself and is embodied in that work itself; nothing else can make the common surroundings of life beautiful, and whenever they are beautiful it is a sign that men's work has pleasure in it, however they may suffer otherwise. It is the lack of this pleasure in daily work which has made our towns and habitations sordid and hideous. . . . Terrible as this is to endure in the present, there is hope in it for the future; for surely it is but just that outward ugliness and disgrace should be the result of the slavery and misery of the people; and that slavery and misery once changed, it is but reasonable to expect that external ugliness will give place to beauty, the sign of free and happy work.[22]

It should not be considered impractical, or overly nostalgic, to see some truth in these thoughts over a hundred years later.[23]

Figure I.15. William Morris

The Building Culture and Contemporary Practice:
The Possibility of Improvement

The idea of wide-scale improvement to the built world has been part of architectural discourse for many decades. The modern movement itself was originally seen partly as a means to counter the ugliness and squalor of nine-teenth-century cities. But modernism had its own problems, including its assumption that culture could be universal and that *place* was not important; as a result, modernism engendered a reaction against itself. Throughout the world, there were local architects—William Wurster in California, David Williams and O'Neil Ford in Texas, Edwin Lundie in Minnesota, Sedad Eldem in Turkey, Knut Knutsen in Norway—who resisted the universalizing aspects of the International Style. These efforts, however, as effective as they were individually, were mostly made within the existing systems of building production and were therefore only symbolic of a genuine resistance to the hegemony of modernism. The growing system of bureaucratic and techno-logically oriented production continued to be given legitimacy by the propo-nents of modernism.

But today there is a renewed understanding of the importance not only of what is built but of the process of building itself. This understanding has come from architects who choose, on leaving architecture school, not to follow a "standard" professional path but to turn instead to community ser-vice or building construction; from builders who choose to work more closely with clients or architects; and from clients who recognize the poten-tial problems in the institutionalization of architecture and building and who deliberately choose architects or builders who are trying to work in more integrated ways.

Figure I.16. Community participation: housing project for cycle-rickshaw drivers at Vellore, Tamil Nadu, India, by ILLAM (The Centre for People's Housing/Tamil Nadu) and CEDMA (Centre for Development Madras)

Figure I.17. School designed by Atelier Iruka, Team ZOO, Japan

An explicit connection between the scholarship on building history and alternative forms of modern practice does not yet exist. But some of these alternatives are, sometimes unknowingly, reinstituting historical modes of production. There are attempts to put craftsmanship back into building, new rules that allow design and building to be done by the same firm, a desire on the part of some practitioners to personally do both design and building, environmental movements that call for sustainable building and planning practice, and new small shops that produce windows, doors, and other "custom-made" building components. Many of these developments arise from a dissatisfaction with various aspects of contemporary practice, and to be sure, many of them are not part of the "mainstream" of building production. But even as they make use of modern tools and modern methods of management, many of them seem to resemble various preindustrial techniques and methods of organization.

Indeed modern society, all over the world, contains many pockets of resistance to the dominance of abstract, central control: communities fighting for their own autonomy and language; architects who insist on working closely with their clients, and staying in their own communities; craftspeople who are more concerned with doing a good job than with maximizing their profits; people working to change archaic zoning laws; architectural educators seeking to connect their students to the great traditions of architecture or to make students aware of how architecture might be a catalyst for contemporary social change. There are entrepreneurs who believe that social responsibility and making money do not have to conflict, farmers who are

Figure I.18. The reintroduction of craft in design and construction: visitors' center at West Dean, Sussex, England, by Christopher Alexander

growing organically and making a go of it, banks that see the importance of making loans to people who have traditionally been cut out of the banking system.

Although these efforts are relatively minor, they take on more significance within a framework of belief in the free market of ideas, which under the right conditions should allow valuable innovations to flourish. It is partly by anchoring these new and fledgling efforts in a historical and contemporary understanding of the building culture that we can connect them to something solid rather than leaving them isolated. One of the purposes of this book is to give legitimacy to contemporary efforts by anchoring them in the building culture as a whole and by showing that they are compatible with processes that have taken place throughout history. And this added legitimacy may help strengthen these efforts themselves.

This book uses the experiences of history to help develop and expand on the model of a healthy building culture. Having such a model will help us understand how the continuing transformation of contemporary building practice might be directed toward fostering a healthy building culture—one that gives dignity to people making buildings, that is respectful of other cultures and of the environment, and that is capable of producing commonplace buildings that can enhance and elevate the spirit and lives of everyone in society.

BUILDINGS AS
CULTURAL PRODUCTS

I

The world we live in, a world of 2 billion buildings, is being continuously built and rebuilt, through processes that seem completely natural to us because we live in the midst of them. A developer subdivides a tract of farmland, puts up thirty houses, and offers them for sale. Additions are built to several houses in each of dozens of neighborhoods in the city. A neighbor installs new vinyl windows in his house, and another neighbor lays a concrete driveway. A new commercial strip development is built along an important road. An office building is erected downtown, and office space there is advertised through local commercial realtors. The local university decides to build a new building to house its law school and hires an out-of-town architect to design it. A large foreign corporation builds a semiconductor plant on the outskirts of town after exerting pressure on the local political establishment to approve it. A successful doctor buys a beautiful piece of land and hires an architect to design a house for her.

Individual actions like this are repeated hundreds, thousands, tens of thousands of times, taking on different form in different parts of the world and resulting in the gradual transformation of the built world. Each of these actions that we see from our car window or walking along the street is just the visible result of a complex system of human relationships and knowledge—a building culture. In the modern world, this culture is highly articulated. It includes large, bureaucratic organizations; millions of construction workers; banks whose profits depend on the marketability of real estate; architects; developers; building departments; insurance companies. Many of the jobs within these organizations are highly specialized. The organizations and the people who work for them operate individually and deal with each other in ways that are understood and predictable. And together they produce buildings, millions of them, that are also understood and predictable.

To begin to understand this enormous complexity, Part I describes several different building cultures in history and in various conditions of social and economic development. Building cultures did not always have the form they do today. They have changed through history, sometimes slowly, sometimes quickly. But at any time, in any particular place, the building culture can be described as a specific configuration of knowledge, institutions, rules, and built results. A brief description of these various building cultures, with their similarities and differences, will begin to define both the nature of building cultures themselves and the way our present building cultures result from a long historical evolution.

In describing any historic building culture, several questions must be asked:

- What was the relationship between the building culture and the society, the larger culture, in which it existed?
- What were the major institutions of the building culture?
- What were the major human roles within those institutions?
- What kinds of agreements did people enter into with each other in the building activity?
- How did money and materials flow?
- How was building activity regulated?

- What was the building operation itself like?
- What were the typical built results of the building culture?

These basic questions include issues of how the culture sees itself, the major social groups, rules of exchange, and rules of behavior within the culture. It turns out that although individual building cultures handle different issues in similar ways, different building cultures vary in the way they work. The differences from one culture to another help illuminate each culture's particular characteristics. In Part I, by revealing the unique identity of different building cultures, we will explore the idea of a building culture itself. And by looking at building cultures from different historical epochs, we will begin to understand the origins of our own.

BUILDING AS A UNIFIED
SOCIAL PROCESS

Traditional Villages and Informal Settlements

A t its root, a building culture may be characterized by fundamental human relationships and social habits, and not all building cultures require large and formal institutions. In this chapter, we will deal with two generic building cultures: the traditional village, which has been the subject of much study in vernacular architecture, and the informal settlements that characterize cities in many Third World countries. Although formal institutions do not play a major role in these building cultures, both of them work as complex and integrated human systems.

The Building Culture of the Traditional Agricultural Village

If there are about 2 billion buildings in the world, there are about 2 million or so villages.[1] Only a few of these villages exist in cultures where there has still been little contact with the modern world; some are in cultures where there has been quite a bit of contact with the modern world but where traditional village life persists; most others are changing rapidly under the impact of agricultural modernization, industrialization, and the internationalization of the economy. This section focuses on the village that exists as an agricultural community and that has tended to maintain traditions that stretch back over many generations, even in the face of agricultural improvements and social change. These are the mud villages of India, some stone villages in the Alps and farming communities in the American Midwest and Plains, rice-growing villages of China and Southeast Asia, villages of kraals in Africa, and wooden villages of the Ukraine and Russia that persisted even through seven decades of Soviet collectivization.

Over the last hundred years, anthropologists and other specialists in vernacular architecture have studied many of the villages in the so-called primitive world. Anthropologists work by "joining" a culture as much as possible, by immersing themselves in the subtleties and minutiae of life, and by writing unique accounts based on these observations. They have shown, dispassionately, the enormous diversity of cultures of the world and have made us aware of the legitimacy of each one. Much of the strength of anthropology lies in this body of work—in the particulars, to the extent that generalizations are often looked at with a healthy and productive skepticism.[2]

Indeed, villages in different cultures may have entirely different religious and social structures, different economies and agricultural systems, different relationships to cities and towns, and people with different worldviews. Villages' settlement patterns and buildings and the way people go about building also differ widely from place to place. This diversity does seem to belie the idea of generalization. But removal from specific situations also gives us the perspective to see commonalities that may exist among them. Although these commonalities may not apply to every village everywhere, some of them are so striking, across villages that are very far apart geographically and culturally, that they suggest principles that may be at least partially acultural.[3]

The size of villages, for example, often depends on the productivity of the agricultural land that surrounds them and the consequent ability of a

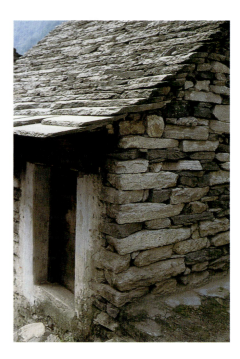

Figure 1.1.
Stone construction in Corippo,
Ticino, Switzerland, 1989

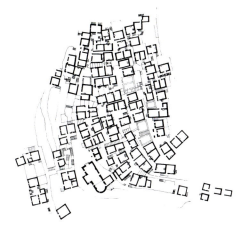

Figure 1.2.
Plan of Corippo

certain number of people to work an amount of land that is reasonably close to the village. In villages based on agriculture, the protection and safekeeping of crops is of major concern, so such villages contain symbolically important buildings for this purpose—ranging from the *laft* of the Norwegian farm, to the granaries of the Dogon, to the protected yam storage huts of the Trobriand Islanders in New Guinea.

In the traditional agricultural village, building both fulfills direct need and affirms the cosmic order connected to daily and annual cycles of life. The timing of building activity may be tied to agricultural cycles and human rituals of birth, marriage, and death. Individual life and beliefs are often subordinate to those of the community. The cosmic order and the functional order of daily life are intertwined.

The form of the village is itself often a representation or reaffirmation of the cosmic order as seen by the culture. Villages so organized are as various as the linear plans of the Nias Islanders,[4] where the chief's house stands at the end of the axis; the square plans of the Creek Indians in the American Southeast, where the vertical axis connecting the underworld and heaven passes through the intersection of the four cardinal axes;[5] and the positions of longhouses in the Amazon rain forest, which anchor the community to its ancestors.[6]

In the village, ordinary building is an ordinary act, even though it may be accompanied by ceremony and ritual. There are no formal institutions and knowledge of building is widely shared. In many cases, members of each family are involved in building and pass this knowledge on to their children by involving them in house construction year after year. Even though the level of skill involved may enable people to consistently produce beautiful things, in many cultures this skill is as basic to life as cooking supper. In some cases, where there is craft specialization, craftsmen live in the village and are known to its people. Agreements are informal and unwritten, but expectations are clear and commonly understood. Learning is by doing and is passed on from generation to generation. Control over the building activity is almost entirely implicit and unspoken.[7]

Little or no money changes hands. Materials are taken directly from the earth or from the by-products of agriculture: mud, straw, baked earth, tree

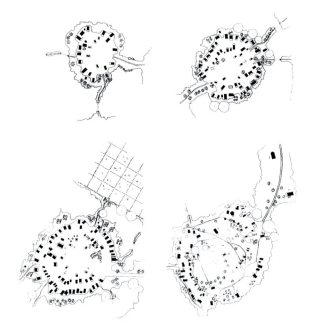

Figure 1.3.
Four circular villages of the
Trobriand Islands, Papua New
Guinea. Yam storage buildings
are located toward the center.

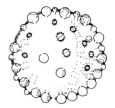

Figure 1.4. Plan of African village.
Seven grain storage buildings are
located just inside the outer ring of
houses.

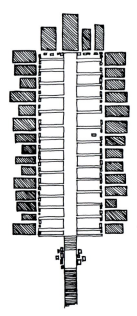

Figure 1.5.
Plan of Indonesian village.
The chief's house is at the top.

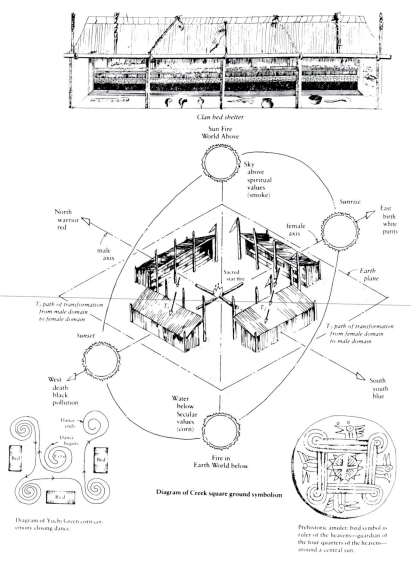

Clan bed shelter

Sun Fire
World Above

Sky
above
spiritual
values
(smoke)

North
warrior
red

Sunrise

East
birth
white
purity

male
axis

female
axis

Sacred
star fire

Earth
plane

T_1 path of transformation
from male domain
to female domain

Sunset

T_2

T_2 path of transformation
from female domain
to male domain

West
death
black
pollution

South
youth
blue

Water
below
Secular
values
(corn)

Dance
ends

Dance
begins

Bed

Fire

Bed

Bed

Fire in
Earth World below

Diagram of Creek square ground symbolism

Diagram of Yuchi Green corn ceremony closing dance.

Prehistoric amulet: bird symbol as
ruler of the heavens—guardian of
the four quarters of the heavens—
around a central sun.

Figure 1.6. Creek Native American square ground symbolism

branches, coconut palm leaves, stone. There is a very limited palette of materials and techniques. Building form is intimately tied to available technology,
and there is little difference between decisions about design and decisions
about construction.[8] And the skill of building itself, while often gender-
specific (in some traditional villages of Africa, for example, it was women
who had primary responsibility for building), is usually not restricted to a
particular professional class but shared across society as a whole. In other
cases, as with the stone shelters of southern Italy or the reed buildings of the
Iraq marshes, builders were members of the small local community. It is not
necessarily the case that in villages of this type, all construction is carried out
by the "users."

Building types are stable over time, similar from site to site, and there is
little individual invention. But within such typological uniformity, no two

Figure 1.7.
Village in Tamil
Nadu, India, 1994

Figure 1.8.
Wattle wall of gristmill,
Ukraine, 1990

Figure 1.9. Village in Papua New Guinea

Figure 1.10. Village of Urych, Ukraine, 1991

buildings are exactly the same. There is also little explicitly understood difference between the pragmatic and the functional, symbolic, or aesthetic aspects of building form. The great pitched-roof houses of Sumatra, with their main floors raised above the ground and gables angled forward, can be analyzed in various ways. The big overhanging roof keeps out water and allows air to rise within. The raised floor allows animals to live underneath. The roof form may be symbolic of the boats that brought people to the islands. The carved ornament on the facade may include metaphors or representations of the human body.[9] Likewise, with the traditional tents of nomads in the Sahara, there are economic "form determinants" (the tent itself is necessary because of the nomadic way of life), physical form determinants (tent fabric was often woven from goat hair, which has particular qualities of strength and stability), and expressions of social organization (men and women are separated into different parts of tents; tents are oriented toward the center of a circle).[10] Like any buildings, these "primitive" buildings have complex reasons for their form and organization.

The village is always in a state of construction. The cycles of growth, building, and decay of a village go hand in hand with those of human life itself. In many cultures, building is a recurring part of the annual cycles of planting, harvest, celebration, and homage to the divine: building often happens at lulls in agricultural activity. Like agricultural production, building materials and the economics of construction fit seamlessly into the overall social and economic life of the village. The annual cycles of production and the passage of time are often evident in villages: buildings that are lived in stand beside others that are falling down and still others that are being built. This real evidence of imperfect and not always beautiful process can belie the bucolic images of villages and village life that people often have.

The nucleated agricultural village of England, which disappeared as a unified economic entity with the land enclosure movements that accelerated

Figure 1.11.
Village of Chenini,
Tunisia, 1994

Figure 1.12.
Temple at end
of village street
in Tamil Nadu,
India, 1994

during the Industrial Revolution, had many of the characteristics that are still present—although threatened and often disappearing—in villages in less industrialized countries.

The village depended on the agricultural economy for its organization and building construction. The number of houses in it depended on the productivity of its agricultural land and on the land lying close enough to the village that it could be accessed and worked in a day. An individual villager's land was divided into thin strips distributed in several fields outside the village center—the result of ancient systems of inheritance practices. It was partly this distribution of land that led to the nucleated form of the village center, which put each dwelling closest to all its lands.

The strips were long and narrow, separated from each other by natural boundaries and verges that developed in the land after years of working it. Adjacent owners worked land at the same time, shared teams of oxen, and shared festivals marking important times of year, including Midsummer and the harvest. This common life, connected to natural cycles, has perhaps been

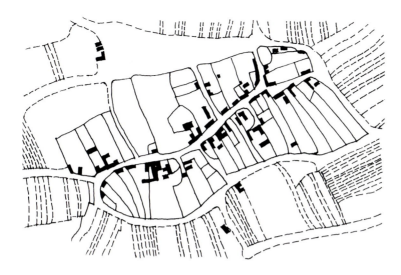

Figure 1.13. The village of Thurlaston in 1717 showing agricultural strips at edge

overromanticized—life may not have been easy or "pretty" in today's terms —but it did provide the context for a building culture in which people knew the same things about building and built buildings in the same way.

The houses people built had evolved from linear, wooden structures whose remains archaeologists have unearthed all over northern Europe. Very early versions of these houses had people and animals housed at opposite ends of the same long space; new forms gradually evolved in which the space was divided, and then the animals moved to a byre of their own. The house maintained a division between major rooms, with an open roof, eventually evolving into a "hall-and-parlor" plan. Such a plan embodied social relations within the house: the hall acted as a more public room, and the parlor (or "chamber") as the private and ceremonial realm for the heads of the family.[11]

The timber construction of the house evolved from a cruck technique in which a single bent piece of wood went from the ground sill to the ridge, to a heavy timber frame in which major hewn members were jointed together to make a rigid structure. In some places, roofs were thatch on a wooden substructure, and walls might have been plastered wattle and daub. The materials used depended partly on the geology of the place, but they were mostly taken from the lands that belonged to the village (timber and stone; thin sticks for wattle) and products of local agriculture (rye or wheat straw for thatch, set aside for the purpose).

Although a timber frame of any complexity or sophistication required the skill of a carpenter, that skill was almost certainly possessed by a person who lived in the village himself and who possibly practiced that craft in addition to farming. Good thatching also requires a high level of skill, but all of the operations in the construction of a house would have involved, in some way, laypeople as well as any skilled craftsmen.

At least from medieval times onward, buildings and techniques were changing gradually, but in the building culture of the traditional village, techniques were commonly and implicitly understood, materials were taken from the land of the village itself, and skills were contained within the village. The building culture and the overall culture were so intertwined as to be almost indistinguishable and mutually supportive, so the system was able to sustain itself until the external forces of industrialization and capital brought it down. This eventual collapse is decried in the poem "Sweet Auburn," by Oliver Goldsmith (1730–74):

> Ill fares the land, to hastening ills a prey,
> Where wealth accumulates, and men decay:
> Princes and lords may flourish, or may fade;
> A breath can make them, as a breath has made;
> But a bold peasantry, their country's pride,
> When once destroyed, can never be supplied.

The nucleated English village disappeared long ago as a unified social and economic entity. This is now becoming true in most other places in the world as well. Villages in which oral traditions and "learning by doing" predominate, with stability over time, have disappeared or changed markedly in today's world. Villages in India (where a quarter of the world's villages are located) have radios and televisions, concrete block and steel rebar, products for sale from international corporations.[12] Wealthier people aspire to move out of their brick courtyard houses into concrete-block houses of modern design. Many young people leave the village to seek prosperity in the city. At the same time, the reach of the world economy is pervasive enough that products of American corporations find their way into the remotest villages. In most places in the world there now seems to be little stability in village life.

Figure 1.14.
Cruck building at
Lacock, near Bath, 1992

Figure 1.15. The landscape of southern England, 1992

The anthropologist Richard Critchfield sees the village in balance with the city as the carrier of the traditions of a culture at large,[13] and he laments the changes that are now changing rural life faster than ever. But some of the qualities that always characterized the building culture in "primitive" society are still present in many villages that survive: a good deal of shared knowledge about building, a link between building practices and religion, oral transmission of knowledge and manual understanding of how to build, and, where the agricultural economy is still prevalent, a strong tie between agriculture and the building process. So it could be that traditional ways of life are disappearing only in part; in part they could be undergoing a transformation into new forms of life that will incorporate traditional ways into their orbits.

The Building Culture of an "Informal" Settlement in India:
Pune 1995

Contemporary change in rural life is of course accompanied by the growth of cities. In rapidly growing cities, building happens in cultures, which, although different from those of villages, are no less coherent. Consider for example squatter settlements in India.

The context in which Indian squatter settlements are formed and grow is similar to that in many other contemporary cities of the so-called Third World, and similar as well to many cases of urbanization in recent history, such as London in the nineteenth century.[14] People move from the country to the city[15] to begin a process of individual development that they hope will take them into the ranks of people who have steady employment, a decent place to live, and the prospect of a better life for themselves and their children—the dream of people all over the world. But when they first arrive in the city from the village, with little more than the clothes on their backs,

Figure 1.16. Market place in Vellore, India, 1994

shelter is far from their highest priority. Most important is a source of income, to buy the food that will consume virtually all of that income. Housing and transportation costs have to be as low as possible, and housing location depends almost completely on place of employment. Though they are commonly regarded as the dumping grounds for the hopelessly poor, to a large extent squatter communities are in fact an efficient means for people to enter the informal economy on which the formal economy depends.

In Pune,[16] as in many other places, settlements form on land where ownership or control is ambiguous in some way. This category may include the banks of rivers and canals, railroad or highway rights-of-way, municipal or even private—often industrial—land that is not in use, and wide footpaths and sidewalks alongside streets. Land is subdivided and allocated in different ways. In some cases, individual families simply establish themselves in a place, almost always where there are people known to the family, perhaps relatives or people who are from the same village or with whom they have other ties. In some cases a "shadow developer" will take illegal control of a large plot of land, subdivide it, and rent plots to individual families. In most cases families do not have security of tenure and may achieve such security, if at all, only after years of struggle.

More than by the conditions of houses themselves, the status of a settlement is defined through this ambiguity of ownership and control. In fact, the settlement itself, as a physical place, goes through cycles of improvement that may eventually turn it into an established neighborhood, with houses, streets, and services that are permanent and well maintained. Security of tenure may even be gained. In this way, the contemporary Indian squatter settlement demonstrates processes of physical development that may parallel those that existed long ago in traditional settlements and cities.

This development occurs through the mechanism of a building culture that is socially intricate and highly responsive to needs. The building culture

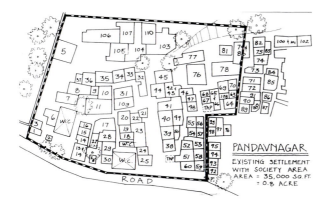

Figure 1.17.
Plan of informal settlement in Pune, India

Figure 1.18. Street in informal settlement in Pune, India, with building materials along the side, 1995

includes clients, money, credit, craftsmen, and materials suppliers—most of the players present in wealthier, more "legitimate" communities. It includes ways of design and construction that are well understood. The culture is also connected to the building culture of the city at large: laborers may work outside the settlement, and materials may also come from outside as well.

In Pune, people tend to build because they want a better house for themselves and increased equity, not so much because they want rental income. Often families will build before a monsoon because the old house is falling down: there may be "lots of building activity before monsoons, lots of relaxing after monsoons."[17] People frequently save money while living in a hovel, then do the improvements all at once rather than undertaking a series of very small improvements. The expense of building a proper house is not one of the major expenses in people's lives—it is still less than they would spend on a wedding or on a funeral. But people might also borrow to build, and their loans may come from many different sources, including advances on their pay.

The houses themselves may be 10' × 10' or 10' × 15' and are often on tight sites; two or even three walls may be shared with other houses. A door is often the only source of light and ventilation. Cooking usually takes place at the back of the house, where the owner will proudly display several shiny pots and pans. The bed is generally at the front; the bathing space might be at the threshold right in front of the door. If the bathing space is inside the house, there will often be half-walls surrounding it, with big water pots on top, giving more privacy. The space is also used for washing clothes. Inside the house there is often a little prayer place—in the form of a small shelf or cabinet nailed to the wall—containing incense, idols, bells, and water.

Sleeping space is not designated; family members sleep all over, on a steel bed and on the floor. The bedding spread out on the floor at night is stored on the bed during the day. There is often a little place in front of the house with stones for washing, places for grinding, places to hang laundry, and a square pot for the sacred tulsi plant. If people decorate the front, this is the area they decorate; if they build a brick house, the front is where they plaster.

Indeed, people hold a strong picture of a "proper" house in their minds, which they refer to during the construction process itself. They are flexible about innovations that do not disturb that picture (they will agree to changes in pragmatic issues of construction that lower the price) and inflexible about things that clearly do not contribute to that picture (they will not agree to leave the front wall unplastered if they have the money to plaster it).

The construction materials used are dependent on where the house sits in the economic range of *kutcha* (cheap, impermanent) to *pukka* (solid, permanent). The cheapest houses might have walls of gunnysack or plastic sheets; better houses have walls of wooden slats from packing crates tacked to a light wooden frame; even better houses have tin sheets lashed to a frame made of acacia poles stuck in the ground. The most expensive houses have walls of fired brick and mud mortar. When walls are plastered, people want colors, since white means one can't afford color.

There are secondhand markets for tin sheets and for the poles that hold them up. There are also markets for good mud, gunnysacks, cow dung, old plastic sheets (which are recycled plastic waste), flattened biscuit tins, thin

Figure 1.19.
Houses in informal
settlement in
Pune, India, 1995

sticks to which metal sheets are attached, flattened oil drums, and stalks to be lashed into bundles that are then lashed to light wooden frames and covered with mud. All these things are bought and sold. Though materials for houses in such settlements may appear to be scavenged, nothing is really free. Bricks are made around the periphery of the city from soil trucked in from river-beds farther away; agricultural waste and coal are used for firing. These bricks are available from small suppliers, who also sell sand. All areas of India have cement and steel plants nearby, subsidized by the government after Independence, and the prices of cement and steel are consistent from place to place.

A house that is at all *pukka*, even one made out of tin sheets, will most likely have a stone foundation. The simplest houses will have floors of smooth earth, with cow dung and mud rendering; more expensive ones will have floors of *koba*, done with a technique where a smooth concrete layer is put onto a level base made from gravel, sand, and broken brick. While the cement is wet, red oxide might be applied to give it color. Tile floors might be used, sometimes with broken tiles acquired in the secondhand market.

Roofs are mostly simple sheds sloping from back to front and often include storage space. The structure is a series of simple purlins made of steel angles, acacia poles, or, in some cases, dimensioned timber. Roofs extend over the walls; masonry parapets are used only for more expensive masonry walled houses. Doors are of folded sheet steel. Although wooden doors are still made, even a good secondhand wooden door is very expensive. Windows are Z-section steel windows. *Jalis* (concrete screens for ventilation) are manufactured in many local yards; *kuddapa* stone lintels are also made.

The level of professional involvement is also dependent on the economic level of the house. The cheapest houses are built by people themselves, and more expensive ones by masons. When masons are involved, they work with small contracts, for fixed amounts. Contractors tend to live in the settlements themselves, but they also work outside. A mason is chosen by the quality of his work and is known by friends and neighbors; this familiarity helps make the contract secure.

To arrive at the contract, the owner and mason talk matters over. Design decisions about the house tend to be made between the husband and the mason, even when these decisions don't affect the husband. The woman, however, is the one who is there during the construction process. Usually the project will be very defined: the contract will say whether or not the house will be plastered; whether or not there will be a "stand-up kitchen" (one with kitchen counters); whether there will be *koba* or tiles on the floor. The mason will come up with a figure; the parties will do some haggling; participation by the family (the family usually supplies water; will the son help with work?) will be determined. Usually payment will be made in stages: materials will be procured first, and the mason will be paid weekly. The mason will hire his own helpers: he is being paid for the job, not by time. For the most part these are just labor contracts, and the family is responsible for procuring materials.

There is a wide range in quality of work by masons. A good mason will lay bricks in straight rows, with proper keying, and will use wet bricks, but this proper, simple brick masonry is very rare. For the most part there is no formal training: often sons do what their fathers have done, most masons learn on the job, and skill levels are low. But masonry is considered to be a decent, well-respected, and well-paid job.

This detailed picture is meant to illustrate that even a squatter settlement in India does not typify the chaotic desperation that is often attributed to it. Even in such a place there are well-established ways of living, supported by commonly understood ways of building houses, that do not depend on the existence of large institutions or highly paid professionals.

The Parts and the Whole

The building cultures of the traditional village and the contemporary urban informal settlement are similar in the local nature of building operations, in the lack of large institutions and firms directly controlling building operations, and in the highly differentiated character of building form that results from typical processes of design and construction. There are also differences, of course. Building forms are different; there are a wider variety of materials and a higher percentage of industrially processed materials in the informal settlement; the informal settlement is influenced by external economic and political forces in ways that the traditional village is not.

It is significant, however, that two situations as outwardly different as the village and the urban slum—one preindustrial and agricultural, and the other the product of an industrializing economy in the context of a large city—could be so similar in many ways. In each case, the building culture is a highly organized and predictable system, even though it does not rely on large institutions to exert overarching control. All aspects of the system are self-regulating, through local market forces, social pressure, and the constraints that come out of available materials and techniques. In both cases these underlying similarities result in settlement forms in which there is a good deal of repetition of typical building designs but also a lot of difference from building to building in the way details are carried out.

Although formal institutions do not exist in either of these building cultures, the parts of these cultures do not operate in isolation from each other. Materials, costs, and desires work together. Building forms serve people's needs, within the constraints of available resources. Knowledge of craft is transmitted to young people. The building culture, as complex as it might be, is a unified social phenomenon, with its own identity, its own rules, and its own typical products.

FOUR BUILDING
CULTURES IN HISTORY

2

From Medieval London to Modern New York

The four building cultures described in this chapter—of the medieval city, Renaissance Florence, London in 1760, and New York in the 1890s—differ from the traditional village or the contemporary Third World informal settlement not only in the kinds of buildings that are produced but also in the much larger role that formal institutions play. This role increased over history, and as knowledge about building became more and more concentrated, the traditional locus of skill and design understanding began to disappear.

The Building Culture of the Medieval City

The building culture of the medieval city was dense and fine-grained; many small-scale transactions served to weave the players together. There were continuities of building form, materials, and techniques. Movement of craftsmen allowed for sharing of techniques and typical building forms. Many members of society shared understandings of building form well enough that simple agreements could be made with confidence directly between owner and craftsmen. It was this fluidity that helped art to emerge out of craftsmanship and allowed the production of the subtle variety that characterizes all medieval building, large and small.

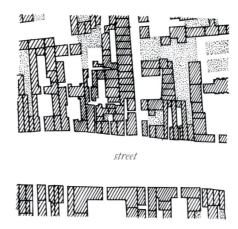

street

Figure 2.1. The building fabric of medieval London

The specialization of craft, and the fine-grained and interwoven nature of economic life and the fabric of the city itself, are the most prominent features of the building culture of the medieval city.

The form of the medieval city reflected the diversity of a rising artisan and trading economy. The London of 1300 included churches, almshouses and hospitals, shops, inns, taverns, stables, outbuildings, permanent market buildings, market stalls, districts devoted to different trades, a waterfront for the transfer of goods, houses that would combine "dwelling" with the business of their owners, and specialized buildings such as tanneries and forges.[1]

Medieval cities included a large proportion of people who were directly involved in the production of goods or artifacts, including buildings. The number of crafts was large. They included, for wood: sawyers, carpenters, joiners, specialist carpenters (carvers, for instance); for stone: roughmasons, stonecutters, freemasons, specialist carvers; for brick and tile: tilemakers, tilers, brickmakers, bricklayers, and laborers; and, more generally, thatchers, plasterers, smiths, and plumbers.[2] Salzman writes that "when Sir Thomas Lucas was building Little Saxham Hall in 1505 he bargained with Alexander Boyn, smith: 'for making of barres of iron, lokettes, hookes, henges, cases, nailes and other things necessary, paying for every lb. of the said cases being wele and clenly wrought and sufficiently rede vernysshed.'"[3]

The typical urban house was narrow-fronted (reflecting the rising value of urban land) and multistoried (allowing for some degree of social segregation between master/master's family, apprentices, and servants) and had a shop or workplace on the ground floor (reflecting the integration of commerce with daily family life). The nondomestic building type that is most associated with the time—the cathedral—was itself larger than previous churches (to accommodate increased numbers of pilgrims), gave increased emphasis to the eastern end (to accommodate the increased importance of the cult of relics), and developed new forms of construction to allow for greater height and more light (to increase the transcendence of the building itself).

Most urban buildings were oak frame on brick foundations. The frames were filled in with wattle and daub for walls and with wooden shutters in openings. Upper floors were wood planks. Roofs were thatch laid onto wooden purlins; after thatch was outlawed, tiles were used. Lime plaster was applied to walls, and there were iron hinges and latches for the shutters and doors. More expensive houses were bigger, had brick nogging instead of wattle and daub, and contained more ornament and interior woodwork, such as paneling, wainscoting, carved ornament in the timber frame, and carefully crafted staircases.

Building tradesmen were organized in guilds. The guild system was to some extent a tool for regulating prices by controlling professional activity. The guild determined who could enter a profession and what the standards of the profession would be. In London there were a few laws that regulated building: the most notable of them prohibited thatched roofs, but this law was not always enforced. By and large, control over what builders did was in their own hands, or the hands of the guilds, which made regular inspections and might tear down work that did not meet their standards.[4]

How prominent was the activity of building in the overall economy? Although the number of people involved directly with the construction of cathedrals may in fact not have been high as is sometimes assumed,[5] the percentage of people involved directly with the production of artifacts was higher than it is today. In Winchester, between 1300 and 1339, about 5 percent of individuals who held and inhabited property belonged to the building trades.[6] In York, in 1381, there were forty carpenters and joiners among a thousand men listed by occupation in a list based on poll tax returns.[7] In some places, stone building was rare enough that a particular town did not have resident masons but instead employed itinerant masons and bands of masons; this is one of the factors that aided the diffusion of techniques from place to place. Workers in the building trades lived and worked in close proximity to each other and to the rest of the population, much of which was itself involved in the production of goods and objects. So even though each of the many crafts protected its own "mysteries," it is likely that there was at least general knowledge of craft and building by many people throughout society.

Most building projects were small enough that the client could deal directly with craftspeople. A person who wanted a house built would contract directly with a carpenter, who would agree to build the house of a certain set of dimensions, and a certain number of stories, by a certain time. The carpenter would be responsible for obtaining the materials, for shaping the frame and joints (sometimes at his own yard, in a different place from the house), and for erecting the frame. Any necessary drawing for laying out the building was done by the carpenter. There would have been separate agreements with other craftsmen, in which the owner might agree to supply materials himself. All of these agreements, even if written, were short and sealed "with a handshake" and left many decisions up to the craftsman.

The process was similar for larger buildings. The greater complexity of the cathedrals, and the fact that many of them were built over time, meant that more money and more craftsmen of different kinds were involved, along with more drawings and more elaborate details. But many building techniques were elaborations of those used in more modest buildings: building materials came from the same places, and craftsmen might expect to

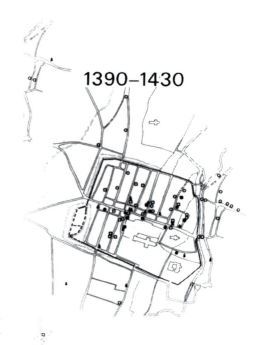

1390–1430

Figure 2.2.
Location of building tradesmen in medieval Winchester

Figure 2.3.
Street in
Winchester, 1988

work on different kinds of buildings rather than specializing in one building type. For example, timber roofs or house plans may have a basic similarity in larger and smaller buildings, but they differ in their elaboration and detail. One basic medieval house plan in London is a simple chain of rooms, with the great "hall" at the center. This basic unit is present in all domestic build-ings, large and small. In small houses, there is just one unit of this chain; in large houses, the chain itself is repeated, the individual parts of the unit are larger, and the individual parts are more greatly elaborated and detailed. Ideas spread throughout society, because buildings of different sizes and classes were being constructed within the same building culture.[8]

Figure 2.4.
Medieval masons

Figure 2.5.
House in Ship Yard,
Temple Bar, London

    The organization of work on a larger building was complex and hierarchical. Although there is now ample evidence of drawings, of people who "designed"[9] and people who oversaw the work of masons, the training and duties of a person playing the role of architect were considerably different than they would be today.

    For example, the laying out of ground plans, the drawing of elevations, and the drawing of patterns used by masons was done by master masons, who were trained in geometry and drawing as these skills applied to stoneworking. Drawings were done as the need for them arose (likely based on measurements of completed work), not necessarily at the beginning of construction.[10] Some master masons rarely cut stones but instead spent their time in the tracing house, drawing and "laying out" stones for other masons to cut.[11] On projects smaller than cathedrals, such as country churches, master masons probably cut stones themselves.[12] This indicates that the master mason, or "architect," did not belong to a separate profession; rather, there seems to have been a professional continuum, from the craftsman who cut the stone based on someone else's drawing to the person who supervised a large project and did drawings but very little stonecutting.

Overall design coherence on large cathedrals, which often took several decades to build, was maintained because different teams of masons were working in a culture with considerable movement of craftsmen from place to place, where copying of buildings and building details was often explicitly called for in contracts and where the overall design intention of the building was apparently well enough understood by the cathedrals' administrators.[13]

Simple buildings were financed directly by the owner, and materials were usually procured by the owner rather than the craftsmen. Most construction materials came from forests and quarries that were relatively close. For example, the Thames Valley had rich clay suitable for making bricks, English oak was plentiful for timber framing, and other wood was available for fuel to fire the bricks. Materials were sold at standard, commonly understood prices; the regulation of these prices was one of the tasks of the guild. Money flowed according to work done and materials bought, and often

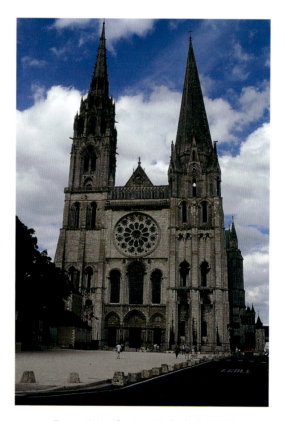

Figure 2.6. Chartres Cathedral, 1997

individual amounts were small, even for large projects: there were many different "streams" of money from the client to different members of the building culture.

Table 2.1, compiled from detailed accounts, shows the character of the overall distribution of money for a medium-sized project.[14] The attention paid to tiny amounts (15 shillings 4 pence for wax and pitch) points to a building economy in which expenses even for what was apparently a simply constructed building were distributed over many recipients, and in which a particular operation that today would be a single account was itself distributed (carpentry = nails + boards + wages of carpenters + wages of sawyers + carriage of timber) and billed individually over several years. Note also that about 70 percent of the total is for labor.

In short, the medieval building culture existed in a context in which craft and production were an important part of society. In some towns, the building of cathedrals and churches was central to the town's identity and economy; in most towns, building craftsmen and the provision of materials were integrated into the economy in a fine-grained way. In cities like London, buildings were timber frame with infill of wattle and daub or brick; large and important buildings were stone. Buildings were based on a few standard, well-understood building types, with a lot of variety in execution and detail. Most buildings were built by individual craftsmen under the supervision of the client; agreements were largely informal and based on personal trust.

Table 2.1. Summary of building accounts for Vale Royal Abbey, 1278–1280 (in pounds, shillings, pence)

	Year 1	Year 2	Year 3	Total for 3 years
Miscellaneous	4.15.10			4.15.10
Tools	0.2.1	0.1.7	0.1.6	0.5.2
Wax & pitch	0.6.4	0.2.10	0.6.2	0.15.4
Iron	3.12.6	4.15.0	5.5.0	13.12.6
Steel	2.18.4	3.0.0	3.3.9	9.2.1
Nails	1.12.3	1.5.5	0.18.9	3.16.5
Boards	3.18.6	1.18.0	3.0.0	8.16.6
Lime	6.4.0	7.18.0	9.12.0	23.14.0
Straw	0.10.0	0.12.0	0.12.10	1.14.10
Carriage				
of timber	5.5.4	3.10.0	2.0.0	10.15.4
Carriage of lime	4.10.0	5.8.9	6.0.0	15.18.9
Carriage of stones	150.17.8	104.11.8	91.10.0	346.19.4
Wages of carpenters	29.0.6	9.16.4	6.0.11	44.17.9
Wages of sawyers	1.10.6	1.16.0	1.2.8	4.9.2
Wages of plasterers	2.6.8	1.12.6	1.14.0	5.13.2
Wages of masons	234.1.9½	200.12.10	260.2.10	649.17.5½
Wages of quarriers	36.15.6	28.10.5½	38.15.10	104.1.9½
Wages of smiths	24.4.3½	16.13.1	24.8.1	65.5.5½
Wages of diggers	58.14.0	50.3.5	57.2.7	166.0.0
	571.6.1	442.7.10½	511.16.11	1,525.10.10½

Source: Douglas Knoop and G. P. Jones, "The first three years of the building of Vale Royal Abbey, 1278–1280: A study in operative masonry," *Trans. Quatuor Coronati Lodge* 44 (1931): 4.

The Building Culture of Renaissance Florence

There were two major differences between the building culture of Renaissance Florence and that of medieval cities:

- Large families now supplemented the church as a source of money for building. In Renaissance Florence, building was a means of recirculating wealth and displaying the status of private patrons, who provided much money for building and centralized control over building operations for major projects.

- The new architectural styles of the Renaissance, combined with the smaller size of important buildings (compared to medieval cathedrals), meant that the building could now be represented more completely before the start of construction. What is not often realized in discussions of Renaissance building practice, however, is that this did not happen universally, and in many building projects a lot of design still happened simultaneously with construction.

The advances of the Renaissance—the emergence of the professional architect, the revival of classical forms, and the codification of architectural knowledge—were gradual advances, made first in a few important building projects, and through more and more projects as time went on. Typical daily life changes slowly, even in a city as prosperous as Florence was, and the architects, artisans, suppliers, and laborers of the city were responding to more gradual change as well as to the most current, stylish innovation.

This gradual change is shown by the building fabric of the city itself, which combined Renaissance with medieval types and included new and reconstructed palazzi, churches, public buildings, and tenements. Since there

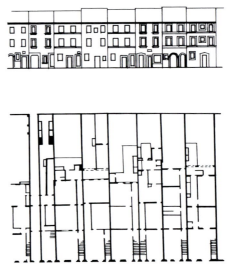

Figure 2.7. Typical houses in Renaissance Florence

was a reluctance to build outside the existing city walls, the existing physical fabric of Florence persisted and became the context for new buildings.[15] Much building took place on properties that had been cleared for the purpose, and the nature of street life changed as many palazzi without ground-level shops replaced older medieval buildings with shops.[16] But many medieval buildings remained: typical domestic buildings were party-wall buildings that resembled the ancient Roman house, often with an interior courtyard and a shop at the ground floor.[17] The renovation of these houses provided the opportunity for ordering and detailing the facade according to new architectural styles, but even with new speculative development, there was a reluctance to deviate much from medieval models.[18]

Up to 10 percent of Florence's workforce may have been in construction—a higher percentage than in some medieval cities.[19] Most construction workers were in relatively small shops; there were few large contractors who acted in a coordinating role rather than employing many workmen themselves. Strong connections of neighborhood and family meant that the same workmen would be hired again and again, and the continuity often extended over generations. This personal trust allowed for the existence of informal contracts.[20]

A single guild, the Arte dei Maestri di Pietra e di Legname, set regulations concerning apprenticeship but did not regulate prices. Presumably it was understood that the market was self-regulating. There were enough artisans of good quality that discerning clients would not be exploited, and there were enough clients that artisans did not have to fight for work.[21] There were also building laborers who did not belong to guilds: the *popolo minuto*, some of whom were recently arrived immigrants, continually searched for day labor.[22]

In a typical building project the client was at the center and employed and managed craftsmen directly. For the Strozzi Palace, Filippo Strozzi entered into dozens of agreements with individual workmen.[23] Notwithstanding the public role of architects like Brunelleschi or Michelangelo, in the eyes of the client the architect was only one of many players and might have barely

Figure 2.8.
Via San Nicolo,
Florence

Figure 2.9.
Via dei Servi, Florence

entered into the otherwise detailed accounts.[24] More important were the *capomaestri*, responsible for day-to-day supervision of building sites and the coordination of workmen and materials. Big projects might have had more than one *capomaestro*, and these workers were supervised by overseers, *soprastante*, who combined the roles of today's architect, contractor, and construction supervisor.[25] Roles tended to overlap. William Wallace points out that it is difficult to draw lines between masons, sculptors, construction supervisors, and sometimes even architects.[26]

Building materials included stone, fired brick, timber, iron, lime plaster, tile, and marble. Brick kilns were located outside the city because of greater access to clay and fuel for firing and because of safety restrictions. Kilns were significant industrial operations, employing brickmolders, firemen, and unskilled laborers. Wood was plentiful in Tuscany, and it did not represent a large part of the materials cost for buildings; it was used as fuel and for furniture as well. A limestone known as *pietra forte* came from nearby quarries, sometimes owned by stonecutters themselves. The demand for stone increased during the Renaissance, spurred partly by the introduction of classical forms in cornices, moldings, and columns. Goldthwaite writes that there "was probably not another city in all of Europe with such a large number of highly skilled stoneworkers as were found in Florence by the fifteenth century, and in fact the emigration of them throughout Italy was a phenomenon of considerable importance for the diffusion of Renaissance taste."[27]

For smaller projects, only a few measurements and a ground plan sufficed, and the craftsmen developed the details as construction progressed.[28] When contracts and specifications were sufficiently precise, the finishing of stone would generally take place not on the construction site but instead in

Figure 2.10.
Palazzo Medici, Florence

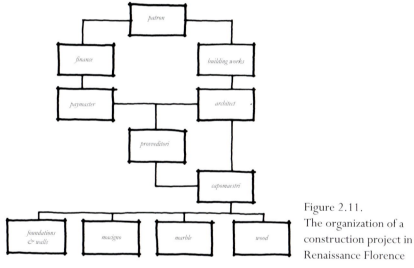

Figure 2.11.
The organization of a
construction project in
Renaissance Florence

the quarry and in the artisan's shops.[29] For larger projects, the architect, who
himself likely came out of the building trades, was in charge and remained
involved with the work on the site. The increasing use of models and drawings arose partly because wealthy patrons wanted to see what they were
going to get; after all, the architect might not have worked full-time on the
projects he designed. Generally, the language of drawing and model was
understood both by patron and craftsmen.

Drawings were of two kinds: general drawings used in the initial conception and layout, and details, used to communicate with the craftsman. But
James Ackerman writes that "drawings were not the chief means of communication between architects and builders. . . . Much of the designing went on
in plastic form. . . . Builders, rather than work with detailed specifications,

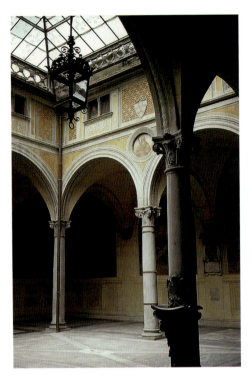

Figure 2.12. Chiostrino at the church of S.S. Annunziata, Florence

got the gist of the design from the model, and when they encountered problems, they simply got the answer from the architect or supervisor by word of mouth."[30] In the case of the Medici Chapel, models, precise drawings, and templates were used to guide the workmen.[31] But for some details, including the detailed carving of arabesques, masks, and certain elaborate capitals, the carvers were allowed to work on their own.[32]

There was apparently no single process of design, or type of design representation, that was universally used. Indeed, Wallace writes:

> There is no clear division between the design and building phases of the Laurentian Library. Once the site for the building was established and a general design approved, work began with many particulars unresolved. . . . A final design, which entailed raising the walls above the main story entablature, was not approved until February 1526, more than three months after work had begun. . . . Drawings for the entrance door to the reading room were only sent to Rome in April 1526, when Michelangelo was ready to have it carved more than two years after the beginning of the vestibule construction. . . . Design and execution were inextricably linked, overlapping rather than successive moments.[33]

To summarize, as in the medieval building culture, in Renaissance Florence the craftsmen were highly visible in the culture, within a guild organization. On small projects, craftsmen were directly employed by clients; on larger projects, craftsmen were supervised by *capomaestri* and *soprastante*, who themselves reported to clients. Architects, who came out of the trades, exerted a growing influence. The building process itself was similar to that in medieval times; agreements were largely informal, based on personal knowledge and experience, and written contracts were generally reserved for larger projects.

The Building Culture of London about 1760

As during the Renaissance, building activity in London around 1760 was local, fine-grained, and at a relatively small scale. Important associations were not between large firms or institutions but between individuals, who operated with informal agreements and relative fluidity with respect to each other.

At the same time, change was imminent, in terms of the accumulation of capital that would allow for larger building operations to take place; industrial operations that would produce more and more manufactured components; the development of professions and professional turf; and a proliferation of building types that would reduce the role of commonly shared knowledge about architecture. These changes were occasioned partly by the growing industrial and financial capabilities of England: in many different ways the stage was being set for large speculative building operations and general contracting.

In 1760 London, which had recovered from the disastrous fire of 1666 and was the incipient center of a worldwide empire, trade and industry were burgeoning, and building activity was everywhere. Much ordinary building was occasioned by the need to house new industrial workers, and building development began to be linked to systems of investment and capital accumulation. An elaborate system of leases and subleases on land put money into real estate cycles as well as into construction. Construction money itself flowed in relatively small amounts, with some barter of labor among craftsmen/developers.

Much speculative building in London happened within the leasehold system, in which large freeholders held their land as the result of favors or grants from the Crown. In some cases, such as the Bedford Estate, this was church land that had been confiscated by Henry VIII at the time of the Dissolution. These freeholders embarked on subdivision and subsequent leases with leaseholders, who entered into agreements with small-scale builder/developers, who entered into further subleases with lessees who directly contracted with builders. Improved property reverted to the lessor after a specified time—often ninety-nine years—but in the meantime, rents were flowing to every leaseholder in the hierarchy.[34]

In a typical lease, no rent would be due for a specified initial period—often a year—which gave the builder a chance to build the house and begin collecting rent before making payments. A small-scale builder could enter the speculative housing market with a minimum of capital. If he did a good deal of the construction himself, his only costs were for materials and for the trades that he did not do himself.

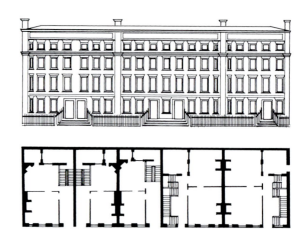

Figure 2.13.
Typical London houses, part of a
small speculative development

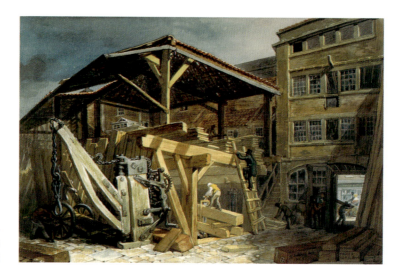

Figure 2.14.
Ingram's
Timber Yard

The bricklayer or the carpenter would often be the person responsible for the overall construction. He performed his own trade but also contracted with plumbers, joiners, and plasterers. Sometimes agreements-in-kind let craftsmen/speculators work on each other's speculations—further reducing the amount of money that had to change hands, enabling more people to become speculators. At a given time, a particular contractor would typically be responsible for only a small number of houses. Large-scale speculative development, in which dozens of houses would be built by a single contractor, was still half a century away.[35]

Many building craftsmen worked within a particular district and belonged to networks in which the same men would often cross paths on different jobs. Men who were particularly skillful might work farther afield, sometimes discovered by architects who would see to their employment on larger or more prestigious projects. As in Italy 300 years before, ordinary craftsmen were trained as apprentices. Training was mostly in the manual craft itself, but some trades, such as carpentry and joinery, required knowledge of mathematics, particularly geometry. Some craftsmen were also trained in drafting and were able to make a drawing of a floor plan or building elevation.

Architecture was not yet a formally established profession, but people who called themselves architects and other people who drew plans existed. Many architects came out of the building trades, and some people who still called themselves surveyors were responsible for the design of buildings.

The principal craftsmen for a simple terraced house were the bricklayer, carpenter, joiner (for stairs and finish woodwork), plumber (for lead roofs and gutters), plasterer, painter, glazier, and ironmonger. Bricks were made nearby, in brickfields that used the rich clay of the Thames Valley. By 1760 much wood was being imported from Scandinavia and the Baltic region because English oak had become expensive following the sixteenth- and seventeenth-century deforestations for shipbuilding. The beginnings of more highly industrialized processes were already in place: lead was refined and made into sheets, and iron bars and crown glass panes were made for blacksmiths and glaziers.[36]

A house was well enough understood that minimal instructions were necessary for the builder, and craftsmen were still working according to traditions that had slowly evolved. Although there were many variations, the plan and construction of a typical house was well established. It had two brick party walls, with built-in chimney flues that extended above the timber roofs; its front and back walls were of brick, and its interior structure of timber. The roof was often made of two gables parallel to the street, with a valley that drained by means of a lead-lined wooden gutter that went through the roof to a leader on the rear. The main part of the building, which was between two and five stories, was two rooms deep, with a space for circulation and stairs along one party wall. The facade was of face brick and spare of detail, with double-hung wooden windows recessed several inches behind

Figure 2.15. Brickmakers

the plane of the wall. Following the 1666 fire, acts of Parliament legislated new building regulations. These were often mentioned in building contracts, and regular enforcement was strengthened with the establishment of the post of district surveyor in the second half of the eighteenth century.

Larger houses and public buildings were also being built; the city had seen a church-building program occasioned by the fire. Neoclassical architects such as William Chambers and Robert Adam were in practice; John Soane would soon appear. They built stone buildings, or buildings rendered in stone and plaster, that were more fashionable than the simple brick terraced house. The larger houses shared details and features with buildings built by well-known architects, because better-educated builders had access to books that described fashionable details and methods of construction.

Figure 2.16.
Bedford Square,
London, built
in the 1760s

Figure 2.17. The portico of the church
of St. Martin-in-the-Fields, designed
by James Gibbs, looking toward
St. Martin's Lane, in the 1820s

In short, the building culture included craftsmen, architects, surveyors, landowners, and building suppliers. It also had the seeds of modern practice. Design and planning reflected academic, Georgian styles and Enlightenment ideas of society. Terraced houses were built of brick walls, with wooden floors and roof; larger buildings were of stone and wood. The building operation itself was usually controlled by bricklayers or carpenters, but architects began to play an important role in larger buildings. Human agreements were informal for small buildings but involved increasingly detailed contracts for larger buildings. Municipal authorities started to have a role in regulation, and as we will see in chapter 5, the precursors of mortgage banks began to form.

The Building Culture of New York in the 1890s

The building culture of New York in the 1890s had many more players and kinds of players than that of 1760s London. It included industrialized products and large institutions: architectural firms, general contractors, and municipal departments to administer building laws. This increased size was connected to changes in professional roles, and with many buildings the architect's role became one of control over all aspects of design and construction—general planning, construction supervision, costs, and the crafting and fabrication of details. Yet, aspects of the building culture were still connected to older sensibilities about craft and to older and more informal methods of operation.

The extremes of wealth and poverty that existed in New York City during the 1890s were evident in both buildings and building activity. The economic engine of the garment, publishing, and other industries, along with shipping and warehousing, needed low-paid workers (partly met by great waves of immigration) and a consequent need for housing (mostly met by tenement construction).[37] By the 1890s, many neighborhoods of Manhattan had already undergone at least one cycle of building replacement and increasing density. Buildings were placed not only on unbuilt fields but also on land made available by the demolition of less profitable buildings. The *Real Estate Record and Builders' Guide* for January 7, 1893, reports many real estate transactions involving buildings: the purchase of a corner property on Broadway near Bleecker Street, including old buildings, for the "erection of modern buildings"; various tenements and flats; a four-story brick dwelling at No. 5 West 16th Street. It also reports conveyances of land: eighty-seven acres for building lots, north of 167th Street; a lot at the northeast corner of Madison Avenue and 77th Street, "the site to be improved by the erection of a handsome apartment house"; six lots on the south side of 80th Street, near Columbus Avenue, "which [builder Robert Wallace] will improve by the erection of seven first-class four story and basement private dwellings"; and lots on 83rd and Lexington, for five-story flats.

Many kinds of buildings were under construction: tenements (housing a dozen or more families, often on 25-foot-wide lots that had been platted for single-family houses), apartment houses, buildings with apartments above and shops below, single-family dwellings, churches, warehouses, factory

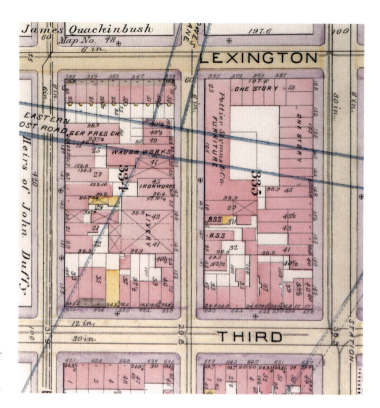

Figure 2.18.
Two blocks of
Midtown Manhattan,
1890

Figure 2.19.
Building under con-
struction on Fifteenth
St., New York City,
prior to 1901.
© Collection of
The New-York
Historical Society.

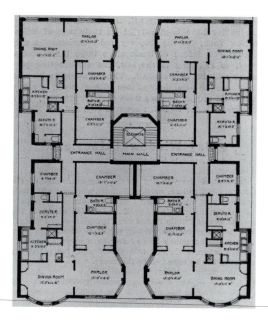

Figure 2.20.
Plan of apartment house
built in the 1890s

buildings, builders' yards, social clubs, libraries, schools, department stores, hospitals, park structures. A map of two blocks of what is now Midtown, published in 1890, points up this diversity.

There were hundreds of building firms in the city, and hundreds of materials suppliers. Just a quick look at the advertisements in a few issues of the *Real Estate Record and Guide* around 1900 yielded the following building trades, suppliers, and services:

annunciators
architects
asbestos pipe covering
awnings
blinds
brick
bronze, brass, wrought
  iron
cabinetwork
carpenters
chimney ventilators
concrete vault lights
contractors and builders
dumbwaiters
electrical contractors
engineers
engines
fire-proof partitions
fireproofing
furnaces
furnaces and ranges
general repairs
glass
grates

hollow clay block
house movers
ironwork
lighting reflectors
lime
linoleum
lumber and timber
mantels
marble works
masons
masons' materials
metal ceilings
metallic cornices and
  skylights
mineral wool
paint
painting and finishing
parquet floors
pipe, fire clay flue linings
pipe, vitrified sewer
plasterboard
plasterers
plastering fiber
plastic slate roofing

Portland cement
preservative coatings
punching and cutting
  machines
ranges
real estate brokers
real estate loans
refrigerators
roof drying frames
roofing
sash, doors, blinds, trim
sheet-metal lath
sidewalks, arches, stoops
stair treads
stone, artificial
stonemason
terra-cotta
tiles
tin, slate, and metal
  roofing
title companies
wallpaper
window cleaning

To this list we can surely add "banks" and "lawyers."

Furthermore, the list shows a significant number of materials that come to the building site having already been manufactured or preprocessed in some way, beyond traditional processes such as the firing of brick:[38]

annunciators	dumbwaiters	paint
asbestos pipe covering	engines	plasterboard
awnings	furnaces and ranges	ranges
blinds	grates	refrigerators
chimney ventilators	lighting reflectors	sash, doors, blinds, trim
concrete vault lights	metal ceilings	wallpaper

Suppliers and contractors were located all around the city. Timber yards were often on the river's edge, enabling them to receive shipments by boat. Large manufacturing works or contractors' yards often had a different address from the main office of the firm, indicating that firms were large and were developing complex internal structures of their own.

The extremes and continuities of the building culture are illustrated by comparing the construction of two buildings belonging to two different economic and social worlds.

The Metropolitan Club, built between 1891 and 1894, was one of a number of rich men's clubs, designed to project wealth and status. The building was designed by McKim Mead and White, New York's premier architecture firm, which also designed Pennsylvania Station, other clubs and public buildings, and houses for industrialists and financiers. The total construction cost was about $1.6 million.[39] The building had a steel frame, brick exterior walls covered with limestone, and elaborate interiors of marble, plaster, and gilding. An accounting of the building's costs prepared on April 13, 1894, lists a figure of $60,000 for "McKim Mead & White and Sundries"; presumably this figure included the architect's fees.

At the same time, the tenement house at 64 Oliver Street, near the Manhattan Bridge, was built by Roderick Green as a speculative investment. It contained ten flats, was completed in five months during 1889, and was

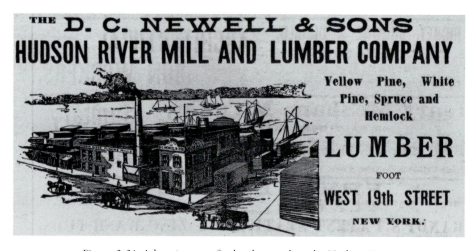

Figure 2.21. Advertisement for lumber yard on the Hudson River

designed by the firm of John Butler Snook, an architect known for many commercial buildings throughout the city. The construction cost was about $6,000.[40] Oliver Street is at the edge of the Lower East Side, and it is likely that the families who occupied the building included low-paid manufacturing workers, perhaps recent immigrants. Like other tenements, the building was of brick exterior walls (including two party walls), and its floors were mostly of timber, with some steel. Its plan was typical of thousands of tenements built at the same time: only a minimal light shaft provided daylight and ventilation to interior rooms.

For each building, an architect drew plans, negotiated contracts with builders, and supervised construction. In both cases building laws had to be followed. However, the Metropolitan Club was one of a relatively small percentage of similar buildings in the city on which attention was lavished. The building on Oliver Street was one of thousands built at around the same time, buildings thrown up cheaply to try to squeeze as much money as possible out of their tenants.

Figure 2.22. Metropolitan Club, Fifth Avenue, designed by McKim Mead and White, 1891

Figure 2.23. Street in Lower East Side, New York City

There were hundreds of drawings done, at various scales, for the Metropolitan Club, but the New-York Historical Society has only about ten drawings—most of those that were done—for the Oliver Street building. The Metropolitan Club took three years, the tenement five months. For the Metropolitan Club, there were at least a dozen contractors (including one in Paris that provided much of the decorative work for the main rooms), working through either the main builder or the architects; for the tenement, there were six (including one contract for $15 for the surveyor—the same surveyor as for the Metropolitan Club—and $7.08 for stained glass—probably around the front door).

In both cases it was the architect and not a general contractor who dealt directly with the various building firms (although in the case of the Metropolitan Club, builder David H. King administered some, but not all, of the subcontracts). For the club, builders submitted formal bids as they do today; asked for progress payments to be approved by the architect, as they do today; and hired workers through building trades unions, as many builders do today.

An architect or draftsman working for an architectural firm would most likely have been trained by working directly for an architect. His first assignments might be to trace designs done by more experienced people in the office. (This tracing was necessary, before the age of blueprint machines, to prepare drawings for various contractors.) In this way the architectural apprentice began to work with the actual material of drawings and building designs without being in a position to make decisions. Through repetitive copying, however, he did begin to learn a language, of plan, elevation, and detail. Within the office, those who were more successful were gradually given positions of more responsibility, eventually perhaps taken under the wing of the principal designer, and asked to do buildings on their own.

The number of drawings for the Metropolitan Club, the time spent on its construction, and the extent of the correspondence files during its design and construction (several thousand letters, estimates, memoranda, and bills) are indicative of the building's cost (over 250 times that of the tenement) and presumed importance.

The tenement was one of thousands built for speculation and to house the working classes of the city. Jacob Riis's *How the Other Half Lives* reported that 3,733 tenements had been built from June 1, 1888, to August 1, 1890, and that the estimated population of the city's 37,316 tenement buildings on August 1, 1890, was 1.25 million, out of the city's total population of about 1.6 million.[41] This is about thirty-three people per building (but the actual density was much higher in many buildings). So if we imagine that the $6,000 cost of 64 Oliver Street was average for tenement construction (it was probably lower), we can estimate a total construction cost for *all the tenement buildings in the city* at about $230 million—only about 140 times that of the cost of the Metropolitan Club alone.

In summary, the vigor of the building culture reflected the strong mercantile/industrial economy of New York; the growing size and complexity of firms was typical of commercial operations in general. Buildings were made to show status, accommodate new and complex functions, and house the many workers who made the economy function.

There were large firms of architects, general contractors, specialized sub-contractors, banks, major commercial and institutional clients, building developers and speculators, municipal regulatory agencies, and insurance companies. Many industrial components and materials were brought in from afar, occasioning elaborate systems of control and accounting.

Agreements were detailed and explicit for large projects, and somewhat less so for small projects, but for most buildings they were certainly more explicit than a hundred years before. Personal trust and informal association brought people together, but agreements themselves were spelled out in detail. Strong hierarchies of control governed building and general contracting firms, and there was extensive regulation by municipal departments.

Among the thousands of buildings built, architectural style was hardly consistent. The neoclassical style of firms like McKim Mead and White conveyed permanence and wealth, but there was a wide variety of styles, including varieties of "Richardsonian Romanesque," French Empire, Gothic, Italianate, and others. Materials included brick of different colors, terracotta, limestone, brown sandstone, cast iron, and glass—and the overall visual impact of the city, layered with styles of different decades and the work of hundreds of different builders and architects, had a vibrancy that represented the richness of the city's building culture and economy. The manufacturing and mercantile sensibilities of the Victorian age had allowed buildings to break away from the visual consistencies of earlier times, resulting in the kind of city that modernist critics two or three decades later would see as confused and chaotic.

Figure 2.24. Building construction near Columbus Circle, June 16, 1897

The Four Building Cultures Compared

From the point of view of architectural style, the four cultures are different in what kinds of buildings they produced. From the point of view of *process*, however, most significant change did not occur before the nineteenth century. Although there were innovations introduced before that, including a growing explicitness of architectural knowledge, and the carrying through of projects by a single architect, no tremendous *procedural* differences existed between the building cultures of the medieval city, Renaissance Italy, and eighteenth-century London. All were organized with independent craftsmen, with control over design in the hands of someone who came out of the building trades, training largely by apprenticeship, and with a minimum of external regulation. In London during the 1760s, hints of change were evident: small-scale builders were amassing enough capital to become small-scale speculators, municipal authorities were exerting more regulatory control, and factory production had begun. But even then, the building culture would have been familiar to someone from the fifteenth century or even the twelfth. As with so many other aspects of society, it was in the nineteenth century that major changes happened, and by the 1890s in New York, the building culture had taken on essentially the form it has today. The architectural profession was emerging as an independent set of institutions from those of builders, building developers, banks, and government regulators—each of which had its own identity and asserted its own authority.

BUILDING CULTURES OF
THE CONTEMPORARY CITY

3

The Making of the Everyday Built World

The previous chapter described how the building culture of 1890s New York included speculative tenement builders that employed immigrant labor and architectural firms that designed major public and private buildings. It included a wide diversity of firms and a construction workforce of thousands. In the contemporary American city, a century later, the building culture has evolved to such a complex form that it has several major parts, or subcultures, each of which is responsible for a different kind of building:

- *Speculative commercial and office development, and standard buildings for large corporations:* These include buildings with space for lease, in downtown areas or along "strip" thoroughfares, shopping malls, warehouses, fast-food restaurants, "big box" retail stores.
- *Buildings designed by architects for particular clients:* These include public buildings such as courthouses, museums, hospitals, schools, airports, theaters; corporate headquarters; university buildings; houses commissioned by their owners.
- *Residential development by merchant builders:* This includes single-family "tract" development as well as multifamily apartment complexes and apartment buildings.

- *Small-scale building and self-building, without architects' services:* This includes house renovation and additions, individual houses built by builders or owner-builders, and other small projects.
- *Manufacture of building components and buildings:* This includes all manufacturing operations that provide components for the above four categories, as well as "manufactured houses," prefabricated house panels and roof trusses, and similar items.

Together, these subcultures produce the vast majority of the buildings in modern society. Although many of the specifics given here are for the United States, similar versions may be found in most countries of the world.

Table 3.1 points up the volume of this work, and the relative quantities of different kinds of building in the United States, for the year 1995.[1]

The various subcultures are not independent, but many attributes in them are different. Agreements are handled differently in different subcultures, money flows differently, different kinds of institutions are prominent in each, and the built results are very different. Far from being monolithic, the contemporary building culture operates in many different ways—and it will turn out, later in the book, that these differences will provide some of the seeds for understanding how the building culture as a whole may be changed for the better.

Commercial and Office Development

Most nonresidential building in modern cities—downtown office buildings, suburban shopping malls and office buildings—happens through a development process guided largely by financial considerations. The process has big players—a large corporation that acts as the developer of a major complex of buildings—and small players—an individual who buys a quarter block of land to erect a small commercial building for rental to a few individual shop owners.

Table 3.1 Construction work in the United States, 1995

	Floor area (millions of square feet)	Contract value ($ million U.S.)	Number of dwelling units (thousands)
Office buildings	113	14,577	
Stores/shopping centers	266	16,436	
Other commercial	320	15,419	
Manufacturing buildings	160	12,374	
Educational	176	21,445	
Hospital and health	69	10,707	
Other nonresidential buildings	171	21,326	
Single-family houses	1,869	110,211	989
Multifamily housing	301	17,562	275

Source: Robert Murray and Kermit Baker, "Architecture market outlook: Two crystal balls," *Architectural Record* 184, no. 6 (June 1996): 37.

Figure 3.1. Urban speculation: Los Angeles

The developer is central, responsible for land acquisition, construction financing, long-term financing, arrangement of design and construction contracts, and the disposition of the finished building. Some developers are concerned with architectural quality, or improving the life of the city, but to a large extent the decisions the developer controls are based on simple variables of profit and risk. Often, this is *short-term* profit, as when the developer builds with the intention of selling the finished project as soon as possible to an entity that might maintain a longer-term commitment.

In this context, decisions about such projects are based on a series of interacting financial variables: the price of land, interest rates for construction financing and for long-term mortgages, current vacancy rates, taxes and potential tax breaks, construction costs, and professional fees. Construction costs are often only a part of the equation, and the project's success may hinge on slight variations in interest rates or tax breaks. With this kind of development, concern for the bottom line promotes:

- Building as much as the site will allow, with the highest possible ratio of rentable space to gross building area.
- Building fast. Since interest rates for construction financing are much higher than mortgage rates, the project needs to be turned into something that can act as income-generating mortgage collateral as soon as possible.
- Building as cheaply as the market will bear in order to keep site development and construction costs as low as possible.
- Building "for the market," which requires flexibility of rental situations over time. Since the rental tenant, who may not be identified until the building is erected, will be responsible for fitting out the rented space, the flexibility of the raw space is important.[2]

These interests guide the developer's activities. They encourage the developer to use zoning rules for his or her own benefit, perhaps investing in the writing of proposals for variances, to increase the allowable building area on a particular site. They promote designs that allow for construction sequences and techniques that are simple, able to be carried out by construction workers who are making as low a wage as possible. They promote designs to be done with a view toward maximum "flexibility." Since the people who will actually use the buildings are not known, the design often comprises simple, large rectangular spaces, with as much unobstructed floor area as possible.[3]

An experienced developer begins by becoming familiar with the local real estate market, the available properties for development, and the rental market for space. He or she will have ongoing relationships with realtors—who themselves profit from large land transactions—and these relationships will provide the developer with knowledge about potential properties that is not yet available to other people. Large developers may put a lot of effort into assembling large parcels of land, perhaps acting in secret or through dummy corporations so as not to drive up prices.[4]

At the same time, the developer will be cultivating relationships with investors and bankers, trying to raise money at the best possible price. Again, ongoing relationships are important, but in all cases the developer needs to produce a detailed financial proposal for the project, laying out the variables of costs and income, to convince potential investors that the ratio of risk to profit is low. This process may involve schematic architectural design and construction cost estimates: at this early stage the design is already strongly tied in to financial variables and regulatory constraints such as zoning. Financial viability depends on the architect's ability to design within these constraints. It also depends on the "image" of the building, which in the case of office buildings may involve little more than the exterior skin (which in typical cases represents, perhaps, only about fifteen percent of the construction cost) and the design of the lobby; in the case of shopping centers it will have to do mostly with the interior design of the "public" space.

The architectural firm will likely be chosen because of its track record with similar projects and perhaps because of previous experience with the developer. Depending on the firm's size, most of the actual design work may fall to lower-level people in the organization; the principal may only supply the financial variables or a very general design concept at the beginning.

Typically, although there will be hurdles to overcome and perhaps, in complex projects, major changes before the start of construction, the overall parameters are thus set early on. The subsequent steps of design, construction, and occupancy will all support these initial decisions.

At the point that financing has been secured and the project has been given the go-ahead, the architect is under pressure to complete the "bid package"—the set of drawings and specifications that the contractor will use. The architect will use consultants of various kinds, including civil and mechanical engineers, space planners and interior architects, cost estimators, landscape architects, and others. Through his or her experience with similar projects, and ongoing relationships with contractors, the architect is also aware of potential difficulties during construction that might be avoided through design.

Although the developer is working in a matrix of real financial constraints, he or she may be in some position to take risks, often with other people's money. The architect is not in such a position and has a relatively small amount of control. A good deal of the "design" of the building is determined by other people and institutions; the architect acts as a manager or coordinator, a go-between, making sure that the separate requirements of all the players are met. This reduces the opportunity for the architect to engage in creative expression or even to specify details and materials that may allow for the level of craft and finish she considers appropriate. In many ways, the architect is an agent, instrumental to the demands of other people and institutions, and the images they want to put forward. Large development companies and major clients, in fact, have their own in-house architects, who help represent the client to the architect preparing the bid package and form another layer of authority between the architect and the head people in the client organization.

Drawings and specifications emphasize standard techniques and components, to reduce costs and uncertainties that contractors feel while bidding. Although project delivery methods—particularly for larger projects—are changing in favor of construction management in which the construction process is controlled more directly by the client than by a general contractor, the next step is typically to put the project out to bid. General contractors who meet particular qualifications (experience with similar projects, construction volume, size of projects, ability to secure construction bonds) will be invited to bid. The preparation of a bid involves knowledge of real costs, experience in estimating unknowns, and no small amount of guesswork. Subcontractors will be asked to bid their portions of the project, applying their own guesswork to the situation, and general contractors will want to work with subcontractors whom they have worked with before, who are reliable, and who they think will not inflate their bid.

The contract is awarded, and the site is turned over the contractor, who then feels the same kinds of pressures that the architect felt up until that point. The contractor's pressures are perhaps greater—a lot more money is involved (over 90 percent of the building budget, as opposed to the 5–6 percent that might go to the architect), and interest now needs to be paid on the

Figure 3.2.
Building for money

Figure 3.3. Suburban commercial speculation: Eugene, Oregon, 1998

construction loan. Now the contractor is working in a tight matrix within which he and the various subs and tradespeople who are working for him have little leeway. He is bound contractually to build according to the drawings and specifications, to the architect's satisfaction. The bank will not make progress payments until it is convinced that a certain amount of work has been done; building inspectors need to check on compliance with codes; the site needs to be kept safe according to government rules; subcontractors must be coordinated with each other; materials must arrive at the right time; change orders from the architect must be dealt with. The general contractor's skill ensures that the building will be built according to specification and within budget.

The buildings produced through such development form an important, everyday part of the context of people's lives, providing space for many commercial and retail activities. They are also an important means of financial investment. Developers are central to this subculture: they help to coordinate the contributions of bankers, architects, general contractors, subcontractors and building workers, engineers, and municipal agencies.

The subculture produces shopping malls and other commercial buildings, office buildings, restaurants, and so on. Often these buildings will be of simple wood or steel frame construction, or perhaps tilt-up concrete slab construction; exterior and interior surfaces will be made of large sheet materials, with standard details and off-the-shelf "special" details and finishes.

To summarize, in the process of building, there is a strong hierarchy of control, starting with the developer and including the bank, and the contractor's organization is responsible for strict compliance with detailed drawings and specifications. Because of the cost of money and the need for the building to be profitable as soon as possible, speed is often critical, and the building's design, along with the use of premanufactured components and standard details, can facilitate this. There is strong regulation by all the institutions that take risks or have exposure: banks, municipal building departments, government bodies that deal with workplace safety.

Buildings Designed by Architects for Particular Clients

With buildings designed for particular clients or users rather than for speculative investment, the architect often retains at least some of her traditional control over the building—and it is for this reason that most architects and architecture students aspire to this kind of work. Although such buildings involve the full panoply of consultants, contractors, and code officials, there is a greater expectation that the architect is central. Even so, the number of building projects that are controlled in a "traditional" one-on-one architect-patron relationship is very small, and most larger institutions and institutional buildings have hierarchies of control, building committees, and consultants to those building committees.

Such a project begins with a client's decision to build for a particular purpose, the formulation of an approximate budget, and the search for an architect. In some cases the architect will be chosen because of previous experience with the client or personal word of mouth; in some cases, there is a public process of asking for qualifications and conducting interviews (this is the usual case with public projects); and with some important projects, a competition is held.[5]

The architectural firm designs the building in consultation with the client. Generally, this consultation consists of a series of presentations of the design at different stages of completion. The client is asked to comment on the design, and on the basis of those comments, the architect may revise it. In this situation, the architect is in control and will tend to only want to make changes that do not fundamentally alter the basic conception of the project and do not increase the architect's design time. The portion of the architect's fee for basic design is only about 20 percent, while the rest goes for design development, preparation of contract documents, bidding, and construction supervision. Since there is often uncertainty in phases of work that follow design, in ordinary cases the architect will be reluctant to spend too much time on design.

Figure 3.4. Designing for a public client: Center for the Arts, San Francisco, designed by Fumihiko Maki

It is with the custom-designed, single-family house, as opposed to larger buildings, that the architect retains the largest amount of control over all aspects of the process. On larger buildings, the architect is at the center of a large network of players during the design phase, consulting with the client, building code officials, materials suppliers, engineers, cost estimators, and other paid consultants, some of whom are preparing drawings and specifications that will become part of the bid package. Once the design phase is finished, the project proceeds in much the same way as others that are put out to bid. There will tend to be more involvement on the part of the architect throughout the process, particularly in the case of buildings that will be particularly visible and that might form an important part of the portfolio of the firm.

The fundamental difference between this situation and that of the speculative commercial building is in the balance of control between the client or developer and the architect. In the speculative situation, the developer is more in control; in the "traditional" client-architect situation, the architect is more in control—although not in complete control. Large clients are becoming less and less willing to give complete responsibility to an external architect, and as already mentioned, they tend to have their own in-house architects to represent their interests.

In both the commercial development and the building designed for a particular client, although the architect and the contractor are each highly skilled professionals, their relationship is wary. The architect may see the contractor as someone who is instrumental to his own ends—the "design" of the building—and may be impatient with the issues that are of concern to the contractor. The contractor may see the architect as someone who is not as familiar as he might be with the technicalities of building and who produces drawings that are incomplete, requiring further interpretation by the contractor. Each of these descriptions often has some truth, and the unfortunate net result is that there is a tension between the two that in many cases prevents all but the most formal, legal sort of relationship.

This subculture produces unique buildings that may be an important means toward the expression of image and status on the part of the client and toward the realization of current artistic ideas on the part of the architects. Usually, these buildings are intended to stand alone rather than in a context of other similar buildings. Architects are more central here, but in other respects this subculture is similar to that of speculative development. There may be more involvement and interest on the part of the client, more shaping of materials and components specifically for the project, but to a large extent the contracting procedures, regulation, building materials, and techniques are the same as those of commercial speculative development.

Merchant House-Building

Most of the housing produced in the United States consists of single-family dwellings built as repetitive units in subdivisions or in apartment developments by speculative developers who operate locally, functioning much like developers of office and commercial buildings. A speculative house developer, like the developers discussed earlier, is at the center of a process that includes bankers, regulatory agencies, contractors, manufacturers, perhaps architects, and house buyers.

The developer begins by identifying a piece of land and doing a financial calculation based on projected costs and income to determine whether or not the project is viable. If it is, a civil engineer will prepare a subdivision plan and work the project through the offices of the local government agency responsible for new subdivisions. This stage is often lengthy, involving sewer permits, water and electricity connections, the fire marshal's approvals, and perhaps environmental impact assessments—all the while checking the proposed plan with the developer and his architect, if an architect has been retained. This is one of the most formative stages of such a project, because it may determine the character of the resulting neighborhood.

The design of the houses is determined by the developer, often by working with a realtor who is familiar with the local market. Developers pay a lot of attention to each other[6] and to other houses that are being built; they

Figure 3.5. Marketing the product, Eugene, Oregon, 1998

Figure 3.6. Speculative rental housing, Eugene, Oregon, 1998

Table 3.2. Characteristics of new single-family houses in the United States

	1971	1995
Average square feet	1,520	2,095
Two-and-a-half or more bathrooms	15%	48%
Garage for two or more cars	39%	76%
Brick exterior	38%	20%
Two or more stories	17%	48%

Source: National Association of Home Builders, *1997 Housing Facts, Figures, and Trends.*

know what is selling and are sensitive to slight changes in user preferences. One developer said that "one of the most common design strategies starts with a few guys getting into a car [and looking around at what has recently been built]."[7] They are largely catering to the center of the market—the so-called typical family, or those who would agree to have a house of a typical family, even if it does not exactly meet their needs. Table 3.2 shows how the center of the market changed over twenty-four years.[8]

Since developers want to reduce their financial risk or the perception of risk, the market is continuously and subtly redefined to exclude the atypical. For example, it is often difficult for nontraditional families, extended families, or people who have businesses at home to find suitable houses. While this is partly a problem of zoning, developers tend not to want to push the issue with zoning officials or to enter into what they see as a risky market situation. The buildings themselves will likely include standard details and construction practices and the most readily available materials, chosen to get the maximum immediate visual impact for the least possible cost.

The developer negotiates a bank loan for construction and submits plans for approval by the building department. The houses will consist of variations on two or three models that perhaps are similar to a successful development nearby, or obtained from a plan service that advertises nationally and provides permit/construction drawings for the house that may require only minor modification to include foundation design and exact placement on individual sites. Architects are not usually involved in the construction process of speculative residential developments. But they do produce many of the designs that make their way into house-building, and their influence in this process is greater than commonly believed. The largest stock-plan services often contract with architects who produce and market those plans to different builders in different places.[9]

Particularly with smaller projects, the developer may act as the general contractor. In other cases a contract will be negotiated with a general contractor. In either case, the contractor will act much as contractors do with commercial and residential projects. He will employ a foreman to organize the construction and will enter into subcontracts or labor agreements with tradespeople. These tradespeople are often individuals that the contractor and foreman work with on a regular basis: excavators, framers, concrete contractors, roofers, finish carpenters, plumbers, electricians, drywall installers, insulators, painters, roofers, sheet-metal fabricators, floor finishers, and many others. Each of the subcontractors has regular accounts with materials suppliers—lumber yards; paint distributors; sand, gravel and cement distributors; hardware houses; plumbing and electrical suppliers; and suppliers of sheet metal, glass, roof shingles. In the United States, typical buildings are wood-frame tract houses with increasing use of engineered wood components and premanufactured sheet materials. Multiple-unit buildings are of concrete block/wood frame, with finishes of similar materials to tract houses. According to its own agreement with the developer, the bank makes regular payments to the developer, corresponding to the progress of the work. The tradespeople are individually bonded and insured, are covered by workers' compensation insurance, and are also entitled to have job safety maintained by their employer. As work proceeds, regular visits are made by city building inspectors, who make sure that the work is in conformance with city law, which likely includes the nationally used Uniform Building Code.

This building subculture produces a large percentage of the dwellings of a town, and its products reflect current values and aspirations—at least in image. But house-building is also an important mechanism for investment and the buildup of long-term equity on the part of many families.

Although the development process is similar to that of other speculative development, many individuals enter into purchase agreements with developers and mortgage agreements with banks, bringing money into the building operation from many different sources. One end of the process, at least—the market itself—has the potential for difference and variety.

Small-Scale Builders and Self-Building, without Architects' Services

A good deal of building gets done with no involvement from architects at all. A sizable percentage of the house-building market, and an even larger percentage of the house-renovation and addition market, is undertaken by small-scale builders without architectural services, and by owners themselves without builders. In 1996, for example, the U.S. house remodeling market stood at $118.6 billion, but architects' invoices for remodeling single-family houses only accounted for $265 million.[10] Assuming architects' fees to be 10 percent of construction cost for residential work, these figures indicate that architects were involved in only about 2 percent of house remodelings. Robert Gutman suggests that about 50 percent of all building is done without the involvement of architects at all.[11] In many places, building permits for buildings smaller than a certain area do not require preparation by an architect or engineer, and such projects go ahead with only the owner and/or builder in charge. Since a certain portion of this kind of building is undertaken without legal building permits and thus goes unreported, the percentage may be even larger than what Gutman reports.

People undertaking small building projects are continually exposed to popular home magazines and other media and to what builders tell them. The ideas that people use may have a connection to the more "artistic" architectural culture or to much more popular understandings of taste. Stock plans are advertised in home magazines, and working drawings are readily available; builders can use these to make bids and to submit to local building

Figure 3.7. Small-scale building takes place all over the world: house addition in Mahdia, Tunisia, 1994

departments for approval.[12] Thousands of products are available through home stores and catalogs. With these products, there may be an emphasis on image, surface treatments, and on items that can be readily installed in the basic structure.

A house built in this subculture is likely of light-frame construction, sheathed with a processed wood product or vinyl, and walled on the inside with gypsum board. The roof is made of asphalt shingles or wooden shakes, the windows of vinyl and glass. This materials palette has many variations, but it is ubiquitous, and builders are familiar with it. Subcontractors—who deal with plumbing, wiring, insulation, heating, flooring, cabinets, ceramic tiles, the hanging and taping of gypsum board, and other aspects of house construction—are also familiar enough with the system that they can operate with minimum instructions. With only a very few constraints, and a minimum of drawings, the heating contractor can install the ducts for a heating system in a day; likewise for the rough plumbing or rough electrical work. This system of house construction is open and easy to work with.

The builder, who perhaps has had an informal apprenticeship with someone like herself, tends to be sensitive to the client's wishes and knowledgeable about what products and materials are available. Until her firm becomes big enough that specialization of tasks can occur, she will handle all the tasks: bidding, purchasing, talking to the client and to potential clients, billing, hiring and paying personnel, dealing with inspectors, and hiring and coordinating subcontractors, in addition to building—and all of this perhaps for several different jobs. Individual builders spend their days building, and driving from job to supply house to job, and their nights on the telephone, coordinating with subcontractors and working up bids.

This subculture of small builders is the most informal of the various subcultures discussed here. Very small projects may be undertaken on the edge of what is legal, without permits; small contracts may be oral; the project may be changed as it is being built; clients and builders are identified almost completely by a word-of-mouth network; suppliers may range from local hardware and "home" stores to the same outlets that larger builders use.

This part of the building culture is nevertheless connected to the wider building culture. Builders may have worked for larger firms and then decided to venture out on their own—the modern version of the old apprentice-journeyman-master story. The small builder will use many of the same materials as the merchant-builder. Subcontractors may also work on larger projects. If drawings are submitted for permit approval, they may be drawn by an architect who is just starting out. The house or kitchen remodeling is one of the ways that young architects begin to build up a portfolio; for these architects, a new house designed from scratch is an important next step.

This subculture operates more informally than the larger sectors of building speculation and large building construction; agreements between parties are often informal. The building operation may have a good deal of give-and-take between builder and client. Building techniques are similar to those of larger building operations, though the level of craft can be higher or lower. Money flows in relatively small amounts, and although materials come largely from local suppliers, they are largely the same as those for larger building operations.

This is the subculture of building that is perhaps most familiar to most people. Closely integrated with everyday life, and through relatively small-scale transactions, it involves small builders, clients, and building departments and produces houses, house additions, and commercial alterations.

Manufacture of Building Components and Buildings

All four of the modern building subcultures already described in this chapter depend on a system of industrialization—a subculture in itself—that has evolved considerably over the last 200 years and produces building materials that are quite different from those earlier in history. Building construction has reached a point where very few materials are brought "raw" to the site, to be shaped by building craftsmen. Instead, a good deal of processing takes place in factories, and the building worker's job is either to cut a processed material, such as gypsum board or plastic laminate, or to install a premanufactured component, such as a vinyl window or wall panel. The manufacture of ready-made parts for buildings accelerated during the nineteenth century, when popular media and railroads started to allow for nationwide distribution of products that required large capitalization for their production.

In the United States, techniques, details, and components are to large extent shared nationally—there is a high degree of dimensional standardization of parts, and manufacturers have plants producing the same things in different parts of the country as well. So a great variety of products is available, and these products can be easily incorporated into a project. But in the same way that speculative projects are themselves conceived "for the market," building components and products, too—particularly the cheapest ones—are designed for what most users will accept. If one looks at the

Figure 3.8.
A large retail building
products store, 1998

range of readily available off-the-shelf window units, floor coverings, hung
ceiling assemblies, exterior cladding materials, bathroom fixtures and finishes—in fact, all the building items that people see every day—there sometimes seems to be a lot more standardization in the built environment than
one would infer from going through the pages of the myriad of manufacturers' catalogs available.

In some cases, manufacture has itself become a building delivery system,
not only a way to deliver individual parts of the building. This development
has many historical threads, including the premanufacture of houses by the
Sears Roebuck Co. in the early part of the century;[13] the massive industrialization during World War II;[14] the large tract-house developments in Levittown, in which construction was essentially based on an assembly-line
method in which building workers moved from house to house; failed U.S.
government programs for prefabrication such as Operation Breakthrough;[15]
and the growing market for manufactured houses in recent decades.

The manufactured-house market has steadily increased to 24 percent of
new houses sold in the United States,[16] and there are places where most new
housing consists of premanufactured housing. The houses are being made in
larger and fewer plants: the number of corporations producing such houses
decreased from 170 in 1980 to 92 in 1995, and the number of plants
decreased from 450 in 1980 to 285 in 1995.[17] The plants are large shed-
like factories, not subject to the uncertainties of weather or difficult site
conditions that slow production, and workers there generally make lower
wages than they would doing comparable jobs on a construction site. Buyers

Figure 3.9.
Panelized house
construction (Donald
Corner, architect),
Eugene, Oregon,
1993

Figure 3.10.
A manufactured
house factory in
New England, 1992

usually have some choice in layout and finish materials, and the buildings are marketed on lots, similarly to automobiles. The buyer may have the house delivered either to her own lot, which will have been prepared with a foundation and utility hookups by a local builder experienced with such installations, or to a manufactured-home "park" where the buyer of the house may rent but not own the site of the house.

In summary, this subculture is closely allied to manufacturing in general and accords with many social ideals of modern culture. Building components and parts are made and marketed in the same way as other products, making them available to many people. Materials and components are the products of highly capitalized industries in which the main players are large manufacturers, product engineers, testing laboratories and building code organizations. Regulation of building components and materials occurs through building codes and testing laboratories, but manufactured houses are sometimes subject to different codes than site-built houses. Production of building materials, building assemblies, and even manufactured houses takes place in factories.

Variety in the Contemporary Building Culture

The character of the contemporary building culture as a whole is illustrated by the relationships between these five subcultures. Each has people and institutions that are not shared by the others: a small-scale builder with a pickup truck and a home computer tends not to deal with large contractors; well-known architects tend not to do small kitchen remodelings; large contractors do not do business with retail home stores; manufactured house salespeople do not deal with architects; electricians may concentrate on residential rather than commercial work. Each realm has its own set of participants, its own place in the building market and the building economy, and to some extent its own language.

Yet at the same time, the same building code applies both to single-family houses and to the large commercial development; the same line of windows goes into the bedroom remodel and the multiunit residential project; the same zoning ordinance applies to all buildings. So this sharing of institutions, and of workers who move from subculture to subculture, ties them together. In this respect, today's building culture may be compared to that of the early eighteenth century, where craftsmen, known to each other, moved from building to building, and from large building to small building.

In addition, the building culture is not monolithic—all parts of it do not operate in the same way. Some parts may be better at innovation than others (architects, large capital); some parts are more responsive to client needs (some architects, small builders, clients themselves); some are better at producing beautiful buildings (some architects and some builders); some are better able to deal with quantity production (large capital, merchant builders, small-scale builders).

However, partly because of the nature of contemporary institutions, the positive attributes that exist in one part of the building culture do not necessarily make their way to others. The variety and responsiveness with respect to buildings that small-scale builders enjoy is not shared by large corporations; small builders cannot as easily invest in a risky new product as a large corporation can. The aesthetic judgment of architects may not be shared by builders. The modern building culture, although it does have elements of diversity, is not nearly as fluid as it might be in the sharing of ideas, techniques, and expertise, and not nearly as responsive as it might be to necessary changes.

The complexity of the modern city arises from the combination and layering of these five interrelated subcultures. The city consists of buildings done by large, multinational development corporations and others done by small investors who want to see if they can make a go of it in the development of a very small project. It consists of a development of half a dozen houses by a local builder, and many basement remodelings and rear decks built by homeowners. It consists of new motels and office buildings near the airport, and restored historic houses in an old neighborhood near the downtown. Even a single building may have been the result of two or more of these processes—an obvious example is a speculative office building that holds a custom-designed set of offices.

This range is much wider than it was in the medieval or Renaissance city. The proliferation of building types during the nineteenth century and a simple increase in the number of buildings built was accompanied by a proliferation of institutions and an increase in the sheer number of people involved in building activity. It was perhaps inevitable that this increase in volume would have led to a divergence of functions among different subcultures.

At the same time that this variety in the building culture makes separate subcultures evident, though, many of the attitudes and procedures are the same from one to another. As we will see in Part II, building cultures are characterized by deep-seated attributes, not always helpful, that emerge partly out of society at large.

RULES AND KNOWLEDGE
ABOUT BUILDING

II

The seven chapters of Part II each deal with a different aspect of building cultures. In these chapters we will look comparatively at the various building cultures already introduced, along with others, in order to better understand the ways in which the people and institutions of the building culture affect the form of buildings and cities. In the Introduction the idea of a healthy building culture was put forward; the discussions in the following chapters will describe how particular attributes may or may not lead to such healthy cultures.

- In chapter 4, the relationship between the building culture and the larger culture in which the building culture exists will be examined, and we will suggest that *healthy building cultures exhibit both autonomy and interdependence with respect to the larger culture.*
- In chapter 5, the institutions of the building culture itself—architecture firms, contracting firms, and so forth—will be examined, and we will conjecture that *as the number, size, and complexity of institutions increases, the ability of the building culture to produce healthy results decreases.*
- Chapter 6 deals with shared knowledge about building form, and examines how the building culture may facilitate both the sharing of that knowledge and its transformation in ways that allow it to be used most appropriately for particular situations of design and building. *In healthy cultures, there is widespread sharing of building knowledge, and that knowledge can evolve in appropriate ways.*
- Chapter 7 describes how the flow of money is related to questions of control and the distribution of value in the environment. *In healthy cultures money is distributed in a wide range of scales and can be spent in ways that reinforce the affective value of different parts of the environment.*
- Chapter 8 deals with human agreements and control, particularly contracts, and finds that the nature of agreements is indicative of basic relationships in the building culture. *In healthy building cultures, strong human relationships are marked by agreements that are based on common sense. Responsibility for the production of the built environment is not overly centralized but distributed over many people.*
- Chapter 9 is concerned with regulation—with how institutions oversee building activity to ensure that basic cultural needs concerning the city and the character and safety of buildings are met. *In healthy building cultures, regulation is based on common sense and does not overwhelm a positive vision for the built environment that people might share.*
- Finally, chapter 10 lays out an expanded view of the concept of craftsmanship, considered in a modern sense, and discusses how it is either enabled or hindered by the building culture as a whole. *Healthy building cultures allow for craftsmanship at all scales—as opposed to the planning and design of the environment according to abstractions and/or bureaucratic criteria.*

Common to these chapters are a few general issues that concern all the processes involved in the making of buildings. These issues have to do with knowledge and control: the extent to which knowledge about the making of buildings is shared among members of the building culture and throughout society at large, the extent to which that knowledge is clear enough that people can understand it, and whether or not decisions about buildings are being made with strong reference to built reality as opposed to abstractions. The term sometimes used is *transparency*: if knowledge is "transparent," one can easily see through it to its intention and effect. That allows for more people to understand and share building knowledge.

Wide sharing of knowledge, in turn, allows buildings and building processes to reflect the wider aspirations and needs of society and permits many different players to do separate jobs in a complex system of production, in such a way that they are not working at cross purposes.

Both implicit understanding and control that is physically or professionally close to the building operation allow for design- and construction-related decision making that is based on the reality of the building and on real contextual conditions.

Ultimately the character of knowledge and control affects all the processes of the building culture and the nature of the built result.

CONNECTIONS TO
THE LARGER CULTURE

4

Autonomy and Interdependence of the Building Culture

Tess . . . started on her way up the dark and crooked
lane or street not made for hasty progress; a street laid
out before inches of land had value, and when one-
handed clocks sufficiently divided the day.

Thomas Hardy,
Tess of the d'Urbervilles

The building culture displays both autonomy and interdependence with
respect to the larger culture to which it belongs. People in the building
culture, in other words, have two kinds of knowledge.

One kind of knowledge is exclusive to the building culture itself and to
the specialists who work within it. People in the building culture have the
ability to frame a hipped roof, or to quickly sketch a coherent plan for a
house, or to ask the right questions so that such a plan can be sketched, or to
interpret working drawings and relate them to current building codes. This
knowledge includes language that allows the members of the building culture to communicate with each other.

The second kind of knowledge comes about because the building culture
is located within a larger culture: "the Renaissance," or "English culture in
the eighteenth century," or "postindustrial American culture." Today, for
example, architects are as vulnerable as physicians to liability actions; many
people view "postmodern" architectural style as a part of corporate image-
culture; the procedures for getting a zoning variance are consistent with
other procedures within local governments. This knowledge includes language that allows the members of the building culture to communicate with
people outside it.

This interdependence with neighboring cultures is essential. A building
culture that attempts to exist only by its own rules, paying no attention to the
culture around it, will become irrelevant. This is what happened to the
experiments in building craft and production of the Arts and Crafts move-

ment. Although Arts and Crafts as an artistic style had great influence, its experiments in production did not, because they turned out to be too small and irrelevant to the dominant industrial establishment. It has been argued that in recent decades, architecture lost relevance because its jargon became exclusive and many practitioners refused to speak the language that most people were using.

On the other hand, one has only to look at buildings in which the "balance of knowledge" has shifted far away from an identifiable building culture, into the realm of bureaucracy, to see both the deadliness of the product and the irrelevance of an identifiable building culture to the making of that product; much building by large, bureaucratic organizations illustrates this point. In these situations, various bureaucracies claim for their own what once were different parts of a coherent building culture, and the strong common intentions about buildings that once were held by the members of a coherent building culture are lost.

The Decision to Build as the Reinforcement of Cultural Identity

In most cultures, building is marked by ceremonies that help reinforce the culture's identity. The persistence of such rituals is indicative of people's need to use the activity of building to reinforce the deeper meaning of their culture.

The most important Shinto building in Japan, the Ise shrine, is rebuilt every twenty years on adjacent sites; this rebuilding helps to perpetuate the highest level of traditional carpentry as well as to reiterate important rites.[1] In traditional Japanese house-building, the service of a diviner helps appease the deities. In one ceremony a plaque known as the *mune fuda*, containing the names of the builder and head carpenter on one side and a prayer asking for the protection of the gods over the house and the family on the other, is fixed to a principal post of the house.[2] Traditional Hindu house construction begins with the burial of unburnt bricks and "the embryo of the house"—a jar with an image of a serpent inside—at a corner of the house.[3] In Thailand, ceremonies ensure that the site on which a house is to built will be exorcised of evil spirits before construction begins.[4] Chinese *feng shui* practice controls many aspects of settlement and house design, combining spiritual and practical rules for house orientation and room placement.

Even in the modern world, important steps in the process of building and building use are marked by rituals or ceremonies. These may include the laying of the cornerstone; erection of the last part of the structure (or "topping out" with a flag or fir tree at the top); ending with a banquet for everyone who worked on the building, around the time of the official cutting of the ribbon. The traditional New England barn raising is a familiar American example of the reaffirmation of the strength of a community. In some cultures the ceremonies of building use take on an annual or even daily cycle: the whitewashing of houses before Easter in Greek island villages; the creation of an ornamental pattern in rice flour, twice daily, outside the doors of houses in parts of India.

Figure 4.1.
The first bricks: ceremony at start of house construction, India, 1993

Figure 4.2.
The last beam: at the conclusion of steel framing of a building to house a university law school, 1998

Rituals associated with building follow a more fundamental decision: the very decision to build. In different cultures, building may come about for different reasons. It may be a means of re-creating the cosmos, as in some so-called primitive cultures. It may result from a desire to strengthen a person's or an institution's social or economic place. It may be a purely functional issue: people may need a place to live or work. It may be a means purely to reap financial gains.

Some purposes for buildings can be met *only* through construction: providing basic shelter, controlling the environment, establishing a permanent connection to place, reinforcing the cosmic order understood by a culture, supporting the basic functioning or status of a family or institution, creating a lasting aesthetic object in the city or landscape, contributing to a city's life or form. All of these reasons are discussed in the architectural literature and taught in schools of architecture: they are the things that make architecture unique among the arts and among other realms of human endeavor.

Yet there are other motivations as well, and some of these can also be supplied by different means. These motivations include the reinforcement of community and institutional self-identity, long-term financial investment, and short-term financial speculation. With these motivations, the building may be central or peripheral; the choices of whether to build, what to build, and how much to build belong to a set of considerations that is removed from the discourse that architects commonly engage in.

In a particular culture, certain motivations may be more dominant, and each of them may be associated with particular "players." When the need for a symbolic reaffirmation of cosmic worldview prevails, those who support this worldview—priests, geomancers, cathedral builders like the Abbot Suger—may be central. When the need is to increase status and image, then financial and political patrons—the Medici in Florence, Louis XIV at Versailles, Thomas Jefferson and "building for democracy," and the town business leader who builds a big house on the hill—may be central. When more functional, domestic, utilitarian, or commercial needs dominate, as in eighteenth-century London or a late-twentieth-century informal settlement in India, then the building culture may be controlled by a wider variety of people. When the desire for money dominates, then the building culture is organized so that "money"—the modern financial institutions that control credit and to a large extent the standards for building itself—is in charge. In all these cases, fundamental decisions about building make links between society as a whole and the building culture itself.

Of course, buildings are not necessarily built to satisfy only one kind of need. Many religious buildings are motivated by both religious symbolism and social power, and it is the interaction and balance between these differ-

Figure 4.3. Schonnbrunn Palace, Vienna: the architecture of status and power

ent motivations that may be more revealing, rather than the simple existence of one of them alone. A city hall may be an expression of municipal wealth; it may be a symbolic expression of power with respect to other institutions, such as royal courts or churches;[5] it may house definable civic functions.

In Renaissance Florence, building and the arts were financed by private wealth that had a particular distribution: many players, a high percentage of whom had money to spend, desire for patronage and civic spirit, and some degree of restraint.[6] In eighteenth-century London or nineteenth-century New York, housing served both the workers' needs and the speculators' desire for profit. But in the nineteenth century, the institutions that could provide the capital for building—banks and building societies—*began to depend on that development to keep their own businesses going.* Building therefore began to become instrumental to purposes completely outside the building culture itself. In recent decades, the speculation in buildings where the need simply did not exist (the office boom of the 1980s) and the artificial creation of need (aggressive marketing of ever larger houses by developers and speculators) has shown that the marketing of buildings is similar to the marketing of any other American product, in which the lead is taken by a manufacturer not only to satisfy the market, but to create the market in the first place.

The differences in the reasons buildings are built lead to differences in the buildings themselves. For example, the more profit is a motivation, the more space may be optimized toward "assignable" ("sellable") space. Certainly this is true for most contemporary office buildings, in which there is a careful intuitive understanding of the relationship between the need for an impressive lobby (which increases the prestige of the building and therefore the amount of rent) and maximum rentable space. But it is also true for modern public buildings in which profit is ostensibly not a motivation but where the controlling nature of rent is still present because a private market exists for

Figure 4.4. University of Virginia: the architecture of democracy

office buildings. In fact, there are few buildings in contemporary society in which an explicitly financial bottom line does not drive the design in some way.

The idea that the building is an instrument toward gaining money is not new; even the medieval cathedral, sometimes regarded as the essence of spiritual building, helped to increase the wealth of the local church. Indeed, building for profit may be socially helpful. People who build a small rental unit onto their house may be not only gaining an additional source of income and providing a place for a student or in-laws to live but also adding to the social diversity of their neighborhood. The investor who builds rental work spaces for small, fledgling industrial concerns may be providing for local employment and keeping creative talent within the community. The developer who takes a risk and converts a historic warehouse into rental retail and professional space may be helping a community maintain its links with the past. For some years a preservation tax credit encouraged projects of historic preservation and adaptive reuse. Zoning itself came about partly because of observations of the effects of building for maximum profit, and ideally, zoning recognizes that profit needs to be tempered with other aspects of the public good.

But motivations that are much more exclusively concerned with financial profit pervade the modern environment, and when a drive for profit rules, the built environment does not improve. Tax policies in the United States have encouraged building for profit alone without consideration as to whether or not the building is helpful in other ways: the assumption is made that profit is inherently healthy. These policies are indicative of a wider understanding, in contemporary society, of the role of buildings. Unfortunately, buildings built for profit alone—or to a large extent for any single motivation except perhaps a spiritual one—may be shallow in their form and meaning. An important goal in the improvement of building cultures will be to restore deeper and more multiple purposes to building.

Figure 4.5. Dallas: the architecture of money

The Cultural Context of Building

On one hand, buildings exist as stand-alone artifacts, and on the other, they are artifacts that express the deep meanings, aspirations, and social order of a culture. Like the building culture that produces them, they are at the same time autonomous and interdependent with the culture at large.

Just as the motivation for building reinforces cultural tendencies, the architectural form of buildings reinforces and expresses the aesthetic sensibilities of the culture as a whole. A culture is characterized by a particular aesthetic sensibility, over and above the specific building types that are usually ascribed to it: the crisp and functional sensibility of Danish design; the explicitness of parts and connections in objects manufactured in France; the precision and clear visual lines of things Japanese. The understanding is a tacit one, hard to put into words, but we know it when we see it.

Pevsner writes about English architecture:

> The flat chancel end of the Perpendicular church has its immediate parallel in the flat-topped tower of the Perpendicular church—something extremely rare on the Continent, but something that to the foreigner is part and parcel of the English landscape. There are spires of course also . . . but the square-topped tower remains England at its most English, also in its absence of demonstrated aspiration, its compromise between vertical and horizontal, and even a certain matter-of-factness. Here, as in the matter-of-factness of Perpendicular space and tracery one may perhaps tentatively look back to the clipped sound of the English monosyllable, to the contrast of chop and cos-toletta. . . . The same compromise between vertical and horizontal also appears in the low-pitched Perpendicular roof and the emphasis on parapets and battlements. It is sufficient to remember the majestic roofs of Late Gothic churches in Germany to feel the fundamental difference.[7]

Christian Norberg-Schulz makes equivalent comments on Norwegian architecture and its relationship to its landscape:

> But the Norwegian place is above all determined by the tension of above and below. . . . To reveal and maintain this in building requires forms that simultaneously possess the safety of home and express the indefinite and savage environment. . . . This problem was solved with the combination of stave and log construction, the two methods that form the basis of Norwegian wooden architecture. . . . Architectonic form can be simultaneously heavy and light, and embody thereby the tension of below and above. In the "loft" at Kultan in Åmotsdal (c. 1790) builder Jarand Rønjom employed timbers laid horizontally to create a secure "cave of wood," while he united the timber ends to form a springy, rising curve. The result is a building that both rests and ascends, thus embodying the Norwegian relation of earth and sky. Here, forms speak the language of the land.[8]

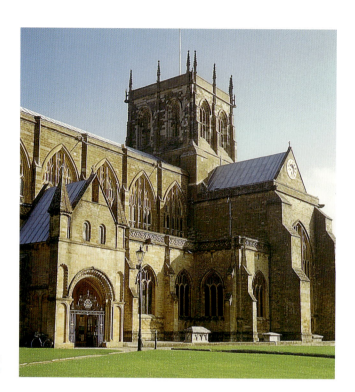

Figure 4.6.
Sherbourne Abbey:
"England at its
most English"

Figure 4.7.
Sherbourne Abbey

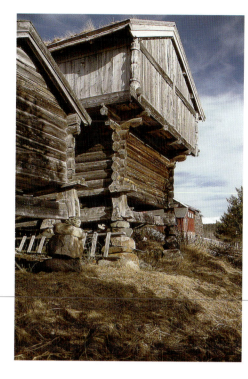

Figure 4.8.
Norwegian farm building:
"the tension of above
and below"

And Juni-chiro Tanizaki follows the same line of thought as he describes the darkness of traditional Japanese houses:

> In making for ourselves a place to live, we first spread a parasol to throw a shadow on the earth, and in the pale light of the shadow we put together a house. There are of course roofs on Western houses too, but they are less to keep off the sun than to keep off the wind and the dew; even from without it is apparent that they are built to create as few shadows as possible and to expose the interior to as much light as possible. If the roof of a Japanese house is a parasol, the roof of a Western house is no more than a cap, with as small a visor as possible so as to allow the sunlight to penetrate directly beneath the eaves. There are no doubt all sorts of reasons—climate, building materials— for the deep Japanese eaves. The fact that we did not use glass, con- crete, and bricks, for instance, made a low roof necessary to keep off the driving wind and rain. A light room would no doubt have been more convenient for us, too, than a dark room. The quality that we call beauty, however, must always grow from the realities of life, and our ancestors, forced to live in dark rooms, presently came to discover beauty in shadows, ultimately to guide shadows towards beauty's ends.[9]

The connection between the building culture and the aesthetic sensibility of the culture at large does not happen only through analogy. In traditional Japanese carpentry, process and product are inextricably linked. It would be

Figure 4.9.
Katsura Villa, Kyoto:
"in the pale light
of the shadow"

difficult, if not impossible, for a carpenter trained to work on Western buildings, even one who does very fine work, to use his techniques for the production of a building in the traditional Japanese way. Such a carpenter knows
that to do this, he would have to not only buy Japanese woodworking tools
but also immerse himself in the Japanese building culture: apprentice himself to a Japanese carpenter, learn new systems of layout and measurement,
study the properties of different woods and their relationships to new techniques of cutting, chiseling, and planing. William Coaldrake writes that

> the process of building in Japan . . . entailed far more than the proce-
> dures of erecting and decorating structures. It became a special way of
> life, a pattern of existential belief which, over the course of many life-
> times, took on the richness of the term Way. This is seen in the obser-
> vance of complex rituals based on Shinto rites throughout the process
> of construction, in the esoteric nature of the organization and training
> of the profession of the carpenter, and in his rituals and reverence for
> tools.[10]

Beyond the general aesthetic nature of which writers like Norberg-Schulz
and Pevsner write, any culture is characterized by particular forms of social
relationships that are expressed in architectural and urban form. In the
medieval town, for example, people of various classes lived in close proximity to each other, and the rooms of a building took on a number of different
functions. Architectural space was dense, and functionally indeterminate: the
street was the locus for any number of activities; servants and apprentices

slept in the same house as their masters, and that house might also include the workshop. Around the centuries of the Enlightenment, this began to change in the service of a society that would have measurable order and where particular people had a specific physical place. Consider a certain kind of transformation that took place in houses and other buildings of western Europe and the American colonies from the seventeenth through the nineteenth centuries. This transformation had two aspects:

- First, an increasing specificity of the functions of rooms and buildings, moving from a situation in which a particular room might house many different functions, sometimes at the same time, to one in which rooms and buildings were assigned exclusively to particular functions.[11] The house itself is the best example of this. A particular room, like a "bedroom," which in the seventeenth century might have harbored a variety of functions, including sleeping, writing letters, eating, visiting, working, and studying, had by the nineteenth century become much more specialized: functions such as visiting and eating would not occur there.

- Second, increased levels of spatial hierarchy, in order to manifest increased levels of social control over certain rooms in a building or streets of a city.[12] This can be seen in the development of institutional buildings as well as in town planning initiatives such as the New Town of Edinburgh (in which streets were designed so that they each had a certain width, a certain kind of inhabitant, and a certain publicness, so that the wealthiest people and institutions were on the widest and most public streets) and the Act for Rebuilding the City of London of 1667 (which classified houses and streets into four "sorts").

These architectural ideas are essentially Enlightenment ideas, in which formal classification begins to fragment a formerly unified picture of the world.

Moreover, the architectural form that buildings take is related to the organizational form that the building culture itself takes. The building culture takes its forms of organization from the culture at large, and the increased explicitness of function in buildings was accompanied by equivalent changes in the organization of the building culture itself. Over the last few hundred years, the tendency has been toward the establishment of formal institutions with more explicit roles, and away from informal and implicit methods of operation. During this period there was a gradual emergence of distinct professionals—surveyors, architects, builders, and contractors—each of whom had more specialized roles than members of the earlier building culture.

The organization of architectural space and the organization of the culture that produced architectural space were both part of a phenomenon that was reordering society during the eighteenth and nineteenth centuries, putting people into an explicitly understood place. People's roles (not only what they were called, but what they actually did) were becoming more defined and circumscribed, paralleling the new ordering of the rooms and streets they inhabited.

The organization and design of today's buildings parallel the organization and structure of the building culture that produces them. The discontinuous and fragmented character of the contemporary built world corresponds to similar qualities in the building production process. If this relationship is not merely a coincidence, then it stands to reason that improvements to the built world depend on fundamental changes to the building culture that produces it.

Business and Professionalism

Most people picture architects as people primarily concerned with the creative act of design and, as such, fundamentally different from other people in business, spending their days and nights over the drawing board, laboring with pencil and triangles and parallel rule. Architectural offices, however—and construction firms—are also part of the culture of business. They enter into contracts with clients that precisely specify what services are to be rendered, for what price—contracts that are very similar in form to those of other businesses. Architects are represented by attorneys who specialize in architectural and construction law but also follow the current rules and standards of the legal profession and legal practice.

Like other businesspeople, architects are concerned with their own balance sheets. They are in a competitive environment and adopt marketing and networking strategies that are similar to those of other businesses. They produce multicolored brochures, have sites on the World Wide Web, and make efforts to have their products recognized in prestigious publications.[13] Their firms have hierarchies of authority and responsibility, standard ways of communicating, and common methods of hiring, managing personnel, figuring costs, and keeping accounts. All of these procedures resemble those of other entities in the building culture and in the business and industrial world.[14]

The contemporary building culture relies on the tools of bureaucratic management, in which roles are defined in explicit job descriptions that precisely delineate a person's responsibilities. There are strict lines of authority and reportage; job rules of labor unions, safety rules of OSHA, standards of architectural licensing boards and professional organizations. Everything is recorded on paper; quality is explicitly defined in terms of performance criteria or specifications; the threat of litigation controls every move. These tools are shared by the building culture as well as by every other major institution in modern society: the social organization of the building culture has similarities to that of the culture of medicine or municipal administration or food provision. In all cases, the particular activity that makes the culture distinct (building, healing, administering laws, feeding the population) is tempered by the same sorts of rule systems that control the basic relationships between people, and the framework in which they do their jobs.

How did this situation come about? Industrializing society during the nineteenth century was moving away from the local and tradition-based methods of regulating the activities of people providing services and making goods. The story is a familiar one: a breakdown of traditional communities and a consequent reduction in the ability for common understanding and trust to guide people's actions; a growing complexity in the tasks that needed to be performed; an increase in explicit scientific knowledge that needed to be applied to professional activity. Professional institutions with explicit standards and clear methods of maintaining those standards were seen as the means of replacing what had formerly been local and human control over professional activity. At the same time that professionals rose to the top, labor sank to the bottom. Industrial concerns employed workers on a salary basis, and the basic relationships between employers and employees changed, away from the guild system and toward a management-labor system (which came to include labor unions and organizing). Those who made things became separated from those who controlled the economic means of production.

This pattern was true of all the professions. It included the assertion of exclusive legitimacy to carry out a set of tasks, the formation of an association to advocate that assertion, the formation of schools to regulate entry into the profession, and the push for government to institute statutory licensing.[15] The argument was often tied into the apparently increasing complexity of the profession—or at least its increasingly "scientific" nature—and the consequent need for people who were highly educated in an academic as well as practical way.

The sequence of steps for the establishment of many professions was similar, and the dates at which these steps occurred in the United States were remarkably close to each other. These time lines are shown in table 4.1.[16]

Society was moving toward an organization in which roles were precisely defined and explicit standards of operation could guide professional behavior. This movement corresponded both with the scientific quantifying mentality that gradually won out over intuitive and "hidden" knowledge and with a centralized, hierarchical industrial system in which the roles of workers themselves became explicitly defined and controlled from above. There was an increasing separation between highly educated people (like engineers) who had professional responsibility, and laborers (like assembly-line workers) whose only job was to precisely follow the orders of others, within a system that the engineers had set up. When the professions finally achieved the legal status they were after, in the first part of the twentieth century, Henry Ford and Frederick Taylor had managed to show the world how human workers could achieve maximum economic efficiency.

Table 4.1. Major dates in the formation of American professions

	Became full-time occupation	First university school	First national professional association	First state license law	Formal code of ethics
Accounting	19th cent.	1881	1887	1896	1917
Architecture	18th cent.	1868	1857	1897	1909
Civil Engineering	18th cent.	1847	1852	1908	c. 1910
Law	17th cent.	1817	1878	1732	1908
Medicine	c. 1700	1799	1848	before 1780	1912

Source: Harold L. Wilensky, "The professionalization of everyone?," *American Journal of Sociology* 70, no. 2 (Sept. 1964): 143.

The crafts and professions of the building culture followed the same trend. Each tried to separate itself from the others, assert its own expertise, and claim a unique niche of the building production process for itself. Organizations such as the Royal Institute of British Architects, the American Institute of Architects, the Chartered Institute of Building, and the Chartered Institute of Surveying formed; each sponsored publications and undertook public relations campaigns to argue the case for its own importance and eventually to argue for statutory licensing. One of the goals of the architectural profession was to establish itself as uniquely in control of buildings and their construction. To some extent it was successful—but much less so than professions such as law and medicine, in which it was easier to make the case for the need for exclusively controlled knowledge. The vast culture of builders, craftsmen, and emerging contractors was simply too pervasive for the architect to establish complete control, particularly over ordinary buildings that did not require the services of a highly trained professional to build them. In the realm of house-building, and much of the small-scale construction that makes up such a large part of cities, architects have never gained as broad a market or as strong an effect as they have sought.[17]

An Example of Early Professionalism: Surveying and the Precise Definition of Property Boundaries

A historical example—the formalization of the surveying profession, which came about partly because of the need to make more property boundaries mathematically precise—shows how social change was related both to the emergence of a particular profession in the building culture, and a particular attitude toward form.

The definition of property boundaries, which are often more permanent than buildings, is one of the most powerful determinants in the establishment of urban form. This was demonstrated after the London fire of 1666, when Christopher Wren's rational plan for the reordering of the old medieval street pattern was abandoned after it was realized that thousands of individual properties still existed under the ashes—and that to implement the plan, a massive program of property acquisition and reallotment would have had to take place.

In the nucleated village/common field system of medieval England, the portions of land belonging to one individual were in the form of long and narrow strips, separated from each other by small verges. These strips were defined, in custom and by whatever documents existed, not through absolute mathematical coordinates but through their relationship with the strips on either side of them. A typical deed read as follows:

> 4 acres in Scutterhith nigh Chichester lying on both sides of an acre and a half of his later of John Heberden, whereof three acres lie together between Chawntregardyn on the south and John Vincent's land on the north and abut on the Lovent on the east and on Gretedipemersshe on the west, another acre lies between John Vincent's

land on the south and a new field fence running from the Lovent to Gretedipemerssh which he has lately made on the north.[18]

Such property definition also existed in medieval urban situations:

I, Adam de Stockbrigge, baker, and Hawys my wife, grant to Alan de Inlonde and Maud his wife a plot which we bought of Claricia, widow of Stephen Bunde, with buildings on it outside Eastgate, Chichester, near the chapel of St. Pancras on the west, between the land which Mr William de Keynesham bought of Agnes Buckehorne and gave to the altar of St. Mary in the High Church and the land formerly of Richard le Sauerir.[19]

These definitions were all that was needed for people to maintain their rights. Common knowledge and memory took care of any disputes. Such disputes would have been rare, however, in a community where people would be doing the same things to their land at the same time, or living together in tight urban situations. There was no need to define boundaries

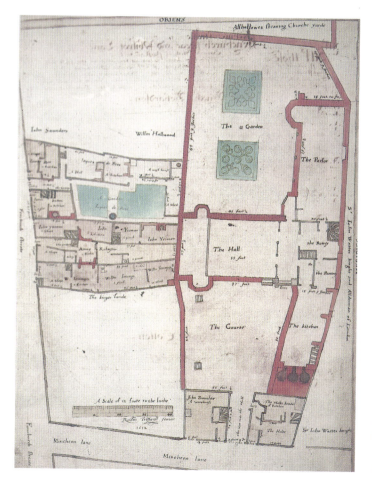

Figure 4.10. Irregular property layouts in early-seventeenth-century London

mathematically: they did not change much, and as long as people were able to carry on their work as they always did, there was no problem. In both city and country, the stability of property definition depended on common understanding rather than on mathematical definition divorced from experience. This understanding was connected to people's basic understandings about each other and was part of the basis for the culture itself.[20]

Even when measures were stated numerically, there was not necessarily consistency. Standard measures varied. As late as the early part of the nineteenth century, a Parliamentary Commission pointed out that there are at least two different standards for the inch: "Another Standard, still less precise in its magnitude for the immediate determination of measures of length, is found in a Statute of Edward 2. It is ordained, that three barleycorns, round and dry, make an inch, twelve inches a foot, three feet a yard," and that

> the custom of interposing the Thumb, when cloth is measured by the yard, had been so universal, that the thumb came to be considered as a part of the measure, and in process of time an inch was substituted for it. . . . It must, indeed, sometimes be almost as impossible to control the despotic influence of custom, with respect to the contents of a measure of a certain denomination, as with respect to the signification of a word of any other nature; and even the terms of number, precise as they necessarily are in their strict meaning, have become liable to perpetual variations.[21]

The idea that a word denoting a measure of length might have the same significance as a word "of any other nature" seems remarkable within our late-twentieth-century legal/scientific mentality. However, it was only during the eighteenth and nineteenth centuries that the separation of scientific "fact," based on numbers and classification, from subjective judgment began to speed up. Before this time, the statement of a particular length could be interpreted in different ways, depending on circumstance and who was doing the measuring.[22] In the case of a piece of land or a plot in the city, the perceived reality of the property, shared among different parties, had a mental status that aided judgment. When properties were defined in terms of others that were abutting, the definition of a particular piece of property affirmed a web of social relations as much as it specified a geometric shape. The highly "irregular" property layouts of vernacular towns and settlements map a dense system of human agreements and understandings.

In the countryside, a gradual process of enclosure accelerated during the seventeenth and eighteenth centuries, legitimized by new attitudes toward work and agriculture. The same attitudes toward scale and efficiency that were driving industrial capitalism were also changing the rural landscape: larger fields belonging to the same owner could be worked all at once.[23] Larger landowners gained title to entire fields, which then needed to be precisely defined by markers and hedgerows, to demarcate differently owned fields.

Small landholdings that were implicitly understood were thereby replaced by large landholdings that were precisely defined. Parliamentary enclosure acts awarded these pieces of land to larger landowners. The awards included precise mathematical definitions of land, like those found in modern deeds. Such precise definitions were necessary, of course, because adjacent land-owners were not in daily contact with each other as they had been before—and this development contributed to the rise of surveying as a profession that was primarily concerned with the measurement of geometric shapes rather than the general oversight of estates. The rise of a specific profession, based on precise and explicit measurement, came hand in hand with the decline of local custom, based on community knowledge.[24]

Ultimately this cultural worldview is reflected in the form of the built world. In the premodern world the definition and security of the center was more important than the definition and security of the boundary of the entire territory. Indeed, in many maps and pictures of the world, the center was surrounded by water; what was known was at the center, and as one moved away from the center, the world became more and more unknown.[25] This notion gradually changed. The nucleated village in England, surrounded by concentric rings of cultivated land, pasture, waste, and forest, was replaced with farms defined by straight hedgerows of hawthorn. The city-state, where the city lay at the center and agricultural lands surrounded it, was replaced by the nation-state, where the city was still the capital but the nation-states were separated by clearly defined boundaries. The boundary, as a mathematically defined line, gradually came to replace the center as an emotionally felt point.

It was perhaps this cultural attitude regarding the relative importance of the center versus the boundary that allowed for the boundary to be defined more "informally" in earlier times. The center was visible; it gave its name to the entire territory; it was the place from which power was exerted; and it was the place with the most symbolic and material investment. It needed

Figure 4.11.
Land surveyor in the
seventeenth century

protection. The boundary, on the other hand, might have been a natural feature: a range of mountains, a river, a forest. It was wide, and the exact line of separation between two territories was therefore ambiguous. When translated into understandings of how properties could be defined, this idea contributed to the characteristic pattern of vernacular settlements, in which a so-called organic overall pattern is made up of individual lot boundaries that are themselves "irregular" and less formally defined.

This small example of property boundaries illustrates how cultural ideas support a type of professional activity that leads to a particular character of form. Discrete professions, characterized by explicit knowledge and rules, emerged out of the scientific, quantifying, and classifying mentalities that came to characterize Western culture during the Enlightenment and the Industrial Revolution. The professions, in turn, acted in ways that were consistent with these mentalities and that eventually led to a built environment reflecting their own discrete and explicit nature.

The building culture's identity comes about partly through the nature of its interactions with other cultures, and particularly the larger culture to which it belongs. In these interactions, it shares knowledge systems, procedures, and attitudes. At the same time, it maintains its own knowledge systems and its own language. Any field of endeavor—law, farming, medicine—has its own language. It is the same for architecture and building—most people don't know the meaning of the terms *valley rafter*, *Palladian window*, *astragal*, *free plan*, or thousands of others. By itself, specialized knowledge is not a problem, but it becomes a problem when communication with cultures surrounding the specialty becomes difficult. And if there were no specialized language at all, the culture itself, which may have a specific goal at its center, would disappear. The interdependence of the building culture with the larger culture, its anchoring in common modes of thought and practice, is essential—but equally essential is the ability for the building culture to assume an identity of its own so that its members can work toward common goals.

Moreover, just as the culture of building draws its strength and character from the larger culture, the reverse happens as well. The culture of a city, or of an ethnic group, or of a nation is healthy partly because it includes a building culture that is healthy, that is making things that have real value to the members of the larger culture and providing creative opportunity to people. But Western culture, and many of the individual national cultures within it, are turning away from the idea that the production of things is at its heart and toward the idea of "service functions," communications, and management.

Our relationship to real things, artifacts, buildings, has become more and more tenuous—and we might question the health of a culture for which artifacts and the production of artifacts, as tangible and valuable entities in people's lives, are not important.

BUILDERS, ARCHITECTS, AND THEIR INSTITUTIONS

5

Transformations of Traditional Practice

The institutions and people of the building culture are ultimately responsible for the form of the built world. They act in predictable ways with respect to design, construction, the financing of buildings, the provision of materials, and the regulation of land and building. By doing these things, they are not only applying the knowledge contained in the building culture to current projects; they are also reproducing and perpetuating the culture itself.

These institutions and roles have changed over history in the following ways:

- People have become more specialized in their occupations, and professions have become more explicitly defined.
- Formal institutions have become larger, with more explicit rules guiding their operations.
- The relationship between individuals and between institutions has become more formalized.

These changes have resulted in increased separations between design and building and a decreased ability of people who are close to the building—in either design or construction or as users—to have the responsibility for making decisions on the basis of their close knowledge.

Master Builders, Guilds, and Apprenticeship

In traditional society, the builder combined the functions of design and construction that are now assumed by separate professionals, and the system of apprenticeship taught people to take these functions on in a way that combined thinking and doing.

The word *architect*, when it was used up to the eighteenth century, usually referred not to an architect in the present-day sense of the word but to someone who assumed overall responsibility for design and construction. Almost invariably, "architects" came out of the building trades, and their responsibility lay not only in the production of drawings but also in work on the building site—work that included the organization of trades and the supervision of workers. Their work was in fact an extension of the role of the craftsman:

> In order to design a cathedral or castle a master mason had to know more, indeed a great deal more, than the average mason working under him. But this knowledge was not of a totally different order from that of the working mason; it was . . . an extension of the skills and knowledge which the cutting and setting masons had to possess. . . . The art of designing buildings and the task of organizing and supervising the labor of the men who would actually construct the buildings were just as much a part of the mason's craft as were the techniques of cutting and setting stones.[1]

In 1703, Joseph Moxon pointed out that a carpenter might sometimes need to refer to books of architecture in order to do his job:

> Being now come to exercise upon the Carpenters Trade, it may be expected by some, that I should insist upon *Architecture*, it being so absolutely necessary for Builders to be acquainted with: But my Answer to them is, that there are so many Books of *Architecture* extant, and in them the Rules so well, so copiously, and so completely handled, that is needless for me to say anything of that Science. . . . *Architecture* is a Mathematical Science, and therefore different from my present Undertakings, which are (as by my Title) Mechanick Exercises.[2]

The idea that architecture is a "mathematical science," that it might be rigorous and precise, speaks to a different idea about architecture than exists today. Indeed, Moxon's very statement that architecture is something that builders need to know obviously describes the opposite of the modern relationship between the two professions. Moxon was referring to the treatises and pattern books that began to proliferate after the Renaissance, which helped to spread classical styles of architecture throughout society. Moxon's observation is telling. In Moxon's world, the person calling himself the builder was central. Contemporary architects see themselves as central and building as something that is instrumental to the architectural idea.

The builder's job combined craft and theoretical knowledge and was learned through apprenticeship, one of the oldest forms of cultural trans-

Charpente.

Figure 5.1. The craft of carpentry

mission. It is through apprenticeship that the Cosmatis learned how to make the exquisite mosaic tile floors for the churches in Rome; through a form of apprenticeship that the medieval stonemasons learned how to carve the columns and capitals of Bourges and Chartres and set them in place; through apprenticeship to Wren that Hawksmoor learned architecture; through apprenticeship to Sullivan that Wright learned architecture.[3] In the world of work and building, the master-apprentice relationship is as fundamental as that between parent and child.

The word *apprenticeship* has two uses. One deals with the economic arrangements that prevailed for several centuries, and the other with hands-on learning itself.

The guilds, which were formal institutions of craftsmen that acted to regulate prices and quality, maintained the standards for apprenticeship. The traditional arrangement involved a simple agreement between the master and the father of the apprentice. The master agreed to give the apprentice food and lodging and to teach him a craft; in return, the apprentice would work for the master for a specified number of years—usually seven. Apprenticeship was a means of economic regulation. An individual master would ordinarily be allowed to employ only a certain number of apprentices at a time. The guilds also controlled the entry of "foreigners" into cities to work. These kinds of control gave guilds economic power by allowing them to regulate the number of workers in their field, thereby keeping prices up. The system gradually broke down, however. The 1667 Act of Parliament following the 1666 Great Fire of London allowed foreign craftsmen into London: this extraordinary move was seen as necessary in order to get the city rebuilt quickly, thereby maintaining its ascendancy in a period of great expansion. Presumably the amount of work that needed to be done was seen to be enough so as not to cause a fall in wages due to the influx of foreigners. The system was further weakened by factory production, and the statute setting out the rules of apprenticeship was finally repealed in 1814.[4]

Since medieval masons were often itinerant, workers sometimes entered that craft through arrangements that were less formal than the apprenticeship systems that prevailed in towns. Knoop and Jones point out that at the Vale Royal Abbey, only 5–10 percent of the masons were local, whereas 50 percent of the carpenters and almost all the laborers were local.[5] Masons often learned from a father, brother, or uncle, or began through labor in a quarry or on a construction site.[6] Control of entry to the craft also helped assure quality of work. The years of training toward the eventual production of a masterpiece meant that a rigorous approach to craftsmanship would be learnt. In 1514 some stonemasons in Germany had to demonstrate the ability to "make a simple vault; to cut the pieces to form a stone doorway; to make a gateway; to cut a projecting cornice; to make appropriate foundation walls for a house and to repair a damaged wall or angle; to know the proper thickness of a wall from its height and make the correct foundation for it."[7] The price level of work was presumably supported by a particular level of quality: the years of training paid off for both craftsman and client.

Through what sort of mechanism is knowledge transferred in apprenticeship? It is based on an arrangement in which the master and apprentice are working together on a real piece of work of economic consequence. This sets the stage for professional responsibility on the part of the apprentice—a responsibility to other people, not just to her own learning. Furthermore, because of this connection to real work in the current market, the latest knowledge and skill is being taught. Certainly in the centuries when the guilds exerted their control, it was easier to be up-to-date because craft knowledge changed slowly. Today, on the other hand, one of the many criticisms made about schools of architecture, for instance, is that they are out of touch with practice—both what clients are interested in and what office practice is about.

Probably the most critical aspect of apprenticeship is the apprentice's involvement with something that is real and not abstract. The apprentice is watching carefully, working side by side with the master. The extremely detailed observation required of an apprentice is suggested in this passage about the fitting of a cast-iron box into the middle of a wagon wheel to receive an axle:

> The wedges (hand-chopped, out of heart of oak) were not themselves allowed to touch the box. Truly, that brittle cast-iron might easily have snapped, if jarred too closely by such a sledge-hammering as the wedges were subjected to. A place having been started by a broad iron wedge . . . the oak wedge was driven into the elm itself, splitting it open slightly. (There was no danger of splitting dry elm too far.) The iron stock-bond prevented the stock from opening outwards at all; only by

spreading inwards, towards the cast-iron box, could the elm make way for this oaken wedge. But this was exactly what was wanted. Until the box was fixed immovable, in its right place, wedge after wedge was driven in; and when at last the wedges came to be chiseled off they fitted so tight that no division could be seen between them and the stock; a difference between oak grain and elm grain alone showed where they were. In that tight grip the box lay embedded in the stock, ready to bear the pressure of tons without moving. Considerable knack, besides experience, went to chopping off the wedges so that they did not splinter or tear. And, at last, a spoke-shave put on the end of the stock gave it the handsome appearance of inlay-work.[8]

This passage, from a classic account of a craft-centered business, describes not only the sorts of observations that an apprentice is making but also the craft itself, which depends on an intimate relationship to the object being made. The book contains similar descriptions where the author cautions that even more details were involved but not recorded. Even if it were possible to write down every step, we would still not know about every movement of the hand required.

In traditional building, this kind of knowledge—and learning—is always present: in the reading of a piece of land to know whether it is a good place to build; in determining the layout of the building; in knowing when and how to make adjustments to the plan, or which piece of timber to use where. These subtleties, which can be described in words, can only be learned by doing.

There may also be a complementary relationship between hands-on learning and theoretical understanding. A man who apprenticed to a pewtersmith wrote that "when polishing became almost second nature to me, Frances began to let me shape the rough cut developments and to sink bowls for her. It was during this time I really had the questions that needed to be answered. During our lunch hour each day it was like a lecture class in . . . pewtersmithing. . . . Gradually I spent more time doing my own work."[9] In building, theoretical understanding has to accompany craft knowledge. In medieval times, however, even knowledge of geometry, required in laying out parts of buildings, was in large part *practical geometry*, learned through actual practice.[10]

In apprenticeship, what is learned is not only what is culturally understood about craft but also the master's particular way of understanding it. In crafted work, as in fine arts like painting and sculpture, one can recognize the particular "schools" or workshops where the work was made, as well as techniques that are more culturally shared. Jerome Bruner comments, "What the teacher must be, to be an effective competence model, is a day-to-day working model with whom to interact. It is not so much that the teacher provides a model to *imitate*. Rather, it is that the teacher can become a part of the student's internal dialogue—somebody whose respect he wants, someone whose standards he wishes to make his own."[11]

In some countries, such as Germany, the master/apprentice system still exists, but it is under threat because the economy cannot support it. However, apprenticeship and the system of making things to which it is

Figure 5.2. Building trades school in Philadelphia. Such schools developed during the nineteenth century to supplement older apprenticeship programs.

connected are not archaic ideas. This way of making allows for things to be precisely shaped—an idea that we will see later as compatible not only with emerging, advanced methods of production but also with the attention and care required for the evolution of a city as a whole.

Building Firms and General Contractors

The increase over time in the size, formality, and complexity of building firms has resulted in the removal of building knowledge from the general public and a fragmentation of the building process itself.

The modern building firm has its origin in the small-scale builder who, before the Industrial Revolution, took responsibility for most aspects of a building's production, including design, the organization of construction, and the execution of at least one of the building's major trades. In eighteenth-century England or America, this builder was usually the carpenter or bricklayer. A typical house or small group of houses built for speculation would have had a builder who not only put up the money but also combined today's roles of architect, general contractor, and tradesperson.[12]

This individual did not necessarily do all the work. Some builders would occasionally hire surveyors to draw a ground plan and occasionally an elevation, and these surveyors would sometimes call themselves "architects." Contracts would be signed for the other trades, so that if a bricklayer were the builder, he would do the brickwork himself and contract with carpenters, plasterers, joiners, and plumbers. Sometimes in small-scale speculative development, craftspeople bartered with each other, so that a bricklayer would work on a house for which a carpenter acted as "contractor," and vice versa. The person in charge was almost always someone who either was doing some of the labor or belonged to the building trades.

The emergence of the general contracting firm was gradual, within a general trend toward an increasing specialization of roles. In the eighteenth century the roles of "architects," "builders," and "surveyors" were much more loosely defined than today, and there was a considerable amount of overlap between them. There were builders who understood architecture, architects who came out of the building trades, surveyors who could draw plans, gentlemen for whom architecture was a hobby along with botany and astronomy, and farmers who took on building to supplement their income. That system transformed into something quite different, in which it was expected that each person would have only one role.

The functions of the surveyor, for example, who might have measured quantities of building materials, drawn plans for buildings, surveyed land, or managed estates, were split up into the roles of "quantity surveyor," "architect," land surveyor, and estate manager.[13] The functions of the builder, who might have laid bricks, drawn plans and elevations, and organized workers on the site, split up into the roles of builder, architect, and general contractor. The functions of someone called an architect, who might have come out of the building trades, drawn plans and elevations, and supervised construction split up into the functions of architect (who did not necessarily come out of the building trades) and general contractor.

In addition to this increasing one-to-one relationship between individuals and individual professional activities, there was the growth of *firms* dedicated to particular activities: building design (architecture firms), construction (general contractors), the measurement of materials quantities used (firms of quantity surveyors), and building inspection (municipal building authorities).

By the last part of the nineteenth century, many contracting firms were large and complex business organizations with subspecialties of their own. The heads of these firms no longer practiced building trades; instead, they were organizers, managers, and negotiators. Firms included principals, estimators, and construction managers. If they employed building labor, there would also be job foremen. Construction firms had formal relationships with architects, and the responsibility of firms with respect to the building was clearly demarcated and limited. The firm's job was to build the building according to the architect's specifications and satisfaction. Although a good deal of skill was required to do this, the building firm's organization was set up to carry out the architect's instructions and, during that process, to protect itself as much as possible from liability or financial loss. By the end of the nineteenth century the relative positions of builders and architects had reversed. Builders were now instrumental to the wishes of the architect, instead of themselves taking charge (and perhaps calling themselves architects), as they did before.

A similar formalization of relations took place between the firm, its own employees, and its subcontractors. In some situations, relationships to craftsmen changed to something akin to today's management/labor arrangement. Building journals and publications of trade unions in the last third of the nineteenth century contain many accounts of disputes between contractors and building workers. Typical was an account of an employer in Manchester, complaining about plasterers during a dispute: "As the plasterers' labourers of this town have turned out, this day, from their employment, I wish to lay the facts of the case before you, so that the public may have an opportunity of knowing the tyranny we are from time to time subjected by those we employ."[14]

By the end of the nineteenth century the typical building firm had much the form it does today. Employers and employees replaced masters and apprentices who were part of the same guild. The firm bid on jobs, based on the architect's specifications; it signed a contract with the owner giving the architect the right to approve payments; it entered into subcontracts; and if it took responsibility for some of the construction itself, it hired building workers who were now protected by organizations of their own—labor unions.

Since then, firms and their work volume have grown. However, in many cases, the general contracting firm, while legally responsible for the execution of the entire construction contract, directly employs relatively few people who work on the building itself. Instead, the general contractor's role is to contract with and coordinate the subcontractors who provide labor, materials, and components for construction. This complex arrangement requires elaborate control systems. These controls, in combination with other constraints with respect to cost, speed, and the execution of specifications, mean that the contractor may have little or no flexibility with respect to the final outcome.

Speculators, Developers, and Banks

The source of money for building has transformed from direct investment by owners to indirect investment by backers; here, projects are financial instruments for profit. This increase in the distance of money from human purpose has affected both public policy and the quality of building that results.

In some form, the construction of buildings for largely financial motives has existed through most of history. The *insulae* of ancient Rome, workers' housing in sixteenth-century Venice,[15] and the growing industrial towns of seventeenth- and eighteenth-century England are all examples of buildings erected for profit *and* to provide housing. However, it is only relatively recently that the scale of speculation became so great that it has controlled the layout of large sections of towns.

For example, through the end of the sixteenth century, most building activity in London was at the relatively small scale of one or two buildings at a time. Near the end of the century, large tracts of land outside the medieval city walls began to become available for private development. Gradually, the new large landowners embarked on the subdivision and "improvement" of their land through elaborate systems of leaseholds that allowed them to retain ownership—and gain rent—but also allowed leaseholders to profit from the actual building construction they carried out.[16]

In these developments, the landowners laid out streets and building plots, then entered into building agreements with builders to lease the houses and do the construction. In some cases, when many houses were involved, the builders entered into further agreements with smaller builders to actually build the houses; these builders then employed craftspeople and laborers. In this way, through a system of nested leaseholds, profit was made at several different levels, although the landowner retained control over the overall form and quality of the development. Since the largest landowners held vast tracts of land, this control amounted to a form of city planning, akin to that of the suburban tract developer of today. Particularly in less exclusive locations, the system of leaseholds often resulted in cheap building, since it was always in the financial interest of the builder to satisfy the building agreement in a minimal way.

During the first half of the nineteenth century, Thomas Cubitt carried this process one step further. Although he was a large-scale builder, he did not enter into leases with smaller builders; rather, he began to control building construction itself by employing many laborers and craftsmen in one firm and by operating factories in which building components were mass-produced. Cubitt thereby combined the operations of the land developer and the large general contractor into one firm.[17]

The ability of people to buy into speculative developments was enhanced by the growth of financial institutions that specialized in mortgages in which real property itself was held as collateral. In England, building societies (the equivalent of the U.S. savings and loan institutions) emerged out of cooperative groups that engaged in building: the group owned all of the houses that were built. These early building societies had some similarities to today's cohousing groups. Gradually, as the societies grew, the lenders and borrowers became unknown to each other, and the institutions lost their direct connection to building, although they remained closely connected to builders who were developing large estates.[18] The societies evolved into institutions that accepted deposits and engaged in financial transactions that did not have to do only with building.

In the United States, up until about the beginning of the twentieth century, most building was financed directly, "out of pocket," or through loans from people who were well known to those undertaking building. However, during the nineteenth century, two related trends increased speculation in building: first, increasing accumulation and concentration of money, which made funds available for large-scale investments in real estate; and second, the growth in urban population, which provided a market for buildings among people who were no longer connected to traditional communities and the building cultures they contained.

Furthermore, American real estate brokers coordinated the growing operation of real estate development.[19] The real estate industry, which had grown partly because of the land deals sponsored by the railroads and intra-urban transit lines,[20] was well placed to coordinate the financing, selling, title transfers, infrastructure development, and construction operations required for large-scale development. Real estate brokers knew that profits could be

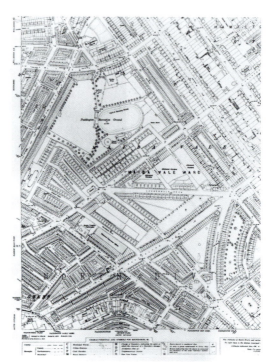

Figure 5.3.
Three stages of property
development in
St. John's Wood,
London: 1868, 1893, 1913

Figure 5.4.
Early-nineteenth-century
brickmaking. Brickyards
were often located at the
edge of the developed
part of the city and moved
outward as the city did.

Figure 5.5.
Thomas Cubitt

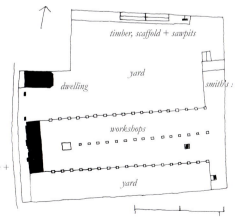

timber, scaffold + sawpits

yard

dwelling

smith's

workshops

*counting house +
showroom*

yard

Figure 5.6.
Thomas Cubitt's works

made through the increased value of land resulting from its "improvement" and that the costs incurred in construction itself needed to be kept as low as possible.

In the United States, large-scale private speculative development has been a major force toward change in public policy regarding building. This happened in several ways: first, private deed restrictions that were used to help sell houses in communities by guaranteeing that properties would not be changed in "unfavorable" ways provided a model for land-use planning;[21] second, developers who had built large speculative developments lobbied for zoning that would protect them;[22] and finally, lobbying for the mortgage interest deduction, highway construction, depreciation allowances, and other measures that favored speculative building activity resulted in policies that, taken together, can be said to have reshaped the landscape as much as any profession or group of professions.

Today, in many cases, developers, with varying levels of civic responsibility, are at the center of the building culture. They provide the coordinating role of the wealthy Medici during the Renaissance, of the small-scale builder in London during the eighteenth century, of the architect with respect to large building during the nineteenth century. The developer coordinates real estate agents, bankers, financial backers, architects, and contractors, and often their relationships with these institutions are determined almost solely by the financial bottom line and by the simple balance between risk and likely return on investment. Unfortunately, attention to the bottom line alone does not guarantee the production of buildings that support and enhance human life and the quality of cities.

The Architectural Office

The gradual emergence of the architectural firm as a unique institution has paralleled that of the general contractor and developer. The profession has gradually become more isolated from society, and the roles of people within it have become less commonly understood.

The growth of architecture as an independent profession has gone hand in hand with the development of the idea of design as an intellectual activity separate from craft and building. Design as invention, as the conscious creation of new form, has existed in most traditional societies as well as modern ones. In building and architecture, there are great works—Amiens, Brunelleschi's dome in Florence, the Great Mosque at Cordoba, the Brooklyn Bridge—that represent conscious and deliberate attempts to solve problems in new ways and to make the solutions beautiful. The role of the *designer* in these situations is clear, but less widely acknowledged is the fact that in each case the designer was working in the context of materials, of engineering, of construction activity, of the real "fabric" of the building, *of the building culture as a whole*. Even when rules needed to be broken or procedures changed to get the building built, the designer was in a position to exert influence. In the twentieth century, the modern profession of architecture has assumed that such invention could happen in an isolated professional context, and this assumption has exacerbated the split between the architectural profession and the rest of the building culture.

The often-made statement that the architect has always existed obscures how the role of the person called "architect" has changed over history.[23] The emergence of the professional architect was not sudden. For many buildings, even through the nineteenth century, construction supervision was up to the builder, and the architects' legal role was not formalized. In some cases, "surveyors" drew plans. In some cases, the "architect" settled disputes but was not responsible for approving payments. In some cases, the drawings were extremely sketchy, or nonexistent. In many of these early cases, the architect seems peripheral to the main business of building and to the main relationship between the builder and the client.

Like some architectural innovations, the transformation of the architectural profession began with larger buildings, or buildings for the wealthy. For larger buildings, the architect's role was formalized earlier than for smaller ones. The contract for the building of the Union Club, Trafalgar Square, in 1822 included thirty-three sheets of drawings and is completely unambiguous about the architect's legal control over the work of the builder and about his role in approving payments from the client.[24] Yet, when this building was being built through arrangements that are recognizable today, most houses were still being built by builders, with minimum if any control by architects.

The development of the modern architectural office has corresponded to that of the contractor and other formally organized institutions of the building culture. The demarcation of the profession's boundaries included the development of exclusive claims to professional expertise, the encourage-

Figure 5.7. Drafting room, offices of McKim Mead and White, New York. "[In the specification room], the specification writer can walk around the room with his eyes on the drawings, dictating specifications to his stenographer."—D. Everett Waid, "The business side of an architect's office."

Figure 5.8. Business office, offices of McKim Mead and White. "The veteran accountant who is skilled in drawing contracts carries unusual responsibilities in keeping tab on estimates, extras, orders, and certificates, aside from all the office accounts which include a notable system of keeping office costs on each building."—D. Everett Waid, "The business side of an architect's office."

Figure 5.9. Reception room, office of Ewing & Chappell, New York. "One device which Mr. Ewing recommends to his interested visitor is a bunch of blank cards which are kept within reach for a memorandum record of first interviews with clients. These cards are larger than a letter sheet and have printed down the left margin a list of items suggesting questions which always need to be asked at the outset of any commission to give a clear understanding of the problem at hand."—D. Everett Waid, "The business side of an architect's office."

PLAN.

OFFICE OF EWING & CHAPPELL.

Figure 5.10.
Plan of office of Ewing & Chappell

ment of clients' use of architects, the adoption of legislation to control both means of entering the profession (statutory licensing) and the exclusive right to practice by the members of the profession (the requirement that only licensed architects can design buildings). To further these aims, the Royal Institute of British Architects was founded in 1834, the American Institute of Architects in 1857, and the first American school of architecture, at the Massachusetts Institute of Technology, in 1868.

By the end of the nineteenth century, the architect was more firmly established as the party with responsibility for designing buildings and for supervising the work of the builder. Even then, all building types of all sizes did not use the architect in the same way, and even though her role was formalized, the architect remained in a continuous struggle for legitimacy that has continued to this day.

The professional organizations pushed for—and attained—statutory registration, so that no one could be called an "architect" without meeting standards of education and competence. A degree from an accredited architecture school became an important part of those standards. While formerly the "architect" could come from different places and operate without formal training, it gradually became the role of institutions to determine who would have that privilege.

As the nineteenth century progressed, the architect—as a formal institution separate from the building firm—gradually assumed a greater controlling role in the building operation. One needs only to look at the operation of the preeminent New York firm at the end of the century, McKim Mead and White, to see this.[25] Every detail and every payment to contractors and subcontractors had to receive the firm's approval; the firm had final say over quality of materials and workmanship; and they produced, for each major building, hundreds of drawings to help them in their control of the outcome.

At the same time, even though this "modern" firm had over a hundred employees; a hierarchy of control; principals, job captains, and draftspeople; memoranda being exchanged; letters flowing in and out; and contractors and vendors coming to visit, it still represented a transitional period in the evolution of the profession. There was still a connection to craft, and the firm still had some of the responsibilities of today's general contractor. As architecture became further severed from other professions and trades, many offices became larger, with the attendant problems of needing to keep people employed, and the control of money flow became even more of an issue. During the early decades of the twentieth century, notions of efficiency, in the form of "Taylorism" and "scientific management," which were generally in the air of the business and industrial worlds, affected the operation of architectural offices as well, partly by further reducing and formalizing their relationship with the building operation.[26]

However, it is not possible to talk about the "modern architectural firm" as if all firms are the same. Indeed, one of the things that characterizes the profession today is a good deal of diversity in the way firms operate, in their size, in the kind of work they typically do, in the way they are organized internally, and in the way they deal with clients.[27] For example, in the United States, architects tend to specialize in one or more building types and may be chosen because of that expertise. Most firms are small, but some are very large. Some firms are organized so that small teams follow jobs through, and others have separate design and production departments.

Although there is also diversity in the relation of architecture firms to builders, by and large, firms tend to "keep their distance" from builders, ultimately dealing with them in formal ways even if informal relationships help guide everyday behavior. In the last few decades, this relationship has become more and more litigious, and many architects and contractors have been reorganizing their work and relationships with others, partly in order to reduce their liability.[28] There are prominent architects who act as design consultants and not architects of record, allowing them to do the schematic design of a building—the aspect of design in which the basic organization and appearance of the building is set—but to then pass the preparation of the construction documents and the site supervision to a firm that will take legal responsibility. For similar reasons, contractors and architects transfer liability for construction details to contractors by specifying performance standards, or to manufacturers by specifying proprietary items to be installed in the building rather than designing details to be crafted on-site. Every party in the process is attempting to reduce its exposure to litigation as much as possible.[29]

As a result, architects have control only over a certain aspect of the building—its image—and buildings in which image prevails over substance predominate. To improve the quality of the built world, this trend needs to reverse, so that architects can be closer to builders and to buildings.

Architectural Education

In *Toward a Theory of Instruction*, Bruner writes,

> The change in the instruction of children in more complex societies is twofold. First of all, there is knowledge and skill in the culture far in excess of what any one individual knows. And so, increasingly, there develops an economical technique of instructing the young based heavily on telling out of context rather than showing in context. In literate societies, the practice becomes institutionalized in the school or the teacher. Both promote this necessarily abstract way of instructing the young. . . . In the detached school, what is imparted often has little to do with life as lived in the society except in so far as the demands of school are of a kind that reflect indirectly the demands of life in a technical society. . . . For school is a sharp departure from indigenous practice. It takes learning . . . out of the context of immediate action just by dint of putting it into a school.[30]

The emergence of architectural education as a formal activity distinct from the apprenticeship that was more typical of the building trades paralleled the development of the general contracting firm and the architectural profession itself. During the nineteenth-century decades when some builders began to call themselves "architects," and when architects as an organized body began to call for formal recognition, there were already two streams of architectural training: one in offices, and one in schools. Well-known architectural offices, which were already separate from building firms, were taking on apprentices, who learned the practice of architecture by doing it. Schools of drawing and architecture also began to emerge, providing courses for people in the building trades who aspired to be architects. These schools offered courses in drawing, architectural history, and other architectural subjects,[31] and they preceded by several decades the founding of the first university-affiliated school of architecture at MIT.

The Ecole des Beaux Arts guided formal architectural education for several decades before and after the turn of the twentieth century. The Beaux Arts system, based in Paris, helped to codify both a certain socially sanctioned content of architectural form—which would last until the advent of modernism in the 1920s—and a particular method of teaching—which in part still exists today.

The educational system of the Ecole des Beaux Arts, and the similar schools that it spawned, may be viewed in the context of *practice*. The Ecole advocated a neoclassical approach to architectural style. It also operated within, and affirmed theoretically, a professional system that was beginning to practice according to this same system. Much more so than the Arts and Crafts movement, the Beaux Arts system saw architecture as a cerebral exercise in which the architect was expected to control the craftsman. It was suited to clients who were the new moneyed elite, and their institutions, that were exerting the same kind of control over industrial labor.

Schools that followed the Beaux Arts system provided a theoretical underpinning for it through courses in history and theory, through highly stylized modes of design presentation, and through competitions that singled out the best work. This educational system was also intimately tied to the emerging profession in which offices took the responsibility for a good deal of basic professional training.[32]

The Beaux Arts educational system was a bridge between old apprenticeship models and the modern university studio system, where students work on projects that will not be built. The system of ateliers in the Beaux Arts, in which students worked under the direction of a particular master, and the corresponding system of competitions, or *concours*, made the core of architectural education studio-based and highly competitive. The modern system, of course, was also greatly influenced by the major school and movement that followed the Beaux Arts, the Bauhaus, which evolved from a system with a strong orientation to craft into one in which basic design principles were combined with an ideology of individual creativity, to be valued over adherence to a particular system.

Modern architectural education is a muddy and usually poorly integrated mixture of the old apprenticeship and Bauhaus systems (in the studios) and the more modern idea of explicit rules and knowledge (in nonstudio courses). And even considering the studios by themselves, apprenticeship does not really work in today's architecture schools. There is usually neither time nor trust to develop the close relationship that apprenticeship demands, and within faculties there is disagreement about the nature of architectural knowledge itself. Instead, schools promote individual creativity and pluralism—educational ideas that sometimes represent well-founded pedagogical intentions, but sometimes are the simple result of faculty failing to agree. The schools face confusion about their roles with respect to the profession;

Figure 5.11. Architecture studio at the University of Oregon, the first American school to reject the Beaux Arts system, about 1920

Figure 5.12. End-of-term studio review at the University of Oregon, 1998

constant pressure from the profession to "train" people to do things in accordance with everyday practice; and resultant conflicts between the public responsibilities of a professional school and the academic freedom assumptions of the university—including the desire of many faculty to be critical of practice. Michael Crosbie writes, "Indeed, it is a particular and widespread current complaint of architectural firms that recent architecture graduates are not very well equipped for what those firms want them to do, and that the firms need to 'start from scratch' in training them."[33]

This conflict adds to the fragmentation of the building culture, and must be resolved for architectural education to contribute to the long-term health of the building culture and the quality of the built environment that results.

Institutions of Control

The institutions that finance, design, and build buildings and that train people for these activities are overseen and regulated by a whole set of other institutions, which are even more distant from the built result than are many of the people in architecture and contracting firms.

Whereas craft guilds were once self-regulating, construction is now regulated by building departments that enforce building codes. Architects are licensed by governments and have professional standards set by professional associations. Architecture schools have accrediting bodies that set and guarantee compliance with explicit rules and standards for the content and conduct of architectural education. All of these groups are large institutions with their own internal bureaucracies and external constituencies.

Professional architectural associations. Such organizations as the American Institute of Architects (AIA) and the Royal Institute of British Architects (RIBA) promote codes of conduct and standard forms of contract and act as lobbying organizations with respect to government.

Both professional organizations are strongly aware of the relationship between the profession and political/market forces and are trying to position their professions better with respect to the market. In the United Kingdom, the RIBA recently turned back a government proposal to deregulate the architectural profession altogether, a proposal that would have allowed anyone to use the title "architect," and to allow market competition alone, rather than the licensing function that the RIBA offered, to determine which firms would control the market.[34] In the United States, in the face of increased competition from large construction firms that employ in-house architects, the AIA changed its policies several years ago to allow for so-called design-build operations, sanctioning architects and builders working for the same firm.[35]

Although the AIA is an independent organization and its standards do not have the force of law, it has a good deal of influence, making it more difficult for individual architects and firms that are not members to appear to have professional respectability. Its rules, proposed fee structures, and standard forms of contract have become the standard for the profession. Even if an individual firm may want to establish a different standard for itself, it does so only at risk, since it may not be able to use an accepted "trademark" that is an important marketing device.

Professional associations of builders, surveyors, engineers, and building code officials. The United Kingdom and most countries in Europe have national building codes, applied to every locality in the country. In the United States, each locality chooses from among several standard building codes promulgated and maintained by quasi-official, nongovernmental organizations.

Associations of architecture schools, and accrediting bodies for architecture schools. In the United States, the National Architectural Accrediting Board (NAAB) is responsible for maintaining standards in schools of architecture. The NAAB evaluates compliance with a set of several dozen pedagogical criteria that it determines. These criteria involve various competencies that students are expected to develop in the course of their professional training; they are satisfied in different ways by different schools and are written so that on the one hand, the accrediting agency may be satisfied that various issues are being covered, but on the other, the schools have latitude in the direction of their programs and the ways in which the standards are actually met.

Insurance companies that deal with building liability. Insurance companies have a tangible interest in the safety of buildings and represent an important lobby in the maintenance and revision of building codes.

There are many other institutions of control: licensing boards for architects, testing laboratories that help set standards for materials, agencies that enforce laws concerning the environment and workplace safety, agencies that regulate bank lending policies, city transportation, and public works and planning departments, each of which maintains its own set of rules and standards with respect to building practices.

Together, these organizations act inside and outside government to control functions that at a different time in history were controlled by a combination of internal institutional rules and shared cultural understandings.[36] Shared understandings have been replaced by formal organizations to protect the public interest by putting a "check" on individual institutions. Although these institutions—and the external rules that control them—are effective in making sure that the public interest is served with respect to individual intentions, the lack of shared cultural understandings means that the institutions may develop individually to the point that they are often working at cross purposes.

Fragmentation

The institutions involved have individually legitimate but often contradictory agendas. Although their procedures are coordinated with each other, the result may represent less a common vision than an unobjectionable compromise. In these respects, the modern building culture takes on the qualities of a modern bureaucracy.

Each of these bodies has a different agenda:

- *Developers and banks* are interested in maximizing the ratio between profit and risk. They do this by concentrating their investment in projects that are predictable and not innovative.
- *Planning departments* are interested in furthering the city's political and economic concerns by developing growth policies, master plans, and zoning ordinances. They do their job by involving development interests as well as citizens' groups in their work.
- *Zoning review boards* are interested in interpreting zoning laws in a way that is in accord with relevant law and constitutional protection of rights. They do this by instructing staff to evaluate project and variance proposals according to strict interpretations of the law.
- *Transportation departments* are interested in keeping vehicles moving smoothly. They do this by hiring traffic engineers who are well schooled in the relationships between street design, traffic control, and traffic flow and by basing their capital funds requests on this issue.
- *Building departments* are interested in minimizing the risk of life-threatening conditions in buildings. They do this by utilizing nationally promulgated codes and by authorizing plan checkers and building inspectors to interpret the law strictly.
- *Architectural firms* are interested in the design quality of their buildings and the life of the city, while maintaining the highest possible profit margin for their professional services.
- *General contractors* are interested in the construction quality of their buildings while maintaining the highest possible profit margin for *their* services. They achieve their aims by developing expertise in bidding and contracting and by building up a network of subcontractors on whom they can rely.

- *The public* is interested in most of the things that concern the institutions. They also want a lively and prosperous downtown, safe and pleasant neighborhoods, and humane and affordable housing.

These separate institutions are further broken apart internally. Large banks have separate divisions that set lending policy, contract with independent appraisers, authorize the loan, and collect payments. The appraiser, or any of these divisions, will have its own bureaucracy, policies, and procedures.

The architectural firm may have a marketing department, a design department, a production department, and a financial controller. It will contract with outside engineers, mechanical consultants, landscape architects, and other specialists; and each of these outside firms has its own internal bureaucracy. The zoning review board has politically appointed board members and a permanent professional staff. Building departments have plan checkers, field inspectors, and a legally responsible building officer.

The needs that these various institutions meet are important, and the argument that supports their existence as separate entities also justifies professionalism: knowledge and expertise are so complex that they must be handled by specialists. One cannot argue with the need for building safety, or with the need for the bank to be conservative with money, or with the importance of protecting the constitutional rights of people and companies. Each institution has its own legitimate claim to authority.

But this proliferation of institutions has several undesired consequences. One is that the explicit and formal communications among institutions take a good deal of time; another is that the litigious atmosphere consumes many resources; and a third, the most important, is that these different institutions do not necessarily have compatible goals with respect to the production of the built environment.

Indeed, individual institutional goals are often in direct conflict. The goal of the transportation engineers to have traffic moving smoothly might lead to the need for streets of a certain width; this goal might conflict with the planner's goal to have well-formed urban space. The goal of the planning

Figure 5.13.
Austin, Texas, 1986:
the environment of
fragmentation

department to have well-formed urban space, with sunlight at street level, might be at odds with the goal of developers to build as high as possible. The goal of the bank to minimize risk might be in conflict with that of the public, which sees the need for affordable housing and lower commercial rent for start-up businesses. What makes this situation difficult is that none of these goals is necessarily by itself unreasonable.

The same kind of conflicts exist within institutions themselves because of their internal fragmentation. The legal requirement of the zoning review board to be fair might be at odds not only with the architects who are designing the building but also *to its own members*, who see the logic of the architects' claim but are legally powerless to allow it, because of the need to interpret the law strictly. The goal of the architectural designer to have a facade of a certain quality might be at odds with the firm's production department, which is concerned with cost and might not understand what the designer is trying to do. The goal of the code officer to follow the letter of the law might be different from that of the field inspector, who sees that a particular piece of work is safe even though it does not follow the letter of the law and who wants to keep things smooth with the builder. What is important about these goals, too, is that none of them is necessarily by itself unreasonable.

In this context, although there may be a common vision of what *will* be built, it does not reflect a common, positive understanding of what *should* be built. The common vision of what will be built is itself a product of institutional compromise—it represents what each of the institutions can accept in light of the needs of the others.

There are several difficulties with the present system of institutions in the building culture:

- The individual institutions, each of which has individual control over its own realm of operation, are not set up to allow a positive vision of the whole to guide their work.
- There are too many institutions, and they are individually too complex.
- The institutions operate according to formal rules, leaving little opportunity for flexibility.
- And finally, the ordinary people of society have only limited means to come in touch with the institutions of the building culture, to make their desires about the built world known, and thereby to ensure that the culture as a whole influences the culture of building in the most appropriate way. The story of professionalism, which has removed ordinary people from those who control expertise, has influenced building in a way that the legitimate concerns of professionals do not necessarily take into account all the legitimate concerns of people in society.

The fragmentation of the built environment is at least partly a result of the differing and often contradictory agendas of the various institutions of the building culture.

SHARED ARCHITECTURAL KNOWLEDGE

6

Tradition and Innovation in Building Form

One of the key qualities of a building culture is that the people in it share architectural knowledge. An important part of this knowledge consists of rules about building form itself. These rules are expressed as types or patterns—commonly understood configurations of building arrangement or construction that characterize the buildings of the culture.

Within a healthy building culture, the rules that govern the form of the built world form a dynamic system that can change gradually over time, as need warrants, and that reflect differences from place to place. Such subtle difference occurs most effectively when the rules themselves are known and understood and when the players in the building culture have the ability to change the rules as needed. This is not to say that building types are changing continuously or rapidly: one of the most obvious characteristics of much traditional architecture is its relative stability over time and its repetitive nature in a particular place. However, as we will see later, that stability is tempered by the ability to change when necessary.

The rules concerning form have three attributes that allow for the maximum appropriateness of buildings to ways of life, the reinforcement of the culture's picture of itself, and the maximum "fit" between form and the culture/place in which it exists:

- The availability and sharing of the rules across society, and the capacity for cross-fertilization of the rules.
- The ability for the culture to change the rules when necessary, thereby promoting innovation across the culture.
- The appropriateness of the rules themselves, which is made possible in part by the first two attributes.

Availability and Sharing of Rules: Cross-Fertilization

The great variety of places and cultures in the world has generated and sustained a corresponding variety of kinds of buildings and construction techniques. One of the things that sustains the precision and appropriateness of the individual type, and the consequent variety among many types, is the interaction between different cultures and the sharing of knowledge and rules. This interaction traditionally came about through the movement of craftsmen from one place to another. When it is happening fully, this cross-fertilization results in great richness of buildings and enables individual building traditions to benefit fully from the ideas and cultures around them.

The variation of building type with geography is a central idea of vernacular architecture. Types, which are commonly understood and shared building configurations, move from place to place, and buildings often demonstrate how a type that had been brought from somewhere else has been modified to particular new conditions. We need only look at the transport of a German house type to Virginia,[1] or the movement of Ukrainian building practices to North Dakota,[2] or the interactions between the Mamluk and Ottoman empires in Islamic architecture.[3] In all cases a conservatism brings the type along, then a transformation allows a version of the type to exist in the new place. Global cultures have only accelerated the geographic diffusion of building types. Anthony King was one of the first to point this out, in his work on the bungalow,[4] and we can also see it in the Japanese penchant for American tract houses and the geographically aspecific character of such buildings as airports, hotels, and office buildings. In these last cases, geographic variation has been suppressed or has disappeared altogether.[5]

The links among building types are human links. People maintain and change building types over time and transmit them from one place to another. These links may be observed along a single street in London, or across the ocean, in the case of large-scale migrations, like those of the English craftsmen who built in particular places in New England. They brought what they knew to the New World and adapted that knowledge to new conditions.

In medieval times, master masons sometimes traveled specifically to get ideas and facilitate the sharing of information. John Harvey writes:

> William Humberville, master mason in 1369–79 for the building of the library of Merton College, Oxford, journeyed to Sherborne, Salisbury, Winchester and London, "with the purpose of view[ing] the library of the Preaching Friars," to get ideas; Pedro Balaguer, architect of the famous belfry or Miguelete of Valencia, was sent as far afield as

Figure 6.1.
Hawksmoor's Christ
Church, Spitalfields,
London

Lerida and Narbonne—some 400 miles each way—to examine towers in 1414; in 1450 Roger Growdon was instructed to view the steeples of Callington in Cornwall, Buckland, Tavistock, and Ashburton, and to use the best of them as a pattern for the tower of Totnes parish church. . . . The long term process involved amounted to a steady downward percolation of design, beginning with royal palaces and chapels, cathedrals and greater monasteries, and passing through lesser churches, priories and manorhouses, to end in small houses and chapels in areas remote from the source of each wave of inspiration.[6]

Hawksmoor and His Craftsmen

The diffusion of techniques in a particular place is seen in early-eighteenth-century London. Christ Church Spitalfields was designed by Nicholas Hawksmoor as one of the fifty new churches commissioned to replace churches lost in the London fire of 1666. Next to this church, in Fournier Street, is the church minister's house, a building also designed by Hawksmoor. These buildings are different, but they have some similar features, including the cornice.

The carpenter for both the house and the church was Samuel Worrall. The mason for the house was Thomas Dunn, and he was also the mason for the church. The plasterer for both buildings was Isaac Mansfield, and the painter for both was James Preedy.[7]

Samuel Worrall was also the carpenter for several other houses in Fournier Street, and in fact he was the developer for some of them, as was the practice for London's craftsmen—particularly carpenters and bricklayers—at that time. It is likely that some of the other craftsmen mentioned were also working on those smaller houses. So this one carpenter, Samuel Worrall, worked on the church, the large house, and smaller ones that he himself built on speculation. The architect worked on both the church and the large house, and some of the other craftsmen worked on a range of buildings as well.

Many other builders in Spitalfields worked on both major and minor buildings. Thomas Ellis did joiner's work at the French Church in Fournier Street, built a house on the street, and rebuilt a house elsewhere. Thomas Denning was the carpenter for a tabernacle at St. Mary's Spital Square and bid unsuccessfully for the work at Christ Church. William Tayler built almshouses for the Weavers' Company, the Three Tun Tavern, and speculative houses. William Seagar was the carpenter for the Seven Stars public house, built seven houses in Folgate Street, and also bid unsuccessfully for the work at Christ Church.[8]

The building culture of early-eighteenth-century London was one that encompassed a good deal of movement of craftsmen, and interrelationships between craftsmen, from building to building. There was practically no steady employment—the expectation of steady employment only came about a century later, with the advent of general contracting on a large scale,

Figure 6.2. Fournier Street, Spitalfields, with Hawksmoor's Christ Church, Spitalfields at end and the minister's house just to the left of the church

Figure 6.3.
Door of house in Spitalfields

and the subsequent rise of labor unions; and depending on their trade, craftsmen could expect to work on a relatively large number of buildings in a particular year. The work of a particular craftsman would appear in many different places and would not necessarily be restricted to buildings of a particular size or type. The nature of this building culture led to a good deal of continuity in building form and detail.

Variation over Function and Economic Class:
Houses and Mosques of Cairo and Tunis

One example of how *a single building type* may change over function and economic class in a particular place is the traditional courtyard building in the cities of the Middle East. Such buildings, which predated classical civilization, were fundamental to urban domestic architecture during the civilizations of Greece and Rome, were maintained in modified form through the various Islamic dynasties, and still survive all around the edge of the Mediterranean.

Consider Bayt Suhaymi, a courtyard house built for well-to-do merchants in Cairo in the seventeenth or eighteenth century. It has an asymmetrical plan, on an irregular site, but is organized around a courtyard that displays considerably more symmetry than the house as a whole. Off this courtyard is a main reception room, the *qa'a*, which is three stories tall, finely crafted, and symmetrical. The courtyard has two adjacent outdoor rooms that are typical of such houses: one, the *taktaboosh*, lies between the courtyard and the garden, and the other is a porch on the floor above the courtyard.

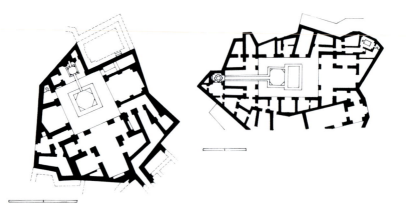

Figure 6.4.
Plans of
houses in
Fustat, Cairo

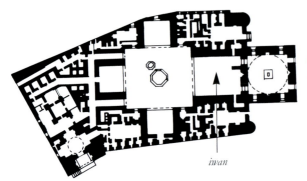

Figure 6.5.
Mosque of Sultan Hassan, Cairo

iwan

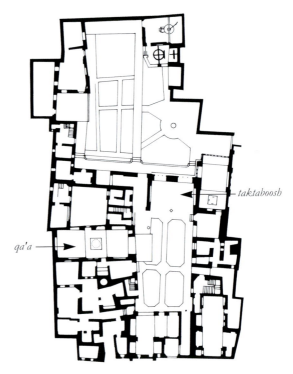

taktaboosh

qa'a

Figure 6.6.
Bayt Suhaymi, Cairo

Formally, this house is in between simple vernacular houses—shown in plans of ancient Fustat—and more elaborate religious buildings like the mosque of Sultan Hassan, which have similar features. The other buildings, too, are organized around bilaterally symmetrical courtyards. Their main rooms are on the axis of the courtyard. The *iwan* of the mosque—the covered porch at the sides of the courtyard—corresponds to the *taktaboosh* of the large house. There are many typological correspondences, both in plan and construction, between the buildings that are vernacular, the ones that are "architectural," and the ones that stand somewhere in the middle.

We can be more systematic by looking at the plans of twenty-eight houses of the sixteenth and seventeenth centuries in Tunis (figs. 6.9 and 6.10).[9] The plans are at the same scale, and their different sizes might be some indication of the wealth of their owners. Certain attributes are present in most of them: a main courtyard with an entrance that allows it to be well hidden from the street, and rooms that communicate directly with the courtyard.

Other attributes show systematic variation through the range of plans. In smaller houses, the courtyard is not necessarily a rectangle, but its sides may be parallel to the sides of the property (whose sides are not necessarily parallel to each other). As houses get larger, the courtyard is more likely to be rectangular. In the largest houses, the courtyard is always rectangular (and often square). Arcades tend not to be present in the smallest houses, but they are *always* present in the largest houses and are sometimes present, to different degrees, for houses of moderate size. Virtually all of the houses have at least one room whose door is directly on one axis of the courtyard, but

Figure 6.7 (left). Bayt Suhaymi, view to courtyard.
Figure 6.8 (right). Bayt Suhaymi, courtyard

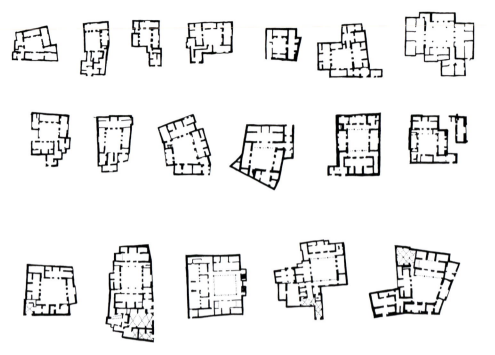

Figure 6.9. Plans of smaller Tunis houses

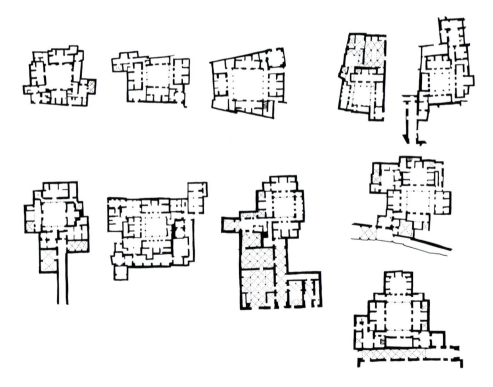

Figure 6.10. Plans of larger Tunis houses

Figure 6.11.
Courtyard of Dar
Othman, a large
house in Tunis

Figure 6.12.
Fountain in courtyard
of Dar Othman

larger houses tend to have more such rooms. In the same way that all houses reinforce the symmetry of the courtyard by putting such rooms on their axes, the largest houses reinforce the symmetry of *these* rooms by putting smaller rooms on *their* axes.

As houses get larger, their basic symmetries are intensified through a recursive process that reinforces the symmetries of smaller and smaller parts of the house. This intensification includes more elaborate ornament related to the courtyard, and to rooms that reinforce the principal symmetries, as the houses get larger.

Certain ideas about form—in this case arising from the fundamental importance of the courtyard itself—pervade the building culture as a whole, making houses of different classes into variations of each other, through the mechanisms of human habit, social aspiration, and craft knowledge.

The Hybrid Wood-and-Stone Buildings of Northern Greece and the Southern Balkans

Another example shows the diffusion of type over a wider geographic area. Between the Black Sea and the Aegean, a particular house type, using a hybrid construction system of masonry and timber, was widely built until the middle of the nineteenth century. The houses had one or two floors with outer walls of masonry, and a top floor of wood; in many cases the wood superstructure extended down to the ground, inside the masonry walls. The lower part of the house, which was more easily heated than the upper, wooden part, was used for winter living, while the upper part, which could be opened to catch the breeze, was used during the summer.

The upper part, which contained the most important room for visitors, was often built with great virtuosity, rotated with respect to the masonry part below, to catch the breeze or a view. The complex framing was handled in an everyday and straightforward way by the craftsmen who built them—members of groups that moved from town to town.[10] The most spectacular examples of these buildings stand in the monasteries of Mount Athos, in northern Greece, where large versions, often with courtyards, are built on constrained and rather inaccessible sites.

These buildings came about partly because of their location in the world and partly because of the movement of craftsmen from place to place. To the north of the Black Sea lie Ukraine and Russia, with their great forests and ancient timber-building cultures, where one can find buildings built very similarly to the upper parts of these hybrids. Around the Aegean are masonry building traditions, including Byzantine tower-houses, examples of which can still be seen in the southern Peloponnese. There, wood, which is rare and expensive, is used minimally, in some places hardly at all.

Figure 6.13.
Hybrid wood and masonry
house in Kavalla, Greece

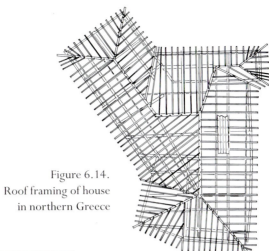

Figure 6.14.
Roof framing of house
in northern Greece

Figure 6.15.
Hybrid wood and masonry
building in monastery at
Mt. Athos, northern Greece

wood

Black Sea

wood & masonry

masonry

Mediterranean Sea

Figure 6.16.
Southeastern Europe: the
meeting of two great
building traditions

The wooden building tradition exists as far south as it can and stops at the point where economics and climate make the use of wood impractical. The masonry building tradition exists as far north as it can. The overlapping area combines the two traditions. In general, *type persists from place to place, to the extent that it can, and changes from place to place to the extent that it must.*

Palladio and the Farmhouses of the Veneto

To extend the point to the interaction between architects and vernacular building traditions, we turn to the Italian Renaissance, in which the typological continuum crossed professional lines, so that architects learned from the vernacular, and the vernacular was in turn influenced by what architects did.

The villas of Palladio combine preexisting vernacular forms with new Renaissance ideas. In the second of his Four Books of Architecture, Palladio wrote about both the location of villas and their "compartment or disposition"[11]—the need to place buildings near good water; the importance of not placing buildings in confined valleys; and the importance of avoiding places with too much reflected sunlight. He writes about the functional importance of porticoes "joined to the master's habitation, that he may be able to go every place under cover, that neither the rains, nor the scorching sun of the summer, may be a nuisance to him, when he goes to look after his affairs; which will also be of great use to lay wood in under cover, and an infinite number of things belonging to a villa, that would otherwise be spoiled by the rains and the sun." In one instance, he wrote that local custom should be followed: "The places for breeding animals, as hogs, sheep, pidgeons, fowls and such like, are to be disposed according to their quality and nature: and in this the custom of different countries ought to be observed."

Other Renaissance theorists also appreciated the vernacular. Serlio's treatise included a volume on domestic architecture,[12] and this book—volume 6—begins with plates illustrating very humble buildings indeed. It has been suggested that these buildings were connected typologically to larger buildings[13] and that this volume influenced Palladio.[14]

Palladio's villas draw on the traditional farms of the Veneto, the countryside inland from Venice (the *terraferma*, to Venetians). The agricultural system of the Veneto was based on large estates that included clusters of farm buildings with residences for the landowner and workers, as well as the working buildings of the farm.

These farms had developed over hundreds of years. Traditionally, on smaller farms, all functions were under one roof. On larger farms, the central buildings were connected and included living quarters for the owner as well as for supervisors, servants, and employed workers; a hayloft; a granary; sheds for animals and implements; a cool place for storing wine; and a threshing floor.[15] They often included a portico to give shade from the hot sun. These buildings were often rectangular, but one had to go outside, under the portico, to get from one room to the other. This arrangement was maintained into relatively recent times. A late-nineteenth-century traveler's account of a farm in the Veneto comments, "You are then taken up narrow staircases and into the granary. The countless windows are opened . . . letting in warm light through curtains of wistaria and of ivy. . . . From the granaries you descend to the *barchesse*: these are immense arcades where all the farm machines, sacks, seats &c., are housed and guarded by a herd of Maremma sheep-dogs. Here, too, are innumerable beehives looking out upon parterres of lavender."[16]

Typical Palladian villas and typical farmhouses of the Veneto share some formal and functional characteristics: the barchessi, dovecotes, granaries, and wine cellars; the enclosed court in front of the house; the use of covered walkways to connect various areas; and views from the loggia at *piano nobile* level.

At the same time, they differ in the presence of symmetries and classical motifs. The loggias and outbuildings of farmhouses are likely to be asymmetrically placed, while those of the villas are symmetrical. The facades of Palladian villas are composed with Renaissance versions of the classical orders, while those of earlier farmhouses may not be. Palladio used these techniques to reinforce the status of the Venetian moneyed families on the *terraferma* as the supremacy of the city of Venice in world trade began to decline.[17]

In Renaissance Italy, the close relationship between the vernacular and buildings designed by architects is not restricted to the Veneto. A different

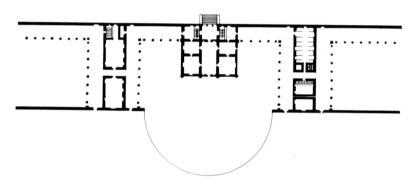

Figure 6.17. Plan of villa by Palladio at Angarano

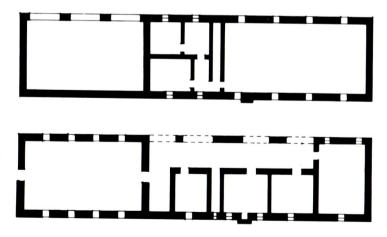

Figure 6.18. Plan of farmhouse in the Veneto

Figure 6.19.
Villa Barbaro at
Maser, Palladio

Figure 6.20.
Farmhouse in
the Veneto, 1981

rural building type, consisting of a rectangular hipped-roof block with a dovecote at its center, projecting above the main roof, and a tripartite plan, was typical of Tuscany and nearby areas. During the sixteenth century, Vignola invented an architectural type that was based on these vernacular elements (and used it for the two pavilions at the Villa Lante, among other places). It became common for landowners' houses during the seventeenth century, then reverted to vernacular usage, including as dwellings for farmworkers. The interaction was strong enough to "[illustrate] the difficulty of distinguishing between monumental and vernacular traditions in the countryside. . . . Because of the fluid interaction between the houses of owners and those of workers, neither can be understood without reference to the other."[18]

Henry Hobson Richardson and American Small-Town Architecture

The movement of ideas from architects to the vernacular is seen in the work of H. H. Richardson, who practiced in the decades after the Civil War. A formal inventor and a precursor of Sullivan and Wright, and often seen as the first genuinely "American" architect, he is famous for the use of continuous surfaces and plastic forms.[19] Buildings such as Trinity Church in Boston and the Crane Library in Quincy, Massachusetts, are powerful and still-admired exemplars of Richardson's mature handling of form and composition and of his role in the development of an architecture that began to depart from the surface styles that characterized the earlier nineteenth century.

Many American cities and towns, particularly those in which a lot of construction took place in the last third of the nineteenth century, have a solid building style, sometimes called "Richardsonian Romanesque," manifested in tens of thousands of buildings. It is characterized by stone walls that are thick or that appear to be thick; arched windows, in groups, separated by rounded stone mullions; arched door openings; rough-cut stone at the building base, at arches, and at other points of focus, such as belt courses. Most of these buildings are not as inventive as those done by Richardson himself, but they are visually pleasing and represent solid additions to urban streets. Even though the deeper architectural and spatial intentions of Richardson did not make it to these smaller towns, the material and stylistic ideas did.

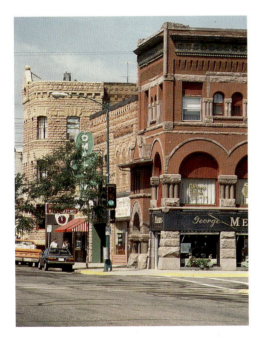

Figure 6.21.
Richardsonian buildings in Yankton, South Dakota

Figure 6.22.
Distribution of granite quarry areas in the prairie states around 1890.

As the building height and density of downtowns increased in the prosperous decades after the Civil War, wooden structures were replaced with brick and stone. Architectural styles that made use of these solid materials were appropriate for marking a town's "coming of age." The materials were available: there were granite quarries in Colorado, South Dakota, Minnesota, Wisconsin, Missouri, and Texas, and limestone and sandstone quarries in most midwestern and Plains states. Large cities could afford to import stone from afar, while smaller places generally continued using local material. The railroad and improved communications systems allowed people and architectural styles to travel more freely from one place to another. The development of an architectural press, including new regional journals in such cities as Chicago, Minneapolis, and Kansas City, also helped this process along.[20]

Hundreds of small-town architects used Richardson's buildings as precedents. This was sometimes done with simple repetition of elements and sometimes with a greater understanding of underlying design principles. Some of these architects had been apprentices in Richardson's office and then established their own practices in other towns. They began to get commissions from even smaller towns; John Hudson points out that "by the turn of the century, Richardsonian courthouses and building blocks were found in more than 150 prairie cities, ranging from north-central Minnesota to southern Texas."[21] Ideas spread down to the smallest town in which civic leaders aspired to respectability, announced with a solid Richardsonian architecture. In the last decades of the century, Richardsonian buildings constituted an everyday vernacular that had made its way from Richardson's office to be copied, repeated, and transformed throughout the country.

The influence of Richardson even traveled outside North America: in Australia, for example, nationalistic fervor and the search for an Australian identity at the end of the nineteenth century led some to look away from England and toward a country that had broken its British connections. Richardsonian buildings, including ordinary brick warehouses, began to appear in Sydney and Melbourne—fully half a world away from Richardson's office in Massachusetts.[22]

Antoni Gaudi, Le Corbusier, and Carlo Scarpa

Finally, even the work of twentieth-century architects, typically considered the most original, demonstrates how the vernacular moved "upward," into the realm of "architecture."

The work of the Catalan architect Antoni Gaudi is rightfully considered the product of a fertile creative imagination. His buildings are unusual and often fantastic: curved forms predominate, simple engineering techniques are employed to emulate natural forms, and richly colored tile is used extensively.

Yet his innovations also depended on the fact that he was deeply embedded in Catalonian building traditions. His father was a coppersmith. He was affected by the landscape around him, the "red earth, the shadowed furrows of its plowed fields, the vines and olive trees with their sculptural, contorted trunks,"[23] and also by the rapidly industrializing—and increasingly politically assertive—society of Catalonia. The use of colored tiles had been introduced by the Arabs and was common in the eastern and southern parts of Spain. Stonemasonry and bricklaying had long traditions in the area, and Gaudi could design with models rather than precisely detailed drawings because he could depend on the skills of masons and bricklayers. The thin-tile vaulting that Gaudi used, which easily allows for the creation of complex curves, was (and still is) an accepted technique in Catalonia.

Le Corbusier was also influenced by the vernacular. The journal he wrote on his first trip to the Mediterranean makes it clear that he was looking at vernacular building with the same eye for form with which he looked at the great monuments. The formal essence of each was revealed equally, in a democracy of forms in which the courtyard of a tiny house could have as much meaning to him as a column of the Parthenon. Describing a house in a Bulgarian village, he writes:

> Each house has its main room: a very large window, wider than it is tall and checkered with windowpanes, opens out on the trees and flowers of the garden, and because of the unique location of this town, the bold and brutal profile of the mountain and a yellow stream are framed in the geometry of the fenestration. These rooms are so small that the window takes up the entire wall, and a balcony is always hung, overlooking the avalanche of houses; this balcony is of fine wood-work, and the contours of the pillars and of the glaze brings to mind the exquisite niches of Islamic interiors. In this charming small space, the men squat on sofas and quietly smoke. They look like a Persian painting in a Moorish setting.[24]

Le Corbusier looked at vernacular buildings in terms of their most basic, irreducible elements: thick masonry walls punctured by small windows; roughly finished surfaces; cubic building forms; high contrast between light

Figure 6.23. Casa Mila, by Antoni Gaudi

Figure 6.24. House from La Chaux de Fonds, Le Corbusier's birthplace, now in outdoor museum at Ballenberg, Switzerland

Figure 6.25.
Detail at Querini Stampalia
Museum, Venice,
designed by Carlo Scarpa

and shade. His own buildings were characterized by a high degree of inventiveness, but many also have a primitive aspect, including simple forms, rough surfaces, and direct juxtapositions of shapes and materials. These aspects of Le Corbusier's architecture were inspired and given justification by the vernacular architecture he saw on his trips to the eastern Mediterranean and North Africa.[25]

Carlo Scarpa, the twentieth-century northern Italian architect, depended on the use of traditional building techniques of Venice within architectural compositions that rejected traditional order. While much modern architecture made a point of rejecting traditional techniques, Scarpa used them as the medium for his designs. In his project for the renovation of the Castelvecchio in Verona, Scarpa worked on-site, developing details as the work progressed and consulting closely with craftspeople who were trained in the ancient Venetian ways of building.[26] Scarpa's strength was in detailing and using materials and in the clear articulation of different materials at joints.

Figure 6.26. Building materials in Venice

Such articulation is typical of much traditional Venetian building, and Scarpa's details were both inventions and transformations of these traditional approaches to materials.

No strong boundary exists between the vernacular and the nonvernacular—all buildings are part of a continuous web in which such distinctions have little meaning. In traditional society, there was a continuity of building types—vernacular and nonvernacular alike—among the different situations within a culture and across geography. This web of building was maintained by a network of people who dealt with each other in the building culture, sharing knowledge and information, and who were in a position to put forward innovations when they were required.

Today's building cultures are not characterized by the kind of diffusion described in many examples in this chapter. As we will see, although much information is made available by modern media, the ability to easily apply and change this information is constrained by the organization of modern practice.

Ability for Building Types to Change When Necessary

In a healthy building culture, the people and institutions who are responsible for making buildings need to have the means to make and test changes as they are needed, without a great deal of hindrance. In much traditional building, this kind of change happened smoothly, if slowly. Before the medieval period, for example, many rural houses in England as well as in vast areas of northwestern Europe were single-roomed buildings that housed both people and animals. Over the centuries, this type became more differentiated. At some point a two-unit plan was introduced, with people in one unit and animals in the other. This plan remained linear, even when the animals were moved out, into a byre of their own, and the people remained in a two-room dwelling: the ancestor of what we now know as the hall-and-parlor plan.

The plan had variants that were characteristic of different regions. In some places the entrance was at one end of the building; in others it was in between the hall and parlor. In some places the service rooms were separated from the main rooms by a cross-passage; in others the cross-passage did not exist at all.

Early versions of these houses were open to the roof, with no second floor—the height was necessary because there were open hearths on the floor. There is evidence that at some point when the fire was still in an open hearth, partial smoke walls were used and that, high up, smoke baffles in the position of the roof trusses, and originally the width of one structural bay, collected the smoke, sent it out the roof, and perhaps even formed a crude draft for the fire. Eventually this arrangement was transformed into the closed fireplace and chimney, as we know them today. As the medieval period progressed, it became fashionable for houses to get bigger and for the hall to be a large open room, high and open to the ceiling. This configuration persisted even as the rooms on either end of the hall might be ceiled over, with rooms above.[27]

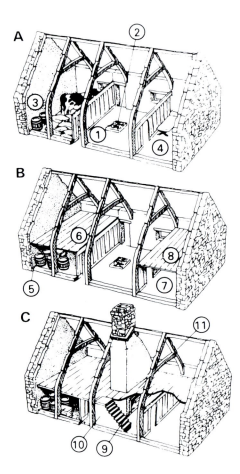

Figure 6.27.
The gradual transformation
of an open-hall house

The technological innovation of the fireplace and chimney allowed for a big change in the plan and organization of the house: once the open roof structure was no longer necessary for smoke, the second floor could be completely spanned for living space. This change was gradual. At first, a second floor would have been inserted into a hall that was built many years before. Eventually, second floors were built with the initial building, and the medieval open hall disappeared. Houses started to have full second floors, comprising a linear chain of two or three rooms, and this closer packing of rooms supported increasing building density in towns and cities.

In New York City during the nineteenth century, a different transformation, connected to the evolution of the English urban house but many generations away, led to the emergence of the tenement. At the start of the century, the party-wall row house, often on a 25-foot-wide lot, was the typical dwelling unit for many families. Like the related "terraced house" in England, it consisted of three or four stacked floors, each consisting of a major and minor zone: the major zone contained the rooms in a line, and the minor zone contained the stair and hall. For the middle and upper classes, such buildings held extended families, plus servants and perhaps other workers, such as apprentices.

Industrialization and the breakdown of the apprentice system forced changes in this basic unit, as many independent workers began to crowd the city. The single-family row house gradually evolved into the apartment house and then the tenement. First, individual rooms in single-family houses were rented to strangers and other families. Then, gradually, versions of the row house were built that had one or two independent apartments or flats on

Figure 6.28.
Row house, New York City

Figure 6.29. Apartment house, New York City

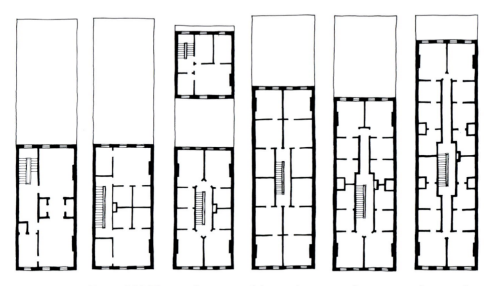

Figure 6.30. The transformation of the row house into the apartment house and tenement, New York City

each floor. In some cases the plan brought two units together, in a 50-foot-wide building with four apartments. Gradually, the row house evolved into the typical tenement and apartment-house plan, which served the needs of immigrants and workers.[28]

In each of these cases, the building culture allowed these transformations to take place. Social need and building technology changed hand in hand because building craftsmen were readily able to make the relatively minor changes that gradually added up to a major typological transformation.

However, building cultures do not necessarily allow for needed innovations. Although the initial emergence of the tenement, which served real needs, happened relatively smoothly because the market easily provided for these needs, improvement of the type was enormously difficult. The miserable conditions caused by lack of light and air eventually forced the adoption of new laws to regulate tenement design, but these legal changes took years of social and bureaucratic effort in what had become a climate of rampant speculation.[29]

Today, rigid zoning rules may prevent useful innovation. In many American communities, zoning does not permit such things as small accessory apartments, home offices, and other small businesses, such as child-care centers or mom-and-pop grocery stores. These needs come out of the changing nature of the population and work. However, it has proven almost impossible for such changes to be introduced within zoning laws that require a strict separation of uses—an example of how typological innovation that may have been natural in another time is prevented by the institutional structure of the contemporary building culture.[30]

The persistence and diffusion of type, and the innovation of type, are two sides of the same coin. In a healthy building culture, *tradition* and *innovation* are not contradictory but complementary concepts. In both cases, building type is allowed to take on the most appropriate form. When change is not called for, then people's conservative habits simply allow existing building types to persist. When change is called for by new social or physical conditions, the culture does not prevent people's ingenuity to make change happen.

A smooth evolution of building type may be facilitated by a fine-grained network of players in the culture. Each player is able to apply individual discretion within a framework of overall cultural understandings. The emergence of Gothic architecture can be traced to a sequence of individual innovations by master masons dealing directly with buildings under construction, innovations that eventually contributed to a coherent style;[31] many variations of the English terraced house plan were executed by many different builders during the nineteenth century;[32] the development of typical designs for concert halls was the result of trial and error over many generations of building, where the designers of such buildings were intimately aware of the successes and failure of buildings that had been built before and of what new problems needed to be solved. In all cases, incisive judgment could be applied to the problem at hand.

Within the diversity of today's building cultures, the necessary delicate balance between tradition and innovation is not easy to find. There is a good deal of innovation in service of the financial bottom line, in realms as disparate as the production of power tools, engineered wood products, and sheet materials; speeded-up methods of project delivery; and the use of computers in architectural offices and in complex construction operations. Innovations in the service of profit happen smoothly, and business firms that cannot innovate in these ways lose their viability.

Some degree of innovation is also visible in architectural practice, and in buildings themselves. There are changes in office design, responding to new forms of business organization; innovations in hospital design, responding to new ideas about healing; innovations in city planning, responding to calls for towns of human scale, in which the pedestrian is not overwhelmed by the automobile. But these innovations are much more hard-won. Today, noneconomic innovations are not so easy or smooth. They tend to require the participation of several institutions—not just a single company that introduces a new product and has the resources to push it through with respect to building codes and testing laboratories. The complexity and formality of institutions in the contemporary building culture may prevent the tentative and gradual introduction of innovations that was a hallmark of traditional building practice.[33]

Appropriateness of the Rules Themselves

When the rules that are known and shared about buildings—the patterns and types, knowledge of craft techniques and commonly used building materials—are appropriate, there is a good fit between buildings and their context. As we have seen, such a fit does not happen automatically but is supported by the free movement of ideas and by the lack of inappropriate restraint against making good rules work. When rules are appropriate, they lead to everyday buildings that enhance culture and place and evoke strong positive feelings and deep affection toward them.

The characteristic of vernacular architecture that has been most thoroughly described is the close fit between buildings and human life—so close that it may become almost impossible to talk about one without reference to the other. Buildings and the way they are used are not "instrumental" to life, but they define it in a profound sense—and may evoke deep emotions as a result. Clare Cooper Marcus writes, "Home is not only a literal place but also a place of deep contentment in the innermost temple of the soul."[34] Consider the simple Berber house, in which the division of space and the placement of every object help reveal basic understandings of men and women, day and night, nature and culture;[35] or the large English country house, which reinforced a complex social order;[36] or the American small town, with its familiar and well-loved shops and houses and schools; and even to some extent the Levittown house, which became gradually personalized and modified over the years. In all of these cases, the building or village and its particular typological configuration are essential and strongly felt.

The ability of architectural works to evoke real affection is not limited to very old or faraway buildings. But to a large extent, the prevalent building types of modern building cultures fail to connect people to their past, to their place, and to each other in a genuine way. They do not result in buildings that deeply touch us.

Figure 6.31. An American shopping mall, 1998

Certainly our buildings are *familiar*. We have a certain set of expectations about a shopping mall: we will be able to park our car when we get there; the mall will contain a few well-known department stores, many more smaller shops that are part of well-known chains, a few locally owned stores, a "food court," and perhaps a movie theater, and plenty of daylight, along with temperature-controlled air. When we enter one of these places, even one that we have not been in before, it is familiar and we know how to behave in it.

This familiarity, however, is not the same as deep feeling. Consider a very common building type that has emerged in the last ten or fifteen years: the convenience store attached to a gas station. It emerged out of well-understood trends: faster American lifestyles, drivers' decreasing desire to stop for a full meal, the changing economy of the gas station business. It can be considered a positive example of innovation.[37] To many people who are on the road every day, these places are useful, familiar, and expected. If they disappeared suddenly, we would miss them. But we would not remember them wistfully; we would not see "a part of our past" disappear as we do when our childhood home is torn down for a new development. Most people's relationship to these places is functional rather than emotional.

This is true for many building types in modern society. Things work; society is not so chaotic that we can't make our way on a day-to-day basis. We move efficiently from home to office to shopping mall, stopping occasionally to fill our tank and buy a cold drink. However, our relationship to most of the buildings we use is not an emotional one. These building types have a curiously abstract relationship to people's inner lives. The idea of the building as an artifact that has affective possibilities is absent.

It is even questionable how well the functional aspects really work. From one point of view, a fast-food restaurant meets our needs perfectly: fast food, located just where you need it; cheap, predictable, clean, well lit; a place

Figure 6.32.
A convenience
store/gas
station, 1998

Figure 6.33. Rue du Jour, Paris, about 1925: architecture in the context of the building culture as a whole. Eugene Atget. *Rue du Jour*, c. 1925. Albumen print, 8 5/8 x 6 13/15". The Museum of Modern Art, New York. Abbott-Levy Collection. Partial gift of Shirley C. Burden. Photograph © 1998 The Museum of Modern Art, New York.

to sit, a place for kids to play. One cannot really argue with this list of needs, but it is also highly abstract and *explicit*. The needs are defined in very precise ways, and design solutions are developed partly as the result of actual human responses to proposed configurations, lighting, and color—and the profitability that comes from such responses. One mall executive said, "We totally redid the floors. We put in skylights, changed the facades of all the tenant spaces, and retenanted many spaces. The increase in sales has been considerable."[38]

When the whole building becomes purely an expression of abstract need and vehicle toward profit, and very little is left that connects people to a familiar past, there may be a large gap between the deep feeling buildings can arouse and the way they satisfy real or perceived abstract needs. The absence of deep feeling toward buildings is connected to the fact that decisions about the design of buildings happen in abstract ways: there is no strongly held image or goal to which decisions can be referred, so decision making itself loses an emotional center.

There are three issues with respect to the appropriateness of building types: first, the satisfaction of definable functional need; second, the satisfaction of undefinable but equally real functional need (the kind that historical continuity traditionally helped to ensure); and third, the familiarity of the building itself, whether or not it meets functional needs in various ways. Modern building types tend to satisfy needs that can be expressed in explicit and quantifiable ways but not needs that are more emotionally felt, that affect people in their hearts and memories.

The Importance of Shared Knowledge in the Building Culture

The continuities between "architecture" and "building," and between buildings of different types, in different places, built by different people, are *necessary for the existence and success of all the buildings in a building culture*.

The story that is usually told centers around how ordinary building is not as good as it can be because it has no great architecture to draw on. It is the story of architects innovating, and of others copying their innovations. Indeed, much "ordinary building" depends on what is happening elsewhere in the culture, including what architects are doing.

But the story that is told less often goes in the other direction: great architecture depends on all the other building happening around it. The power and beauty of great works of architecture comes about partly because of the vast amount of experimentation that is done in the building culture as a whole; because of the techniques and materials that are made available by the building culture; because of the community of craftspeople who are available, competing with each other, and trying to make beautiful things.

The usual interpretation of the idea that great buildings emerge "within a tradition" is that it is happening within a tradition of architecture, where architecture is defined as narrowly as Pevsner defined it. *The point here is different. Great buildings emerge within a tradition of building, which often includes architecture.* Great buildings do not happen in an intellectual or material vacuum, and architecture cannot be removed from the great volume of ordinary building that happens around it—and architects who aspire to great architecture cannot remain aloof from that building.

It is perhaps most accurate to say that the success of *any* building within a building culture depends on all the other buildings in the culture.

If the culture is functioning well, if knowledge is being shared and can be continuously improved, any building can be influenced by buildings and techniques in all different places within the culture, present and past. Most important, the ability of that building to evoke deep feeling ultimately depends on the health of the building culture as a whole.

VALUE AND THE FLOW OF MONEY

The Economics of Quality

To a large extent the transactions of the building culture are economic ones that involve labor and the production of wealth, the flow of money, the value given to different things in the culture. Buildings and the built world represent a good part of the wealth of modern societies, and construction activity represents a good part of ongoing economic production. However, in the United States, and other countries as well, the total square footage of new construction has greatly increased, even as its total cost has slipped—raising questions about how the value of buildings is understood.[1]

In this chapter, the building culture will be examined from three different economic points of view:

- The distribution of value in the built environment. How does the distribution of economic value in the built world correspond with the meaning and affective value that people ascribe to different parts of the built world? How does the building culture support the most effective distribution of value?
- The value added in the construction process. Where is value added, what is the balance between materials, labor, and capital in different parts of the process, and how does this balance affect the nature and quality of the built result?

- The flow of money between the building culture and the larger culture in which it exists. To what extent is the money spent for the construction of buildings helpful to the local culture in which the building is being built?

The Distribution of Value in the Built Environment

About fifteen years ago I went to visit an office of the New York City Department of Parks. This office was responsible for all of the tiny planted squares where two streets meet at a diagonal; the planted boulevards like Upper Broadway in Manhattan; in fact, all such public pedestrian space— thousands of individual sites throughout the city. These sites are often unnamed, too small to fly a kite in, but they provide a breath of air, a bit of visual relief—they are important places even though left over from decisions about street layout and property subdivision made decades before. The office turned out to be a single room on the upper floor of an old office building, with peeling paint and flickering fluorescent lights, occupied by two people who were together responsible for the ongoing upkeep of these thousands of places. I must have appeared surprised, because when I walked in, one of the two people said to me, "Yes, this is the last outpost of the public realm."

This state of affairs reflects how by and large, in this century, the investment of money in the American built environment has had to be correlated with the probability of economic gain *as a direct result of that investment*. The parts of the public realm that have received the most attention are things like the interstate highway system (highly promoted by the trucking lobby) and airports (supported by the airline and business communities); places like small planted squares in New York City have been neglected. This shift in investment is directly connected to the cultural idea discussed in chapter 4: that decision making is based on measurable, explicit criteria rather than factors that may be deeply felt but are more difficult to measure.

An idea prevalent in modern architecture—that buildings are mere objects, independent of each other, and separated from each other by swaths of space that do not have particular meaning—is consistent with this. When each object has its own independent identity and that identity is to a large extent economic, then the distribution of money is discrete and scattered rather than continuous.

The same is true of public spaces within buildings. Since the profit on an office building is dependent on the quantity of net leasable space, it is beneficial to that profit to reduce as much as possible the amount of nonleasable space within the building—public lobby and circulation space. The prestige of a building, and therefore its rental rate, may of course be increased by an elaborate lobby and public space, but again, the lobby is seen purely as a financial investment. When there is no profit to be made from office or work space, as in government buildings, public space and "amenities" disappear altogether, and design is guided solely by explicit and measurable criteria of space standards, ventilation needs, and fire codes. In all cases, the expenditure of money is justified by direct return on investment, in terms of either profit from rent or the basic ability for government employees to carry out their jobs.

Since the value of the built environment can only be partly measured in terms of money, investment in the built environment needs to take into account values other than financial ones.[2] Although the circulation space of a building, for example, does not directly bring rent, it is important to the life and community of the building and may deserve more investment than if it is only considered necessary for movement. The same is true of urban streets, squares, and parks that do not themselves add to the property tax base of a city.

The success of many historical places depended on a broader measurement of value. Consider Hyde Park in London, or Bernini's fountains in the Piazza Navona in Rome, or the elaborate investment in the courtyard of traditional Islamic houses, or the emphasis on facades rather than side walls in many urban vernacular buildings, ranging from brick houses in London to wooden houses in Norway.[3] In these places investment is not based on the prospect of immediate financial return, and its distribution corresponds to the distribution of meaning and value in the environment.

Fortunately, a wider recognition of the value of such investment is becoming evident today. Bryant Park, behind the New York Public Library

Figure 7.1. An old public place in France, 1922: simple investment in the public realm. Eugene Atget. *Place due Tertre*, 1922. Albumen silver print, 7 x 9 ⅜" (18 x 24 cm). The Museum of Modern Art, New York. Abbott-Levy Collection. Partial gift of Shirley C. Burden. Print by Chicago Albumen Works, 1981. Copy print © 1998 The Museum of Modern Art, New York.

at the very heart of the city, at Fifth Avenue and 42nd Street, has been reclaimed by a private foundation and turned into a vital public space.[4] The promenade along the Hudson River in Lower Manhattan, developed by the quasi-public authority that developed the office and apartment buildings at Battery Park City, provides a place for people from those buildings and from the financial district beyond. The Boston Redevelopment Authority found, in planning the redevelopment of that city's Central Artery site, that commercial land value—and the total tax base—would rise if not all land was developed for profit, but if some were left for public space.[5] In some of these cases the financial bottom line depends on investment in the public realm. But in others the financial bottom line is not explicitly present—even the New York City Parks Department has begun once again, with the help of local volunteers, to take care of the odd bits of public land in the city.[6]

In well-formed historical environments, not only is the distribution of investment more continuous, encompassing public space as well as buildings, the circulation space within buildings as well as rooms built for a specific purpose; but the distribution of investment is broader, with more participants and a wider range of sizes.[7] This variety reinforces spatial and functional hierarchies and allows small buildings and "interventions" at the edge of large ones to tie the large ones into the fabric of the town. Examples include small commercial buildings at the edges of large mosques in traditional Islamic cities (these buildings often provided rent for the mosque complex itself), almshouses and other buildings in English cathedral closes, and ordinary commercial spaces in front of movie theaters in American small towns. As shown in fig. 7.3 the scale of the large building is mitigated in a way that spreads investment over more smaller projects. This is quite different from typical modern public development, in which large urban projects sit bare, without being brought down to scale.

This is also true within buildings where necessary spatial hierarchies require a varying distribution of resources, as opposed to projects where it is assumed that all spaces should receive the same level of finish. In many great works, ranging from Chartres Cathedral to the Great Mosque of Kairouan to many traditional agricultural settlements in which the storehouse—the place of wealth—received the most lavish attention, architectural intensity is correlated with level of investment.

Christopher Alexander has made this clear in projects where the distribution of a budget is based on the intensity of centers or places, from the point of view of feeling and function.[8] Describing where to cut in the case of overruns, in order to maintain an overall sense of unity, Alexander writes,

> Very early on, the client begins to appreciate that, to pay for some luxurious item, other items must be rough. Great buildings always have some luxury, and some roughness. The money must be distributed so that some areas are intensified, receive a little more care, are made more beautiful. As a result, less money will be spent on other areas. But this is not a bad thing. It is a good thing because—as in the Alhambra—the reduced areas provide a necessary counterpoint to the intense areas, allowing them to shine.[9]

Figure 7.2. Battery Park City, New York, 1998: reinvestment in the public realm

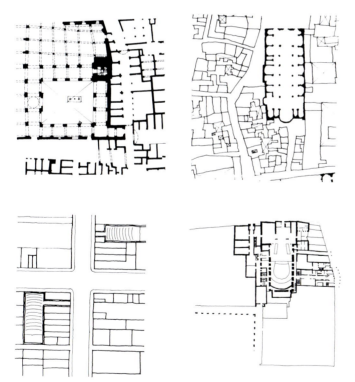

Figure 7.3.
Smaller buildings forming an edge to the Great Mosque in Tunis, the church of S. Maria sopra Minerva in Rome, two movie theaters in 1948 Eugene, Oregon, and a theater at Covent Garden, London, in 1808

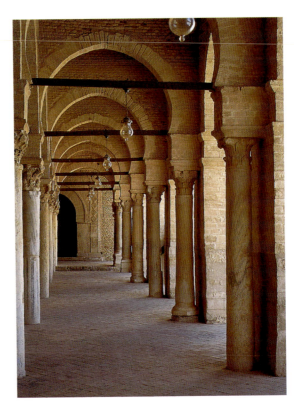

Figure 7.4.
The Great Mosque
of Kairouan

This necessary variation in monetary distribution, in the environment as a whole and in individual buildings, has implications for the way that the institutions of the building culture carry out their business. It means that financial backers and city agencies should not necessarily favor large projects; that the production of drawings and specifications and the organization of work on the building site should not necessarily promote uniformity; and that there should be as much flexibility as possible in the way that money is controlled and distributed.

Historically, the distribution of money in building has shifted from many small amounts of money, widely spread, to large amounts of money that flow through single institutions. In chapter 2 we saw the extremely fine-grained distribution of payments, even on large projects, in medieval building cultures. In Renaissance Florence and eighteenth-century England, local projects were accompanied by local control. The money that large Renaissance Florentine families put forward for their own projects was accompanied by direct control: the client or a representative was involved in overseeing construction on a day-by-day basis. They did not borrow money for their construction projects, and they themselves determined how their money was being spent. There was little speculation, and banks were not organized so that investment credit could be channeled to subcontractors.[10]

In eighteenth-century England, sources of money for building included the craftsmen themselves (including loans to each other), builders' merchants, and some lending by banks (although banks were not inclined to make long-term loans, at least in the early years of the Industrial Revolution).[11] In provincial towns, loans were made by local people rather than at long distance;[12] they were small and were secured "only by a bond or a promise to pay."[13] In London, loans by banks and individual backers began to be contingent on the quality of the work. On the Southampton Estate, leases were granted for construction "provided [the houses] were 'good and substantial' and built within two years according to a plan laid down by Charles Fitzroy."[14]

The growing involvement of financial backers who were separate from the actual building operation was accompanied by the lender's specifying more conditions regarding the quality of the building, in order to ensure value when the lease reverted to the lessor or in the case of default. Since money came from local sources, though, these conditions were not unreasonable; they only served to reinforce solid, common practice. At the same time, the seeds for the partial control of building by financial backers were being planted.

The contemporary system of mortgage loans is characterized by large, national financial institutions that engage not only in lending directly to borrowers but also in buying mortgages from each other in the secondary mortgage market, as purely financial instruments.[15] To minimize risk while keeping interest rates as low as possible, these institutions put stringent, explicit requirements on loans, including specifications about buildings. These specifications tend to consider the local market as a statistical aggregate and do not necessarily take into account particularities of buildings that might in fact be of high quality—and high financial value—but may not exactly fit a statistical profile. Since the lending institutions are not really local, it becomes difficult for even their local representatives to base decisions on an intuitive understanding of buildings or the local market, or on personal trust. Developers therefore have an incentive to build for this statistically determined market, which sometimes makes it difficult to be innovative or even to serve a small sector of the market.

Moreover, construction loans are more expensive than mortgages, partly because banks see a higher risk in lending on something in progress, with attendant contractors and possible liens, than on something that can be much more easily sold in the market. This high cost of construction money means that contractors are under pressure to work fast; this will guide the development of building systems and may lead to shoddy work. At the same time, the bank's willingness to use the real property as collateral for a mortgage means that the bank will also put constraints on the design of that real property so it can be easily sold in the case of default; this tends to discourage diversity of the building stock.

The distribution of money, meaning, and value in the built environment are strongly related. The fragmentation of modern cities, and the concentration of building activity in certain places, result from particular attitudes toward financial investment. Building investment needs to be distributed in large and small projects, in ventures that are spread widely over the public and private realms, in ways that correspond to real human needs and feelings, not just profit.

Where and How Value Is Added in the Building Production Process

In the traditional agricultural village, many materials are used with minimal processing after their extraction from nature. In most other cases, including the contemporary world, there are several stages between the raw extraction of materials and their final transformation into the building. The finished building represents more value than the initial raw materials, because labor has added value to those materials through processing and shaping. Building cultures differ from each other lies in the point at which value is typically added to materials. Over time there has been a gradual movement toward adding value earlier in the process, farther from the fabrication of the finished building itself. The trend to premanufacture parts of the building away from the building site has accelerated in the last 200 years and is still accelerating. This has corresponded with a growing tendency for both capitalization and professional expertise also to be remote from the actual site of construction.

In so-called primitive cultures, houses are often built of one or two materials taken directly from the site or nearby and processed in simple ways by the builder. Examples are the Marsh Arabs of Iraq, who use reeds from the marshes to build their houses; the villagers of Alberobello and other towns in Basilicata, southern Italy, who use stones from the fields to make *trulli*; and people of the Rajasthani desert in India, who use mud and water to make houses.

In most cultures, where more complex buildings are the norm, different materials go through different processes before they assume their final form. Compare a stone-and-timber English farmhouse from the late seventeenth century; a small London house of the eighteenth century; and a modern wood-framed American house on a concrete slab. In all cases, the number of different materials used in the house has grown dramatically over time, as shown in table 7.1.

The three examples in table 7.1 can also be compared in terms of how the materials were processed for use in the building.

In the fifteenth-century English house, timber structural members and pegs were prepared roughly by sawyers, relatively near the building site, and finished by the carpenters who shaped joints and laid out and assembled the frame. Thatch was prepared from material taken from local fields and was put in place by skilled thatchers. Lime plaster was prepared from lime and sand; the lime was prepared in nearby kilns, and the sand came from quarries and river bottoms. The plaster itself was mixed at the building site by the plasterer and his helpers. Casement windows would have been made by a skilled local joiner. Iron hinges and latches, which represented a very small amount of material, were made by the village blacksmith with iron from the Weald of Sussex or the Forest of Dean[16] and furnace fuel from nearby woods. Most materials came from nearby, and if they were processed, they were processed nearby.

The most skilled labor—those who prepared the frame and did the plastering and thatching—worked at the construction site itself or at nearby timber yards. The presite preparation of materials required much less skill.

Table 7.1. Materials used in three typical houses

15th-century farmhouse	18th-century London house	Modern American house
Stone rubble walls	Fired brick	Concrete
Timber structural members	Lime mortar	Rigid insulation
Pegs for structural members	Lead sheets	Engineered wood joists
Thatch	Wood double-hung windows	Solid sawn studs, joists, rafters
Lime plaster	with glass	Wood and plastic windows with
Wattle	Lead gutters	glass
Daub	lime plaster	Gypsum wallboard
Stone	Oil paint	Gypsum wallboard joint
Timber shutters	Iron hinges and latches	compound
Iron hinges and latches	Iron railings	Bricks
. . . not much more	Stone paving	Cement mortar
	Varnish	Latex-based paint
	Cut nails	Plastic pipe
	Chimney flue pipe	Pipe cement
	. . . not much more	Cast iron pipe
		Pipe compound
		Plumbing fixtures
		Sheet metal ducts
		Sheet metal gutters and leaders
		Plywood
		Nails
		Wood siding
		Asphalt shingles
		Electric cable consisting of
		copper and wire and insulation
		Lighting fixtures
		Switches and outlets
		Carpet
		Laminate for countertops
		Glue for laminate
		Weather-stripping for windows
		and doors
		. . . and quite a bit more

Figure 7.5.
Construction of an eighteenth-century
London house

The Bricklayer.

Figure 7.6.
Early-nineteenth-
century bricklayer

Figure 7.7.
Early-nineteenth-
century brickmaker

The Brick Maker.

The Carpenter.

Figure 7.8.
Early-nineteenth-
century carpenter

The Plumbers.

Figure 7.9.
Early-nineteenth-
century plumbers

Sawyer.

Figure 7.10.
Early-nineteenth-
century sawyer

Figure 7.11.
Early-nineteenth-
century stonemason

The Stone Mason.

A typical relationship between labor and materials costs is shown by the accounts for Mapperton Rectory, a later building built from 1699 to 1703, in which labor cost £135.2.10 and materials cost £81.17.11, a proportion of 60 percent labor and 36 percent materials (transportation of materials cost 4 percent).[17]

On the face of it, the London house of the eighteenth century was not very different from the earlier house in terms of the number or character of materials and components used. But more materials came from farther away: wood for joists, partitions, and rafters came from the Baltics and Scandinavia; lead for roofs came from mines in northern and southwestern England, and the plumber shaped them and fixed them to the roof. The bricks were bought ready-made from a local brickyard or supplier, but the on-site preparation of mortar was similar to that of the lime plaster in the earlier rural house. Items such as nails and glass were commercial products manufactured away from the site, and oil paint was mixed by the painter, who knew about color and the formula for pigment, binder, and oil. With the eighteenth-century house, few if any materials come from the site, but some of the processes of materials preparation were still known by the person who was responsible for applying those materials to the building.

In their description of the construction of early-eighteenth-century houses in London (where industrial techniques were more advanced than

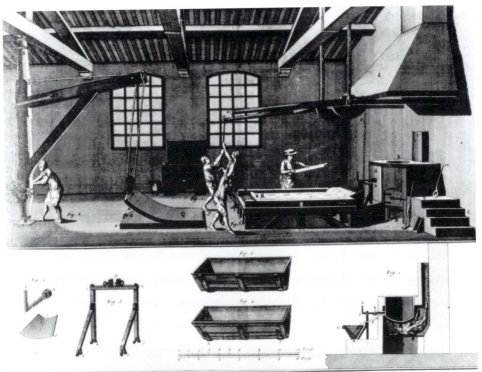

Laminage du Plomb, l'operation de Couler le Plomb en Tables et Coupe du Fourneau &c

Figure 7.12. Lead sheet manufacture in the eighteenth century

they were in the country), Cruickshank and Burton point out that "the high value of materials (all of which, whether sawn timber or hand-moulded bricks, reflected a lot of hard toil and man hours in manufacture) also explains why it was common practice to pack all manner of hard bricks and parts of bricks into the construction of a house even when, to modern eyes, it would seem to have been easier, as well as better, to use whole items."[18] They also note that for carpentry and joinery, one-third of the cost was for labor.[19] This suggests a greater percentage of value in materials than for the rural house just a few decades before.

The processes involved in the manufacture of the materials that came from locations far from the building were becoming more capital-intensive. Glass furnaces, nail manufactories, and sawmills all involved either expensive machinery or a somewhat elaborate structure, or both—quite different from the anvil and fire of the village blacksmith, or the chisels and adz of the carpenter. This higher level of capitalization goes hand in hand with the removal of the process of preparation from the process of actual construction.

The modern American house is very different from the first two examples, both in the sheer number of materials involved and in how few of them come to the site in raw form, without having been prepared in some way beforehand.

Gypsum board, for instance, is made through a highly capitalized industrial process, produced in sheets that are of precise modular dimensions, predictable in their character and performance. Concrete is typically batched at nearby plants and delivered to the site in a large mixer mounted on a truck. Materials come from cement manufacturers and sand and gravel sources that are not too far away. Many other materials are produced through highly automated and capitalized manufacturing processes: rigid insulation, engineered wood joists, paint, plastic pipe, electric cable, carpet, laminate for countertops. A few components are produced in shops that are much more local, from materials that are processed elsewhere: sheet-metal ducts, gutters and leaders. Some components come to the site in almost raw form, having been changed only in dimension: mostly solid sawn wood members, joists, studs, rafters.

In all three examples the building culture is strongly anchored to the culture of production as a whole. With the farmhouse, the provision of building components was connected to the cycles of agricultural production, the clearing of woodlots, and the blacksmith's manufacture of iron tools and wagon parts. With the London house, wood was one of the items actively traded between the countries around the North Sea; the manufacture of glass and lead depended on the same fuel that powered the machinery that was driving England's Industrial Revolution. With the modern American house, building products are produced like many others, as part of large industrial/financial conglomerates. Building materials are unique to the building culture but are also connected to the wider economic system.

In the sixteenth and seventeenth centuries, strong interactions existed between the English building culture and the shipbuilding industry as the great demand for oak for thousands of ships for the fleet drove up the price of the large oak members that had traditionally been used for making house frames. Techniques of timber framing changed to allow smaller members to

Figure 7.13. Modern gypsum board production

Figure 7.14. Carved plaster and leaded glass on house in Cambridgeshire

be used in walls and roofs, and the Tudor "black-and-white" half-timbered buildings began to disappear in favor of buildings that were faced with stucco or brick. This stylistic change was linked to an economy much larger than the building economy itself.

Much later, the manufacturing operations of the London speculative developer Thomas Cubitt during the first part of the nineteenth century represented a further change in how value would be added to buildings. Cubitt, who subdivided large tracts of land and built identical houses on them, owned large fabrication plants where workers made such building parts as

Figure 7.15. Eighteenth-century window glass production

Figure 7.16. The control room of a modern float-glass production plant

windows and doors, cast-stone pieces, moldings, marble slabs for staircases and sideboards, plaster cornices, iron girders, baths, cisterns, plumbing equipment, plumbing fittings, and iron railings.[20] In many cases these parts represented expensive details that would otherwise be made individually by craftsmen. Cubitt set up a system of identical manufacture, removed from the building and from the control of the actual builder.

The capital investment in manufacturing plants producing building components grew rapidly during the nineteenth century, in both England and the United States,[21] and the number of premanufactured building components

Figure 7.17. Advertisements from the 1890s

increased. This was the case with items as diverse as house paint,[22] wooden window sash and blinds,[23] wire lath, plumbing fixtures, concrete block, wall and ceiling coverings, elevators, heating and electrical equipment, and many others. The mass-production techniques used in the manufacture of these goods were being applied at the same time to goods of every stripe, not just building materials.

During the twentieth century the building became more and more a site where workers assembled pieces that already had value added to them through craft and/or manufacture. Today it is often the stated intention to reduce value added at the site as much as possible. This is justified for several reasons:

- The control of quality that is possible in factory conditions.
- The reduction of contractors' and architects' liability for defects.
- The increase of choice in available products, by utilizing national and international markets that could only exist with large manufacturing operations.

The quality control that comes along with modern windows and other modern building parts is laudable, but choices are limited by the economics of mass production. For example, in any particular style, the off-the-shelf availability of window sash by big window manufacturers is confined to a limited matrix of sizes, and the number of styles is limited. It is difficult for

Figure 7.18. Pattern shop for precut ornamental woodwork, Sutherland's Steam Mill, Denmark, Nova Scotia

individual players within the building culture to affect what products are available; product choice is more easily altered through changes in an identifiable market.

The great variety of available products has allowed a lot more people—and classes of people—to enjoy the fruits of good design. The commodification of the building culture, however, was not restricted to building components or even to entire houses (as, for example, the Sears "kit" houses). It began to pervade ideas about buildings themselves and the ways people were expected to live in them. These ideas entered into popular publications as products became to be associated with choices about lifestyle and self-image that people were expected to be able to make. The creation of desire by marketing and advertising meant that one could buy a lot more than just a physical object. From one point of view, the product orientation of today's building culture, in which ways of life are implicitly being sold along with kitchen cabinets, bathroom fixtures, adobe-style houses, or shopping malls with a New England village theme, is the simple continuation of the advertising imperative made necessary by highly capitalized production. Manufacturing firms, developers, and, to a large extent, architects are participants in a culture in which the physical settings of people's lives—buildings and places—have been turned into negotiable commodities.

A great choice in available products exists, but it is not clear that buildings gain in quality when more than a certain percentage of their materials is shaped off-site. Nineteenth-century American houses that utilized the new industries of sash and blind manufacture probably did not suffer for it, and in those buildings, premanufacture of certain components existed alongside site-based craft. In some cases, even for simple buildings, carpenters modified pattern-book designs for their own purposes.[24] Sears kit houses—which today usually cannot be distinguished from "normal" site-built houses—were put together out of many parts by local builders. Their construction required skill, and they needed to be fit to their specific sites. Even with the value of modern manufacturing in the building production process, any building needs a certain amount and quality of on-site shaping—a certain amount of value added on-site. Enabling this process contributes to the quality of the building—and, as we will see next, also helps the building culture itself.

The Overall Flow of Money Inside and Outside a Building Culture

Finally, there is the relationship between the activity of building, particularly the ways that money flows in the building culture, and the larger culture and place in which the building culture exists. In some situations, the activity of building regenerates the larger culture, financially and otherwise, and is also regenerated by it. In others, the activity of building has little effect on the larger culture or, worse, drains it of life and vitality.

In Renaissance Florence, virtually all the subcontractors, craftspeople, and sources of materials, and many of the sources of investment in buildings, were located within the relatively small area of Florence and its hinterland. Wealth was being created in two ways: through a strong industry (the production of cloth, although increasingly with wool imported from abroad) and through a strong commercial sector (trade between northern and southern Europe). This growing wealth was widely distributed over a large number of families with a bootstrap effect on building. Goldthwaite writes:

> As the men who made their fortunes in the forward sectors of the economy spent more and more of their wealth, a consumption linkage was opened to other productive forces in the economy. Because building was the most expensive of their new tastes, the construction industry received a major stimulus, and it, in turn, activated its own set of linkages, both backward to the building-material industries and forward, by complementarity of use, to the craft industries producing all those goods men needed to fill up their new and enlarged built-environment. This forward linkage from construction created new demand, therefore further strengthening the consumption linkage originally derived from the staple. In other words, by that marvelous process of "one thing leading to another," an upward shift in overall demand was induced within the local economy that resulted in the growth of the luxury-arts sector, which included the new palazzi of moneyed families.[25]

One reason that the construction sector could be strengthened to such an extent was that its parts were located largely within Florence itself. Not many construction materials were imported from far away, and craftspeople and laborers who came from Florence in search of work wound up contributing to its economy. As we saw in chapter 2, craftsmen were residents of the city and often long-term residents of particular neighborhoods; stone and brick came from nearby quarries and kilns; many specialty building products were made within the city itself. Wealth came to Florence, was generated within Florence, and was recycled within the Florentine economy, including the construction industry.

It is not necessary, however, for a healthy building culture to be completely local. The construction of buildings in New York during the 1890s involved a highly articulated economy of wealthy investors, builders, manufacturers, materials suppliers, bankers, and many others. This economy was increasingly a national economy, in which large industrial concerns, helped by advertising, mass marketing, and the railroads, were beginning to make building products available in many places.

Advertisements in the *Real Estate Record and Guide* for March and April 1900 show firms manufacturing building components in the following places:

Richmond, Virginia (bricks)
Pittsburgh, Pennsylvania; Port Murray, New Jersey
   (terra-cotta fireproofing)
Burlington, Vermont (venetian blinds)
California (redwood shingles)
North Carolina (pine flooring)
Bangor, Pennsylvania (roofing slate)
Farmingdale, Long Island (bricks)
Rochester, New York (mail chutes for apartment buildings)
Keasbey, New Jersey (brick, tile, fireproofing)
Jersey City, New Jersey (artificial stone)
Newark, New Jersey (elastic rubber roof cement)
Pittsburgh, Pennsylvania (plate glass)

Granite and marble from Vermont and lumber from New England were also sold. The national trade in building components had started many decades before, with the development of improved transit networks and the steam engine.[26] As the port of entry for most immigrants, New York's construction labor force was international: stonemasons from Italy, bricklayers from Ireland, carpenters from Germany and Scandinavia.[27] There was a good deal of back-and-forth flow between New York and the national and international economy.

New York was prosperous, though, and was apparently not being financially drained by its imports. It was expanding and had a strong manufacturing sector of its own that produced building materials as well as clothing, books, and many other things. For many building materials, value was still being added to them locally. Money that cycled through the economy of the city itself was balanced by money that included the city in a larger national cycle. As a result of this balance, the building economy of New York, like that of Renaissance Florence, was strengthened by the economic interactions among its players and between it and other cultures.

Consider now a contemporary phenomenon: the factory manufacture of houses that are then shipped to faraway sites. In some rural counties of Oregon, for example, such houses represent a large majority of new houses produced. Among some scholars of American housing, manufactured houses represent a positive new trend, one that needs to be supported by appropriate building codes and zoning legislation. Manufactured houses do provide inexpensive housing to people on tight, fixed incomes—people who would otherwise be shut out of the housing market by high costs.

These arguments, however, see the house purely as an industrial product or commodity and not as something that has significance *in its making* other than by providing employment for factory workers. Although these factory workers contribute to the local economy in which they do their job, the components and materials they use—metal or wooden studs, various laminated sheet materials, aluminum windows, asphalt shingles, insulation, plumbing fixtures, electrical fittings—are, as we saw in the last section, themselves the products of mass manufacture that come from different places again.

The building economy/building culture of the place where the house is "erected" may be virtually nonexistent. The building economy/building culture of the place where the house is manufactured consists of a source of capital (for plant, machinery, and tools) and money that flows from buyers to local workers and other well-capitalized corporations that may be far away. In none of these places does money recycle as it did in Florence or New York; the construction of a building is by no means a part of a locally regenerative economic—and cultural—process.

The fragmentation between source of investment, place of construction/manufacture, and place of ultimate use is devastating to the quality of the built world. This is true not only for manufactured housing but also for buildings where little of value comes from the local place. This fragmenta-

Figure 7.19. Vinyl windows on construction site in Eugene, Oregon, 1996

tion may mean that the motivation for investment is more likely to be financial than geared toward improving the environment in a qualitative way; it may mean that the product is divorced from the qualities of place in which it will be used; and it may mean that the reinforcement of artistic and cultural life that can result from increased financial investment—and the relationship between this investment and a particular culture—will not take place. Banks' "redlining" of minority neighborhoods in American cities was a major factor in the disinvestment and eventual decay of many of those neighborhoods. The fragmentation and disunity of much of today's built environment is not only a failure of design or "urban vision"; it is also intimately tied to the nature of investment in the contemporary built environment and to the ways that money flows.

The availability of materials may also be influenced by much larger cultures, operating on a worldwide scale. The timber industry, for example, is becoming more and more internationalized: large American companies have begun cutting forests in Siberia, and Japanese companies, which have long operated in the hardwood forests of Indonesia and Malaysia, are now importing wood from Siberia as well. The production and pricing of cement (perhaps the single most indispensable product in modern construction) is controlled by a powerful international cartel.[28] The prices of petroleum-based building products, like asphaltic roofing materials, are dependent on the geopolitics of oil.

Some of this remote and large-scale operation is genuinely destructive to the environment[29] and exploitative of vulnerable local building economies. A rise in cement prices may mean the difference between a house and no house, or between a better house and an impermanent shack, for tens of thousands of families in a country like India, where building with cement has become the norm.

But large-scale operations in building materials and components are not ipso facto bad, and all materials do not necessarily have to come out of the earth close to the building site. On the contrary, balance is needed in the realm of materials, just as balance is needed between knowledge that is contained within the building culture itself and knowledge that is contained in other cultures and subcultures that interact with it. Large companies do have the ability to invest in research and development and to be responsive to markets. The industrial production of building components may have taken craft away from the building tradesman at the site, but it has also allowed many laypeople who are not building tradesmen to build and remodel their own houses. The development of modern insulation materials, engineered wood members, efficient heating systems, and many other parts of a modern building has depended on the ability of large companies to produce and market individual technical innovations on a large scale. Ideally, these companies have one foot inside the building culture, evaluating buildings and listening to architects and builders, and one foot outside it, applying basic research and innovations from other fields and understanding issues of mass production and the human organization of complex manufacturing operations.

In a healthy, contemporary building culture, money flows in two ways: first, internally, in ways that reinforce the capabilities, economy, and social life of the building culture itself; and externally, in ways that bring in the best innovations, and good products that cannot be capitalized within the building culture itself, from outside. A balance is needed that results neither in isolation and stagnation nor in the elimination of the local building culture altogether.

In today's commodity culture, the humanity and beauty that many people would like to see in buildings are often subjugated to money, which seems a more permanent and intractable force. With a deeper understanding of how quality in buildings comes about, coupled with even small initiatives that attempt change, money—and value—could be distributed in better ways. Such a distribution would involve large and small pieces, in public and in private, throughout the building process and both in large factories and at the place of construction, and in cultures close to the building as well as those farther away.

This kind of distribution of money, in turn, corresponds to a different distribution of control, one in which those close to the building are able to make decisions about its shaping and in which all sizes of buildings and building parts can be most appropriately shaped.

Figure 7.20. The American dream?

AGREEMENTS, CONTRACTS, AND CONTROL

8

Human Relationships in Construction

> Our fair readers must forgive us if we halt a moment
> here and endeavour to unearth the idea hidden under
> the Archdeacon's enigmatical words: "This will destroy
> That. The Book will destroy the Edifice."
>
> Victor Hugo,
> *Notre-Dame de Paris*

The building contract is a map of one of the most fundamental relationships in the building culture: that between the builder and the client. A modern building contract formalizes that relationship by precisely specifying the building. Even for small buildings, contracts can be extensive, with many pages of general conditions and agreements, dozens of sheets of drawings, and a sheaf of specifications. Historically, such contracts were much shorter and often verbal. This difference is indicative of fundamental changes in building cultures over time: changes in shared understandings and in the nature of control over the building operation. The more explicit contract is necessary in order to enforce centralized control over the building's construction, in a situation in which shared cultural understandings and informal social sanctions are not strong enough to guide construction.

Building Contracts

What follows is the entire text of a contract to build a house in London in 1510. The contract includes no drawings at all. Italics are mine.[1]

This Indenture made betwene the Prior of the house of the Salutacion of oure lady called the Charter house of London on that one partie And William Dewilde Carpenter on that other partie Witnessith that the same William couenauntith and grauntith by these presentes to make and sett up or doo to be made and sett upp for the same prior *w^t in the parisshe of seynt Benett beside Baynardes Castell* of London where the same prior will name and assigne *a house of Newe Tymebre* at the costes and charges of the same prior on thisside the Fest of seynt Mighele tharchaungell next for to com after the date of these presentes that is to say the same William couenauntith and grauntith by these presentes *that the same house shall have two loftes and one ouersett w^t ij stayres to the said ij loftes and ij dorres on the strete side and also to make as many playne windowis as the same prior shall think most necessary for the said house. And the same hous shall conteyne in length from one end to the oder xl fote of assise and in bredth xxij fote of assise and betwene the groundsell and the hevesinges xxiiij fote of assise in hight.* Whiche said house shalbe in all thinges redy made and fraymed to the setting upp in Kinges Towne upon Thamys, and so from thens to be brought and sett up in London as it is aforsaid. And for almaner of carriages concernyng the same house during all the tyme that it shalbe in making and settyng upp to be borne and susteyned at the propre costes and expenses of the same prior. And the same prior covenauntith and grauntith by these presentes to save and kepe harmles the same William agaynst the Wardens and occupacion of Carpenters of the Cite of London during all the tyme and space that the forsaid house shalbe in setting upp wt^in the Cite of London as it is abouesaid. For the whiche house so raysed made and fynysshed in the forme abouesaid onthissid the date aforesaid The same prior couenauntith and grauntith by these presentes to content and pay or doo to be contentid and paid unto the same Wylliam his executours or assignes *tenne poundes sterlingges* in forme folowing that is to wete to be paid alway as the same house goeth forward in making and setting upp. In witnesse wherof the parties aforesaid to these indentures sundrely haue put their sealles. Youen the viij^th day of Julii in the secunde yere of the Reigne of King Henry the viij^th.

How is it possible that such a document could be legally binding? The builder is to build "a house," but no drawing is provided to indicate the plan of the house or what it should look like. The builder is to put in windows as the client shall direct, within a fixed price. The builder is to put in two stairs, leading to each of two lofts, without any specification of the size or position of either the lofts or the stairs. The sizes of certain pieces of the timber frame are specified, but others are not. Even the location of the house is not precisely specified.

Take, for example, the word *house* itself. In today's building world, it is not expected that any two parties to the building contract understand that word in the same way. Indeed, the word need not appear in the contract at all; reference is often made to "the work" rather than to the name of a particular building type. This was apparently not true in 1510. Then, the word *house* was well enough understood that it could be written in a contract, unambiguous enough that two parties could put their signatures to it. In 1510 the word—a symbol of the kind of shared typological understanding described in chapter 6—had a specific, unambiguous legal meaning. This meaning could set into motion a whole chain of events, calling on a particular set of knowledge.

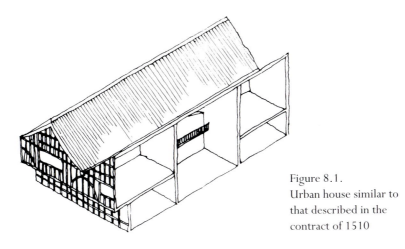

Figure 8.1.
Urban house similar to
that described in the
contract of 1510

Any agreement to build must include certain information: the work to be done, the compensation for doing it, and the means for determining that it has been done. But all of this information is not necessarily contained in a *written* contract. Nonwritten contracts and agreements are common and may be no less binding than written ones. In preliterate societies, all contracts are verbal or implicit. In literate societies, many contracts are verbal: they range from a carpenter's informal agreement with a house owner to repair a porch to a restaurant owner's phone conversation with a fish supplier to make arrangements about the next day's delivery. We enter into such agreements every day, and they allow us to transact everyday business with others. Even though noncompliance may result in social rather than legal sanctions, such agreements are normally taken seriously by the parties to them.

Throughout history, such implicit agreements were common in building practice, and most contracts have combined written and unwritten information. This includes information that is explicitly stated and written in the document and information that is implicitly understood, or verbally stated, and not written in the document.

Major Forms of Contract

English building contracts of the eighteenth and nineteenth centuries took two major forms: *contracts by measure* and *contracts in gross*. The differences between them epitomize the major transformation to the building culture during the nineteenth century.

The earlier form, the *contract by measure*, was used for buildings of any substantial size or complexity. Agreements were made with individual craftsmen, and payment was based on measurement of actual work, according to rates that were well understood and often standard for a particular place and time.

The *contract in gross* saw increasing use during the nineteenth century. The price for the entire job is fixed in advance. Such a form became prevalent as the *general contractor* began to dominate the building world, entering into competitive bidding procedures to get work.

These two forms of contract differ in human terms. The contract by measure gave craftsmen a more direct relationship to the client; the contract in gross put the general contractor in between the client and the craftsman. The contract in gross and the competitive bid remove commonly understood measurement as a basis for the price and require the general contractor to come up with an exact total price before beginning. To do this, the building must be so completely specified that precise measurements can be made on the basis of the drawings and specifications, rather than the completed building itself. But as any modern architect or builder knows, bidding is as much a human game as it is a technical science, and when it was first instituted, the contract in gross was bitterly criticized for its effect on client-builder relationships and on the quality of the finished building.

The Evidence of Contracts

Two dozen London contracts, from the middle of the seventeenth century to the late nineteenth century, provide evidence of how the human relationships in building changed. The contracts are for small houses and larger public buildings; buildings where architects were clearly involved and those where they were not; buildings for which the client was a large estate, and others for which the client was an individual proprietor. The following attributes of the contracts changed in clear ways over time: (1) the inclusion of drawings and reference to them; (2) the quantity, nature, and precision of specifications; and (3) professional responsibility for the building.

(1) The Inclusion of Drawings and Reference to Them

In a modern building contract, drawings are central. They are dimensioned precisely, are constantly referred to during construction, and are legally binding. However, in the late seventeenth century, drawings were not typically part of the contract for small houses, and it was only in the nineteenth century that they took on the central role they have today. The drawings themselves have changed as well, and they took on an increasingly detailed character as the decades progressed.

A 1668 contract,[2] for a five-story building, refers to the drawing only once: "according to a ground Draught hereunto annexed." Apparently the ground plan alone, along with about a page of specifications, was sufficient for the construction of the entire building. Almost six decades later, the 1734 contract for 10 St. James's Square,[3] a considerably larger building, made reference to "the drawings of plans Elevations and Sections" and also called out features of those drawings more specifically: "with two clossetts . . . each side the chimney in the two little rooms according to the plan . . . and cornice to the doors in the two best rooms and to two doors in the hall with closetts in the hall and back room framed with double deal as is drawn in the said plan" and "portland stone Cornice, Doorcase, Stepps facias, window stools and copeing to the front according to the said drawings."

By 1822, the contract for the Union Club,[4] a relatively large building designed by Robert Smirke at what is now Trafalgar Square, included thirty-three drawings and also the explicit prospect for more: "shall and will for

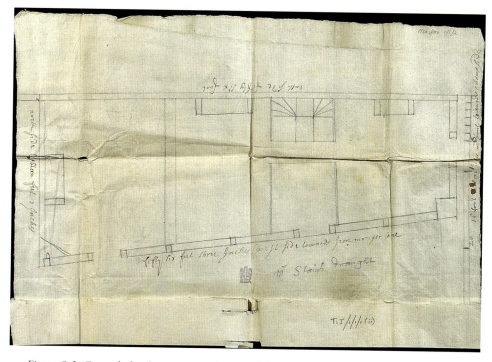

Figure 8.2. Ground plan from contract between Thomas Steane and Joseph Titcombe, 1668

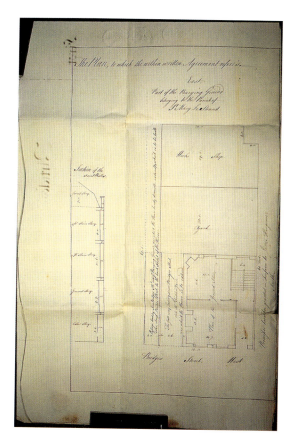

Figure 8.3.
Ground plan for contract for
building on west side of
Bridges Street, 1748

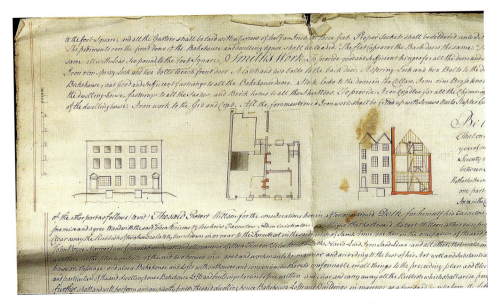

to the foot Square, and all the Gutters shall be laid with a [....] of half an Inch [....] three feet. Proper Sockets shall be soldered unto [....]
The pediments over the front doors of the Bakehouse and dwelling house shall be leaded. The flat [....] over the Back doors the same. [....]
same, all worth Lead [....] pound to the foot Square, a Smith's Work. To provide good and sufficient hinges for all the doors and [....]
Iron rim spring Lock and two bolts to each front door. A latch and two bolts to the back door. A spring Lock and two Bolts to the [....]
Bakehouse, and good and sufficient fastnings to all the Bakehouse doors. Stock Locks to the doors in the Cellars. Iron rim Brass knob [....]
the dwelling house, fastnings to all the sashes, and Brick turns to all the Shutters. To provide Iron cradles for all the Chimney [....]
of the dwelling house. Iron work to the Gib and Crab. All the forementioned Iron work shall be fitted up with screws Nails Staples [....]

Bi [....]
That on [....]
year of [....]
Seventy [....]
between [....]
Rotherhithe [....]
one part [....]
Anne in the [....]

of the other parts as follows (to wit) The said Robert Willson for the considerations herein afore mentioned Doth for himself his Executors [....]
promise and agree to and with the said John Somme[?] by his heirs Executors Administrators [....] Masons that he the said Robert Willson at his own pro [....]
clear away the Rubbish of two houses lately burnt down in or near to the Fore street in the said [....] Parish of Saint [....] time [....] then in the occupation of [....]
John Joyce Mariner [....] and [....] dwell and all manner of Stone Timber Tiles Bricks [....] Nails Lead Iron Lead Lime and all other Materials [....]
house in the place or site of the said two houses in a good and workmanlike manner and according to the best of his Art well and substantial [....]
house or Messuage and also a Bakehouse and Lofts with out houses and conveniences thereto conformable in all things to the preceding plan and Elevati [....]
and particular of the said dwelling house Bakehouse Lofts and buildings herein before written and clear and carry away all the Rubbish which shall arise from [....]
further shall and will perform and completely finish the said dwelling house Bakehouse Lofts and Buildings in manner as aforesaid [....]

Figure 8.4. Contract for building in Fore Street, 1770

Figure 8.5. Union Club, Trafalgar Square

that purpose execute do perform provide and fully complete all and singular the works and materials respectively described specified required and set forth in the said specification and drawings or thereby to be referred to or to be implied therefrom or be incidental thereto And also according to such explanatory instructions and drawings as shall or may from time to time be provided."

(2) The Quantity, Nature, and Precision of Specifications, and the Character of Language

Along with drawings, a detailed set of written specifications is an ordinary part of a modern contract. These describe aspects of the building that drawings cannot: choice and quality of materials, proprietary items, standards of workmanship. In the late seventeenth century, a typical contract would include only one or two specifications, usually concerning the quality of brick and mortar. Over the subsequent 200 years, specifications became more extensive, and the precision with which an individual specification was stated increased.

For example, in 1706 the specification for brick was quite minimal: "and shall Build all such new Buildings soe to be made with good and well burnt Bricks."[5]

In 1734 the specification called out different parts of the brickwork: "The walls to be all flusht solid and faced with the best grey stock bricks with Arches over the windows, and the shafts and Tops of the Chimneys done with Grey stocks."[6]

And by 1872, there was even more detail:

The principal front and Chimney Shafts are to be faced with the best yellow malms and all other external & unplastered brickwork with the best of the Stocks carefully selected for shape and color. All brickwork not intended to be plastered is to be finished with a neatly struck joint cut off clean straight and of uniform thickness. . . . The several walls piers, arches chimney stacks and chimneys are to be built with the best sound hard and well burnt Stocks and such facing bricks as are hereinafter described all to be truly laid and well bonded in mortar or cement, thoroughly flushed up and filled in at every course and grouted at every twentieth course.[7]

A similar increase of specificity occurred for mortar, roofs, ironwork and hardware, and other building components. Although London buildings after the last part of the seventeenth century had brick exterior walls, their floors, most of their interior walls, and their roofs were made of timber.

The timber specification changed in remarkable ways. The 1668 contract called for

Good sound and well seasoned Timber Boards . . . and in such manner and forme as shall be according to the aforesaid Act of Parliament for . . . the Third Sort of Building . . . with strong and substantiall joyests and board them with whole and well seasoned Deale Boards . . . and

shall make and put up good Seeling joyests in the Garrett . . . and lay
Timber sufficient to beam the said Balcony.[8]

By 1710 a contract[9] included a detailed table for timber scantlings, as
shown in table 8.1, below.

And the 1872 contract[10] specified how the girders under partitions were
to be assembled, including the sizes of bolts: "Provide and fix under partitions where shown girders formed of 12" x 9" fir sawn down the middle and
reversed and bolted to 3/4" boiler plates with 3/4" screwed bolts, head nuts
and washers complete."

Not only is there increased detail; in addition, adjectives that call for subjective interpretation disappear. Words and phrases like *good, well burnt, strong
doors, proper Hinges and Fastnings, Good and Sufficient Fastnings* appear in the earlier contracts. In later contracts, such adjectives are eliminated and replaced
with quantitative descriptions or with qualitative descriptions that go into
considerably more detail. Specifications for a gutter in 1748[11] called for the
builder to "lay the Gutters with lead not less than seven pounds to the foot
superficial & make good lead rain water pipes as low as the upper part of the
Ground Floor to convey the waters down to the drains." In 1770[12] a similar
specification told the craftsman what would actually support the water and
allow it to flow: it said that "the lead for the said Gutters shall weigh at least
seven pounds to the foot square, and all the Gutters shall be laid with a Current of half an Inch on three feet. Proper sockets shall be soldered into
Ditto to lead the water in the Trunks." This specification still uses the word
proper in describing the gutter sockets, but it includes far more quantitative
details—details that would not have been specified at all in earlier contracts.
The discretion of the craftsman is still being called for, but in matters that
are becoming more and more localized in the building. There is less ability
for the craftsman to make general decisions about the layout or design of
parts of the building.

Table 8.1 Timber specification from contract of 1710

If Timber fronts	Plates 7:12	oak	
	Corner posts 18:sqr.		
	Breasts summr 12:14	yellow fir	
	Story posts 12:8		
Cellar floor through 4th floor	Girt not to exceed 10½ feet long nor lye above 12 inches asunder	Girders 12:0 Girt 7:3 Trimmers+c? 7:5 Do Girt	yellow fir
	Girt not to exceed 10½ feet long nor lye above 12 inches asunder	Girders 08:14 Girt 8 ¼:2½ Trimmers+c8¼:4	yellow fir
All the Lintalls front + rear of yellow fir 6:8 without Wains			
If a Girt Roofe	Principle Rafters 7:9 Purleyns 10:8 Single Rafters 3:4		

Source: Agreetment with William Long, abutting on Covent Garden market. Greater London Record
Office, Covent Garden leases: CG/L206/2.

Figure 8.6.
The Essex Serpent

Figure 8.7. Buildings in Bow Street

A modern contract leaves very little to the discretion of the builder and does not assume many shared, implicit understandings between the builder and the client, or between the builder and the architect. In the late seventeenth century, there were shared understandings of quality, and the builder was allowed to act on the basis of a specification worded to ask for *a desired performance, rather than a desired physical form.* Over time, less and less was left to discretion and shared understandings, and performance specifications dealt with more and more detailed aspects of performance. In a discussion of early American building contracts, Catherine Bishir points out the sufficiency of nonspecific language for guiding the construction activity.[13] Words like *convenient, sufficient,* and *needful* all had meanings, in the context of the particular item at hand, that were apparently well enough understood by craftsman and client alike that the craftsman could proceed.

Sometimes specifications were stated in terms of comparison to other buildings. In 1715, a contract[14] asked for building "in the same manner as the said messuage or tenement now standing." The 1734 contract[15] for 10 St. James's Square called for the "best stairs finisht as Mr Turners is done." Such clauses may have helped to continue the tradition of the wide sharing of knowledge of architectural type.

The specification that allows for the least discretion on the part of the craftsman is for a proprietary item that is not to be crafted at all but simply installed in the building. Notably, no contract in those studied through 1773 includes any proprietary items in its specifications, but such items were included in contracts of 1872[16] ("Tye & Andrews" or "Antills patent stench trap"; "Seyssel Asphalte") and of 1886[17] ("Haywards illuminated gratings in footpath over front area").

Figure 8.8.
St. James's Square

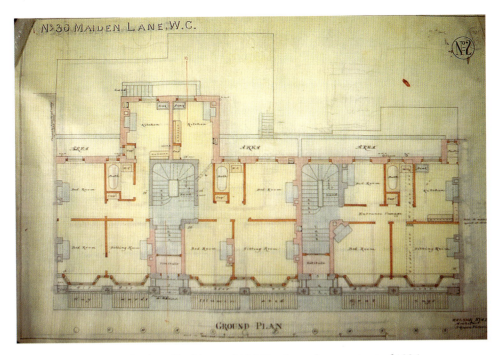

Figure 8.9. Plan of building at 36 Maiden Lane, from contract of 1886

Figure 8.10.
36 Maiden Lane, London

Various cases litigated over the years point to the increasing difficulty of subjective performance specifications. Over the years the precision of the terms required for courts to determine that a contract had been met increased. In an early case, during the realm of Edward IV, "it was said by counsel, 'If I promise to build a house for you, if I do not build it, you shall have a remedy by subpoena.' To which the chancellor is reported to have answered, 'He shall.'"[18] This implies that around the years 1460–70, the word *house* was specific enough in a contract to be enforced.

By the year 1794, such performance could be found only if the agreement were "sufficiently certain." Lord Chancellor Loughborough, in the case of *Mosely v. Virgin*,[19] said, in reference to another case: "It was an agreement to build a parsonage house for the improvement of a living. It is not to be too large nor too small; and I can conceive such a decree as the court made there by reference to two clergymen to define, what is a proper parsonage house. But to lay out £1000 in building! What building? It is not said. I suppose, a house was meant. It is not said, whether a manufactory would have answered, or not. I cannot tell."

Although the law was changing in favor of contracts where specifications were more and more precise and less "discretionary," this change was by no means universally understood, or even desired. The 1734 contract[20] for 10 St. James's Square contains a passage indicating that even explicit instructions do not explain adequately the detailed reality of the building: "And as it is next to impossible to enumerate or insert every particular work and thing requisite to be done in and about the building and compleatly finishing the said premises pursuant to the said drawings plans Elevations and Sections and Agreement before mentioned It is mutually agreed between the said parties to these presents that the same shall be left to the care and management of the said Henry Flitcroft to see the same duly performed and executed according to the intent and meaning of these presents."

(3) Professional Responsibility for the Building

The explicitness of specifications is linked to the question of who makes decisions. Over time, the contracts demonstrate increasing certainty about who is responsible for the interpretation of and compliance with the contract, and later contracts are unambiguous in assigning this role to the architect.

In the late seventeenth century, the question of professional responsibility was often not explicitly part of the contract at all. If anyone was named, it was the client herself or an unnamed person whom the client would appoint, who may or may not have drawn up the specifications. In one 1638 Massachusetts contract, many decisions were left up to the builder. The following are typical words of that client: "Concerning the frame of the house . . . I am indiferent wheter it be 30 foote or 35 foote longe; 16 or 18 foote broade. . . . You may let the chimnyes by all the breadth of the howse if you thinke good. . . . It makes noe great matter though there be noe particion upon the first flore; if there be, make one biger than the other."[21] Over the years, the responsibility for such decisions became more and more explicitly assigned to the architect.

The increasing specificity of contracts was also linked to the development of building regulation. In the years following the 1667 Act of Parliament for Rebuilding the City of London, many contracts made explicit reference to that act. In 1668:[22] "According to the intent and meaning of the Act of Parliament made for the rebuilding of the City of London"; in 1706:[23] "According to the best second Rate of Buildings sett downe in the Act of Parliament for Building the City of London"; in 1715:[24] "And that the brick and timber work shall be of height of stories . . . proportions and scantlings as are directed and appointed . . . by the Act of Parliament heretofore made for building the City of London." In 1872, a contract requires a builder to "execute all artificers works in the best and most workmanlike manner in strict conformity with the provisions of the 'Metropolitan Building Act' and the 'Metropolis Local Management Act' applicable thereto."[25]

The growing legal role of the explicit specification of the building in the contract made the professional architect's work indispensable to the building process and helped take control away from the builder. In publications throughout the nineteenth century, the growing antagonism between architects and builders is a constant theme. The following excerpt from an article in *The Builder* in 1856 is just one small voice in this ongoing conflict:

> In all contracts a spirit of antagonism is had. . . . Even when a contract is entered into honestly, clauses will have different readings to the opposite interests affected by them. Respectable men, when reading over the specification, generally require explanations of ambiguous stipulations; and, if they are not satisfactory, obtain an alteration of them, or provide accordingly; but it is far different with the unscrupulous, who rather pass such clauses over sub silentio, in the hope of getting their version of them adopted afterwards. . . . The result of the system of public competition for the execution of buildings [which depended on a firm bid and a contract in gross] has been to deteriorate workmanship, to introduce bad materials, to provoke disputes, to involve litigation, to offer a premium to rascality, to disappoint those embarking in building speculations, and to lower the tone of moral principle in masters and men.

Ability to Shape the Building during Construction

In addition to setting up rifts among builders, clients, and architects, the change in contract form affected the architect's ability, during the construction process, to develop the building according to the contingencies of the situation. George Saunders[26] stated as much in testifying before Parliament against the system of lump-sum contracts: "In the ordinary course of business, while the Work is in progress, there is the opportunity of considering and laying out the detail of the construction; but under a contract in the gross, the Architect cannot, unless he has the contractors consent, vary from what has been settled, or order what has been admitted in the specification, without an alteration in the sum agreed for."[27]

Such "consideration and laying out . . . while the Work is in progress" was not uncommon. Richard Norman Shaw had a close relationship with his builder, Frank Birch. At one point during the construction of Pierrepont, a large country house, Shaw wrote that "it would be better not to do these steps at present, I should like to see the doorway built and the general surroundings."[28] In 1891, during the design of the Metropolitan Club by McKim Mead and White, the secretary of the club's building committee wrote to another club official that "in order to ascertain which height [of the ground floor] is the best a platform at the different levels will be erected by Monday on the ground & you are requested to ascertain by trial which level you deem the best."[29]

Figure 8.11. Pierrepont, a country house designed by Richard Norman Shaw

Figure 8.12.
Metropolitan Club, New
York, designed by McKim
Mead and White

Early contracts allowed for the kinds of adaptations that are associated with traditional vernacular architecture. The balance between typological uniformity and formal variation in vernacular architecture has a procedural counterpart in the balance between constraint and freedom indicated by these contracts. The craftspeople had a good deal of responsibility for the interpretation of drawings and the development of details. They were not free to do anything, however, but were constrained by what was commonly accepted. There might have been reference to details in pattern books, for example, but within a system of social constraints, each craftsman was responsible for carrying out his own craft. Compliance was informal, and little hierarchy or explicit mechanisms of control were present.

With earlier contract forms, the shared knowledge existed as a framework that limited the actions of the individual players, and two factors prevailed: (1) individual players had more freedom within the constraints; (2) the top-down control mechanism was looser with respect to details of the building.

Control of the building's construction was historically largely in the hands of craftsmen, but over time that control became more and more dispersed, codified, and fragmented. Although the craftsman may have maintained his skill and responsibility for executing individual parts of the building in a "workmanlike manner," he was no longer called on to make judgments or affirm common understandings about the overall form of the building, the layout of rooms, or even, in many cases, the shape of individual details. Increasingly, these decisions were made for him.

As history progressed, more and more of the building came to be specified explicitly in the contract, and the discretion of the builder was gradually removed. At a certain point the meaning of the word *house* itself was lost, and the client could not rely on the builder's good judgment anymore. The plan of the building, and perhaps now the elevation as well, needed to be included in the contract. However, construction techniques and details were still commonly understood, and strong common understandings could still be relied on for matters of construction. This was generally the case around the beginning of the nineteenth century, but later, even the knowledge of the details could not be assumed to be common, and they also needed to be specified. Contracts have now evolved to the point where *everything* is specified. Both the common knowledge of the type and the ability of the builder to exercise discretion during the process of construction have disappeared.

The Dispersion of Control

During the nineteenth century, the roles of architect and builder diverged from each other, so that each was in a particular position of control with respect to building operations. The architect moved toward a position of greater and greater control in buildings specified by contract. With the speculative development, the builder moved toward a position of greater and greater control.

The emergence of the contract in gross, competitive bidding, and increasingly detailed contracts went hand in hand with an increase in the number of players in a building project. They began to deal with each other at greater distances and in more formal ways. As the arbiter of the building contract, the architect was central—but paradoxically, because the building had to be specified completely for the purposes of the bid and contract, the architect's role on the building site was less one of shaping the building and more one of checking on compliance with the contract. The explicit formalization of relationships was accompanied by restrictions on ways in which people could operate.

By the end of the nineteenth century, the reorganization of the system of control was almost complete, and control over most aspects of buildings, apart from some details, was no longer in the hands of the craftsmen. The New York firm McKim Mead and White, for example, which some scholars consider the prototype of the modern architectural firm, attempted to maintain complete control over all aspects of the building's design, materials, and production. This control was maintained through the mechanism of drawings, in which little was left to the discretion of craftsmen. For the construction of such prominent buildings as the Metropolitan Club and the Morgan Library, for example, drawings were made at three different scales, done at different points in the construction of the building: 1/4" drawings for the bidding and the overall layout; 3/4" drawings for such operations as the exact placing of the stones and openings in the exterior walls; and full-scale drawings for giving instructions to the craftsmen who were making details such as cornices, window trim, and interior plasterwork.

With such details, there was still some design input from craftsmen. Many of the detail drawings—for example, those for ornamental plasterwork—did not have the precision of the final work, with all critical dimensions called out. These drawings were sometimes sketchlike and were used by craftsmen to make exact models, which were then submitted to the architects for final approval before the construction of the detail. Even though the architect made the sketch, the craftsmen were still responsible for giving precision to the design, subject to the architect's approval. They were still in a creative role, however small. Finally, in the twentieth century, the full-scale details have largely disappeared from the architect's responsibility as building detail was simplified according to the principles of the modern movement. Shop drawings were now done by the fabricator to specifications of the architect.

In the construction of late-nineteenth-century buildings, the architect was at the apex of a hierarchical control system in which the traditional knowledge of the craftsman had been reduced to knowledge of technique without the need for knowledge of "design," or type. In the case of the Metropolitan Club, the architect was handling the accounts; approving payments from client to contractors and subcontractors; producing drawings and details as required; checking work on-site; dealing with suppliers of bricks, stone, and other materials; and dealing with ongoing client demands and changes. Although there was a builder, David H. King, who was handling some of the basic construction operations and himself employed several subcontractors, the architectural firm was central to design, construction, and the flow of money through the project.[30] Apart from the contract

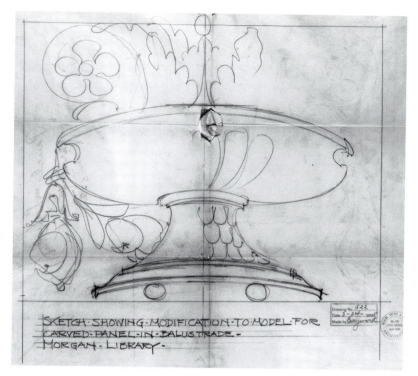

SKETCH·SHOWING·MODIFICATION·TO·MODEL·FOR
CARVED·PANEL·IN·BALUSTRADE·
MORGAN·LIBRARY·

Figure 8.13. Full-scale detail of Morgan Library, designed by McKim Mead and White. © Collection of The New-York Historical Society.

with King, many of the contracts were directly between the client and individual subcontractors; in these contracts, the architectural firm was explicitly named as arbiter. So in a sense, McKim Mead and White was acting as general contractor—or at least construction manager—as well as architect.

Similarly, in cases of speculative development, the builder was in charge. Large-scale builders like Cubitt, for example, even when he sublet sites, maintained control over individual builders.[31] In some cases he supplied the bricks, specified the quality of construction, and approved such details as iron railings.[32] As builders began to erect larger numbers of houses, they saw the economic advantages of repetition, which in turn required tight control over workmen. Teams of workmen were organized according to traditional trades and were supervised by foremen who reported to the builder. This hierarchical system was similar to that for large buildings built under contract.

As the system evolved further, the role of the general contractor grew at the same time as the architect's connection to the building site and connections to craftspeople lessened. Today, the architect is responsible for design and for continuously monitoring contract compliance on the part of the contractor. Although recent years have seen different arrangements for the construction of a building—including "design-build" contracts in which architect and builder belong to the same firm, and different varieties of construction management where construction managers who handle subcontracts are used by the client—the standard arrangement is one in which the client signs what is essentially a single contract with the general contractor, who then coordinates all of the subcontractors.

But where a contractor like Cubitt used to be able to maintain control over details through his foremen and his own manufacturing processes, and where McKim, Mead and White were able to maintain control through the medium of drawings, many typical building operations today have become so large and complex that it is virtually impossible for either the architect or the general contractor to maintain real control. There is neither a strong individual nor a strong set of commonly held cultural ideas at the center, holding things together.

The architect, still nominally in between the client and the contractor, is in fact juggling the competing, legitimate demands of various other players. There is often little control over overall form, which may result from a combination of financial calculations and building and zoning codes. And in the case of certain building types, there is little control over internal arrangement: that role may be assumed by specialists or space planners. Likewise, the contractor has overall responsibility for construction, but real control lies with such entities as regulatory institutions, banks, labor unions, and manufacturers of proprietary components.

In some cases, in fact, the roles of architect and builder are formally dissolving: the architect designs the building but then gives up control and becomes a design consultant who does not actually stamp the drawings; and the contractor gives up control by passing liability along to subcontractors and manufacturers.

In simplest terms, the system of control between client, architect, and builder is shown in figure 8.14. This diagram shows a direct relationship between the three organizations. But as we have seen, the client, architect, and contractor are often large and complex organizations themselves, in which hierarchies of control often separate legal responsibility from detailed knowledge of the building. Each of the subcontractors and consultants may have a similar organizational structure as the architect and the general contractor, with its own hierarchy and lines of authority. This structure is shown in figure 8.15.

Figure 8.15 shows that the people who are most in touch with the reality of the building are not the same people who have signed the legal agreements. The people who have their hands on the building may never even talk to each other. The junior architect who is happy to be given the job of designing a special detail will never know the name of, much less meet, the carpenter who builds it or the painter who paints it. Once that detail leaves the drawing board of that architect, it may be gone forever from her responsibility: a different member of her firm may handle the site supervision, and if any problem arises, the architect who originally drew the detail will most likely not be asked to resolve it.

The people at the "top" who have signed the legal agreements may have the least to do with the actual making, much less using, of the building. The people who are at the "bottom," farthest from the people who have legal responsibility, are most in touch with the building itself: the users who will come in touch with it every day, the architect who designs it, and the tradespeople who build it. These may be the people whose emotional relationship

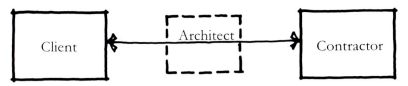

Figure 8.14. The basic contemporary client-architect-contractor relationship in which the architect acts as an intermediary in the legal relationship between client and contractor

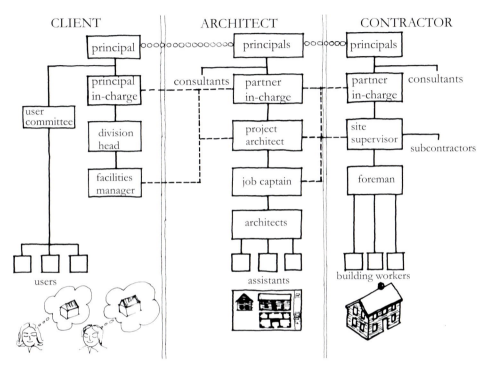

Figure 8.15. The actual contemporary client-architect-contractor relationship, which prevents people who are directly involved with the building from communicating with each other

to the building is greatest, who are most in touch with its reality, and who are in the best position to make certain kinds of decisions about it.[33] But they have been pulled farther and farther away from the ability to make such decisions. There is a tension, within each organization and within the building culture as a whole, between people at the bottom and those at the top.

This tension may have a healthy aspect, in that the people at the top maintain an important overview of budget and intention, and the back-and-forth negotiation between principals and subordinates helps to balance the overview of the whole and the concern for the parts. But the relationship is often one of control—it usually has to be so—than of an honest give-and-take between two equally legitimate sets of concerns about the building, and the real concerns of the people at the bottom are thus lost. This is true for the architect who does the actual drawing, the tradespeople who shape the details, and the people who will use the building.

The more distant loci of control, the increase in the quantity and specificity of abstract documents of control, and the growth of a litigious atmosphere in the construction industry and in the building culture as a whole have developed hand in hand. Together they have removed people's ability to carefully apply human discretion to the making of the building and have contributed to the abstract and fragmented nature of the modern built landscape.

REGULATION

Implicit and Explicit Rules

9

With the growing number and fragmentation of institutions, and the resultant dispersion of knowledge and control, *implicit knowledge* and *explicit knowledge* have changed differently.

One of the effects of the modern movement in architecture was to sharpen the distinction between explicitly stated rules (like building codes, sun angles, and functional adjacencies, which are understood to be social and/or legal imperatives) and implicitly understood knowledge (like the aesthetics of a building, which has come to lose any imperative it may once have had). Modernism helped legitimize things that could be measured and tried to liberate the architect's individual creativity with respect to things that could not. This split has been sharpened even further in the so-called postmodern era, during which discussion (much less common agreement) about things that cannot be directly measured has become almost impossible.

Modern building regulation is concerned with issues such as health, safety, or "nuisances" (environmental factors such as density, noise, or lack of light) that affect people in ways that can be clearly defined. In general, regulations can be described precisely in terms of measurements such as floor-area ratios, decibels of noise, and footcandles of light. Governments, as they have developed statutory and bureaucratic methods of operation, have seen their role as one of maintaining such rule systems.

In more general terms, regulation is the system of social constraints that guarantees that a certain set of knowledge and rules will be followed by the building culture, and it may take three different forms:

- Social constraints and understandings that are not codified. This kind of regulation is most common in preliterate societies. It is also common in modern society, however, as "neighborly behavior."
- Common-law or other codes that are based on custom and adjudicated on a case-by-case basis. Such codes prevailed in many traditional societies. No sharp boundary divides these codes and noncodified constraints; often common-law doctrines are simple formalizations of traditional practice.[1]
- Explicit codes in which contingencies that might distinguish individual cases from each other are not taken into account. Such rules were written more and more during the nineteenth century and form the basis of modern regulation.

The balance among these three forms of regulation did not always exist in the same way. The first two examples in this chapter demonstrate that historically there have been systems of building regulation that operated very differently than present ones do.

Regulation and the Formation of the Traditional Islamic City

To the Western observer accustomed to cities with a rectilinear geometry, traditional Islamic cities may appear random, irregular, and unplanned. Yet these cities exhibit both physical order and procedural precision. This comes from local regulation, based in religious custom, combined with the use of commonly understood rules about building form.

In a city such as Tunis, the physical order of residential districts is very specific:

- The area devoted to houses is maximized.
- Although houses may be on irregular lots, their courtyards tend to be rectangles or squares.
- There are dead-end alleys, with about half a dozen houses.
- Houses are one, two, or three stories tall.
- The position of the front door does not allow the courtyard to be seen from the street. Windows do not overlook a neighbor's courtyard.
- Front doors along an alley are not directly opposite each other.

These attributes and others define with a fair amount of precision the physical order of residential districts. This is a *fine-grained* structure: a map of the whole district appears so complex that the nature of its complexity is not understood, but the ordering rules become more understandable at smaller levels of scale. Although it does not have the global geometric order of Chicago or Haussmann's Paris, it nevertheless has a deep order.

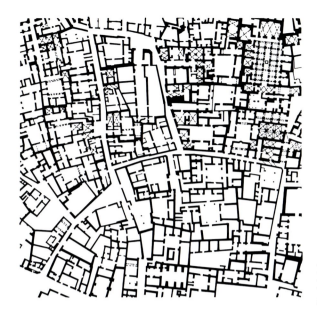

Figure 9.1.
Part of the old
city of Tunis

The source of this order lies in a give-and-take between the private and public realms, through a system of regulation that operated not through central administration but at a very local level. On one hand, each family wanted to give its own courtyard good shape and to make maximum use of land. On the other hand, access to each property was needed, and that access had to be wide enough for loaded animals and wheeled carts. Where houses abut, neighbors' needs were worked out not by statute but through shaping each individual situation according to a commonly understood set of intentions.

Because the rules were applied locally, the result is a fine-grained organization. The rules are of several different kinds. Some are elements of Koranic law dealing with relationships among neighbors. Some are economic, dealing with the desire to maximize equity and/or rent. Some are concerned with status and symbol, and still others with the position of women and family life in society. These factors are not applied to the overall "design" of the district; instead, they make themselves felt in every individual act of building, thousands of which add up to make the district what it is.

The absence of an overall municipal administration to uniformly administer a statutory zoning ordinance meant that disputes were settled by a local judge, who was looking at the actual situation and how similar disputes had been resolved in the past. This reference to things people could understand helped maintain the common understanding of the rules.

Table 9.1 describes various rules, with their origins and impacts on physical form.

Let us simulate the impact of such cultural rules on the growth of a district. For simplicity's sake, we will assume that we are beginning with a still rural settlement, perhaps on the outskirts of a city, on which just a few houses have already established themselves.[2]

Table 9.1. Rules and their effect on the form of local districts in Islamic cities

Rule	Origin of the rule	Impact of the rule
Take up as much building area as possible with the house	Economic tendency to make as much use of land as possible	Narrow alleys and streets; little emphasis on street as important public space
Make a symmetrical courtyard	Courtyard as center, as principal architectural expression	Courtyards have more symmetry than overall house shapes
Don't allow view of the courtyard from the street	Social/religious strictures on privacy	*Skifa*: narrow passage that connects entrance with courtyard
Don't allow doors on an alley to face each other	Social/religious strictures on privacy. Codified in Koranic law	Blank walls are opposite house doors
Keep the street wide enough for two loaded donkeys to pass each other	Need for access and importance of commerce	Minimum street width often followed; street no wider than necessary for this purpose
Make the house one, two, or three stories tall.	Results of laws concerning privacy and available building technology	Relatively low scale of overall district
Invest a lot of money in the ornamentation of the courtyard	Courtyard as center, as principal architectural expression	Streets are simple and plain; courtyards elaborate with respect to streets
Don't allow view into neighbor's courtyard	Result of laws concerning privacy	Courtyards are very private spaces

It is of course difficult to know the exact sequence of decisions that generated a cluster of houses. Here, we simulate a series of steps that seem plausible, given what we know about the rules themselves and the importance of certain elements.[3] In the example illustrated here, we assume that several houses in a cluster are being developed simultaneously. Steps 1 through 8 are illustrated with diagrams.

Step 1. Initial situation: a few simple houses.
Step 2. Decision to place a house in a particular location.
Step 3. Establishment of approximate location of street right of way.
Step 4. Establishment of courtyard; decision about rough size and approximate layout of courtyard. The courtyard is located first, before the rooms, because it is the most important space in the house. In the analysis of twenty-seven Tunisian houses in chapter 6, for example, the courtyard tends to have the most symmetry and elaboration, compared to the other rooms.

Step 1

Step 2

Step 3

Step 4

Step 5

Step 6

Step 7

Step 8

Figure 9.2. Sequence showing the possible emergence of the dense fabric of a traditional Islamic city, based on locally applied rules and laws. During Steps 7 and 8, new houses are laid out adjacent to the original ones.

Figure 9.3.
Sousse, Tunisia,
looking down on
the densely packed
pattern of narrow
streets and court-
yard houses

Step 5. Placement of the entrance. The entrance is designed to do two things: it does not allow views into a neighbor's entrance, and it does not allow views into its own courtyard from the street.

Step 6. Layout of rooms around courtyard. The rooms are laid out roughly, allowing for the most efficient use of space between the courtyard and the outer "boundaries" of the site—boundaries that are not yet precisely set. The idea is to use as much land as possible, while respecting neighbors' rights and leaving a minimum width for the street or alley.

Step 7. Adjustment of street width and lot boundaries; negotiation between overall size of house and width of street, and adjustment of house shape to fit neighboring houses. Now, as the boundaries are set exactly, the rooms take on their detailed shape.

Step 8. Construction of house. The construction of the house begins when the ground plan, determined in steps 2 through 7, is finished.

Step 9. Architectural elaboration of courtyard. This happens after the walls of the courtyard are up and is accompanied/followed by the finishing of the rest of the house. This completes the initial construction of a one-story house.

Step 10. Later addition of second-story rooms.

Step 11. Later rebuilding of parts of the house.

Step 12. Later adjustment of lot boundaries, including a back-and-forth trading of rooms from house to house.

The result shows not only that tiny, individual steps can result in the growth of a coherent district but also that such coherence is partly the result of regulation—rules that come out of social norms—that is handled in a local and contingent way, with each act of building. The rules are based in intention, not numbers, and require that attention be paid to the immediate context of a building act. This is very different from modern zoning—to be discussed later in the chapter—but similar to a doctrine of English law, to be discussed next.

The Doctrine of Ancient Lights

A centuries-old doctrine of English common law helps to protect the access of light to buildings. The *doctrine of ancient lights* prohibits a neighbor from blocking the light to a window that has been in place for a long time. This simple statement of intention was a bridge between commonly understood custom and locally applied regulation based on the actual situation.[4]

The law evolved so that it applied only to certain cases. It applied to daylight but not to sunlight; it did not protect views, only light; but it did work across streets, so that a person could not build a building across the street from a window that had enjoyed light for a certain period of time in a way that materially damaged the amount of light coming in to the window.

The earliest origins of the law are unknown, but it may have been formalized with the growth of the English textile industry. Work with textiles—weaving silk, sorting wool—requires very good light, and before good artificial light it had to take place in daylight. The law's origin was in customary practice: a social compact made among people who agreed about the importance of good light. In some ways it is similar to the rules in Islamic cities, based on intention and performance rather than an explicit numerical standard.

Because the doctrine restrains the construction of adjacent buildings that block the sky, it keeps building heights down. It has been conjectured that this law is one reason that the scale of central London remained so low at a time when other large cities, such as New York, were growing very high.[5] It also led to unique building configurations, which often entailed keeping one

Figure 9.4. Narrow street in Spitalfields, London. The ancient lights doctrine preserved access to light across streets.

Figure 9.5.
Apartment building near Hyde Park,
London, designed by Delissa Joseph.
The part at the left is low to allow
light to the building across the street

piece of an otherwise large building low, in order to allow light to an adjacent building.

The administration of the law shows how discretionary judgment allows for fine-tuned decision making. The judgment was always made by looking at the individual circumstance rather than applying a numerical standard for amount of daylight. (Such numerical standards were sometimes introduced to support arguments, but they were never required by law.) Sometimes the affected room was visited by a judge, who would sit in a chair reading a newspaper. Someone would hold up a panel in a position that would block the same amount of light as the proposed building, and the judge would make his ruling on the basis of whether or not he could continue to read the newspaper.

There are important principles at work here:

- There is common understanding of what constitutes unacceptable loss of light. Within these understandings, distinctions could be very fine; the account of one case stated, "He found that before the building the room 'was just a light room; but by the loss it has suffered it has become a slightly less than light room.'"[6]
- The common understandings could change over time, in a natural way—in the same way, perhaps, that building types evolve. This quote from the judge in a case argued in 1967 makes this clear: "I think the notions of mankind on the subject of light have changed and are changing. Possibly it is connected with improvements in electric light; because the standard of artificial lighting has gone up,

Figure 9.6. Reconstruction of ancient lights dispute: *Senior v. Pawson*, Sheffield, 1866. Judgment was for the plaintiff. (The proposed building is shown with a dotted line, and the affected window with a circle.)

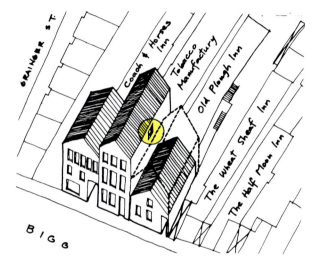

Figure 9.7. Reconstruction of ancient lights dispute: *Dickinson v. Harbottle*, Newcastle, 1873. Judgment was for the defendant.

the standard of natural lighting has gone up too. I do not think that ordinary people would accept now for a living room and office on the outskirts of a town like Gravesend the daylight standard which was accepted 12 years ago for an office in the centre of the City of London."[7]

- The intention was clear, and it applied to rich and poor alike. It deals with everyday life in a very commonsense way, one that makes it accessible to ordinary citizens. One judge said, "It was no defence for the defendants to say that the building injured was only a miserable cottage; the lights of a cottage were as much entitled to the protection of the law as those of a mansion."[8]

In the United States, the ancient lights doctrine was carried over at Independence, but in 1838, a case in upstate New York effectively put an end to it in American cities.[9] The judge ruled against the doctrine because it would prevent economic growth by limiting the maximum use of land for building and because it was seen to be unfair for one person to have any kind of control over the land of his neighbor. Obviously, the nineteenth century took the principle of land as a vehicle for profit very seriously, and by the beginning of the twentieth century, city governments realized that regulations were needed to protect public health and welfare. The spirit of the times had to do with numbers, efficiency, and mass production—so zoning regulations, which spelled things out in great mathematical precision and could apply to all neighboring properties in the same way, became popular.

With the ancient lights doctrine, the process of coming up with the judgment is itself an affirmation of human community in a way that modern explicit regulations are not. This idea is expressed in a quote from a surveyor who dealt with such cases:

> How different this is from the rigidity of regulations. . . . Running through all the expert evidence and judgments is . . . the affirmation that no exact prescription of angles and no specific codes can entirely meet the requirements of any case. There must be a judgment on the facts. . . .
>
> We should . . . keep our minds steadily on the true foundations of man's relationship to man in an ordered community . . . in which the principal element is not sanctions, but sanctity of contract between man and man . . . the ordering of the affairs of the community so that one man is not injured to another's profit. . . . Justice should not only be done but should be seen to be done; in this respect the judgment of a court carefully arrived at and elaborately stated in all its nuances is far healthier for a community than the administrative decision arrived at in secret and for reasons not disclosed, in pursuit of a policy hidden from the parties affected.[10]

Modern Zoning

In contrast to the performance-based and locally applied ancient lights doctrine, modern zoning involves the uniform application of explicit standards for which the intention may not be generally understood.

Land ownership is rarely absolute: the owner is not absolutely free to do whatever she chooses on her land. Land ownership is more accurately defined as a particular bundle of rights and obligations, balancing the rights of the individual with those of the community. The ownership of 10,000 square feet of land in downtown Manhattan is not the same as the ownership of the same amount of land in central London: in each case there are different constraints and obligations associated with the land.

These constraints include historical methods of control as well as modern zoning. In American cities, zoning ordinances came about as a reaction to the crowded and unsanitary conditions in cities that had developed during the great industrial expansion at the end of the nineteenth century. The legal justification for municipalities to control—and limit—building on private property was government's "police power" to safeguard public health and welfare, affirmed by the Supreme Court in 1926, in the famous case *Euclid v. Ambler*.[11] Zoning ordinances have two broad functions: the control of *build-*

ing form and placement, so that density and the provision of light and air are appropriate, and the control of *land use*, so that buildings with compatible functions are grouped together.

Zoning ordinances control building form and placement through uniform requirements that are applied to all properties within a *zone*—the city having been divided into zones allowing certain uses (residential, commercial, industrial . . .) and a certain intensity of use or density of building (single-family residential, multifamily residential, light industrial, heavy industrial, airport . . .). These uniform requirements are usually stated numerically and tend not to state their intention. For example, one provision in the zoning ordinance of the the city of Eugene, Oregon, reads:

9.544 (c) *Projecting building features.* The following building features may project into the required front yard no more than five feet and into the required interior yards no more than two feet; provided, that such projections are at least eight feet from any building on an adjacent lot:

1. Eaves, cornices, belt courses, sills, awnings, buttresses or other similar features.
2. Chimneys and fireplaces, provided they do not exceed eight feet in width.
3. Porches, platforms or landings which do not extend above the level of the first floor of the building.[12]

In this and similar ordinances, the statement of the rule does not include its intention: nowhere is it stated why chimneys projecting into required yards may be up to eight feet wide, but no wider. One may infer the intention. *But even if one makes such an inference, a design that meets the intention of the law but not its letter will not be allowed.*

Furthermore, the rule may be administered in a way that does not require direct contact with the situation. Compliance with setbacks is checked first on drawings. The building inspector's job is then to make sure that the building's position is in compliance with the drawings. Neither the plan checker nor the inspector has the option of making a judgment based on a contingency of the actual place—for example, a condition near the property line that might suggest that a smaller setback would actually be acceptable. Even a neighbor's agreement might not allow for a variation from the rule.

Indeed, even if individual discretion on the part of the zoning staff member were seen to be desirable for the quality of the outcome, and even if it could be shown to be fair enough to meet constitutional provisions of equal protection, the efficiency of administrative processes might still mitigate against using such discretion. It is cheaper for a staff member to determine the legality of a particular building proposal by working in an office over plans than it is for her to do it on-site.

The absence of discretionary judgment in American zoning is mandated partly by the state "enabling legislation," which permits municipalities to have zoning ordinances. Such legislation was first drafted in the 1920s and has subsequently been used more or less intact by most states.[13] An example is California's, which reads, "All such regulations shall be uniform for each class or kind of building or use of land throughout each zone, but the regulation in one type of zone may differ from those in other types of zones."[14] Zoning ordinances are constructed in this way because of criteria, arising partly out of equal protection provisions of the Constitution, requiring that "the police-power regulation of land use can be legally enforced only insofar as it is predictable and certain in its enforcement, and on condition that administrative discretion is guided by established standards."[15] On top of this is the difficulty of the variance process, which generally cannot be used unless one can show that the property would be harmed (i.e., its economic value reduced) if its owner were required to follow the strict letter of the law.

American zoning ordinances act to prevent potential problems rather than to deal with problems as they arise or to require that buildings conform to a particular positive vision of a community. Richard Lai points out, "This use of the police power as a preventive remedy rather than a corrective one was a significant expansion of its applicability."[16] So not only is the rule separated from its intent, but the rule will apply in all cases, even if the conditions that prompted it do not exist.

In the United States, numerically explicit standards make the constitutionally mandated doctrine of equal protection easy to achieve. Where every property within a zoning district has the same rules, equal protection becomes an administrative rather than discretionary matter. This helps explain the nature of zoning law, but it also reveals the difficulty in changing it. Any performance-based system would also have to be completely fair, protecting everyone's rights equally.[17]

The land-use aspect of zoning ordinances results in a different sort of difficulty. The prescription that buildings of particular uses may be located only in particular zones (grocery stores in commercial zones, one-family houses in low-density residential zones, eight-family apartment houses in higher-density residential zones) leads exactly to what the modern movement set up as an ideal: cities in which particular functions had particular places. All this was done with the good intentions of preventing incompatible uses from being near each other, but the results have often turned out to be unsatisfactory. Cities—and people's everyday lives—are fragmented by design. And today a neighborhood of single-family houses is often prevented from containing second apartments in existing houses, or small corner groceries—either of which might be genuinely helpful in improving the livability of the neighborhood or the economic viability of a household.

Although the ostensible purpose of zoning is to protect the livability of cities, the close relationship between modern zoning and economics—particularly the idea that zoning should not affect similar properties in a zone differently—is demonstrated by the ability to sell and trade air rights, particularly in major downtown areas, where millions of dollars may ride on a tiny change in what is allowed by the zoning laws. In New York City, zoning rules lead to a particular imaginary "envelope" within which an owner or developer may build "as of right" for each property. The familiar "wedding cake" shape of stepped-back New York buildings, for example, resulted from the 1916 Zoning Resolution. In these cases, developers tried to build as much as possible to the maximum allowed "envelope." But more recent zoning has not only changed the allowable envelopes but has also permitted the trading of air rights—the volume of space in between what is actually built and the imaginary envelope of what could be built as of right. This volume of space has financial value, and it can be sold to allow a nearby property to *exceed* the "as of right" envelope.[18] In similar manner, developers have been permitted to make buildings higher if they provide amenities like plazas, public lobbies, or subway stations that they would not otherwise build. However, in some of these cases, the value of the public amenities is of dubious value compared to the value of additional space gained by the agreement.

Figure 9.8. Suburban development in Eugene, Oregon, 1998: subject to requirements for street width, minimum lot size, setbacks, sidewalks, drainage, and many others

Figure 9.9.
Stepped buildings in New York showing impact of the 1916 Zoning Resolution. Photograph taken from the Empire State Building, 1984

The involvement of large-scale residential developers in the formation of zoning ordinances was already mentioned in chapter 5. There is a close relationship between the original purposes of zoning—to protect the basic environmental qualities through use of the government's police power—and its effect on the value of real estate. The line between those original uses of zoning, and zoning as an economic tool, is not always a clear one. Again, in New York a perception that the Midtown East Side was becoming overbuilt led to changes in zoning rules that allowed and encouraged higher buildings on the West Side—and enabled developers to profit from those buildings. And the use of zoning to restrict social and economic diversity in American cities became so severe that it needed to be stopped by the New Jersey Supreme Court.[19]

The ability to manipulate zoning, and the ability to use zoning as a technique of manipulation, are connected to the divergence of the means of zoning from the publicly understood *intention* of zoning. The use of zoning for economic purposes is connected to the inflexibility of zoning when it is being applied to physical design and environmental purposes. Abstract rules either act as roadblocks to decisions based on reasonable discretion or are used for purposes other than those for which they are intended. Modern zoning has gone hand in hand with both the abstractly defined functional separations in cities and the emergence of unused and disconnected urban space.

Building Codes

Before the evolution of modern building codes began, the building type itself had the same social status as the particular rules that governed the quality and safety of the building's construction. All aspects of a building—those relating to its structural integrity, those relating to its function and the quality of its materials, and those relating to its aesthetics—were held by builders in the same or similar knowledge systems and were regulated in the same way. Over time, certain things got called out for more and more explicit specification (initially relating to fire safety and structural safety, and later relating to infectious disease), while at the same time, other things, relating to less quantifiable aspects of a building's performance (functional suitability, aesthetic pleasure), were left more and more to the individual creative talents of the architect.

In the medieval building world, the guilds themselves, which were responsible for training the builders, were also responsible for regulating them. Government's role for the regulation of trade extended to such acts as specifying the size of bricks. In cases when the municipality took responsibility for certain aspects of building safety (as London did at various times even before the Great Fire of 1666), the people responsible for maintaining the standards were drawn from the crafts, when such people were specified at all. In London, it was only in the eighteenth century that the establishment of the formal post of District Surveyor led to a distinction between regulating bodies and the trades themselves.

In the Renaissance and the centuries just after it, the codification of architectural ideas, relating to the composition and aesthetics of buildings, began to be more widespread. Even though this codification did not take on the role of laws maintained by government, it was still consistent with those laws. The most graphic instance is the London building laws following the 1666 fire, which together with ideas of Georgian style resulted in a particularly London kind of building. The codification of architectural ideas was similar to legal building regulation in that both represented external, explicit rules controlling the work of architects and builders.

In London toward the end of the eighteenth century, explicit building codes legislated and maintained by government began to have more of an effect. The codes, instituted in 1667, 1707, 1709, 1724, 1764, and 1774 and intended to prevent the spread of fire, were concerned with building heights and their relationship to street width, party walls, timber sizes, fireplace flues, and exposed woodwork on the exterior of buildings.[20] Each law included more rules, or made existing rules more explicit. At the same time, the aesthetic codes that began to be written down in the Renaissance became more widespread in the form of builders' pattern books.[21] A widespread codification of building knowledge took place—some of it in laws maintained formally by government, and some of it in books that represented the social standard for building.

By the end of the nineteenth century in New York and London, the explicit regulations had become extensive. They now dealt with fire, structural safety, light, air and ventilation (the New York tenement laws were hard-won examples of this), plumbing, and electricity. In 1867 the Superintendent of Buildings was granted discretionary powers over new tenement construction; a new Department of Buildings was established in 1892; the first electrical code was introduced in 1891.[22] Building inspection was an established occupation. By this time, however, particularly in the cities, the explicit *design standards* that had come in the form of pattern and plan books were not as important in a collective sense. The numbers of building types, as well as choices of materials and premanufactured building components, had greatly proliferated. Increasingly, the only standards held by the culture as a whole were the explicitly defined building codes, regulating measurable and objective characteristics of buildings. By the first decades of the twentieth century, the idea of commonly accepted standards for design had begun to diminish in cities and in the world of architects (but not yet in the world of builders). The situation was ripe for the modernists, who deplored what they saw as architectural chaos.

Today, building codes—which may include separate electrical, mechanical, and engineering codes—are themselves only one of many regulatory systems that directly affect buildings. Others include:

- Rules of government agencies, such as Housing and Urban Development (HUD) in the United States and housing ministries in other countries, that finance building construction;
- Testing standards that often lie behind building codes and that specify the characteristics of particular materials;

- Bank standards that specify design requirements in particular markets;
- Rules by government agencies that regulate workplace safety;
- Rules that result from negotiations with labor unions, specifying what kinds of work their members can do and what kinds they cannot, and under what conditions.

This means, in turn, that there are various people involved in seeing to it that standards are met: plan checkers and building inspectors; testing engineers; insurance appraisers, who help set rates; people who write building codes; bank appraisers and personnel who determine lending standards; safety inspectors; engineers who work for industrial concerns and manufacturers' associations.

Building codes and the materials standards they contain are developed by boards of experts that include people with experience as builders, inspectors, materials engineers, and representatives of the insurance industry. As far back as the nineteenth century, insurance companies—which try to reduce their exposure and potential liability as much as possible—played a strong role in the formulation of building codes.[23] The boards rely on large testing laboratories, such as the Underwriters' Laboratory, for the development of fire ratings and structural standards.

Like professional organizations such as the AIA, the conference of code officials and the Underwriters' Laboratory act on a national—or at least widespread regional—basis and are highly centralized, bureaucratic organizations.[24] They have explicitly prescribed rules for operation and are also subject to lobbying by powerful interests such as materials manufacturers and insurance companies. Building codes are a part of local law in thousands of individual jurisdictions, which have the ultimate legal power to modify them as those jurisdictions, and their constituents, see fit. However, the codes have their origin in highly centralized organizations, procedurally very far from these jurisdictions. Indeed, since architects and construction professionals are not nearly as locally based as they used to be, there are now calls for all jurisdictions in the United States to adopt a single building code.

The tendency has been to develop building codes that increase safety, that reduce the potential insurance exposure of contractors and building owners, that can be uniformly administered, and that reduce the responsibility a user of the building needs to assume. These codes are enforced even if initial construction costs will increase as a result, which they often do. In the climate of an enormously litigious society, it is difficult for building owners—and the insurance companies that underwrite them—to expect building users to assume any more responsibility than necessary for accidents while they are in the building. For example, a series of articles in *The Building Official and Code Administrator* describes the need for smaller widths of guard-rail openings. These articles are accompanied by extensive statistics and reports of accidents and court cases. In one of these articles, the author states, "The ideal design is, of course, a solid, smooth guard with no openings or projections upon which children can climb or be injured during a fall against the railing itself."[25] That opening is indeed ideal, assuming no responsibility on the part of children or their parents.[26]

Figure 9.10.
Museo Civico, Bellinzona, Switzerland. This stair would not be allowed
by modern American ordinances.

What the argument about guard rails does not take into account is the ideal balance of responsibility between the building owner and the building user. A well-intentioned rule that is written for a particular, singular constituency is not necessarily the best, when examined from the point of view of the culture and built world as a whole.

Building regulations—in the form of zoning and building codes—help to ensure that public expectations of health, safety, and basic environmental amenity are met in buildings. Older forms of regulation did this while remaining integrated with the commonly understood knowledge systems of the building culture. The origin of modern regulation paralleled the emergence of the architecture and building professions and became necessary as building knowledge became more and more fragmented. The form of such regulations, although they do usually meet the intentions for which they were written, often also has unintended, negative effects. Regulations may promote standard rather than specific solutions; they may lead to an overemphasis on the reduction of risk; and they may hamper innovation because of difficulties in modifying the rules and because of the costs involved in meeting them. What is necessary is regulation based on performance, in which the intention is clearly stated and is guided by common sense rather than fear of litigation.

SHAPING BUILDINGS AND CITIES

10

A Modern View of Craftsmanship

So Architects do square and hew,
Green Trees that in the Forest grew.

Andrew Marvell,
"A Dialogue between the
Soul and the Body," 1681

The institutional, typological, economic, contractual, and regulatory systems that have been described in the last several chapters all converge on the actual shaping of buildings: the processes through which drawings are made, brick is put upon brick, concrete poured into formwork, windows installed in a wall. *These processes and the built result are given their character by those systems: and in the end the systems determine the extent to which the making of the building is the product of craftsmanship, considered in a broad and modern sense.*

The usual idea of craftsmanship has to do with handcraft, and the idea therefore sometimes seems an archaic reference to an earlier age. In a more basic sense, however, craftsmanship has to do not with old processes but with characteristic relationships between the artifact and the person or people who are shaping it:

- A sense of responsibility toward the artifact.
- Immediate feedback from the emerging reality of what is being made, as it is being made.[1]
- The ability to make judgments about how tools are applied to the artifact, as a result of this feedback.

These ideas are not archaic, but twentieth-century processes of production have eliminated them from the production of most artifacts. This is not

Figure 10.1. A village in France: the careful shaping of a place. Eugene Atget. *Chatenay, rue Sainte-Catherine*, 1901. Albumen silver print, 7 x 9 ³/8" (18 x 24 cm). The Museum of Modern Art, New York. Abbott-Levy Collection. Partial gift of Shirley C. Burden. Photograph ©1998 The Museum of Modern Art, New York.

to say that craftsmanship is not present somewhere in the process—in industrial design or the design of machine tools, for instance—but most contemporary buildings in the world, and modern cities as a whole, are not themselves the product of craftsmanship.

This chapter will explore how the idea of craftsmanship may be generalized beyond the idea of old-fashioned handcraft, into the more modern ideas of judgment, feedback, and control that might be applied to contemporary processes of design and construction. If the building culture supports such ideas of craftsmanship, then the notion that craftsmanship applies to an individual artifact can be expanded to a new idea that the building culture might act as a "craftsperson" with respect to the city itself.

Discretion and Human Judgment:
The Essence of Craftsmanship

At whatever scale, craftsmanship is characterized by implicitly understood and intuitively executed decision-making processes that are allowed to operate locally, close to the actual site and building. Neither long-distance control, which removes the architect or builder physically from the reality of the building, nor explicitly determined decisions, which may remove the architect or builder mentally from the reality of the building, can wholly allow for this kind of discretion. With craftsmanship, feedback is smoothly and continuously exchanged between the emerging reality of the building and the person or people who have the responsibility for its emerging form.

One of the most essential aspects of craftsmanship is the relationship between, on one hand, decisions about the artifact and the artifact itself, and, on the other, the fact that *the craftsman is in a position to allow the present state of the artifact itself to be evaluated in order to make the next decision, large or small.*

A carpenter building a roof valley is measuring, cutting rafters, checking them against the real roof, putting them in place, looking at their spacing. He is doing this according to commonly understood techniques of carpentry, to which intuitive judgment is applied.

A pianist playing a Mozart sonata on the stage of Carnegie Hall has mastered technique, has heard and played the piece hundreds of times, has practiced many times for this particular recital, and may not vary in note or tempo from what Mozart wrote. But the particular rendition played that evening has a life of its own, one that arises because the pianist is not a player piano, with programmed instructions about notes, tempo, and dynamics—she is applying her own judgment, as quick and intuitive as it is, to the sonata as it is being played.

A cardiovascular surgeon repairing the septum of a heart has a vast array of instruments, knowledge, protocols, and accepted technique to help him. But the moment-to-moment operation depends on a judgment of reality, of the real heart, the vital signs. The precise action taken may depend on this moment-to-moment judgment.

An architect sitting at a drawing table designing a house is also making, and responding to, an artifact—the drawing. This drawing will certainly correspond to the physical reality of the building, but the architect's decision making may or may not correspond to the experiential reality of the building. The artifact in front of the architect is the drawing, and with respect to the drawing the architect is a craftsperson. She is looking at the drawing in front of her, responding to it, and drawing the next line based partly on this response.

All of these people are craftspeople in the way I have been describing. The things being produced at the moment—the roof valley, the sonata performance, the heart repair, the drawing of the building—are all essential to the decision-making process.

With this understanding, we see that Mozart may be called a craftsman with respect to the written sonata, but not with respect to the sonata's performance: these are two different artifacts, although closely related. The architect who drew the roof valley may be called a craftswoman with respect to the design of the building, but not with respect to the precise connections in the framing of the roof valley: these are two different artifacts, although related. A cardiovascular surgeon who worked years ago may be called a craftsman with respect to the technique that today's surgeon is using, but not with respect to the repair being carried out today. The technique and the repair are, in a sense, two different artifacts.

The traditional craftsperson, who was working neither in isolation nor in a backward way, was part of a system as intense and complex as those described above. The craftsperson was solidly anchored in commonly accepted technique but was also, ideally, "clever": her knowledge of technique was deep enough that she could solve small and large problems that involved reconciling type and context.

When the craftsperson is solving small problems, responding to particular conditions, she is already more than an automaton and is able to operate independently. When she is solving large problems, she is being inventive. If the invention is concerned with a problem that other people are also dealing with, then she may be inventing a new type.

This means that there is a continuum between two different senses of the word *craftsmanship*. On one hand there is work that is carefully done—surfaces that are smooth and plane, joints that do not show gaps between pieces of material. This requires extremely local and continuous judgment: the judgment about where a surface that is not quite level needs to be planed, for instance, and the judgment about the number of passes with the plane that will do the trick. But this all may be in the service of a predetermined standard, set by the carpenter or perhaps by the architect. On the other hand, there is work in which the craftsman has a good deal of creative control over the shape of the whole, which may be somewhat unpredictable. Both of these are aspects of craftsmanship; the first has to do with the solution of small and local problems, while the second may have to do with typological invention.

So the craftsperson may be essential not only with regard to fitting type and pattern to context in the individual building but also with regard to the development of new types. The design of the flying buttresses at Notre Dame—among the first flying buttresses in Gothic cathedrals—were solutions to particular constraints concerning elevation that presented themselves to the builder.[2] Brunelleschi was well enough schooled in the traditional techniques of building churches to know that he had to find a new way to make the dome in Florence. The builder Jacob Holt, who worked in Virginia and North Carolina during the nineteenth century, was successful partly because he was prepared to introduce into his work both technological and stylistic innovations that were being demanded by the market.[3] His ease in introducing these innovations came partly because he maintained a hands-on attitude toward his own work and partly because he was personally aware of the competitive market.

Craftsmanship in Terms of a Particular Craft

The way craftsmanship has changed over time may be understood in more detail by looking at the evolution of a particular craft. Carpentry is the shaping and assembly of wood for structural purposes in a building: the building frame, roof structures, floor joists and subfloors, room partitions. Traditionally, the craft of the carpenter is distinguished from that of the joiner, who made nonstructural "finish" building components: wainscots and paneling, cabinets, handrails and balustrades, doors. The distinction was in the use of the plane: the joiner used tools similar to those of the carpenter, plus planes to achieve smooth finished surfaces, while the carpenter used only saws, chisels, adzes, mallets, measuring tools, and marking tools, but not planes.

Carpentry has been important even in building cultures that are primarily based on masonry. In southern Europe, although the building shell is often almost completely masonry and tile, structural wood is often used for roofs and beams. Consider the flat roofs of traditional small houses on islands in the Greek Aegean: Sifnos or Crete, for example. In some places the wooden structure is made with small, straight tree trunks that are minimally shaped before installation. One piece is used as a kind of "summer beam" to reduce the span of smaller beams that are used as joists. In many cases these smaller beams are of slightly different lengths to compensate for the shape of a room that is slightly trapezoidal in plan. This roof frame is then covered with a sheathing made of smaller pieces of wood; this sheathing supports layers of earth and waterproofing material. In more refined buildings the smallest wood pieces are boards shaped with a rectangular section, rather than unfinished pieces.[4] In at least some of these cases the person who did the carpentry also did the masonry, and in fact built the entire house, perhaps with some help from others.

The carpenter was working within a tightly constrained system in which there was virtually no choice of materials and in which building plans were simple, widely understood, and predictable. This system included a rule-of-thumb knowledge of allowable spans for tree trunks of various diameters, of appropriate room dimensions, and of how trapezoidal a room could get before it became unacceptable. Finally, it included knowledge of technique: what material to place between a beam and the top of a wall to prevent the beam from rotting, how to fix the joists on top of the main beam.

The carpenter thereby held intuitive knowledge of both architecture and engineering, in addition to building. This knowledge was intimately tied to the immediate feedback and judgment that is a feature of craftsmanship, made possible through the integrated nature of knowledge and through the fact that the constraining rules of materials, design, and engineering were part of the knowledge system that the carpenter knew intimately. Constant

Figure 10.2. Wooden roof of house in Sifnos, Greece, 1988

decisions are being made about real things. The choice of a piece of wood was based on whether or not it could span a room. (This decision was probably made after the walls were built, but the walls were laid out partly with the knowledge of what sizes of wood were available). The length of the wood members were cut individually to allow for the irregular shape of the room; so were the planks that covered these wood members. This was craftsmanship, applied to the building itself as it was being built: the carpenter was responding directly to conditions as they arose.

Consider now the carpentry of a medieval timber frame building in London. It was almost always of oak, and in detail, it was considerably more complex and refined than the Greek roof: the principal wood members were sawn to rectangular section, and they were fastened to each other with complex, pegged joints. The higher level of skill required for this task was gained through a lengthy apprenticeship, and the job is executed by someone who can now rightly be called a specialist—different from the builder who made the Greek roof.

This specialist was working within a cultural system of craft knowledge that was becoming increasingly complex. Structural analysis was not done for each building, because buildings were largely done with similar dimensions, spans, and timber members: intuition based on habit could suffice. But the layout of the frame and its joints required knowledge of geometry and drawing, acquired during the apprenticeship—abstract knowledge systems

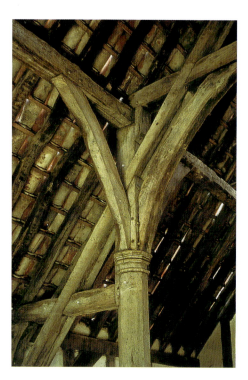

Figure 10.3 (left). Arcade-post with molded capital, Edgar's Farm, Stowmarket, Suffolk
Figure 10.4 (right). Barn at Great Coxwell

that are not required in the simple Greek island case. To a large extent, the medieval carpenter bought wood that had already been sawn to rectangular section[5] and often built and fitted the pieces of the frame at a place other than the building site. The medieval period witnessed an increasing standardization of timber dimensions, which helped the manufacture of frames outside the city, away from the building site.[6] In general, timber sections decreased in area throughout and after the medieval period,[7] partly because of the increased use of oak for shipbuilding. An ordinance issued in 1607, which attempted to prevent the construction of new buildings in London, required that buildings put on old foundations "bee lesse subject to danger of fire, and cause lesse waste of timber (fitter to be reserved for the shipping of his Realme)."[8]

This system of craft knowledge includes rules that are coming from outside the craft itself, and the materials that the carpenter uses are coming to him with some value already added, having already been processed to certain typical dimensions. The carpenter is indeed a craftsman: he is required to apply a high level of judgment to his work, and as with the Greek island houses, the plans of ordinary medieval London houses show that the carpenter would have been required to respond, on the spot, to dimensional variations that would not have been predicted in advance. (See Figure 4.10.) In addition, many parts of the structural frame were typically left exposed, including the roof of the open hall that was the main room of houses. Par-

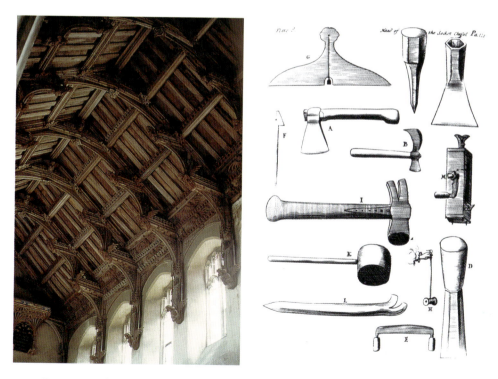

Figure 10.5 (left). Double hammer-beam roof of St. Mary's church at Woolpit, Suffolk
Figure 10.6 (right). Tools of the carpenter

ticularly in larger houses, the exposed timber work provided the opportunity for carpenters to show off their craft: they did so in ways that marked individual styles, including finials, beam chamfers, and other details. But the carpenter was also working alongside agents of expertise and production that were external to the craft—ranging from the workers who shaped logs into beams and delivered them to the site of fabrication of the frame, to explicit building laws that regulated the dimensions and quality of building parts.

Around the end of the seventeenth century and the beginning of the eighteenth, the house carpenter was in charge of both design and construction of small timber houses, to the extent that "design" was simply considered a part of the building operation. The detailed sequence of construction is laid out in Joseph Moxon's *Mechanick Exercises*, published in 1703. He describes a sequence of operations as follows, beginning with the ground plot itself:

- The ground plot is measured with the use of a ten-foot rod.
- Measurements are noted on a sheet of paper.
- Consideration is made of what "Apartments, or Partitions, to make on your Ground-plot." This is an act of design: "Suppose your Ground-plot be a Long-square, 50 foot in length, and 20 Foot wide: This Ground-plot will contain in its length two good Rooms, and a Yard behind it 10 Foot long. If you will, you may divide the 40 Foot into two equal parts, so will each Room be 20 Foot square: Or you may make the Rooms next the Front deeper, or shallower, and leave the remainder for the Back-Room: As here the Front-Room is 25 Foot, and the Back-Room 15 Foot deep. . . . But what width and depth soever you intend your Rooms shall have, you must open your Compasses to that number of feet on your Scale." Moxon states that the master workman must consider the client: "For a Gentleman's House must not be divided as a Shop-keepers, nor all Shopkeepers House a-like; for some Trades require a deeper, others may dispence with a shallower Shop."
- Cellars are dug, if the house has cellars.
- Cellar walls are brought up by a bricklayer.
- Major timber members are shaped. "The Foundation being made good, the Master-Workman appoints his Under-Workmen their several Scantlins, for Ground-plates, Principal Posts, Posts, Bressummers, Girders, Trimmers, Joysts, &c. which they cut square." Moxon devotes a page to precise dimensions as specified in the 1667 Act for Rebuilding London.
- Ground-plates are framed into each other.
- The main frame is erected.
- Chimneys are brought up by the bricklayer, who also tiles the house.
- Windows are framed. The 1510 contract quoted at the beginning of chapter 8 specifies that the carpenter will build "such windows as the client may direct."[9] The client would most likely make this decision when the main frame was already up, although Moxon suggests that windows might be drawn on elevations when the ground plan is prepared. The timber framing system allowed for decisions about

window openings to be made after the principal members of the building had been framed, and there were frequent differences between finished buildings and drawings that might have been done at the time of design.[10] Moxon goes on to describe the finishing of the frame: "The square Corners of the Frame next the Glass is Bevell'd away both on the out and inside of the Building, that the Light may the freelier play upon the Glass. And upon that Bevel is commonly Stuck a Molding (for Ornament sake) according to the Fancy of the Workman, but more generally according to the various Mode of the Times."

• Stairs are built.

Three features of Moxon's description are important here:

1. The central role of the carpenter in the design of the house, and the way in which design was an activity of building.
2. The ambiguous relationship between carpenters and architects. In one place, Moxon suggests that the carpenter might be able to draw a perspective; in another he says that the carpenter should consult books of architecture; in another, writing about the construction of stairs, he says that "Carpenters (as Carpenters) only work by directions prescribed by the Architect."
3. The acceptable level of precision of the carpenter's work. In his introduction to carpenters' work, Moxon writes that "we see Joiners Work their Tables exactly flat and smooth, and shoot their Joint so true, that the whole Table shews all one piece: But the Floors Carpenters lay are also by Rule of Carpentry to be laid flat and true, and shall yet be well enough laid, though not so exactly flat and smooth as a Table."[11]

In some cases, carpenters were closely involved in the building design through knowledge systems that allowed the carpenter to lay buildings out using commonly understood "grammars," or generative rules. These rules dealt with the basic layout of the house, as well as its details, and allowed the architectural features of a particular type to result from actual, standard operations carried out by the carpenter. Within this system, dimensional variations could occur within the framework of rough overall dimensions and shapes: hence, architecture was embodied in the rules of the carpenter's craft itself.[12]

The eighteenth-century carpenter worked in a building culture that was facing a great deal of change. Traditional methods of building organization persisted in the country and on smaller buildings in the city.[13] Changes had occurred in framing techniques and in the size of principal members, but the craft was not very different than in medieval times. Although building regulations were now impinging on the carpenter's craft from one side, and architects were beginning to assert their authority with respect to design on the other, carpenters of small buildings were still operating more or less the way they had for hundreds of years. They used the same tools, framed buildings in about the same sequence, and were in charge of shaping the building from

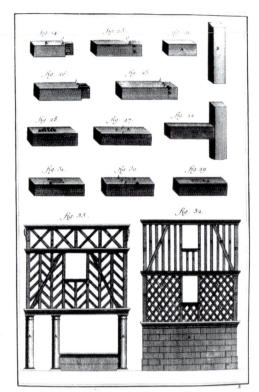

Figure 10.7.
Typical joints and frames
of French carpentry

its conception on the ground down to the small details of the frame. Incipient changes in regulation and in professional dominance and expertise were still small enough that they could be absorbed within the carpenter's traditional systems of knowledge.

With larger buildings, however, the split between architect and carpenter was well under way by the beginning of the eighteenth century. In chapter 8, we saw that control was taken away from the craftsperson first with the largest features of planning, then with smaller features of planning, and eventually with decisions about the shaping of details and connections themselves. Larger and urban buildings preceded smaller and rural buildings in the lessening of the carpenter's creative role.

As early as the Renaissance, for example, architects were familiar with framing techniques, paid notice to them in their sketchbooks, and used techniques that they had seen elsewhere. Serlio's design for a floor framing system in which no member needed to span the entire width, printed in his *First Book of Architecture*, was used by various English builders and architects. Christopher Wren's father, the dean of a church, drew and used a trussed roof when the church was reroofed. Inigo Jones, who had visited Italy and knew Palladio's drawings of trussed roofs, incorporated similar designs into his own buildings.[14] Of Wren's father's work, David Yeomans writes, "What is significant here is that a churchman, with no particular background in architecture, should have chosen to experiment with this novel roof form when he could more easily have called upon the services of the carpenter to design the roof as well as build it, the normal practice of the day."[15]

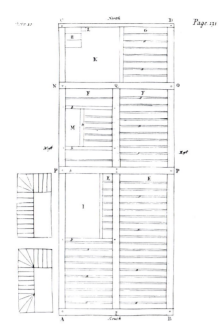

Figure 10.8.
Framing layout shown in
Moxon's book

Figure 10.9. Joseph and Margaret Scott Manor House, Bedford, Nova Scotia,
eighteenth century

By the nineteenth century the profession of engineering had come into
its own, along with that of architecture, and structural calculations were
becoming common. In addition, the larger scale of many building operations meant that the individual carpenter was now likely a member of
a larger organization. By the end of the century, in larger buildings, the
design of even small details of carpentry were the province of the architect.
The following excerpts from letters from V. J. Hedden, who held the carpentry contract for the Metropolitan Club in New York—a building that cost

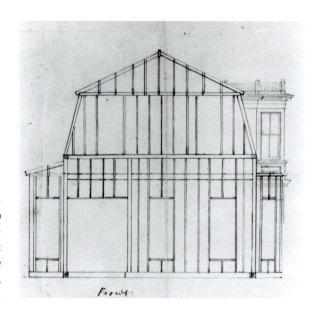

Figure 10.10. Framing elevation of Benjamin Franklin Childs house, Massachusetts, 1877. It is unlikely that the carpenter, who likely did the drawing for estimating purposes, would have followed it precisely.

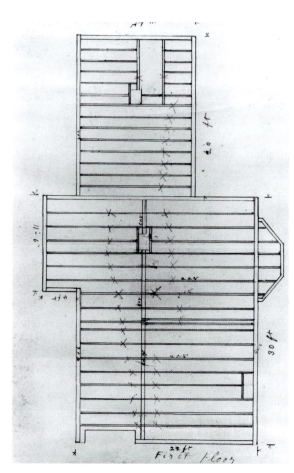

Figure 10.11. Framing plan of Childs house

$1.6 million at the time—to McKim Mead and White, the architects of the building, make this clear:

- October 5, 1893: "We have received a detail from you among others for a wall rail in connection with the stairway from the first story, to the Ladies dining room. . . . As this was neither specified nor shown in the drawings, we did not include it in our estimate."
- October 24, 1893: "Please send us sketch showing divisions of sash in extra partition windows between bath rooms and corridors, on Apartment floor, Metropolitan Club, also stating the kind of glass required for same, and send also details for wainscot on stairs."
- March 20, 1894: "In answer to your letter requesting an approximate estimate for a Cigar Case between Office and Waiting Room. We met Mr. Goelett [*sic*] at the building yesterday, and he requested that a design be submitted him for this. Therefore if you will furnish us with a sketch of what is required, we will at once give you an estimate for putting it in."[16]

By this time the carpenter's relationship to the building had changed altogether. Even though the quality of much carpentry work was still fine, the carpenter had become an instrument of the architect, who was now working in a complex matrix that included engineers and elaborate building codes and who saw the contractor and craftspeople as instruments of his own wishes. On many buildings, factory-made woodwork and subcontracting systems based on piecework diminished the carpenter's traditional authority.[17] The architect, on one hand, and factory production, on the other, pushed the carpenter away from a central position in the making of the building.

A modern framing carpenter for a typical tract house or small commercial project is concerned with speed and the ability to lay out and erect the frame to which various sheathing materials will be fixed and finished. This carpenter has most likely been trained on the job, beginning as a carpenter's helper and gradually moving into a position of taking responsibility for framing. She works to instructions and drawings provided by the architect. These instructions will generally include the position and specifications for the framed wall, but not the exact position of every wooden member. For example, the specification "2 x 6 studs 16 inches on center" is open to interpretation with respect to the exact position of those studs, the precise way that pieces of wood will be attached to each other, and even to some extent the level of acceptable tolerance at joints between pieces of material. A small gap between pieces of wood in a sill or wall plate might be acceptable. Since it is understood that the entire frame is going to be covered with siding or gypsum board, the framing members themselves do not have to fit together "perfectly" or even look very good. The level of finish of the carpenter's work exists so that the *next* operation in the building sequence can be finished to a high level of precision; the work can be rather rough as long as the plane to which sheet material will be nailed is true.

The system of light wood stud framing that the carpenter uses is the result of a long historical evolution, during which the complete modern system was first introduced in the first half of the nineteenth century. It is often

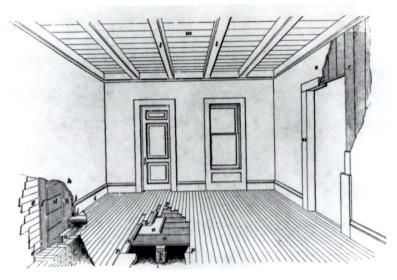

Figure 10.12. Stud framing covered by lath-and-plaster wall

mentioned that the steam-powered sawmill, which allowed for the rapid production of wood members of small section, and the development of the wire nail, a cheap fastening device, facilitated the system.[18] (Historically there are two principal systems of light wood framing in the United States—balloon framing, which came first and in which vertical members run from the ground sill to the eave, and platform framing, in which vertical members are interrupted by the framing of intermediate floors.) But a reduction in the size of wooden members had been taking place in England for a long time, resulting in the simplification and even elimination of complex wooden joints,[19] and the invention of the present-day system followed a gradual evolution in which specific innovations played crucial roles at various points.

How is the modern framing carpenter a craftsperson? In the framing of a 2 x 6 wall, a good framing carpenter works very fast, laying out sill, plate, and studs on the ground; measuring; sawing with a hand-held circular saw; using the nail gun to fasten the pieces together; raising the assembly up; using braces in the right positions to hold it in place until the next piece of the frame can stabilize it. He can look at the lumber and tell in a few seconds where he needs to cut out knots and where he doesn't; he knows that he can bang a misaligned stud back into place with a few whacks of his hammer; he can react quickly to a change in floor level or to the jog in a wall. In this process, there is craftsmanship: knowledge of type and technique and the ability to respond to actual conditions of the artifact itself, as they arise.

However, the product of the carpenter's craftsmanship is hidden from view. Indeed, the purpose of the frame is to provide for finished surfaces that are predictable; variation on those surfaces is much less acceptable than variation in the frame itself. What is visible of the finished building is not allowed to show the "mark of the maker" nearly as much as the light wood frame is. Even though the carpenter may take pride in her work, she is to a large extent an instrument of a purpose other than the work itself. Her relationship to the job may indeed be somewhat abstract. She may be a union member (but in residential work most likely is not); paid by the hour; supervised by a foreman to make sure that her output is where it should be. In these ways, her job is similar to that of a factory worker outside the construction industry, contributing to the production of something that has been completely designed and specified by someone else.

The light wood framing system is often described as being enormously flexible, allowing for any design to be realized through a forgiving system of construction, one in which the modularity of timber framing does not exist. The building is almost as fluid as a pencil sketch, and the construction system is an instrument that can help realize this sketch. This is perhaps the ultimate triumph of the modern designer: the ability to use a construction system toward any visual purpose at all, with no constraints on form imposed by the craft. But the meaning that is part of the construction system itself thus disappears, and so does the connection that the carpenter—and the architect—might feel toward its production.

On the whole, the craftsmanship that exists in modern buildings is hidden, and it does not allow for a sensitive, place-specific shaping of the building. It may exist in the framing carpentry, or in the skill applied to the architect's drawings, but it tends not to exist in those aspects of the building that are seen and felt by people. In fact, the opposite is true: the parts of the building that are seen and felt are the products of a very different kind of control, finished with materials that do not allow for craftsmanship, all done

Figure 10.13.
Framing in modern house,
Eugene, Oregon, 1989

Figure 10.14.
Gypsum board in modern
house, Martha's Vineyard,
1998

Figure 10.15. Modern tract-house construction

Figure 10.16.
The "clean-up man" banging
a misaligned member into
place in a tract house

with the intention of not allowing the kind of variation that is the result of craftsmanship. But if such variation is necessary to allow the building and its parts to assume their most precise fit, and if craftsmanship is necessary to allow the craftsman his fullest expression, then the modern building is problematic regarding both its formal content and the human content of the building culture itself.

The Shaping of a City through Urban Craftsmanship

A city may be no less the product of craftsmanship than a building or a piece of furniture is. A city requires careful attention at every point of its development, at every level of scale. The placement of a building along a street may contribute the most to the life of the street if its height can be carefully adjusted according to the existing buildings, and if the mix of functions in the building can contribute the most to the vitality and economy of its neighborhood—in addition to making a profit for its developer. The decision to fill in wetlands at the city's edge for a new semiconductor plant is a delicate one, like the careful shaping of a room: it should be done only with careful consideration to the urban ecology as a whole, to the patterns of development that would result, to the effect on the urban and national economy. The construction of a highway, the development of a residential neighborhood, the institution of a zoning ordinance that will affect the shape of new buildings, the redevelopment of Times Square, the closing of a busy city center to car traffic, the conversion of an old warehouse into apartments—all of these acts, large and small, contribute in very specific, nonabstract ways to the life of the city. If good decisions are made, the city improves; if good decisions are not made, the city worsens. And a good decision requires sensitivity to the reality of the effect it will have, feedback based on that reality, and skill in responding to the feedback. Each decision is an act of urban craftsmanship.

In this respect a city is like a well-crafted artifact. But the entity with responsibility for shaping this artifact is not a single artisan but the building culture as a whole.

The building culture is the artisan of the city. If the building culture is fragmented—if its various institutions are working at cross purposes, *even if they are individually effective*—there is no reason to believe that "craftsmanship" can be effectively applied to the artifact as a whole. The reason is that none of those institutions is empowered to individually deal with the entire reality of a place or situation—only with some abstraction of it. But effective craftsmanship requires a response to reality, not to an abstraction of reality. In the case of a building culture, whose job is the creation not only of individual buildings but of the city as a whole, this means that its various institutions need to be working in ways that are consistent with each other, that represent some common intention with respect to the reality of the built result, and that can respond to the entire reality of places and situations.

As an individual artifact, a building in a traditional "vernacular" building culture—a stone-and-plaster house on a Greek island, or a one-story, two-

Figure 10.17. The city carefully shaped: Venice, 1990

room, hall-and-parlor house in colonial New England—is simple. It is made of a small number of materials; its plan can be described with just a sentence or two; from a formal point of view, it consists of just one or two simple volumes. It is built through the culturally shared competence of craftsmen, not the individual invention of architects. When compared to a building like Palladio's Villa Emo, or Frank Lloyd Wright's Robie House, it is "unsophisticated." It is this kind of comparison that helps to support Pevsner's distinction between "architecture" and "building"—one apparently requires a great deal of knowledge, talent, and aesthetic judgment; the other seems so simple that a naive child could have done it.

Suppose, however, we look at the Greek island *village* or the New England *town* instead of just the house, and at the house and village or town *types* instead of just the individual artifact. Here we find a high level of evolved complexity. There are many more levels of complexity than in the house alone; there are subtle adjustments among the different parts. The village or town displays continuity over time, even as individual buildings within it change and disappear. In these cases the *configuration of many buildings*—rather than the individual building—contains the same amount and level of complexity as the individual building does in the "architectural" situation.

This comparison becomes even more striking when we look at the *production* of the respective artifacts: the individual piece of architecture and the vernacular town or village. Within a vernacular building culture in the Greek island village or a New England town, any individual is not expected to take responsibility either for the formation of the entire artifact (village, town) or for the evolution of the type. That responsibility lies with the culture as a whole, with all the players in the building culture acting in concert with each other.

Figure 10.18. The building culture is the artisan of the city: Canaletto, *The Stonemason's Yard*; Santa Maria della Carita from the Campo S. Vidal, c. 1728

The locus of knowledge in many building cultures has shifted. The artifact that is the town or village itself was once the result of a highly coordinated system, with the ability to make subtle adjustments and achieve a unified physical order. This high level of coordination came about because of both the knowledge contained in the culture as a whole and the knowledge of how to make individual buildings, in the minds of individual builders. But individuals were not given responsibility for the complex artifact as a whole: that responsibility was reserved by the culture.

The historical shift had two aspects: First, individuals (and individual architectural firms) became responsible for artifacts that were almost as complex as those things that entire cultures formerly took care of. This by itself is not necessarily a problem, since the complexity of the new building types (public and institutional buildings, buildings with complex structural and mechanical systems requiring a high level of integration) was different from that of traditional building types, and that difference required centralized control over design.[20]

But second, at the same time, the culture as a whole absolved itself of responsibility over the things *it* formerly had taken care of. These included both the artifacts that were made in coordinated ways by many people—the cathedral, the village, and the town—and the knowledge that represented collective understandings: the building type itself. Complex form, and complex decision making, moved from the public to the private realm.

An Expanded View of Craftsmanship

The old-fashioned concept of craftsmanship has been extended in two ways:

- Craftsmanship is connected to the modern idea of "feedback": it is the ability to make nonabstract decisions about design and construction, based on actual knowledge of the experiential, material, aesthetic reality of the situation.
- An individual within a culture may be a craftsperson. But the culture itself may also engage in craftsmanship, and it has done so at times—for example, for complex artifacts like villages and towns.

The ability to have a direct connection with the reality of the city, building, or building detail has in fact existed through most of history, in many different cultures, and at many different levels of scale. Even the Roman urban grid, which is often cited as the precedent for more contemporary, abstract rectilinear systems of land division, was based on cosmology and helped to tie the city in with geographic features that themselves had strong cultural significance.[21] The fundamental layout of a city was not an abstract act but a very real one, responding directly to the greatest structures of the natural world.

When the various institutions and systems of the building culture are operating well—that is, producing good physical results in the physical shape of the built world and in its ability to sustain and improve human life, and in the personal and social fulfillment that comes through working in the building culture itself—then those institutions are operating in a way that is analogous to craftsmanship. The discussions in the preceding chapters imply that certain characteristics can be seen in building cultures that produce good results and tend not to be seen in building cultures that do not. These characteristics are all different ways of describing craftsmanship, in a modern sense:

- *Institutions of the building culture that allow for human groups to function in a way, internally and with respect to each other, that does not put undue constraints onto ordinary human interactions.* The institution is not overburdened with rules that defy common sense, and people can use common sense to deal with situations as they arise.
- *Building types that are culturally appropriate and that respond directly to new conditions and contexts.* These building types demonstrate appropriateness of building form and can easily respond and change according to place and culture. How is this an aspect of craftsmanship? The culture is responsible for maintaining common building types, and it can do this either smoothly or with difficulty: it can allow for the emergence of new types as required, or not, and it can perform these tasks with the understanding of the real forces in society, or not.
- *Financial transactions that maintain a balance between necessary controls on investments and the ability for those who are directly responsible for designing and shaping the building to respond to the realities of people, site, culture, place, materials.* In a culture with this characteristic, loans are based more on personal trust and less on abstract rules; money is flowing and recycling within a particular community; and the profit motive is balanced by nonmonetary intentions.
- *Contracts that are based on genuine human relationships and recognition of genuine expertise.* This may involve decentralizing control; using shorter and simpler contracts; allowing for individual discretion and for situations to be resolved as they arise; and rethinking the position of various institutions in the building production process. And it may result in a less litigious climate than we currently endure.
- *Regulation that is based on a desired intention rather than explicit statutory rules and that exists within a system that can change as social needs and conditions change.*
- *And finally, a modern version of craftsmanship itself—one that might recognize the value of both contemporary technology and emerging systems of management and organization to the design and construction of buildings that are appropriate and always carefully made with respect to their own contexts of people, place, and culture.*

In Part III, we will look at contemporary projects that display these characteristics.

These final three chapters of the book consider several questions: How might all the participants and players in the building culture be put in a position where they are similarly concerned for buildings and their quality? How might today's building cultures be modified so that they as a matter of course more effectively allow people to make better buildings and places? And how might this happen in a way that does not require people to give up modern culture altogether, recognizing that along with all of its problems, many aspects of it are positive and life-affirming?

Since the Arts and Crafts movement, in which there was a deliberate attempt to change the process of production as a reaction against industrialization, the idea that innovative process is as important as product has been a recurrent if minor theme in architectural thought. But for most of this century, the operative assumption has been that architecture must follow the means of production rather than lead it; this, after all, was Le Corbusier's rallying cry in *Vers une Architecture*:

> A great epoch has begun. There exists a new spirit. Industry, overwhelming us like a flood which rolls on toward its destined end, has furnished us with new tools adapted to this new epoch, animated by the new spirit. . . . The problem of the house is a problem of the epoch. . . . Industry on the grand scale must occupy itself with building and establish the elements of the house on a mass-production basis. We must create the mass-production spirit. The spirit of constructing mass-production houses. The spirit of living in mass-production houses. The spirit of conceiving mass-production houses.[1]

This idea has largely been realized in building types that Le Corbusier envisaged and in others he did not. Although most buildings are not made on assembly lines in factories, like automobiles, their production uses many of the same principles. Many architects, and many people in construction, dream of an even more "rationalized" building process—one that features greater interchangeability of parts and a broader use of prefabrication.

To a large extent, however, the idea of craftsmanship as described in the last chapter is antithetical to mass production and centralized control. It points instead to greater localism, to buildings being different from each other in response to different clients and different places, to materials that support these differences. In recent years there have emerged architects and builders who are seeking the same kind of localism and craft in their own way of working, who are developing buildings and processes based in local culture and human need, and who see the importance of a close and real connection to the building during its conception and construction.

Such processes need not be inconsistent with the idea of globalization; we are members of more than one community at the same time. Indeed, they will be successful only if they are economically competitive and if the cost-benefit equation can be shown to be comparable, *over the long run*, to present processes. They also need not be inconsistent with the careful use of advanced technology. Fortunately, there are enough people working with ways of building and planning and finance that such processes are already in the marketplace of ideas. These final three chapters are not a polemic for things that cannot be achieved but a description of things that are already happening. Ultimately, the marketplaces of ideas and economics will determine which of them will become part of ordinary practice.

Like most societies before it, contemporary society allows, however grudgingly, initiatives that fall outside its rules. There are many people—builders, architects, planning officials, educators—who recognize that serious problems exist in the ways things are built. Some of these people see the structural nature of these problems. Others are working in more specific realms, attempting to make just one thing work better, with perhaps just a distant view of the larger picture. Some work inside existing institutions, others outside them. It is important to put all these separate initiatives into a framework that recognizes the worth of each and that relates them with the common intention of improving the building culture as a whole. It is, after all, in the nature of a healthy building culture that innovation may emerge from different sources, in fits and starts; but the various separate experiments should eventually coalesce around some new, commonly accepted paradigms of action.

POSTINDUSTRIAL CRAFTSMANSHIP

Innovations in Process

11

Thiss chapter elaborates on the idea that craftsmanship can be seen as a modern process, and involved with more than just the production of individual artifacts. The idea of a process of careful shaping based on feedback from reality may be applied to client interactions, the construction of buildings, or the development of neighborhoods. The chapter focuses on process rather than product with examples that include the unique design of individual buildings, the reintroduction of carefully shaped materials, along with the careful shaping of housing and building groups and consequent variety in the environment as a whole. These examples point to a new idea of *postindustrial craftsmanship*, in which large-scale production at acceptable costs does not necessarily require Henry Ford–like repetition but in which the detailed and unique shaping of the built world may happen in the context of modern society and new industrial techniques, side by side with the reinvigoration of traditional crafts.

Design and Building as a Continuous Process Based on Reality

The most fundamental characteristic of craftsmanship is that thought ("design") and action ("building") are so intimately related that they do not represent two separate phases of a project. The need for such a close relationship arises partly because of the need to respond as carefully and directly as possible to the reality of the site, building, and clients. This reality includes the deep needs and desires of communities or clients themselves, as opposed to conclusions drawn from statistical analysis or group processes that result in a weakly-agreed-to compromise. It includes the experiential reality of sites—of views, quality of light, the subtle feeling created by the way that the site slightly rises and falls, or the way that a copse of trees, a neighboring building, and a distant view work together to give a place directionality and enclosure. It includes the sense of graciousness of a room that can already be felt when the room has just been framed and that might be destroyed if that feeling is not carried through in just the right way in making decisions about finishing the room.

In a process that respects these realities, the maker of the building must be in a position to respond to them in the most appropriate way, to make changes in the design or building when the need for them is recognized. In addition, the process must be open enough to the real conditions of the project to encourage talking frankly with people about their dreams and being open and respectful of what they say; spending enough time on the site and in the community to be able to listen; and being sensitive to the material reality of the emerging building.

Eishin School, Tokyo

In the last twenty or thirty years, user participation has been seen as a means of bringing human realities to the attention of architects, countering purely top-down processes that assumed architects do not need input from people who use the buildings they design. Unfortunately, in many cases participation does not fundamentally alter the architect's views, and results in projects in which lip service to the client's views, rather than buildings based on mutual respect, are the result. In the best cases, however, participation is a means of drawing out the dreams and visions that are already present in the clients' minds, thereby respecting and extending, rather than altering, their reality.

In the work of Christopher Alexander and his colleagues, participation is essential.[1] Unlike many typical processes, in which people's views are not necessarily regarded as central, the process of participation in the development of the program for the Eishin School resulted in a program that reflected a strong, collective architectural vision.

This high school was about to move to a new campus on the outskirts of Tokyo when the architectural team, headed by Christopher Alexander, entered into an intensive series of discussions with the clients.[2] These lasted six months and involved many people at the school—the administration, students, teachers, parents, gardeners. The discussions concerned not only the measurable aspects of life in the school—what needed to be next to what, how much room certain functions occupy—but also ideas of buildings, places, and rooms that could be translated into verbal images. These images, taken together, formed a strong overall vision for the project and guided the development of the design when it began, on the actual site. This

Figure 11.1.
Classroom at the Eishin
School (Christopher
Alexander, architect,
with Hajo Neis, Ingrid
King, Gary Black,
Artemis Anninou, Eleni
Coromuli, and others)

Figure 11.2.
Stakes marking
positions of build-
ing corners during
on-site layout,
Eishin School

overall vision guaranteed that everyone involved in the project was seeing the
same thing and that the real wishes of the community would be translated
into buildings.

A portion of this vision, provided to me by the architect, follows:

- The interior character is warm and subdued: wooden columns,
  floors, and walls in places; pale yellow wall color, comparable to
  golden chrysanthemums, paper, or silk; near-white sliding screens
  and ceilings.
- Floors of many buildings are raised, slightly more than usual, off
  the ground.
- Classrooms have polished wooden floors or carpets, and shoes are
  not worn inside the classrooms.
- All homebase classrooms have big windows facing south.
- Many rooms have gallery spaces to one side, where light comes in
  beyond and shines through screens.

Figure 11.3. Pedestrian street at the Eishin School looking toward the main entrance gate

- Many walls and other surfaces are wooden, with natural unfinished wood.
- The classrooms and other rooms are furnished with very solid wooden desks, which several students share.
- In the larger buildings, there are mirrors where students see themselves.
- Outside the buildings, there are often flower beds.
- And inside, here and there, throughout the school, there are surprising soft highlights of color, shining out among the subdued colors of the rest: a figure painted in pale kingfisher blue in one place, a golden yellow iris in another.

Each of these statements represents the dream or vision of an individual or group connected to the school. The role of the architects was to help articulate something that was deep in the hearts of people, to draw the program for the school itself out of the people who would use it. Such a powerful architectural vision, consonant with the views of a community and describing its life, forms the mental framework of a place; people then use this framework in developing the actual design and construction. Although this type is project-specific, it is like a traditional type in that it represents the shared values of a community. The program included a space budget and monetary budget, but unlike modern architectural programs, which tend to be more abstract and leave the vision of the whole in the control of the architect, this program resulted in architect and client working toward the same goal long before the actual design began.

   This drawing out of the reality of the community, culminating in a program for the school that represented a vision of its life, was followed by analogous work with respect to the design of the site. The layout of the

Figure 11.4. The central square of the Eishin School looking back toward the main entrance gate

school took place largely on the site itself, with flags marking the corners of main spaces and buildings, leading toward the development of a physical design, consonant with both the vision of the school and features of the site that could be seen and felt. This work allowed the participants to together imagine the buildings in place, responding to the reality of the place and adjusting the ongoing design based on that emerging reality.

These processes of programming and site design are versions of craftsmanship. They require a professional stance of great sensitivity and immediate response both to subtle hints from people about things that are close to their hearts and to the felt aspects of the site. Together these lead to a careful fit between people and buildings and the land.

Housing Project in Mexicali

During the construction phase of the Eishin School, following programming, site, and building design, there was a greater-than-usual level of interaction between architect and contractor, but the goal of a complete integration between design and building was only partly met. A housing project in Mexico during the 1970s carried out by Christopher Alexander and colleagues[3] organized the construction of houses that could be individually designed and built by the families who would live in them, at a price not greater than that for government-built, repetitive housing. This project was developed so that *throughout the entire process*, families were in a position to make their own decisions based on their own realities and their own perceptions of their houses as they were being built. The project encouraged variety from house to house, and several attributes of the construction system were specifically developed to foster a direct connection between the direct

Figure 11.5. Manufacture of soil-cement blocks in Mexicali project, 1976

Figure 11.6. Forming roof vaults in Mexicali project, 1976

visualization of a building on site, and its construction, without the medium of drawings.

The construction system was developed so that a building could be staked out on the ground during the course of design, based on the visualization of rooms in their place at full scale, and built directly from those markings on the ground, without the need for drawings as an intermediary. This was done to make it as easy as possible for laypeople to have control. The houses were all different, designed according to the individual wishes of the families. Because of the flexibility of the system, the people were in a position to make choices for themselves about the size of their house, layout

Figure 11.7.
Passage to courtyard,
Mexicali project, 1976

of rooms, relative size of rooms, relationships to outdoor spaces, position and size of windows, and level of interior finish. The quality of the buildings was tied to people's own specific choices.

The construction system consisted of standardized operations and details that allowed for continuous variation in room and building dimensions. It included the development of mortarless, interlocking block walls that could be erected by the families, lightweight concrete roof vaults, and a minimal use of wood for windows, doors, and concrete formwork. The system was approved by the local authorities, who agreed that they did not need to review individual construction drawings for each house, as long as a few basic construction parameters were followed.

In this project, professional time was spent in the development of the system itself, not in the design of the individual houses, which were built within originally budgeted amounts. In the immediacy and direct connection between design intention and construction, the project was similar to traditional vernacular building.

Experimental Forms of Contract

The experimental projects of Alexander and his colleagues, in which design and building are aspects of a single integrated process, have required modification of the typical legal arrangements between client, architect, and contractor. The new processes require that the person in charge of design also be in charge of construction; that design and construction proceed simultaneously, so that construction may begin relatively early and design may continue to take place relatively late; and that as much as possible, decisions are related directly to the physical reality of the project, beginning with the layout of the building(s) on site and continuing through the final details and color.

These unusual procedures result in new contracts with the following characteristics:[4]

- The architect acts as the construction manager and is responsible for the hiring and management of subcontractors. This is intended to ensure a combined responsibility for both design and construction. The subcontractors work directly for the construction managers so that "the details of their work can be planned flexibly, and that changes and subtleties are being worked out continuously, between our team of managers and the craftspeople, while the work is going on."[5]
- Half the money for a particular operation is advanced to subcontractors at the start of that operation; most of the rest comes after about half the work is complete. This is intended to allow subcontractors relief from the pressing need to complete an operation as fast as possible as a result of advancing their own money.
- Cost allocation precedes design and continues through design and construction. This is intended to guarantee that within a total overall budget, there will be a reasonable distribution of money across all aspects of the project, instead of a lack of money in some critical areas—landscaping, for example. Within this process, cost overruns in one area are not allowed to reduce costs in another. In the case of overruns, as far as possible, money is taken from areas that are very close to what is being overrun. "Either quantities are reduced—if that is feasible, to make up for the overrun—or items are reduced, simplified, in other areas of the building—always with an eye to preserving the feeling of the building as a whole, and its essential character. This guarantees cost, in a form rarely accomplished by contemporary architecture."[6]
- Design changes may be made during construction. From a financial point of view, this is accommodated by a system of cost allocations in which total costs—and the cost of each operation—are guaranteed. This means that the architect/construction manager must be sensitive and attentive to the budget at the same time that she is inventive with design during the course of construction. However, legal responsibility for cost control lies with the subcontractor.

This contractual system represents an attempt to form a legal context in which design and building may be reintegrated. The distribution of money and the nature of its allocation to subcontractors eliminates the general contractor as a middleman in the relationships that surround design and building, while allowing maximum flexibility during construction.

In mainstream practice as well, the system of construction management is allowing for the reforging of relationships between architects and subcontractors, often fabricators and manufacturers, who play a more direct role in the character and quality of material assembly than the general contractors do.[7] This system is compatible with the renewed emphasis, in some European countries, for example, on the individual fabrication of industrial components for buildings, and it allows for a modern renewal of the historic relationship between architecture and craft.

Japanese Construction Practice

For construction of the Eishin School, a modified version of a standard contract with a general contractor was used, which included the right of the architect to carry out construction experiments and mock-ups on the site and the obligation of the contractor to provide help for this purpose. These experiments, which were taking place continuously as construction proceeded, formed the basis for discussions with the contractor that led to on-site modifications. Within the context of standard Japanese construction practice, these kinds of modifications were considered normal.

Indeed, the standard building process in Japan is characterized by a high level of give-and-take between architects and builders.[8] Japanese practice is based partly on the long-standing tradition of craft in Japanese building, and partly on the nonlitigious nature of Japanese society. There is a close relationship between architects, contractors, and manufacturers: it is expected that the various parties will work things out together, on-site, instead of simply seeing the construction process as the fulfillment of a contract that had already completely specified the building.[9] In many cases the architect maintains a continuous presence on-site, as contrasted with the once-a-week visits that may be typical of American firms. Long-standing relationships exist between architectural firms and contracting firms, along with the personal respect that grows out of such relationships. Most graduates of architecture schools, in fact, go to work for construction firms, so in dealing with construction firms, architects are talking to professionals with training similar to their own.

Because the culture's atmosphere is not litigious, it is possible for the initial set of drawings to be less detailed than it would be in the American case and for many aspects of design to be worked out during construction. Drawings produced by the architect will often be redrawn by the builder,[10] and as in other countries, many shop drawings will be produced during the course of construction, based on measurements of relevant parts of the building as it is being built. In addition, full-scale mock-ups are typically used to look at details, materials, surfaces, and color.

A close relationship also exists between the building team and fabricators and manufacturers, and there is an expectation that components designed especially for the individual building may be readily produced. This is true for traditional crafts, such as wood and tiles, as well as modern materials, such as stainless steel. Within a highly advanced, technological economy, many fabrication shops remain small, and even large factories are prepared for special orders. Such shops prepared special tiles for one of Arata Isozaki's buildings and sheet stainless steel for the roof of two of Fumihiko Maki's buildings. In the case of the stainless steel roof, the specifications developed by Maki in collaboration with the manufacturer were later applied to buildings by other architects as well.[11]

During construction, it is expected that changes to the original design will take place. They take place in the context of contractual agreements that rely as much on the strength of human relationships as on the fine print in the contract. Dana Buntrock writes that "at least one major architect has been quoted as saying he will not accept projects when the client uses a lawyer in negotiations. Subcontractors and architects also enter into projects with little more than a verbal agreement, further eroding claims to legal rights that Westerners consider necessary."[12]

These kinds of relationships alone cannot guarantee great buildings, and Japan is no different from other modern cultures in the wide range of design quality that exists. However, some of the attributes of building contracts and arrangements in preindustrial Western culture are also present in modern, industrialized Japan: close, "informal" human relationships that are accompanied by a much greater degree of flexibility and hence a greater capacity for innovation and experimentation than in other countries. Even despite the litigious nature of modern American society, there are renewed arguments for reintroducing "common sense" and making room for discretionary decision making in our own culture. In Japan, such an approach is not precluded by a high level of industrialization.

The Precise Shaping of Individual Buildings

Today the word *precision* has particular connotations of advanced engineering and suggests objects that are highly "mechanical" in their nature, with simple geometries and tiny tolerances, allowing for complete interchangeability of parts. The idea of craftsmanship in this book is one that also leads to precision—whether it results from a fifteenth-century carpenter shaping mortises and tenons in a house frame or from a contemporary process in which advanced computer technology is used to give an exact shape to the wing of a jet airplane. One of the characteristics of artifacts produced in a healthy building culture is that they exhibit a strong and careful fit to their physical and cultural contexts. *Precision* is another way of describing this fit and results from processes in which craftsmanship has taken place. In its own context, a traditional Greek village of stone and whitewash is as precisely shaped as a modern Swiss highway bridge is in *its* context.

The search for such new processes is not restricted to a particular kind of technology but generally involves the development of techniques that allow for feedback and action based on that feedback. Some of the following techniques are more connected to tradition, and some are more modern, and it seems useful to consider how they might evolve together.

Innovations in Building Techniques in Japan

A series of construction experiments carried out by Hajo Neis over several years in Japan has attempted to introduce innovations that utilize materials that can be shaped and detailed in a way that design can proceed during the course of construction. The innovations are concerned with basic structural systems as well as finishes. They emerge from a respect for traditional architecture and construction and the emotional impact that traditional construction has on people's experience of buildings. At the same time, since contemporary costs often prohibit the use of traditional craft, the projects often include a search for ways in which modern technology may be transformed so that some of its efficiencies may be applied to the individual shaping of buildings. Often worked out during the course of construction itself, these innovations were developed according to the needs of particular projects.

One project, the Sakura Tsutsumi experimental building, involved the development of a diamond-shaped wall tile, inspired by traditional *kura*, or solid masonry storehouses. Neis writes that the wall system was developed to meet three needs: "Thermal comfort, the structural aspect of creating a solid shear resistant wall system; and, an aesthetic aspect namely the feeling of

Figure 11.8. Traditional Japanese *kura*

Figure 11.9. Experiments with diamond tile wall, Sakura Tsutsumi Building

Figure 11.10.
Adjusting size of window
openings during construction,
Sakura Tsutsumi Building

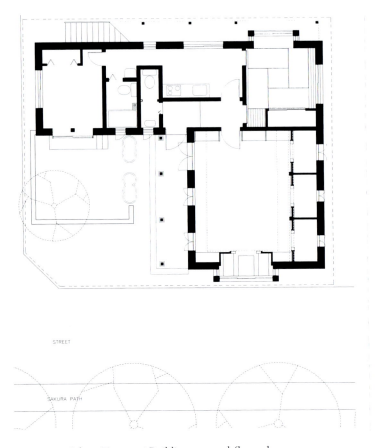

STREET

SAKURA PATH

Figure 11.11. Sakura Tsutsumi Building: ground-floor plan

Figure 11.12.
Sakura Tsutsumi Building:
finished building

presence and solidity in the outside wall and the feeling of comfort and pleasantness in the inside wall."[13] It is a composite system, including wall tile on the outside and wood on the inside, with insulation and a concrete shell in between. The concrete shell takes the shear forces, and vertical forces are taken by the wooden structure. The double-diamond wall tiles were developed in full-size mock-ups, using cardboard and paint, trying different combinations of shapes, proportions, and colors. Neis writes:

> Different color combinations of the two diamonds were tried—warm dark-gray and gray-green, red and dark gray, yellow and off-white. Giving the small diamond a separate color, however, felt a little noisy when the tile was put together in larger quantities on the building shell. Finally an off-white color, combined and contrasting subtly with a warm, light gray, felt most at peace in the small as well as in larger quantities put together.[14]

Much of this innovative work has involved the use of concrete, making use of its plastic properties in ways that allow the architect/builder to shape the building in detail during the course of construction. Concrete is normally used in large-scale projects, either with repetitive precast elements or with repetitive formwork that allows massive amounts of the material to be poured in place. In such typical use the emphasis is on quantity and production efficiency. Neis's experiments represent an attempt to find a middle ground between the efficiency of concrete's application (pouring, precasting, spraying) and the idea that if the formwork or finishing receives more attention and craft than usual, the result might start to approach the quality and feeling of traditional construction.

The potential of computers in the detailed shaping of buildings is only beginning to be realized. Right now, computers are used mostly to speed production and save money. Drawing programs allow for better coordination between architect and consultants, for efficient changes to drawings, for the drawing of many repetitive elements, and for the coordination of different systems of a building. Some programs allow for materials takeoffs. Others allow contractors to keep track of budgets, construction schedules, materials flows, and correspondence with architects and subcontractors. All of this is aimed at efficiency—and in the construction industry, which has traditionally not been known for efficiency, these advances are important.

Manufacturing is now also seeing a trend connected to the new customer orientation of business: the use of computer-controlled processes to make unique products, one different from the next, on an automated assembly line. An example of such a process in building is automated timber-framing systems in Japan, which control the production of all parts of a jointed timber frame laid out to a particular set of dimensional specifications, which can vary from building to building.[15] Because the process is computerized, the parts can be cut for ten individualized houses as easily as for ten identical houses. These production lines, which require three people to man them, can turn out a house frame in eight hours. This process allows for both traditional construction detail and the production of variety from house to house. These plants are capital-intensive, and they are not local, like a carpenter with saws and chisels—but they do go part of the way toward the individual shaping of buildings and toward reconnection with traditional techniques.

However, these innovations do not address the freedom and liberation that the "computer revolution" was supposed to bring about. In addition to speeding up work that is already being done, computer technology might be used to do work that is conceptually more complex, *that would otherwise not be done.* Malcolm McCullough writes that "work has begun on making our data constructions coincide with our abstractive powers of visual thinking. Visual

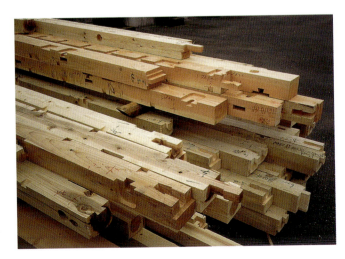

Figure 11.13.
Timber members
with joints cut on auto-
mated production
line, Japan, 1995

computing has expanded our capacity to visualize abstract symbolic structures as physical images. It lets ideas become things."[16] The computer, according to McCullough, is on its way to becoming a tool in which there might be a direct relationship between visualization and actuality—a relationship that might become *more fluid* than conventional processes of design:

> Where a discrete trial-and-error process, such as drawing successive iterations of a design on layers of tracing paper, involves some preconception, or some explicit quantitative specification, a continuous exploratory process such as realtime sculpting a spline-controlled curved surface depends much more on qualitative recognition and discovery. Note that although vision's technological context becomes thoroughly externalized, its arresting capacity remains internal. . . . This ability to develop an image in the mind's eye from which to give form to artifacts in the outer world, by means of discovering appropriate states of continuously manipulated materials, should be a far better acknowledged aspect of electronic art, digital craft, and computer-aided design.[17]

This is different from the simple speeding up of conventional production. We are not yet at the point where such immediate feedback between mind, hand, and object is possible with the computer, but there have been important efforts in this direction by software developers, through modeling programs that allow for visualization and manipulation of three-dimensional images.

Beyond direct object visualization, there are other ways in which the computer has been useful in allowing architects and engineers to work more deeply and not just more quickly. The project for the Eishin School, for example, utilized finite element analysis, a numerical technique for the analysis of statically indeterminate structures that must be carried out on computers, for the engineering design of the timber roof structures. These were the largest timber roofs built in Japan in several decades, and they included complex trusses, akin to the great timber roofs of medieval Europe, that could not be analyzed in other ways. Similarly, the architect Abdelwahed el-Wakil utilized computer techniques for the design of *muqarnas*, the elaborate sculptural squinches found in traditional mosques. Islamic decorative elements depend on iterative geometries, but as these can get quite complex in three dimensions, the computer can be of help in generating designs. In el-Wakil's case, the elements themselves were shaped by craftsmen working with traditional techniques, using the designs that had been generated by the computer.[18] Similarly, computers were used to generate the patterns used by stonecutters at the Cathedral of St. John the Divine in New York City when the work on that building resumed at the beginning of the 1980s.[19]

For a new museum in Spain, Frank Gehry's office used a program—CATIA—that has been used by the French aerospace industry for the design of complex, three-dimensional shapes. The program allowed for the digitization of complex physical models made in a model shop; the digitized models then formed the basis for engineering development and fabrication. This process allowed for a close relationship between engineering and aesthetic design—to the extent that the engineering consultants were able to allow for a +/−300 mm tolerance in the final placement of structural members, allowing the architects to make fine adjustments at the end of the design process.[20] One need not make a judgment about the building to recognize that this process points to more fluid relationships between design, engineering, and fabrication. Other innovations allow a person to adjust a three-dimensional virtual environment while standing within it. Still others allow builders on-site to view a three-dimensional representation of the next step of construction projected onto the building itself through the use of video goggles. This supplements, and perhaps reduces reliance on, two-dimensional drawings contained in contract documents. Catherine Slessor comments, "The notion that uniqueness is now as economic and easy to achieve as repetition, challenges the simplifying assumptions of modernism and suggests the potential of a new, postindustrial paradigm based on the enhanced, creative capabilities of electronics rather than mechanics."[21]

These techniques require the explicit analysis of the physical or mathematical systems that lie behind the forms—the kind of analysis that would have been only implicitly carried out by traditional craftspeople. It is possible, however, as McCullough suggests, that this explicit analysis may come to be incorporated into implicit systems, in which the designer or builder has control over detail. These programs are empowering because they encourage ways to look at a building that are intuitive *and that reunite disparate parts of the building production process*—design plus materials ordering; schematic design plus engineering; design plus actual building visualization.[22] They also have the potential to demystify the building culture (if not to demystify the computer culture) and to put critical decisions into the hands of laypeople. Of course, it remains to be seen how far such techniques can go in connecting the mind of the designer with the material of the building, but the innovations described here may be a first step toward that goal.[23]

"Low-Tech" Processes and Traditional Techniques

At the same time that these high-tech processes are emerging, "low-tech," traditional processes are also making a revival. Mostly operating on a small scale, these processes involve craftspeople and tradespeople who insist on working closely with clients and architects, maintaining a high level of craft, and manufacturers of building materials that are owned and operated locally. The point is not the use of traditional materials or traditional craft techniques for their own sake but, rather, the use of materials and techniques— old or new—that might increase the individual control that people have over the shaping of the building.

In England there has been a revival of thatching, along with a growth of interest in the preservation and restoration of traditional buildings. A historically accurate replica of Shakespeare's Globe Theatre has been built, using traditional framing techniques; it is the first thatched building to be erected in London since before the Great Fire of 1666.[24] In the United States, the historic preservation movement has helped maintain and revive traditional crafts such as ornamental plastering, timber framing, stonemasonry, painting, blacksmithing, fine joinery and sash-making, and many others. There are companies that manufacture historical paint colors using traditional ingredients, and others that have revived the production of terra-cotta. Some of these craftspeople and products are in great demand, and sometimes they are used in new construction as people become aware of their availability and ecological appropriateness.

In developing countries, where a large contrast exists between traditional, vernacular techniques and ubiquitous concrete-and-rebar construction, initiatives have introduced local production of components, which becomes a new source of income and/or a way to reduce the price of the buildings. Laurie Baker, an English architect who has been practicing in southern India for the last fifty years, has developed a series of low-cost construction techniques, including a way of making brick walls in which bricks are stacked so that their wide dimension shows on the face of the wall. This reduces the amount of brick in a wall by about one-quarter and can be used on buildings up to two stories tall. In addition, he has developed a way of hinging window

Figure 11.14.
An up-to-date English thatcher, 1992

Figure 11.15. Thatched houses in Abbotsbury, Dorset, 1988

shutters with a simple set of pins that allow the shutter to move, and a system of ceiling/roof spans made with "filler slabs," reducing the amount of expensive material in the roof.

Baker's techniques have been picked up by local Indian architects and by the national housing bureaucracy, HUDCO, which promotes them in its own projects as well as through a national network of building centers. Similarly, the housing project in Mexicali set up an on-site factory for the manufacture of a new design of soil-cement blocks. The Community-Based Building Program in Papua New Guinea helped set up schemes for the local production of wooden shakes and blinds. In some projects in India, groups of women work in the production of ladis—concrete planks—for the roofs of their houses.

Over the last twenty years in the United States, there has been a revival of timber framing: many companies offer services ranging from a frame "kit" to a finished house. Some of this work is done with solid-sawn, first-cut timber; some with recycled timber; and some with engineered, composite timber members. The traditional timber frame is often combined with a technologically advanced stressed-skin panel wall, resulting in a traditional structure with a high-energy-performance skin.

Although these "low-tech" processes represent a small percentage of total production, they are quite diverse, and when they appear in buildings they make a large difference. Except for the deliberately low-cost techniques of Laurie Baker in India, many of these are more expensive than standard construction. However, if successful, such techniques tend to spread through society and may thereby contribute to the emergence of a culture in which highly crafted buildings are more prevalent.

Houses of Quality That Can Be Built in Quantity: The Production of Variety among Many Buildings

The production of unique artifacts and buildings leads to variety in the environment and the most prevalent buildings in cities, houses and apartment buildings, are basic to the generation of difference and urban variety. However, a principal assumption in modern housing—that exact repetition is necessary to control costs—has prevented approaches that respect the uniqueness of people and communities and would thereby combine precision (of response to client groups) in the individual building with the ability to make many such buildings at reasonable cost. Since the 1960s, architects such as Lucien Kroll, John Habraken, and Christopher Alexander have attempted to develop systems through which individuals could be responsible for designing their own dwellings—to develop such uniqueness—within the context of a larger collective production system.

In a few projects—still too few—the people in charge work carefully with community groups to ensure that housing meets their social and economic needs. Some of these projects take place within the existing systems of design, production, and finance—but stretch these systems so that the built result is shaped very specifically to meet clients' needs. In the United States, many of these projects are sponsored by local groups rather than government agencies, and the most successful ones involve a good deal of cleverness within a context of continuous, direct involvement with all the parties. The principals of these projects are not managers or architects working at arms' length but instead are deeply involved with the communities and the detailed reality of the work. In some of these projects the successes arise when the desires of several different constituent groups are all resolved together. The result is housing that is crafted to fit a particular community in its physical, social, and economic details.

Michael Pyatok, United States

One example of crafted housing is the work of Michael Pyatok, an architect in Oakland, California, who is committed to the design of housing for people who have traditionally been excluded from conventional housing markets. Pyatok views design as a relatively small part of a much larger process that also includes community organization, finance, and production. He works closely with local groups to develop building programs that clearly reflect community needs; with banks, foundations, and nonprofit organizations to put together financing packages that make the housing affordable; with contractors to ensure a combination of high quality and low costs. He "pushes the envelope" as far as possible within the existing systems of design and building production. His projects fit into their neighborhoods, because they are built largely within existing zoning constraints, with familiar materials and techniques that are known to local contractors, and their design is usually subject to an active public process which helps ensure that local people find the project acceptable.

Hismen Hin-nu Terrace in Oakland, California, built for low-income tenants, is typical of such projects.[25] It was funded by a variety of lenders; involved participatory design workshops; and comprises materials and

Figure 11.16. Courtyard of Hismen Hin-nu Terrace, housing project in Oakland (Michael Pyatok, architect) 1997

details that make the project compatible with its surroundings and show a level of craft that is not typical of low-income housing projects. It consists of fifty apartments of varying sizes that are carefully fitted onto a tight site. Although the density is higher than in the surrounding area, the local response is positive. The project shows that low-cost housing may be compatible with neighborhood wishes as well as with the personal needs of modern families.

This work shows that it is possible to work *almost completely within the existing building culture* and produce unique results that fit particular situations. It is an unusual body of work, however, requiring a greater-than-usual level of attention and effort. The complexity of the financing package and the persistence required in dealing with local authorities mean that projects like this are still exemplary models rather than the commonplace vernacular.

Avi Friedman, Canada

In projects like Pyatok's, uniqueness of the project as a whole is achieved through the careful work of architects, but this process does not necessarily yield unique dwelling units or allow for the gradual transformation of those dwelling units over time. In many healthy building cultures, however, uniqueness appears at the level of the individual dwelling unit, and buildings develop further uniqueness over time. Although various contemporary initiatives have attempted to do this, most of them have not proven to be economically viable on a large scale. Avi Friedman's work, in Canada, combines the goal of low initial cost with evolution over time. In this way, the user is in charge of gradually crafting the building over time and thus developing its uniqueness.

Connected to the ideas of John Habraken, who developed a prototypical production system based on an architect-designed and contractor-built structural framework for mass housing that would be filled in with individual dwelling units by the dwellers,[26] Friedman has been working closely with Canadian developers to market small houses that are within financial reach of young families of modest means, and as of 1996, 5,000 such houses had been built in and around Montreal.[27] These houses are very simple in design, but they allow for relatively high density, as well as for additions and transformations over time. Because initial land development costs (usually a high percentage of overall housing cost) are low, overall costs are reduced, and the house can take on its personal character over time, as the family's means improve.

In these houses, structural spans are relatively short, and because the internal spaces do not depend on intermediate supports, their configuration can be changed at will. Structural and construction components are not specialized and are easily available. The houses make sense to people in an ordinary and everyday way.[28] They are modest, with well-lit rooms of reasonable size. Circulation among rooms is easily handled. Houses stand on their own piece of land, allowing for gardens and outdoor spaces, and work together in groups to create a pleasant streetscape. The simple system is designed so that the houses can be changed over time, and analysis of completed houses shows that this has indeed happened.[29]

Figure 11.17.
"Next home" of Avi Friedman

Figure 11.18.
Variety of possible plans
in a "Next home"

In fact, the invention of a modern system that allowed the house to develop over time under the control of its owners was invented at least as far back as the 1940s, when "Levittowns" were constructed in Pennsylvania and in New York. The typical Levittown house, built in thousands of identical units through what were essentially mass-production processes, was extremely simple and conducive to change: few houses among the thousands originally built remain unchanged. The houses were of simple stud frame construction, with room arrangements that did not constrain additions and extensions. Tract houses built later—in the late 1960s, for example—by the same development company did not encourage the same degree of transformation. These houses were larger to begin with and had more complex plans, so they changed less—helping to validate Friedman's point that the careful initial design is critical in stimulating change by occupants.

The Growth of New Neighborhoods in Venezuela and Colombia

Projects such as those of Michael Pyatok represent the careful production of housing variety by architects, and the "grow home" of Avi Friedman represents the production of housing variety among individual units by clients. Neither of these projects deals with the subtle variety that is seen in settlements and cities as a whole: the careful fitting of building to building, *and* of buildings to the landscape. In the last chapter, we saw this variety as an aspect of modern craftsmanship, and in chapter 9 we saw how the step-by-step growth of the traditional Islamic city resulted from local rules that allowed for local decisions based on real situations.

In two projects—one of which was built—in South America, a modern version of a process of piecemeal growth for entire neighborhoods was simulated.[30] In these growth processes, a few rules guide the step-by-step placement of houses, ensuring that individual houses will form good outdoor space and allow for growth over time, while at the same time ensuring that streets and community spaces are well formed. In this way, the development of a neighborhood plan is based on understandings of the real place and the actual houses and can take place without an abstract master plan. Large-scale form emerges through local processes happening all over, each of which is based on its own reality, but all of which are following similar rules of growth.

The projects described in this chapter are on a variety of scales and emphasize different parts of the building production process. Some are concerned primarily with the shaping of materials, or "traditional" craft; some with contracting and construction; some with architecture and design; some with the ways in which people's needs help shape building form; some with larger-scale planning. It may be unusual to consider these sorts of projects together, but they are each aiming at a different aspect of postindustrial craftsmanship, in which the realities of buildings and cities can be considered in direct ways that allow professionals and communities to react to them. In this respect, the shaping of a housing complex according to the social needs of children who will live in it is similar to the careful adjustment

Figure 11.19. Gradual sequence of house development in a small neighborhood in Venezuela project (Christopher Alexander, Artemis Anninou, Hajo Neis, Center for Environmental Structure)

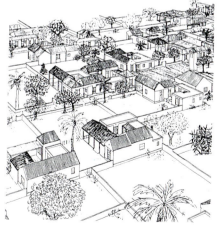

Figure 11.20.
Possible results of sequence of neighborhood development in Venezuela project

of the position of a window according to the actual light conditions in a room, and similar to laying a street out in a way that takes advantage of a view toward a distant mountain. All of these tasks require direct knowledge of the situation and a process that allows the person in charge of making the building to respond to that knowledge in a straightforward way. In all cases, a good result is precise within its own context.

CULTURALLY APPROPRIATE BUILDINGS

12

Innovations in Design

In the last chapter we looked primarily at *process*—at innovative techniques and initiatives, at different scales, that allow buildings to be carefully and individually shaped. Such techniques do not by themselves guarantee that the *content* of the built result is culturally appropriate. The quotes from Pevsner, Norberg-Schulz, and Tanizaki in chapter 4 were poetic expressions of the idea that the building culture—and the architecture within it—reinforce the larger culture of which they are a part. Although in modern society, this intimate relationship exists, and our buildings do represent our culture, the nature of our commodity culture does not allow for necessary connections between people and their own pasts, the places where they live, and larger communities. Buildings that foster such connections are not the norm.

Contemporary projects that make these connections are the focus of this chapter, which includes:

- New building types that are based on emerging people-centered attitudes toward work and health care.
- Buildings that draw their human meaning from tradition, where tradition is seen not as an archaic set of forms but as familiar connections to people's own past—and therefore to each other.
- Buildings that are rooted in culture and place, acting not as isolated objects in the world but as ways of making a larger physical, social, or natural order more connected and whole.

In 1995 Francis Duffy wrote:

> The architectural profession . . . can only justify itself in terms that relate to the unique nature of architectural knowledge; that is, to using building design to anticipate the unfolding demands of users, clients and society for the buildings they need to house themselves and all their activities in the most effective, beautiful and sustainable way. . . . It is absolutely necessary for architects to define architectural knowledge in a way that commands public respect. . . . Developing architectural knowledge, freely shared through voluntary association, will make confidence in the future as easy and natural as honouring the past.[1]

It is a particularly telling commentary on the last few decades that there has been a need to assert that people should be taken more into account in architecture and building. A strong and growing voice has pointed out that buildings do not serve people well[2] and that the abstractions of modernism and the mechanical/bureaucratic nature of the building culture removed the human element from architecture.

This voice is not necessarily based only on a perception of the inadequacies of the built environment. Duffy reports on an analysis of the difficulties that the architectural profession itself is having: "In the RIBA's detailed studies of the performance of the most 'successful' architectural practices, we found that the cleverest, the most able architects still do not feel impelled to relate their design skill to what it does for their clients." He goes on to say that "some architects, desperate to survive, had become accustomed to giving away, or at least spectacularly discounting, their chief intellectual property—conceptual design ideas—in order to buy the busy work of detailing, working drawings and contract administration which they imagined would pay the bills and keep their practices busy."[3]

Duffy's comments hold true for the United States as well. Table 12.1 shows a typical breakdown of fees for architectural services in the United States.[4] The production of the legal contract—the construction documents—accounts for the largest single part of the fee. The two items at either end of the process—schematic design, which often involves the bulk of client contact as it relates to the functional and aesthetic design of the building, and construction administration, or the architect's oversight of the contractor's compliance to the construction documents, are relatively small in comparison.

For example, only 20 percent of the fee goes into schematic design, and architects are often interested in getting through that stage quickly, because they know that they will need as much fee as possible in subsequent stages of the project. But one other service is not even included in the standard fee package and hence is usually not adequately performed. This is architectural programming, or an accurate determination of the client's needs as they pertain to building. Such work has become increasingly necessary as social institutions change more and more quickly, but the architectural profession has not been in a position to respond effectively to that need.

Table 12.1. Typical breakdown of architectural fees
in the United States

	Service as percentage of construction cost
Schematic design	2%
Design development	2%
Construction documents	4%
Bidding	0.5%
Construction administration	1.5%
Total fee as percentage of construction cost	10%

Several recent, positive trends in business management, however, are leading to greater responsiveness toward people in the design of buildings:

- A new emphasis on client satisfaction in the way businesses are run.
- The breakdown of structures of hierarchical control in businesses, in favor of task-oriented work groups that are responsible for their own success, within the general goals of the organization as a whole. In some cases, this includes the elimination of "top-down" management.
- The recognition of the importance of knowledge at all levels of a business, including implicit knowledge that does not always make its way into official procedures, and the knowledge of "low-level" workers who might not ordinarily be consulted.[5]

These trends are affecting the design both of businesses and of buildings to house them. Specifically, new initiatives with respect to two building types—offices and hospitals/clinics—reflect new, more people-centered attitudes.

Offices and Hospitals

Offices and hospitals are among the most singularly purposeful building types in modern architecture. They are designed for one purpose only, and other purposes that might ordinarily be important to buildings are hardly considered. In the case of hospitals, buildings have been designed around the idea of efficiency of a highly mechanized, scientific approach to patient care and healing. In this view, the human body is considered in a functional, mechanical, chemical way, to be acted on by highly trained technicians who have at their disposal sophisticated tools, equipment, and chemicals. The building is often designed to facilitate Taylorian principles of efficiency, applied to a patient seen as a flawed system of chemical and biological processes.[6] The design of Kaiser hospitals in California during the 1960s epitomized this approach: the plans featured two separate circulation systems, one for visitors (along the outer edge) and one for staff (on the inside, so that their steps would be minimized), with the patient rooms, which had no exterior windows, in between. The idea was partly to allow the staff to "do their jobs" without interruption—but the patients were removed from contact with the outdoors, and the families of patients were removed from casual contact with the staff.

Similarly, the office building is designed to provide maximum business efficiency and to allow for the changes to business organization that take place over time. Modern office building design began with its own logic of efficiency, exemplified by such buildings as the Larkin Building and Johnson Wax Headquarters, in which regular ranks of office workers performing repetitive clerical functions could be easily supervised. The advent of the "office landscape" or "Burolandschaft" allowed large organizations to be housed in spaces that had only minimal structural divisions—but such spaces tended to be highly impersonal even as they permitted easy variation in the layout of particular work groups. Probably the most famous reaction against impersonal office space in recent decades was the Centraal Beheer office building by Hermann Hertzberger, in which group and individual work spaces were defined—but not enclosed—by primary structural elements of the building. This allowed for a balance between large-group identity and the ability to personalize the individual or small-group work space.

Such innovations, however, represent the exception rather than the norm. The tendency has been toward larger and larger floor plates, reflecting the desire of larger organizations to be on as few floors as possible. The job of space planners is to maximize the efficiency of layouts, attempting, as with hospitals, to reduce movement. But there are two problems with this scenario. Larger floor plates mean that fewer people in the organization have good daylight or a view of the outdoors from their work space, and maximum efficiency of movement may be just the opposite of what is needed in a modern organization that is trying to engender creativity through more human interaction.

With both building types, the norm is being challenged. Healing is not simply a mechanical or chemical procedure; it involves the whole person. Likewise, the office worker has environmental, social, and aesthetic needs as well as the need to carry out a particular set of functions. In addition, business organizations are changing in ways that are reducing hierarchical control and putting responsibility into the hands of groups and individuals. In these new organizations, group space and space for casual interaction take on much greater importance because it is recognized that creative work happens as much as the result of informal experience and implicit understandings as formal rules.[7]

Office design and hospital design are beginning to change. In both cases the narrow singularity of purpose is disappearing, and attributes of aesthetics, environmental quality, and the realities of social interaction among the users of the building are becoming important. As a result, *new building types* are emerging. For hospital and clinic design, this often means that the qualities of buildings that are important even in nonclinical situations—connections to nature, the hospital corridor as a place of daylight and human interaction, the waiting room and patient room as places that might help relieve anxiety—are taken into account.[8] Technical requirements are still effectively taken care of, but in a context that respects people's humanity and does not assume that they are to be abstracted into systems that are only physiological in nature.

Figure 12.1.
Corridor in new health
center in Melbourne
(Greg Burgess, architect)

1. Entry terrace
2. Bus shelter
3. Courtyard
4. Foyer
5. Reception
6. Waiting
7. Ramp
8. Medical Reception
9. Meeting
10. Kitchen
11. Store
12. Activities
13. Workshop
14. Occupational therapist
15. Physio office
16. Physiotherapy
17. Chest room
18. Podiatry
19. Ethnic Health worker
20. Interview
21. Social worker
22. Community Health worker
23. Quiet room
24. Library
25. Staff
26. Treatment
27. Dental
28. Office
29. Photocopy
30. General office
31. Medical records
32. Co-ordination
33. Executive officer
34. Garage
35. Carpark

Figure 12.2. Plan of new health center in Melbourne

Likewise, changes in business culture are affecting the design of office buildings and the spaces within them. Public spaces, natural light, and connections to the outdoors are important. Group work spaces allow for more flexible work arrangements, permit people to work together more of the time than an isolated "conference room" would imply, and also provide individual places. In these buildings, the user of the building is put back at the center. They may be the forerunners of new, commonly understood building types that will support institutions in which the individual is more respected.[9]

Tradition as Innovation

Innovations in office and health care buildings are the product of invention, of architects' working closely with clients and observing carefully what people are doing, in order to come up with new designs. Appropriateness to modern life does not, however, necessarily depend on the invention of something new. In some cases, what is most appropriate is the continuity of traditional forms—an idea that of course was taboo in mainstream architectural practice for over half a century.

How the public responds to traditional ideas in architecture and how architects respond to those same ideas can be very different. Although the Prince of Wales was heavily criticized by the architectural establishment for his views in favor of traditional buildings, one poll showed that 75 percent of people agreed with him. What the Prince of Wales saw in tradition was buildings that have the capability to be liked, that are familiar to people, and that can be replicated. In describing the ability for replication, he said:

> There are builders all over the country who know about that quality, especially family firms where skills have been passed from father to son. There are bricklayers, carpenters, plasterers who are every bit as skilful as those of past generations, but who are seldom asked to deviate from the norm. The norm is what we see in ever-increasing numbers on the edges of our precious villages, or squashed like bad sets of irregular teeth between the cottage and the school.[10]

This point was elaborated by Roger Scruton, who says that the worth of classical architecture lies in the *reverse* of the elitism that is often ascribed to it:

> How, then, shall we define the classical vernacular? Briefly, I mean a tradition of patterns, adapted to the uses of the ordinary builder, and capable of creating accord and harmony in all the many circumstances of potential conflict. These patterns have emerged from the steady adaptation of the vertical Order—based on column, base, architrave and cornice. . . . Buildings ought not to be designed for the *cognoscenti*, but for the mass of mankind; and the practice of architecture does not lie in the hands of geniuses, but in those of ordinary and half-talented people, whose task is to make us feel at home. Architecture must call,

therefore, upon what is widely understood, easily repeatable, and successfully combined. Its problems are far from the self-created intricacies of a Valéry or a Schoenberg; they arise naturally and inevitably just as soon as stone is laid on stone or brick on brick. This is not to say that architectural problems are easy, or that genius is not as necessary in this art as in the concert hall and the museum. But although it requires genius to solve the problems of the builder, the solutions, once discovered, become the common property of the semi-talented.[11]

It is understandable that architects would react against this idea. Most architects practicing today were trained in the modernist canon, and although most appreciate the beauty of classical architecture, only two varieties of it are readily available. One consists of expensive buildings often made for wealthy clients. The other consists of cheap, ill-proportioned, poorly made details that can be nailed onto any standard tract house. Neither of these alternatives has, at the moment, the attributes that Scruton ascribes to the "classical vernacular"—those of aesthetic harmony arising from the work of builders (although not necessarily "semi-talented" ones) who have at their disposal a well-worked-out system of building based on a commonly appreciated formal canon.

It is most helpful to look at traditional ideas in architecture not in terms of style, but within a context of popular familiarity and connection to other critical trends. Leon Krier's propositions, for example, are explicitly in conflict with two major tenets of modernism. He rejects the idea of the "object building" in favor of well-formed urban space, and he rejects the abstraction of functional separation and zoning in favor of the mixed-use nature of historical cities. Krier's tenets have been presented in actual design proposals and in visual analyses of urban structure, including issues of density, building height, and the distribution of areas to different kinds of urban space, street pattern, and building typologies. In fact, many cities are now recognizing the importance of these ideas.

While Krier's views are sometimes dismissed as a romantic attraction to the past, it is important to look at the ideas themselves rather than the unattainable and undesirable utopian world they might evoke. His "School for 500 Children" at St. Quentin-en-Yvelines, France, was based on the idea that instead of being a large building set apart from the town, the school should be a small district of the town itself. The various functions of the school—"work, rest, health, play and restaurants"—are separate buildings within an urban district that would be available to the town at large when the school is not in session. This project represents a typological reaction against Enlightenment/modernist school planning, in which society saw the school with the same rational mentality that it saw the factory and the hospital and developed bigger and more "efficient" institutions and buildings to house them. Krier writes:

Modern architects have always shown a strong tendency to reduce any public programme to a single form, housed under a single roof. . . . The resultant typological and "artistic" monstrosities were then rationalised a posteriori through all sorts of technical justifications relating to safety, health, climate, fire prevention and so on. Thus it is not by accident that these over-sized buildings have become synonymous with bureaucracy and repressive institutions.[12]

Significantly, this idea has received architectural and educational expression elsewhere. The Eishin School, described in chapter 11, is made up of about twenty buildings arranged around streets and squares. Within educational circles in the United States, there is a strong movement toward smaller schools in which human interaction rather than abstract pedagogical efficiency is paramount.[13] In this case as well as in larger urban design ideas, a strong connection exists between the classical ideas of theorists like Krier and those of architects and others who see more familiar buildings and cities as a means toward an architecture that is more anchored in contemporary life.

Rasem Badran: Traditional Identity in the Modern, "Developing" World

Similarly, the Jordanian architect Rasem Badran has done a number of projects that:

- pay careful attention to the urban context, seeing the building as a means to heal rifts in the urban fabric and create new and useful urban space;
- use familiar elements: screen walls, ornamental brick, simple geometric forms to help make connections to architectural traditions that people understand;
- do not attempt to be reproductions of historic buildings but are clearly contemporary in architectural form and construction technique.

The Great Mosque and associated urban redevelopment in Riyadh, Saudi Arabia, first of all sets a place of worship into the urban fabric, as a continuation of a long tradition of Islamic cities and an expression of the idea that religion is an integral part of social life. The building uses traditional courtyards, minarets, prayer hall, and arcades—and modern construction. It incorporates natural light and ventilation, and air-conditioning ducts are contained in columnar structures and beams. Badran talks about this project in a modern way and sees it as arising out of analysis of the reality of the place:

My first task was to research the special character of the area, by surveying existing historical examples. . . . Islamic architecture is by its very nature "human" architecture, answering the needs of the community without neglecting those of the individual, caring for the whole without denying the particular, and retaining a balance between the spiritual, psychological and physiological needs that people have—within a specific cultural paradigm. I want to avoid trivial historicity and literal copying of the Najdi style.[14]

Figure 12.3. Model of redevelopment of Riyadh, Saudi Arabia (Rasem Badran, architect), showing careful insertions into existing urban fabric

Figure 12.4.
Sketch of area around Great Mosque in Riyadh, showing relationship to existing urban fabric

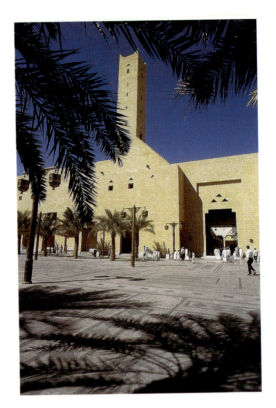

Figure 12.5.
Great Mosque in Riyadh

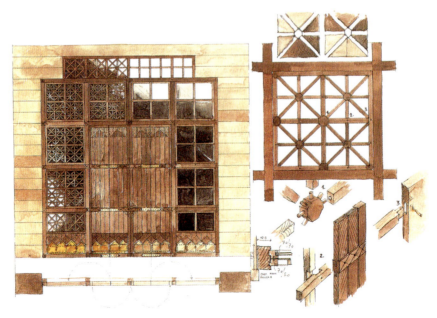

Figure 12.5a. Construction details (Rasem Badran, architect)

Badran achieved continuity with the past not through direct copying but through looking at which aspects of the present, in terms of urban and religious life, were continuous with the past. For continuity of type to have validity, it must be accompanied by continuity of the social reasons for which type existed in the first place. Badran's analysis of contemporary life in Riyadh revealed to him the roots of type, and his design makes reference to history because some of the same conditions exist today in earlier times.

New Urbanism and Traditional Neighborhood Development

The use of traditional form to provide innovative solutions to contemporary problems is perhaps nowhere near as striking as in the New Urbanism/Traditional Neighborhood Development movement in the United States. New Urbanism has involved the development of community prototypes as alternatives to the car-dominated American suburban model of development. These prototypes are based on the clustering of communities around nodes of public transportation—often new light rail lines—and on techniques of lot configuration that allow for a greater-than-usual density without sacrificing privacy or useful outdoor space. The prototypes, some of which have been based on nineteenth-century American towns, arrange a large percentage of houses within easy walking distance of a community center that includes commercial facilities and public buildings as well as the rail station itself—in a similar fashion to some early American suburbs, which were built around extensions of streetcar lines.

This work has sparked widespread interest among developers, but municipalities have been slower to make the large public investment required to extend rapid transit lines.[15] Some of this work has been criticized because it has been done largely for private developers and there is no public ownership of streets and public spaces. These communities have been restricted to generally high-income people, so the ideal of a public Main Street with rich and poor alike has not been achieved. Also, deed covenants require that all buildings be built according to a set of guidelines based on historical precedents—often late-nineteenth- or early-twentieth-century buildings. Strong justifications for this requirement are offered, on the basis of issues of architectural scale, hierarchy, street edge, warm materials, and so on, but the resultant environment is often characterized as a historical pastiche. After all, real cities have rough edges, poor people, industry, a diverse building stock, real competition in land transactions, and continuous change.

Such criticism is justified, but despite its faults, the work must be seen as an important potential first step toward a valuable new approach to suburban development. With careful design it *is* possible to use less land; it *is* necessary to reduce use of the automobile; it *is* possible to rethink standards for street widths and required front and side yards. It may well be desirable and marketable to put front porches back on houses. These projects are propositions that can test in the real world whether or not what architects and other cultural critics have been saying for a long time about the automobile and the disappearance of community is true.

Furthermore, in many communities across the United States, examples of the neighborhood centers advocated by the New Urbanists, in which pedes-

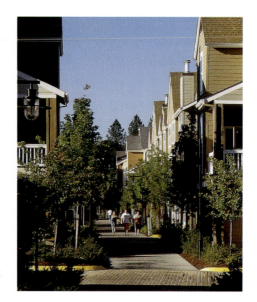

Figure 12.6.
Transit-oriented development
in Beaverton, Oregon, 1998

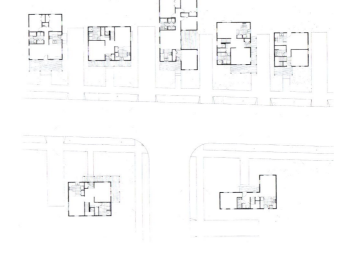

Figure 12.7.
(top and bottom)
Field of Dreams,
Eugene, Oregon,
a new project
based on ideas
of traditional
neighborhoods (Peter
Keyes, principal architect
and site designer)

trian life takes center stage, are emerging spontaneously, through market forces—showing that at least in some situations, the economics of development do encourage some reversal of a trend toward increasing sprawl.

Danish Row Houses, Charleston Single House

Traditional house types are sometimes the most flexible and appropriate. Jørn Orum-Nielsen makes a strong argument for the continued usefulness of traditional house forms—not because they are historic but because they continue to work for people. They are generous enough in their accommodation of use that they can be subjected to continuous transformation over time.

The English/American row house has enough longevity that it endures even into contemporary designs. The type is characterized by two parallel party walls perpendicular to the street, divided into major and minor zones; the major zone is made up of a chain of rooms from front to back, and the minor zone provides circulation. Historically this type has many different manifestations, including the Georgian/Victorian terraced houses of England; the row houses of Boston, New York, Baltimore, and other East Coast cities; and Victorians in San Francisco. Even the Charleston single house, a freestanding structure positioned beside a garden in order to allow ventilation across the narrow dimension of the building, is spatially a close cousin of the basic row house arrangement.

The row house provides enormous flexibility in the way that rooms may be used and combined. The separate circulation zone serves all rooms so that privacy can be maintained; the linear adjacency of rooms means that they can be combined or left separate; when floors are stacked, a house may be easily divided into separate apartments, or separate apartments recombined into a single house.

Orum-Nielsen makes a similar point with respect to traditional Danish houses, called *laenge*. He defines the *laenge* as "a narrow, one- or two-story building, with a loft under a steep, gabled roof, and made up of varying

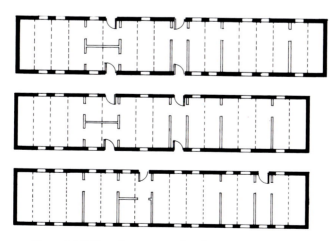

Figure 12.8. Transformations of traditional Danish *laenge*

Figure 12.9.
Traditional *laenge* in
Aerøskøbing, Den-
mark: variety of build-
ings following basic
layout and structure

Figure 12.10.
New ecologically
sound housing in
Denmark, "Tubberup-
vaenge," based on
laenge (designed
by H. Marcussen,
A. Storgaard, and
J. Ørum-Nielsen)

numbers of transverse structural bays."[16] This type turns out to be very
adaptable and combinable, and it provides good light on both sides. It has
been used over the centuries in simple and elaborate ways and continues to
be used for housing in Denmark; many contemporary projects are based on
the *laenge* type.

The Charleston single house type has been used for successful contemporary projects in Charleston. "Infill" housing designed by the architects
Bradfield, Richards & Associates in Atlanta, which won an AIA honor award
in 1986,[17] was designed as low-income housing in the historic district of
Charleston. The buildings included historic details done with inexpensive
materials and retained the traditional orientation of the single house, with its
long dimension perpendicular to the street. This arrangement both provided
a sense of security and made use of a building form compatible with its surroundings.

Although architects are sometimes uncomfortable with the ordinariness
and familiarity of these sorts of projects, they are almost always welcomed

Figure 12.11.
The porch of a traditional
Charleston single house

Figure 12.12.
New low-cost housing
in Charleston based on
traditional single house,
1994

into communities. In these cases, certain types remain appropriate *because of* the familiarity of their forms and because of the flexibility their plan arrangements offer over time.

Rootedness in Culture and Place

In the "developed" and "developing" worlds alike, development has almost been synonymous with the wiping out of identity based on place and local culture. An argument sometimes offered against architecture rooted in a region or place is that contemporary society is so mobile that the idea of place has lost its meaning and that communities of people no longer need to be physically together. An extreme version of this view argues that global communications, and the transformation of the global economy from local companies to international corporations without a geographic base, make architecture based on the characteristics of local place archaic.

A version of this attitude was one basis for the International Style of modernism. But even during the decades when the International Style reigned, there were architects who insisted on maintaining a strong connection to place. They included David Williams and O'Neil Ford in Texas, Edwin Lundie in Minnesota, John Gaw Meem in New Mexico,[18] and others. These architects would, by their desire to work locally, be relatively unknown, particularly outside their own regions. Architecture schools and publications were influenced more by international trends. But these architects got their work primarily through local connections—and the work is significant precisely *because* of its connection to local history, local building techniques, and the realities of the local building economy.

In developing countries, such architects as Sedad Eldem in Turkey, Geoffrey Bawa in Sri Lanka, Charles Correa in India, Hassan Fathy in Egypt, Charles Boccara in Morocco, and many others attempted to develop a new architecture based on local vernacular traditions, partly as a reaction against the internationalizing and homogenizing tendencies of the modern movement. In some cases these architects responded to their countries' political need to build or restore a sense of regional or ethnic identity in postcolonial situations.

Bawa, for example, learned from the traditional vernacular architecture of Sri Lanka. This architecture grows out of the hot and humid climate of the region: low-pitched, hipped, tile roofs with wide overhangs; open walls; verandas and a high level of integration between indoor and outdoor space:

> The beauty of some of these buildings, gardens and landscapes leaves
> a considerable residue of subconscious understanding in the mind—a
> help to solve some present need; for the right placement of a building
> on the site; for the need to frame and emphasise a view or to open or
> construct a space; a wish to get a definite degree of shadow in a room.
> . . . I like to regard all past and present good architecture in Sri Lanka
> as just that—good Sri Lankan architecture—for this is what it is, not
> narrowly classified as Indian, Portuguese or Dutch, early Sinhalese or
> Kandyan or British Colonial, for all the good examples of these peri-
> ods have taken the country itself into first account.[19]

Bawa's statement is strikingly similar to one made by David Williams in Texas many years before:

> These houses have shady places—wide verandahs and porches along
> the wings that run off to the rear on the west side, forming shady
> courts and little gardens. . . . They have slatted shutters which are
> closed into the deep reveals of the thick stone walls, during the heat of
> the day, to keep out the glare of the sun; and ample chimneys to cheer
> the winter through. . . . It is better to throw away our habit of suppos-
> ing everything beautiful in Texas had a foreign origin, and to admit

that these little houses are not French or Spanish or even English at all, but are natural, native Texas art, suited to our climate and indigenous to our soil.[20]

The thread of resistance to homogenization and the elimination of place and local culture as a factor in design has continued. During the 1980s, Kenneth Frampton argued that modernism in architecture is not incompatible with a strong response to place.[21] The journalist Tony Hiss has written about the need to restore a sense of place in human experience.[22] More recently, sociologists such as Manuel Castells and Saskia Sassen have pointed out that the international economy, although it appears to be all-pervasive, in fact exists in *real places*—London, New York, Hong Kong, Tokyo, Singapore, Los Angeles—and employs real people from communities that are not tied into the global economy but that nevertheless are greatly affected by it.[23]

The idea that buildings should be rooted in place and culture forms the guiding philosophy of several contemporary architects working in four different countries—Canada, Australia, England, and Japan. These architects have all done projects based on extensive involvement with local communities, the use of local materials and techniques and/or a serious response to environmental issues, and an attitude toward site planning that allows the building to contribute to and enhance the site's larger physical order. Some of these projects are not "traditional" in their final form—but in their particular, detailed responses to their local and global contexts, they demonstrate the depth to which a building may take its meaning from the way it is anchored to the physical world and culture around it.

Patricia and John Patkau, Canada

The Seabird Island School, designed by Patricia and John Patkau of Vancouver, British Columbia, for a local native community of Coastal Salish Indians, is strongly anchored to its place through site planning, climatic response, and building form.[24] The building reinforces the north edge of a large gathering space and acts as a center for the local community. Its position allows sunlight to penetrate many of the important spaces of the school, giving life to the edge that faces the community. The building is of heavy timber construction, much of it laminated timber members, and some of its most visible parts are expressive of branching trees and the forests of British Columbia. The roof forms help to visually connect the buildings to neighboring mountains, and much of the building's exterior is covered with cedar shingles, a traditional material. The largest room—the gymnasium/assembly hall, which also serves as a community hall—is located to the north and helps act as a buffer against strong north winds. But this room also helps to anchor the building to its place *symbolically*, through its shape: it is evocative of something elemental and alive.

The community participated in the programming and design of the school and built it under the direction of a construction manager who worked for the Canadian Bureau of Indian and Northern Affairs. The architects "feel that the band [native community] did a better job than a conventional contractor, who might have been intimidated by the complexities."[25] A

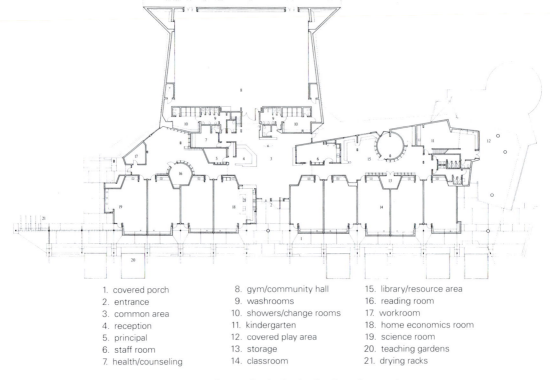

1. covered porch	8. gym/community hall	15. library/resource area
2. entrance	9. washrooms	16. reading room
3. common area	10. showers/change rooms	17. workroom
4. reception	11. kindergarten	18. home economics room
5. principal	12. covered play area	19. science room
6. staff room	13. storage	20. teaching gardens
7. health/counseling	14. classroom	21. drying racks

Figure 12.13. Plan, Seabird Island School (Patkau Architects)

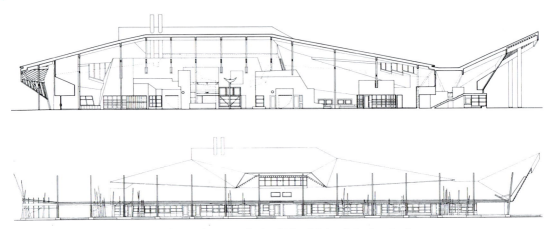

Figure 12.14. Sections, Seabird Island School (Patkau Architects)

Figure 12.15.
Seabird Island School

Figure 12.16.
Seabird Island School—
view of south edge

clearly contemporary building, the school is "of its place" in climatic, social, and cultural/symbolic ways and does not make nostalgic reference to an unattainable and perhaps nonexistent past. It shows how a straightforward building may take on powerful qualities of local place, qualities that enhance the community's connection to the landscape itself.

Greg Burgess, Australia

The Box Hill Community Arts Centre in Melbourne shows how the deep involvement of members of a community may turn a modest program for the extension of an existing building into the creation of a place of great spirit, helping to reinforce the community itself. The building, located in a suburban area, was a collaborative effort between the architects, the community arts officer, and an artist/landscape architect who worked with local artists and community members in the design and construction of many details of the building. It was an important public art project, involving ceramics, glazed bricks, jigsawed fence pickets, woven seat covers, copperwork for gutters, and timber joinery. All of these pieces were handled through separate subcontracts.[26]

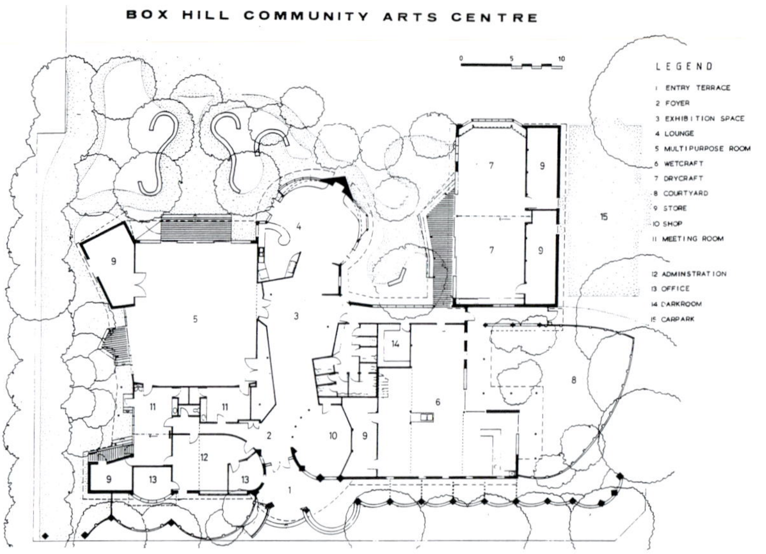

BOX HILL COMMUNITY ARTS CENTRE

LEGEND

1 ENTRY TERRACE
2 FOYER
3 EXHIBITION SPACE
4 LOUNGE
5 MULTIPURPOSE ROOM
6 WETCRAFT
7 DRYCRAFT
8 COURTYARD
9 STORE
10 SHOP
11 MEETING ROOM

12 ADMINISTRATION
13 OFFICE
14 DARKROOM
15 CARPARK

Figure 12.17.
Box Hill Com-
munity Centre,
Melbourne, plan
(Greg Burgess,
architect)

Figure 12.18.
Box Hill Community
Centre, Melbourne (Greg
Burgess, architect)

Figure 12.19.
Box Hill Community Centre, Melbourne (Greg Burgess, architect)

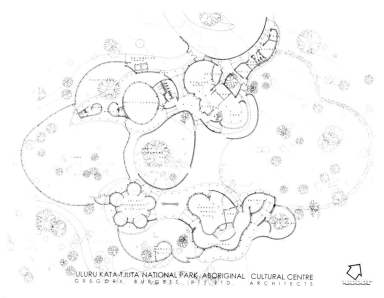

ULURU KATA-TJUTA NATIONAL PARK ABORIGINAL CULTURAL CENTRE
GREGORY BURGESS PTY.LTD. ARCHITECTS

Figure 12.20. Uluru Visitors' Centre, Ayers Rock, Australia, plan (Greg Burgess, architect)

Figure 12.21.
Uluru Visitors'
Centre, Ayers Rock
in background

The building has a simple overall plan, centered by an entry/circulation spine that is curved in section and irregular in plan and focuses one's path toward a fireplace in the main lounge. The unusual nature of the plan, and the variety of crafts used, might have the danger of giving the building an overly idiosyncratic feeling. But that is not the case at all; the feeling is one of vitality and light, and the building exudes a sense of welcoming and ease. Simple materials such as curved plywood come together with strong colors and the many special details, all resolved in a building that serves as the active center for a suburban community. The building now accommodates over sixty organizations, connected with a variety of ethnic groups, and is used for weddings, christenings, and other events of all kinds.[27]

Another building by Burgess, the Uluru National Park Cultural Centre at Ayers Rock, expresses the culture of the Anangu, the aboriginal people of

Figure 12.22.
Uluru Visitors'
Centre, interior

central Australia. Before designing the building, the architectural team spent over a month at the site, to understand it themselves and have it explained to them by local people—through paintings and song as well as stories. Preliminary layouts of the building were sketched in sand. The site is at the edge where the desert meets the scrub and trees of the mountain. The building's form, based on the imagery of snakes, creates a strong sense of place without disturbing the endless continuity of the landscape. The building itself disturbs the land as little as possible but at the same time complements the form of gigantic Ayers Rock beyond. The plan is curvilinear and sinuous, respecting the shape of the sand dunes and forming, within the building, courtyards that will be shaded by vines and brush. By helping to knit visitors into the powerful landscape, the building becomes a strong demonstration of the place-sensitive nature of this aboriginal culture itself.[28]

One part of the inventiveness of Burgess's work clearly comes out of a strong and imaginative talent. But another part is rooted in communities and places, which he respects enough to make the inventive forms so convincing as to seem almost necessary, and even inevitable. In this respect the creative talent of the architect is being used not to make arbitrary form but to discover and uncover things that are latent in the place.

Feilden-Clegg, England

Most of the buildings discussed so far in this section are connected with a desire to resist globalization and reinforce local culture and place. While not rejecting the idea that buildings must be strongly anchored to place, the environmental movement is making architects realize that buildings must be designed with an understanding of how their production and use affects systems and cultures in different places. That idea is part of a larger concept

Figure 12.23 (left). Bengough's House, Bristol: sheltered housing for the elderly, with balconies to courtyard gardens (Feilden-Clegg, architects)
Figure 12.24 (right). Bengough's House, Bristol: internal hall as focus of activity

that concerns the overall sustainability of cultures—and of the earth—and the need for architects to design buildings that reinforce environmental and cultural sustainability. The *rootedness in culture and place* that this section refers to may be extended to the earth itself as an environmental system that must be maintained. Buildings that are "environmentally friendly" may be regarded in the same framework as the other buildings described here: they are all efforts to see architecture as a means of healing and strengthening systems, places, and cultures that are larger than the buildings themselves.

The literature on issues of sustainability is now large, and many important buildings have been designed as "green architecture." The architectural firm Feilden-Clegg, based in Bath, has done a series of projects that are not only environmentally sensitive but also anchored in communities and carefully designed for their clients.

The Olivier Theatre in Petersfield was designed for the Bedales School, which has a tradition of oak-framed buildings, including a library designed in the Arts and Crafts style in 1928. The theater has an oak frame built using green lumber and steel connectors and is clad inside and out with sustainable home-grown Douglas fir and English larch. The building is also naturally ventilated, partly with an underfloor system to store cool air and a tall central structure that provides a stack effect to draw the cool air through the building. The theater is one of the largest timber frame buildings erected recently in Britain and was built through a three-way collaboration between Feilden-Clegg, an oak framer, and a timber restoring firm; the school's students participated in its construction.[29]

The firm has also designed the offices of Greenpeace in London and an office building for the Building Research Establishment. The latter was

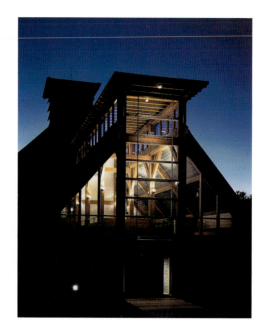

Figure 12.25.
The Olivier Theatre, Bedales School,
Petersfield: entrance foyer at night
(Feilden-Clegg, architects)

Figure 12.26.
The Olivier Theatre:
auditorium

Figure 12.27.
The Olivier Theatre:
student working on beam

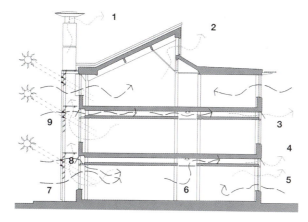

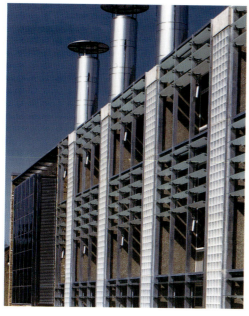

Figure 12.28.
The New Environmental
Office, Building Research
Establishment, Garston (section)

Figure 12.29.
The New Environmental
Office: active facade

designed as a prototype for an environmental "office of the future," which minimizes electricity use for lighting, fans, and cooling and enjoys more daylight penetration than similar buildings. All of the building's systems are designed to optimize energy performance. The building used recycled materials—secondhand bricks, recycled concrete aggregate, and recycled wood block floors. A system of adjustable louvers on the outside of the building can control the penetration of light—and heat—into the building at different times of day and year.[30]

One thing that distinguishes these projects is their use of contemporary materials and components to achieve buildings of human scale and carefully articulated purpose. Peter Clegg sees the work of the firm as combining two trends in English architecture: Arts and Crafts, as exemplified by such architects as Shaw and Voysey, and nineteenth-century engineering, as exemplified by Joseph Paxton and his Crystal Palace.[31] By continuing the optimistic stance of modernism, Feilden-Clegg's buildings demonstrate a pragmatic acceptance of contemporary production systems. But they also seek to stretch those systems, insisting on a responsibility toward communities and the environment as a whole, and entering into contractual arrangements that allow them to work more closely with subcontractors and fabricators.

Team ZOO, Japan

Team ZOO is a loosely grouped set of Japanese architecture firms that has designed schools, community buildings, houses, and hotels. Collectively, their work represents a powerful alternative to much of contemporary Japanese architecture. Many of the buildings are personal and playful, use warm materials, are carefully designed according to the activities of the people who will use them—frequently young children—and are designed so that even a large building is broken down in scale, to fit often complex contexts in old urban neighborhoods or villages. The buildings are deliberately designed not to be "corporate" or "bureaucratic." Local craftspeople are often employed, and in some cases new workshops are set up for the manufacture of personalized building components, like roof tiles.

In the Kodo Elementary School in Izushi, Hyogo Prefecture, by Atelier Iruka (Dolphin) of Team ZOO, the school's parts are broken into villagelike pieces that help to form many outdoor spaces for learning as well as direct connections between most indoor spaces and the outside. Detailed observations using videotape of actual usage of spaces in the existing school helped the architects understand the importance of nonprogrammed spaces to students, and the results of these observations were incorporated into the design.

The Uchijima Public Housing in Kinosaki, Hyogo Prefecture, also by Atelier Iruka, is a rental project where the residents participated in the design

Figure 12.30. Kodo Elementary School, Izushi, Hyogo Prefecture, Japan, 1991 (Atelier Iruka, Team ZOO, architects)

Figure 12.31.
Kodo Elementary School
(Atelier Iruka, Team
ZOO, architects)

Figure 12.32.
Kodo Elementary School
(Atelier Iruka, Team ZOO,
architects): site axonometric

Figure 12.33. Housing project at Uchijima, Kinosaki, Hyogo Prefecture, Japan, 1989–94 (Atelier Iruka, Team ZOO, architects): elevation

Figure 12.34. Housing project at Uchijima

Figure 12.35. Iwaya Junior High School, Awaji Island, Hyogo Prefecture, Japan, 1993 (Atelier Iruka, Team ZOO architects)

Figure 12.36. Iwaya Junior High School: students working on stair

and where the architects conducted observations of how the residents were altering their own dwellings. The buildings are arranged to form a community street and are linked by covered walkways to shelter paths from heavy snow. The residents also participated in landscaping the project. The success of this project led people in a different public housing unit nearby to begin to manage their community in the same way.

In Taiwan, the large administrative complex for I-Lan County by a different firm of Team ZOO, Atelier Zo (Elephant), is broken into individual pieces, each of which has a distinct sense of place. The building includes an almost parklike landscape on the roof, with pavilions, plantings, and places to sit, where employees can enjoy lunch and coffee breaks. The building helps to humanize a large institution by giving its separate parts a distinct identity and by incorporating individually crafted elements into its construction.

The work of the Team ZOO firms shows possible architectural results of the support and revival of local craft techniques. Team ZOO's buildings are not quaint or archaic in feeling, but they do subdivide buildings that are often seen as institutional into pieces of smaller scale, pieces that support the life of individual groups within large institutions and communities.

Figure 12.37.
Administrative complex for I-Lan
County, Taiwan (Atelier Zo,
Team ZOO architects)

Figure 12.38. Administrative complex for I-Lan County, Taiwan. Pavilion on roof

The Role of Architects

In history, the most aesthetically and spiritually powerful building traditions developed step by step, innovation by innovation, within cultural frameworks that allowed the gradual growth of intimate relationships between building and culture. In today's world, which does not have such culturally rooted processes, exemplary buildings are even more necessary to point up the importance of new processes. Individual buildings have a potentially powerful effect on the building culture as a whole. Architects' influence may extend outward, through the popular press and mass communications, the professional press and criticism, and the schools. Even though today a successful building may involve a difficult struggle, it can bring about a shared desire for more of the same, driving procedural and institutional innovations that will make such successful buildings easier to make. *Architects are the only players in the building culture who are now in a position to articulate a physical vision that can drive innovations in all the processes of the culture.*

The idea that buildings might elevate the spirit in a way that can be felt and not measured has been anathema in a world that depends on the satisfaction of explicit standards and functional demands. The contemporary building culture has been good at basing design on standards that can be explicitly described: zoning regulations, building codes, space standards for public housing, daylight standards, results of time/motion studies for factories and fast-food restaurants, retail economic analysis for shopping centers, cost analysis and "value engineering" for construction systems. The need to be explicit in a society that is driven by money, paper, and litigation has caused the more unquantifiable qualities of beauty, cultural meaning, and deep affective feelings to be put aside as things that are unimportant and "subjective."[32] The position of the architect has been made much more difficult by the basic split between the objective and the subjective—but this only points up the importance of the architect's task.

From one point of view, the role of architects is simply to make the "subjective" important again, to make buildings of such emotional power and usefulness that they become necessary.

HUMAN-BASED INSTITUTIONS

Emerging Frameworks for Building

13

Many of the innovations described so far, although important examplars of process or product, are unique and were achieved at great expense: higher architectural fees or construction costs, fights with the bureaucracy, the need for particularly enlightened clients or extensive research and development. That extraordinary activity does not play a role in most building, and in order for such innovations to spread, institutional change is needed. This chapter deals with institutional change that can positively transform the way most buildings get built, by supporting and encouraging the kinds of innovations already described:

- Communities themselves, all over the world, are reconnecting themselves to the strength of their own identity and the role that buildings and construction might play in their social and economic development.
- Institutions like banks, architecture and contracting firms, and agencies that administer zoning and building codes have introduced changes that allow decisions to be made on the basis of common sense applied to actual situations and that allow for improved communications among the institutions themselves.
- Education in architecture and building is beginning to recognize the need to develop understandings of more aspects of the building culture than just design alone and to help knit design and building back together.

Communities and Cities Anchored by Building

The most important institutions of the building culture are human communities themselves. In the past, communities—the people of an agricultural village in China, the patrons and citizens of Florence, the members of a New England town—supported building cultures that were understood, that embodied the community's values with respect to building, and that helped renew the community itself. In modern society, building cultures are divorced from their communities. People look to professionals or governments or banks to take care of the built environment. The idea that building is a fundamental expression of community identity and that a community might improve its own life through building activity is elusive: people have only limited control over the making of their own built world. Yet in both the "developed" and "developing" worlds, new initiatives point the way toward reanchoring the activity of building in the culture as a whole instead of abstract institutions, and of building as a means of healing the community itself.

Healing Communities in India and Papua New Guinea through Building

A common view of slums in India is that they represent nuisances, affronts to established society, and should be eliminated. Looking at a slum from the inside, however, one finds people with hopes and aspirations, like people everywhere, who are trying to make their way in the world, and many of them are vital contributors to the national economy.[1] As described in chapter 1, the slum may be a place of active growth, with a building culture that is largely well adapted to people's desires and means. In fact, more so than people in other modern communities, slum dwellers know what to do when it comes to providing shelter for themselves. They have precise ideas about what they want, know how much they can afford to pay, and understand the market of materials and labor. Although not everyone is a builder, the necessary skills are available within the community. Slum communities are capable of self-directed growth and the development and reinforcement of strong cultural traditions. However, what slum dwellers often do *not* have is the means to build, or the freedom to do so. They do not have access to credit, which makes it more difficult for them to build than people who do have such access, and they do not have land tenure, which makes their houses continuously subject to demolition.

Several organizations centered in the state of Maharashtra are working together to help communities become able to support fully functioning building cultures, in which the impediments of lack of credit and lack of land tenure disappear. These initiatives depend on direct social organization, grassroots savings schemes, and the development of enough political clout to gain land tenure and infrastructure.[2] They involve close work with people and builders for the introduction of better techniques for individual houses that are being repaired or reconstructed. It is detailed and sensitive work: a tiny detail can mean the difference between affordability and excess and can also make a big difference in people's lives. One intention is to develop particular building examples to generate a widespread awareness of designs and techniques so that through simple emulation and example, the slum may be improved through the efforts of people themselves.

An organization in Tamil Nadu, the Centre for Development Madras (CEDMA), has been involved for over twenty years with extremely low-income communities in the slums of Madras and Vellore. CEDMA has sponsored savings schemes, housing improvement schemes in which families borrow money, housing improvement schemes in which loans come in the form of materials, and actual housing projects among such groups as slum dwellers displaced from railroad rights-of-way. All of these projects have exhibited a recognition that shelter is only one part—albeit an essential part—of people's development and that strategies for providing shelter must recognize the ongoing process of people's individual and social development, within communities that are becoming more empowered.

One of these projects involved the direct participation of a community of cycle-rickshaw drivers and their families in designing a new settlement plan and the families' own houses.[3] The settlement plan was based both on traditional housing patterns in villages and urban slums and on the families' own desires for freestanding houses with particular layouts. The work took place at the point that the families had a secure livelihood and were able to pay off their loans. This effort was similar to the Mexicali project described in chapter 11 in that the families designed their own houses, but dissimilar in that it used local, well-understood methods of construction.[4]

The Community-Based Building Programme (CBBP), directed by David Week and Ken Costigan, began operation in Papua New Guinea in the early 1980s. The idea of the organization was partly to set up situations in which the activity of building would help to improve the local economy, through the use of local materials in the production of building components. This firm was based to some extent on the project in Mexicali and involved many

Figure 13.1. On-site layout of new settlement at Abdullapuram, near Vellore, for cycle-rickshaw drivers and their families

Figure 13.2.
Building doors and
windows for new set-
tlement at
Abdullapuram

Figure 13.3.
House construction at
Abdullapuram

Figure 13.4.
A family at its
new house at
Abdullapuram

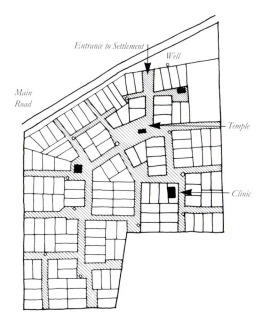

Figure 13.5.
Site plan of new settlement at Abdullapuram

Figure 13.6.
Shake-splitting line, Gavien Resettlement Scheme, East Sepik Province (Community Based Building Programme, Papua New Guinea)

Figure 13.7.
Erecting frame, Kumul Lodge, Enga Province, Papua New Guinea (Ken Costigan, UDC Architects)

305

Figure 13.8. Extended-family house cluster under construction for Sinai and Bungtabu Brown, East New Britain Province, Papua New Guinea, 1996 (Pacific Architecture, Sydney)

of same principles of on-site layout and responsibility on the part of families. At one point the CBBP was responsible for most of the public building work in one province of the country.[5] The work is being continued through projects that incorporate training programs, innovative methods of project management, and the employment of indigenous craftspeople and entrepreneurs. Ken Costigan writes, "People are still close enough to their ancestral heritage to re-invigorate that increasingly dormant or decaying source in a modern context, as part of what has been called a renaissance of indigenous cultures."[6]

These projects are attempting to use professional expertise in order to empower communities—and thereby liberate them from exclusive dependence on such expertise. In this respect, knowledge does not simply flow from the professional in a way that leaves the community and its individuals dependent. Instead, the projects' goal is that dependence on professionals is decreased, that more knowledge is shared, and that communities develop the capacity to make building decisions for themselves. The methods and the outward results differ, but in all cases there is an increased awareness or increased capability and eventually, perhaps, a strengthening of a healthy building culture. And these lessons might be useful not only in developing countries, but in the developed world as well.

Copenhagen and Portland

The ideas that a city may represent the shared view of a community that might come to some kind of agreement about its built environment may seem to be opposed to modern ideas of social diversity. However, in our present commodity culture, it is a myth that a city with fewer explicit controls on design and development is more democratic or more "free." Even in twentieth-century cities like Houston or Los Angeles, buildings are guided by controls that come, if not from zoning, from the rules and pragmatics of marketing, development, building codes, and finance. These cities have tightly constrained systems that produce characteristic sets of forms. The question is not whether or not there should be controls, but what kinds of controls should exist—and whether those controls represent a positive vision that emerges from the community itself or a means of exercising the intentions of external agents and corporations.

The city of Copenhagen, for example, has come to a set of common understandings concerning the preservation of the natural environment, the enhancement of pedestrian life, and the promotion of economic and social diversity. These understandings are expressed in policies and rules that guide building and planning and result in a gradual strengthening of the city's urban life. Tax revenues are shared regionally. The government supports housing and urban revitalization projects that directly involve community residents and are intended partly to retain as residents people who cannot pay high rents. Public transportation is excellent; the public works director sees his role as keeping traffic out of the city; bicycles are everywhere; and the amount of space dedicated to pedestrian use increases every year.[7]

Portland, Oregon, is in some respects the American version of this approach. It has a lively downtown; a historic building stock that has to a large extent escaped the ravages of demolition and redevelopment; livable neighborhoods; a good public transportation system; higher ridership on public transportation than the national average; and a high level of public involvement in decisions regarding planning and building. The seeds for this success were planted in 1972, with statewide land-use legislation that required municipalities with populations larger than 25,000 to contain their growth within urban growth boundaries. In addition, public funding for

Figure 13.9. Copenhagen: streets not overwhelmed by cars

Figure 13.10. Copenhagen: an active square in the center of the city

Figure 13.11. Light rail in Portland

public transportation allowed for construction of light rail lines to the suburbs. Within the downtown area itself, public transportation—comprising
the light rail line as well as buses—is free, with certain streets restricted to
buses.

Because these larger-scale planning initiatives have limited the land available for development, the downtown is taken seriously by businesses as a
place to locate. Public investment in downtown public space, including Pio-
neer Courthouse Squre, has made it even more attractive. New buildings are
designed in conformance with guidelines administered by the Planning
Department that help ensure that buildings' massing and materials and con-
tribution to the streets are helpful. While these guidelines are not universally
liked by architects, there is a general attitude of responsibility on the part of

many architects and developers to the larger health of the city, beyond the particular intentions of individual projects.

Neighborhoods and Groups of Neighbors

There is also a growing sense of local involvement in issues of planning, livability, and the built environment at a more local level than the city as a whole. Community-based organizations—ranging from neighborhood design review boards (for example, in the Back Bay area of Boston and the Georgetown area of Washington, D.C.), to local community development corporations in poorer neighborhoods, to groups that form on an ad hoc basis to protest the construction of a new highway or "big-box" retail store, to cohousing groups that form for the purpose of building themselves places to live—are all modern examples of the old idea that building emerges primarily out of the wishes and needs of a community. One positive effect of the elimination of large amounts of money from the federal government for new housing has been the development of smaller "infill" projects and the need for strong local coalitions to bring together money for these projects, along with more involvement from representatives of these coalitions.

In many of these cases, from India to Copenhagen to American neighborhoods, the effort of the community is not merely instrumental to the building issue at hand. The work the community does, and the built result, feed back into the community itself, strengthening ties among neighbors and promoting a longer-term rootedness and stability. In the best situations, the community has a stronger presence than any of the institutions of the building culture that exist within it—and is thereby able to exert its own values on the building culture, and not only be the unwitting recipients of processes outside its control.

Finance, Architecture/Construction, Regulation

Inside and outside mainstream institutions, there are efforts to make practice more responsive to real situations, to break down barriers between institutions, and to allow members of the building culture to have a more direct relationship with the quality of the built result.

Community-Based Banking

Large-scale financial institutions today base loan approval largely on abstract factors: statistical analyses of comparable situations, or prejudicial views that deny money to people living in particular neighborhoods. Positive initiatives have looked creatively at the question of collateral and have also been aggressive in getting construction money to people who had been shut out of the system for reasons not connected to their individual situations.

Hundreds of millions of people are shut out of the credit system not because they have no income but because they have no collateral. Many poor people in countries like India and Bangladesh have incomes, however small, from a wide variety of jobs. But they cannot save much because they spend most of the money they earn, and they have few or no assets that can be put up as security for a loan. They are therefore caught in a cycle of poverty that prevents them from ever having the capital to start a business or build a house. In Bangladesh, the Grameen Bank has pioneered a unique approach to this problem. Its loans, which are often very small but are enough to allow a person to start a tiny business, rely on *social rather than financial capital*. Loans are made to women who belong to groups, for individual projects such as the start-up of a small business, *and the group as a whole is responsible for ensuring that the individual lendee repays the loan*. If the group does not do this, then loans are not made to other members of the group. Social pressure, rather than the threat of foreclosure or repossession, guarantees repayment of the individual loans. The approach has been enormously successful in terms of rate of repayment (97 percent), number of loans made, and new businesses started, and recognition of the value of this approach has been spreading in international development circles beyond Bangladesh and in the West.[8]

This approach is successful for several reasons: it recognizes the importance that small amounts of money can have for large numbers of people at the grassroots level; it builds community by encouraging people to be responsible for each other; it recognizes that meaningful economic development might emerge locally, out of people's own skills and local culture. At the local level, the Grameen Bank thereby represents an alternative to the long-distance, abstract control that characterizes other banks. The bank is concerned with housing as well as economic development, and it sponsors low-interest loans for small houses, in groups of five families, each of which has to repay the loan before any of them can get a further loan.

A different kind of relationship to communities has been demonstrated for the last twenty years by the South Shore Bank in Chicago. The urban decay experienced by American cities in the decades following World War II was accelerated by the disinvestment of banks and other financial institutions in cities, particularly the redlining of parts of cities with large minority populations. The South Shore Bank, which was acquired in 1973 by a group of activist bankers and is minority-owned, adopted the approach that sound banking—and profit for the bank—is not incompatible with the idea of investment in minority communities. In collaboration with an affiliated real estate company and nonprofit developer, the bank has made significant inroads toward restoring the housing stock of a neighborhood that had been undergoing serious decay.[9]

The efforts of the Grameen Bank and South Shore Bank may seem minor in a building world that is dominated by powerful and profit-driven real estate interests, banks, and developers. These initiatives, however, have had a large impact in their own communities. Their influence goes beyond the provision of construction money to people who are cut out of conventional systems; it includes the very enfranchisement of people and groups.

Architectural and Construction Practice

In mainstream practice, some firms are attempting to construct bridges between themselves and clients and their communities, between parts of their own offices, and between themselves and builders. Some architects take jobs no farther than a certain distance away in order to maintain familiarity with building practices, knowledge of contractors and trades, the ability to maintain close contact with clients, and the ability to closely follow construction. One architect who insists on working close to home in New Bedford, Massachusetts, writes that "one sees every day the improvements for which one has been responsible. There is a connection to time, place and people. . . . If small cities are to survive, more people must choose this path."[10] Some deliberately take on work with a strong community orientation: low-income housing, work for minority communities, active participation in local planning issues, design of community centers. Much of this work pays little or nothing. These architects recognize that for the built environment to be in good health, a diverse population must have decent places to live, and issues of land use and downtown planning must be appropriately solved for everyone.

The culture of an architectural office may be a factor in the character of the result. The office of Behnisch + Partner in Stuttgart, a firm that designs buildings that are very light, transparent, and sometimes playful in feeling, relies on an office organization in which young designers are expected to play creative roles, creative exploration is encouraged, and the energy of all members of the office is respected. Within a modernist aesthetic, the firm's buildings arise out of a careful attention to human activity and, now, environmental concerns. According to one former member, people in the firm believe that there is a connection between the open character of the work that is done and the way the office is organized.[11] The office of Feilden-Clegg in Bath has included a small building firm as well as specialists in historic preservation, all of whom inform the office culture in matters of construction.

Architects who do not act as general contractors or take legal responsibility for construction may have relationships with builders in which a good deal of informal give-and-take occurs during the building process, even when the construction documents are highly specific and detailed. Particularly with smaller projects, the construction documents may be more minimal, with the expectation that a lot of things will be worked out on-site between the architect and the builder.

A small house I designed for myself was an example of a highly interactive process between designer (HD) and builder (TS). HD produced a minimal set of drawings, enough to get the building permit and allow TS to do a cost estimate of the house, which formed the basis for a construction contract. As construction proceeded, many decisions were worked out mutually between HD and TS: each party contributed his own expertise, with respect for the other's needs and skills. The building was built for the original estimate.

The architecture firm Line + Space, in Tucson, Arizona, has extended such arrangements by providing both architecture and construction services but requiring that an atmosphere of trust exist between the firm and client before the firm will undertake construction. The firm takes a fixed fee for its construction services, so cutting costs will benefit the client while not increasing the firm's profit. During construction, adjustments to the design

Figure 13.12. House designed by the author in close collaboration with builder

are made without the formality of change orders, and members of the firm work directly with craftspeople and laborers.[12]

In larger projects, a technique of collaboration known as "partnering" brings all of the major parties to a construction contract together at the onset of the contract, in informal meetings, to get to know each other and to understand mutual expectations and needs. This is intended to minimize conflict, not to change the relative roles of architect and contractor or their legal relationship. Putting architect and contractor into the same room helps them to find common ground.[13]

Improved relationships with contractors are only one aspect of a necessary reorientation of architectural practice. By continually asserting an exclusive claim to expertise, the architectural profession has isolated itself from other institutions of the building culture that have gained more control. The marginalization of the profession will not be reversed if architects continue to ignore changes in society and the business world that have resulted in different ways of conducting business. The profession has been reactive rather than creative and proactive in responding to the whittling away of its traditional responsibilities by contracting firms, government institutions, and other entities. A proactive stance, which many people are calling for, might include the following changes. They would not necessarily require a tempering of the profession's business orientation, and might even strengthen it:[14]

- *The reorganization of firms to allow specialized knowledge to be easily brought into play*, through consortiums that could easily form among different firms. In addition to large firms offering a wider array of architectural services ("full-service" firms), this change would promote the development of smaller, perhaps more specialized firms, with strong connections to each other, that could work together on specific projects.[15] This corresponds to other developments in business and anchors the architect more firmly in a professional culture of skilled people and professions, including building contractors, subcontractors, and manufacturers.

- *The active involvement of architectural firms in research that advances the field.* In combination, the conventional idea of architecture as art and the strong business orientation of the profession have not encouraged the type of investigation and dissemination of useful information seen in fields such as medicine, where research/teaching hospitals ensure that research is relevant to practice. Apart from being helpful to practice, a positive attitude toward research also helps to unify the culture itself through the collegial exchange of information. The firm Feilden-Clegg regularly contracts to do research on energy in buildings. This brings a culture of new knowledge into the office and allows for its easy application in new design projects.[16] Francis Duffy's firm, DEGW, does the same with the relationship of new technologies to the design of offices.[17] The office of Renzo Piano actively works with fabricators and engineers in the development of new construction techniques.

- *The reorienting of architecture firms from business to public service as their primary mission.* This does not mean that firms should cease making money— only that they might see their primary purpose as service to clients, communities, cities, and society as a whole. If the previous two innovations would help to anchor architectural practice more firmly into the building culture, this one would help anchor practice more firmly into the culture at large.

Implementation of these ideas would result in strengthening rather than weakening the architect's role—and this strengthening would not come at the expense of other professions.

Regulation

In the last two or three decades, traditional zoning ordinances have been stretched and modified in different ways. Changes have been introduced that allow small businesses in residential neighborhoods, recognizing the changing character of work, which has resulted partly from the downsizing of corporations.[18] The use of special districts and overlay zones has produced a geographically finer grain of zones to allow for a finer fit between zoning rules and the physical and social realities of a community. These overlay zones have included, for example, historic preservation districts, alley districts in neighborhoods where there is a desire to develop properties along back alleys, and zones for solar access.

Overlay zoning does not by itself change the procedures through which zoning is administered, since there is still an expectation that rules will be written in an explicit enough way that they can be administered mechanically. Some cities, including Portland, Oregon, have instituted *design review*, which deals with the quality of buildings as they affect the public realm.[19] Design review combines less explicitly defined standards with more discretionary judgment. Most municipalities are wary of laws that require human discretion for their administration—but many people are coming to realize that there may be no substitute for simple common sense and trust, within a framework of common intention.

The idea that regulation should be based on intention rather than on explicit rules lies behind *performance zoning*, which does not necessarily separate functions by zone but requires that projects of any kind need to meet minimum performance standards regarding such things as drainage, density, floor-area ratios, and buffers between uses. A form of performance zoning has been applied to Midtown Manhattan, based partly on expectations of light for streets and building interiors.[20] In Havana, Florida, such an ordinance has helped revitalize the town by making project approvals easier. Actual standards are derived from the nature of development; density and buffer requirements depend on the adjacent land use.[21] Zoning based on the immediate context of the building is also part of the residential zoning ordinance passed in San Francisco in 1979. Some of the regulations require, for example, that rear building setbacks be based on the setbacks of buildings on either side of them. This is done to avoid situations in which a building would project so far forward that an overly enclosed yard would be created on neighboring properties. The idea of a local relationship—rather than an absolute number—determining the standard is different from a regulation's being applied completely independently to all properties.

A different way of specifying the standards of a community is incorporated into some New Urbanism projects, which were discussed in the last chapter in terms of traditional forms. A major innovation in the new town of Seaside and subsequent developments by Duany and Plater-Zyberk is the use of prescriptive standards, as stated in the "urban code" developed for each project. This code requires certain materials and architectural elements, porches on houses, and specific positioning of houses relative to the street. Variety is permitted in the houses; certain types of houses are allowed on certain streets, and the code has different specifications for each type.

Compared to the subtle, internalized social codes that guided building in more coherent building cultures of the past, Seaside's rules are a crude approximation. However, they represent a bold social and legal move. Although zoning has had clearly definable architectural effects on the shape of communities, it does not specify architectural forms explicitly—the cultural and physical constraints that once helped the community maintain its own picture of itself do not exist any more. Hence the idea of the urban code.

Legally, Seaside's code is incorporated in deed restrictions rather than in zoning ordinances. Can such codes—and the ideas of community they imply—be applied to the more open and messy situation of cities, which have real constitutional limits on the amount of restriction they can impose and on the way that restriction may be maintained? Jerry Frug argues that "a primary city function—*the* primary city function—ought to be the cultivation and reproduction of the city's traditional form of human association."[22] In other words, it is the rightful place of government to support laws that foster community.

The question is whether a commonly understood set of prescriptive design standards is appropriate as a social idea—whether it is appropriate for a community to regulate what happens on private property more closely than the traditionally defined police power of zoning ordinances has. Zoning ordinances themselves go beyond issues that were important at the turn of the century, when slum dwellings fostered genuinely unhealthful conditions. They establish the character of neighborhoods, and the line between the traditional police power of government and such issues as aesthetics and character has become a fuzzy one.[23] It is now generally recognized, however, that a community has the legal right to establish and maintain a certain character. So the question becomes the nature of the standards' contents, not just their existence.

Performance-based regulation is also now being applied to *building codes*. As an alternative to the explicit specification of materials and techniques, these codes will state the *intent* of the rule—for example, wind loads and seismic loads the building needs to endure—and it will then be up to the architect to meet that intent, and show that it has been met.[24]

Innovations in Architectural Education

Finally, some hopeful initiatives are emerging within architecture schools and in alternative models outside architecture schools. Architecture schools cannot depart too far from the values and standards of the profession. However, there are many tensions between what the schools (and some individual faculty members within them) believe and what the profession (and many individual architects who practice within it) believes.[25] It is within this tension that cracks of resistance appear and initiatives that propose an alternative view are formed.

Some educational initiatives are attempting to define more appropriate architectural types and innovative technologies. These include work at the University of Miami on "traditional neighborhood development"; the emphasis at Notre Dame on principles of classical architecture; a series of studios at Berkeley dealing with new forms of suburban neighborhoods;[26] research carried out at architecture schools in Florence, Venice, and Versailles aimed at understanding the development of cities in terms of historic typologies; research at McGill University on new housing types to meet affordability requirements; research at the University of Tasmania on timber construction; and research at many schools, including Berkeley and Oregon, on energy use in buildings. These efforts are significant in their support for the idea that architectural knowledge can be explicitly understood and used, in the nonarbitrary yet exploratory nature of much of the work, in the attempt to be explicit about useful types and techniques, and in the systematic way that design work is linked to theoretical principles and rule systems.[27]

Within architecture schools, the traditional focus on design is being extended by studios that simulate conditions of actual practice, including the multiplicity of participants and the constraints of money and regulation. In some places, architecture students learn that they may have important roles outside traditional architectural offices—as people who help shape public policy about buildings, as programming consultants, as researchers and teachers. Outreach programs allow participation in public schools, assistance to neighborhood organizations (Pratt Institute's center in New York City was one of the first to offer such assistance), and situations that foster relationships to real clients.

Robert Gutman suggests transferring some of the job of architectural education from the schools to practice.[28] One initiative at the University of Oregon is connecting students with real projects. Oregon has dozens of small rural communities located far from major urban health care centers. Many of these communities have vulnerable populations—elderly and poor—in need of health care. However, they do not have the expertise or the money to buy the professional services that are needed to attract or develop health care facilities. A program run by Professor Jenny Young, the Rural Health Care Design Group, has employed students in internship positions to provide planning and design services to these communities.

These initiatives recognize that architectural practice is part of a much broader matrix of politics, production, and regulation. Students work in the context of community politics, client needs, and budgets. In some cases this work was instrumental in helping clients to think through their needs in a way they otherwise would not have done and to put together proposals that attracted resources for developing their buildings. They make connections between the university and the community at large[29] and begin to break down some of the barriers between architectural theory as taught in architecture schools, and architectural practice as it happens in the real world.

The involvement of architecture students with actual construction is sometimes seen as peripheral or even unnecessary to architectural education, and few architecture schools regularly allow for such experience as part of

Figure 13.13.
Design-build project on
the University of
Oregon campus

the professional program. Schools have mostly adopted the attitude that the profession has held since the end of the nineteenth century, which has separated design from building as much as possible and has assumed that the builder is simply an instrument of the architect's wishes. Even though the teaching of architectural history is taken seriously, a clearer understanding of how architects were trained and their historical relationship to the building process has not been emphasized.[30]

At Berkely, the Building Process program, headed by Christopher Alexander for twenty years from the early 1980s until 1998 with Hajo Neis playing an important role since 1992, allows students to engage in an integrated experience combining design and building at different scales. Other schools, including UCLA, the University of Washington, and Yale, have

Figure 13.14. Design-build project for camp in British Columbia (Stephen Duff, instructor)

Figure 13.15. Design-build project for camp in British Columbia

Figure 13.16. Stonemasons at the Cathedral of St. John the Divine in the 1890s

included direct construction experience as a required or optional part of student's curriculum.[31] At the University of Tasmania, design-build activities are linked to ongoing research in timber construction.[32]

At the University of Oregon, design-build projects run by Professor Stephen Duff have been based on the idea that design judgment in general will be enhanced when students have had experience dealing with real, full-scale buildings. Within this view, design and construction are not separate processes but instead proceed simultaneously, in a process of *craft*, and there is almost immediate feedback from the built state of the project at any moment, and the next step of design/construction. Projects involve full-scale mock-ups and the layout of buildings directly on the site, as well as actual construction.

At Auburn University, Samuel Mockbee has been directing a studio that combines design-build experience with community service: students undertake the design and construction of houses for needy rural families.[33] Schools like the Yestermorrow School in Vermont, outside the architecture school establishment, offer laypeople as well as architecture students and professionals direct construction training. Yestermorrow offers hands-on workshops of various kinds, ranging from basic house carpentry to environmentally friendly building systems. The school recognizes an important fact about the American building culture—that a good deal of residential construction and remodeling happens outside the established architectural profession and building trades.

And finally, the Cathedral of St. John the Divine in New York City, built with traditional stone techniques, has been under construction since 1892. Like the cathedrals of the Middle Ages, construction has proceeded in

Figure 13.17. Modern stoneworks and apprentices at the Cathedral of St. John the Divine

phases that have depended on the availability of resources. In the late 1970s the cathedral—which had been completed enough to be usable as a building and had become a strong social force in its neighborhood—undertook a new cycle of building. It brought over a master mason from England, who had been in charge of the restoration of a medieval cathedral, to direct the stonework. He used this opportunity to institute a unique program, the training of apprentice masons, many of whom were from poor neighborhoods nearby.[34] In this way the building's construction not only provided employment but also provided for the regeneration of a local building culture and the revival of a trade that was needed for the preservation and restoration of stone buildings.

Firms, governments, and university departments are inertial, and change of institutions is usually much harder to achieve than a unique innovation carried out by a determined individual. Indeed, strong institutional change sometimes relies on a single charismatic or powerful person—as with Gropius's transformation of the architecture school at Harvard, or Robert Moses's transformation of the character of public works in New York, or the deliberate efforts by CEOs of many innovative corporations to change the culture of work. But in most cases today individuals with power do not have vision, and change must come from the grass roots, slowly and painfully, relying on good ideas that gradually capture people's attention and imagination. If the building culture and its institutions are to be accurate expressions of the deep values and desires of people, positive changes to those institutions must be able to effectively use the knowledge and energy of the millions of people in them.

CONCLUSION

Cracks in the Concrete Pavement

> The attitude of Hindus to new doctrines has been to
> approach them with the thought that most probably have a
> trace of truth in them, worth absorbing, but that in the pro-
> cess it may be modified, as food is when it is cooked and
> eaten. If the result of combining other people's ideas is con-
> tradictory, they take the view that the contradictions of life
> have to be accepted, even though this can produce discon-
> certing results, in politics for example, where everybody
> seems to disagree, and then they vote unanimously for a
> motion they have argued against.
>
> —Theodore Zeldin,
> *An Intimate History of Humanity*

During the early part of this century, beliefs and attitudes about art, philosophy, and science gave justification to emerging trends in architecture, building production, and the formation of cities. Those trends—
industrial production and mass fabrication, zoning, the emergence of the
architectural profession as an institution divorced from craft—were not
invented from scratch by Le Corbusier, Walter Gropius, or any other master
of the modern movement. In addition to designing their own buildings,
these architects acted to legitimize existing trends. Scholars often explain this
course by saying that architecture was simply responding to the zeitgeist, or
spirit of the times, and could not have taken a different path.

However, to some extent, *a conscious choice was made* in the field of architecture, a choice that helped ensure the success of emerging trends and forces
of production. It is unclear what would have happened if different architectural philosophies had been supported more strongly.

If our present building culture is only a passive result of the present zeitgeist, how can we imagine improving the way buildings are made, without
fundamental social and cultural change? Doesn't one basic premise of the
book—that buildings emerge out of their larger cultures—mean that nothing can be done about the predicament architecture and building are in?

Accepting the arguments of this book seems to put us into a state of paralysis or resignation, forcing us to accept the building culture as it is.

Even within the ideas of this book, however, it is possible to believe in a more hopeful set of ideas. Such ideas reject the notions that conscious thought cannot be brought to bear on difficult human problems and that our culture is something so monolithic that it might prevent its own transformation from within. These ideas support the belief that a conscious choice *can* be made about buildings and the ways they are built. They also recognize that there is a good deal of diversity in contemporary society—a diversity of subcultures as well as of ideas—which, if respected, might provide the seeds of positive change.

The dominant culture of today, which works through the building culture to prevent the production of a humane and deeply felt environment, an environment of "belonging," is not completely monolithic. It has aspects of pluralism in which individuals and groups have been able to assert their own identities. Some unhelpful hierarchies are breaking down, and different views and people are beginning to mix. The culture contains, however tentatively, new attitudes and procedures, like little flowers poking up through cracks in a concrete pavement, that point to the possibility of positive change.

What are these positive attitudes struggling to make themselves felt?

- The recognition of the importance of non-Cartesian modes of thought.
- Science dealing with complexity and whole systems, instead of purely reductionist models.
- The wish for local community along with globalization.
- Serious concern for sustainability and the environment.
- A renewed appreciation of tradition and craft.
- Changes in the business world, with businesses becoming more client- and worker-centered and moving away from top-down management.
- Attempts to break down barriers between institutions.
- A desire for plain-speaking common sense instead of bureaucratic gobbledegook.

These attitudes, which are shared by many people, work similarly with respect to the transformation of different social and cultural institutions. In health care, there is a new emphasis on the "whole person" and on teams of professionals working closely together. In business, new management strategies allow for a decentralization of control within a framework of common goals for the organization.[1] In law, the need to incorporate commonsense systems of legislation and administration is being recognized.[2] In education, there is a movement toward smaller schools where people know each other and where parents and members of the community can participate in policy and the everyday work of educating children.[3] In politics, local communities are taking control of functions once handled by larger organizations or government.[4] In architecture and building, these attitudes have helped to seed the initiatives of the last three chapters, which together are the basis for new cultures of building that may emerge out of existing ones.

Through what sort of mechanism can these initiatives can be taken seriously, supported, and modified? It will be gradual and evolutionary rather than revolutionary.[5] Inside and outside the existing institutions of the building culture, an effective mechanism will respect helpful diversity and the tiniest hints of positive actions and experiments. Architects, builders, educators, and others in the building culture, sharing an intention of improvement, will be alert to helpful changes and innovations and will act to support them. In different communities all over, new building cultures will gradually emerge out of existing ones in which each culture respects the realities of its own situation, learns from other cultures, and is capable of producing buildings that suit its particular place and people.

Because of the nature of this gradual transformation, we cannot invent a healthy building culture from scratch. Indeed, it has not been the aim of this book to encourage the invention of a particular, singular building culture. Such all-encompassing experiments are bound to fail, because they do not respect the realities of existing systems of production.

Consider the production-oriented aspects of the Arts and Crafts movement in the 1880s, or the alternative-lifestyle building movement of the 1970s, with geodesic domes and attempts to subvert building codes, or Hassan Fathy's experiments in Egypt. All were valuable experiments: well-meaning attempts to provide alternatives to systems of production that were inadequate in various ways. They also represented rejections of the dominant larger culture. To a large extent, the Arts and Crafts movement represented a rejection of English industrial society and connected itself with other social experiments that had similar views. The alternative-lifestyle builders of the 1970s were protesting the American corporate capitalism that was implicated in the Vietnam War. Fathy was looking strongly to the Egyptian village past and particularly to traditional methods of construction that were not part of emerging modern life. The housing project in Mexicali described in chapter 11 was similarly separated from the dominant systems of building production around it.

For example, the failure of Fathy's project at New Gourna, near Luxor, is often attributed to its *location*: the people for whom the project was intended did not want to move one or two kilometers from their village of mud huts near the Valley of the Kings, because such a move would deprive them of their livelihood, selling artifacts from the tombs to tourists. But if the *method of production*, using traditional construction techniques, was such a good idea, why was it not taken up in other projects nearby? Why could the Egyptian government not get other families to move into the houses? Why did the technique, which was known up and down the Nile Valley, not take hold? Although it was still used in traditional Nubian villages, south of Luxor, until they were flooded during the construction of the Aswan Dam, it may have become too unfamiliar to people outside those villages, seen as producing buildings that were not durable and not "modern." The method of asking craftspeople to use traditional techniques instead of concrete frames and brick infill was just not enough a part of contemporary practice for people to feel comfortable with it. In other words, there was nothing for people to grab onto, nothing familiar within which they could see other things changing; perhaps there was not enough connection to the buildings that they actually aspired to. Although the existing culture of concrete-and-brick building had certain aspects that were problematic, it also may have had other features that were working well: familiarity of buildings, durability (or perceived durability) of buildings, culturally shared knowledge of techniques.

Certainly such experiments are useful in that they point up ideals and develop new techniques. But often they do not themselves represent a model that can be generally applied.

How, then, can positive change occur? If the wholesale replacement of an existing building culture by a newly invented system of production is doomed to failure, then we must look to much more evolutionary changes, ones with the following features:

- They do not reject the positive features of the existing production system.
- They allow for their own evolution and change by respecting the skill and intention of people who will take them up—people who may not have originally instigated the changes or invented the new technique.
- They are introduced gradually enough that the building culture can tolerate them on its own terms.
- They support existing positive social trends.

This is not to say that wholesale change in the system of building production is not necessary or possible. It only means that the reality of the existing building culture, *no matter how objectionable it may appear to be*, must nevertheless be taken very seriously, even as one looks forward to such wholesale change. This is possible if one sees the culture not as a monolithic and unchangeable system but as a system that *includes*, in and among its problems and dominant institutions, all the attempts at change and resistance—the cracks in the concrete pavement.

Advocates of pluralism often claim that it is the most natural state of people and groups to be so different from each other that the most important thing social institutions can therefore do is support those differences. Suppose, however, that we see today's version of pluralism not as absolute and timeless but, instead, as a timely and political accompaniment to contemporary social movements. Suppose we assume, in fact, that a typical pluralistic culture needs to find more common ground and that it will do so. Then pluralism itself becomes the cultural vehicle through which appropriate shared cultural rules will emerge through a kind of natural selection, in which new ideas are freely offered and then accepted or rejected in a marketplace in which many people participate. This idea of pluralism as a "genetic vehicle" through which the most valuable types and processes will gradually emerge and continue to evolve, through the actions of many people in the culture, might be regarded as the great and unique opportunity of modern pluralistic society. The encouragement of appropriate forms and techniques will lead not only to more appropriate building cultures but also to the emergence of differences among building cultures themselves.

Throughout most of history, innovation has occurred mostly within the framework of commonly accepted type and technique, and so far this book has argued that such a framework is essential. Here we take the optimistic point of view that today's pluralism may be a vehicle toward the emergence of such shared understandings, because in the *absence* of commonly accepted types and processes, a pluralistic framework allows for the visibility and testing of many different ideas by different people.

Therefore any well-intentioned effort, no matter how improbable-seeming, needs to be looked at seriously—and nothing can be ruled out as a potential contributor to a new, emerging, shared culture of building. If we develop a more commonly shared set of intentions about the deep meaning that the built world might have to people, and about the need for shared values of community in our buildings and cities, we need not fear new ideas and experiments, which will simply win or lose when measured against those intentions. If those shared intentions do not exist—and they do not yet exist in a common enough way—then there are no criteria for evaluation, arguments lose their grounding, and the debate becomes one based on power and will rather than on reason.

The first shared understanding might be that the 2 billion buildings in the world, and those still to be built, are all important. They are not just neutral containers for human activity; nor are they just the aesthetic icing on the cake of other things that are more worthy of serious attention. They are important in fundamental ways, intertwined with our lives and communities—so much so that it often becomes difficult to understand the changes that have taken place in the connection between buildings and the cultures that make them.

We have become accustomed to thinking about buildings as physical commodities to be bought and sold and about the process of making buildings as something that is only instrumental to the built result. That is the assumption of modern systems of production and consumption—and the legacy of architectural modernism, which is itself the result of several hundred years of changing thought. But in fact there is a reciprocal relationship between *buildings* and *building*, between the built world and the cultures that produce it. A healthy building culture produces beautiful and genuinely useful buildings, and the production of such buildings itself reinforces the health of the culture, in turn strengthening the ability of the culture to make more such buildings.

In the end, the beauty of the built world comes from the people in it, and they all have a stake in its beauty and its ability to improve their lives. If this concept begins to be recognized by those concerned about the built world, then there is a chance that the hints of new and healthy ways of making buildings—the flowers growing through the cracks in the concrete—will begin to grow and develop into new and sensible building cultures that can make beautiful things as a matter of course.

NOTES

Introduction

1. There are 6 billion people, most of them in families of four, five, or six. Most families live in individual houses, with some in apartment houses, yielding around a billion houses; then there are workplaces, outbuildings, public buildings, shops, factories, warehouses, farm buildings, and so on.

2. The literature that is critical of the modern built environment is vast and ranges from popular books to academic texts, across the fields of architectural criticism, sociology, urban studies, and others. The beginning of this criticism is often attributed to Jane Jacobs's *The Death and Life of Great American Cities* (New York: Random House, 1961) and also included such books as Brent Brolin's *The Failure of Modern Architecture* (New York: Van Nostrand Reinhold, 1976) and Peter Blake's *God's Own Junkyard* (New York: Holt Rinehart & Winston, 1964). More recent books include the Prince of Wales's *A Vision of Britain* (New York: Doubleday, 1989) and James Kunstler's *The Geography of Nowhere* (New York: Simon & Schuster, 1993). Many works in environment-behavior studies deal with the failure of the environment in social and psychological terms.

3. Although the idea of a building culture may seem apparent, and it is perhaps implicitly understood that such cultures exist, there are not many written works in which the term *building culture*, as it refers to the human systems described in this book, explicitly appears. One work that does use the term is an article by Jane Morley, "Building themes in construction history: Recent work by the Delaware Valley group," *Construction History* 3 (1987).

4. Nikolaus Pevsner, *An Outline of European Architecture* (Harmondsworth: Penguin, 1963), 15.

5. There are various definitions of vernacular architecture. Some of them have to do with the idea of *place*: buildings that are "indigenous," built of local materials, responding to local climate and customs—"primitive building," like the mud huts of Africa, the stone houses of southern Italy, the longhouses of Malaysia. Some have to do with professional roles: buildings that are built by "ordinary people," not by architects or builders. None of these definitions really does the trick: it is in fact extremely difficult to draw boundaries between the vernacular and the nonvernacular. The definition usually used here is "buildings most likely to be built at a particular place and time." This definition recognizes the importance of foreign influences; it allows for architects who are themselves "just designing" ordinary buildings; and it recognizes the pervasiveness of modern systems of production.

6. The resistance of architectural historians to deal with connections between their own specialties and the vernacular, or, for that matter, with links to other styles and cultures may be due to a scarcity of documents regarding borrowing and diffusion in history in general. "The profession has systematically underestimated the range and role of diffusion in history. This tendency has been reinforced by the parochialism that concentration on a single literary tradition is bound to induce. . . . The literary record therefore tends to divide humankind into separate and more or less watertight compartments. Everyone who depends on texts for evidence will be impelled to overlook or minimize the borrowings across cultural and literary boundaries that did, in fact, occur." William H. McNeill, "Diffusion in history," in Peter J. Hugill and D. Bruce Dickson, eds., *The Transfer and Transformation of Ideas and Material Culture* (College Station: Texas A&M University Press, 1988), 77–78. This point is made in another way by Michael Camille, "Prophets, canons and promising monsters," *Art Bulletin* 78, no. 2 (June 1996): 199: "Liminal works, that is, works which are both spatially marginal and which cross or come between two distinct periods, often fail to achieve canonical status."

7. Christopher Alexander, *The Timeless Way of Building* (New York: Oxford University Press, 1979), and *The Nature of Order* (New York: Oxford University Press, forthcoming).

8. See Aldo Rossi, *The Architecture of the City* (Cambridge: MIT Press, 1984), and Rafael Moneo, "On typology," *Oppositions* 13 (Summer 1978).

9. N. J. Habraken, *The Structure of the Ordinary: Form and Control in the Built Environment* (Cambridge: MIT Press, 1998).

10. A seminal article is Fred Kniffen, "Louisiana house types," *Annals of the Association of American Geographers* 26, no. 4 (Dec. 1936): 179–93.

11. Henry Glassie, *Folk Housing in Middle Virginia: A Structural Analysis of Historic Artifacts* (Knoxville: University of Tennessee Press, 1975). See also his "Eighteenth-century cultural process in Delaware Valley folk building," *Winterthur Portfolio* 7 (1972): 29–57, and "The variation of concepts within tradition: Barn-building in Otsego County, New York," *Geoscience and Man* 5 (June 1974, 1974): 177–235.

12. Recent books that deal with building history include Richard Goldthwaite, *The Building of Renaissance Florence* (Baltimore: Johns Hopkins University Press, 1980); C. W. Chalklin, *The Provincial Towns of Georgian England: A Study of the Building Process, 1740–1820* (Montreal: McGill-Queens University Press, 1974); Catherine Bishir, Charlotte V. Brown, Carl R. Lounsbury, and Ernest H. Wood III, *Architects and Builders in North Carolina* (Chapel Hill: University of North Carolina Press, 1990); Linda Clarke, *Building Capitalism: Historical Change and the Labour Process in the Production of the Built Environment* (London: Routledge, 1992), an analysis of London's development; and James Ayres, *Building the Georgian City* (New Haven: Yale University Press, 1998).

13. William Coaldrake, *The Way of the Carpenter: Tools and Japanese Architecture* (New York and Tokyo: Weatherhill, 1990), 128–31.

14. Teresa Osterman Green, "The birth of the American paint industry" (M.A. thesis, University of Delaware, 1965).

15. The point is made in many places. For a description of technology as a social process in American architectural history, see Martin Harms, "1770, 1870, 1970: Craft, the machine, and human transaction in the technology of three Philadelphia buildings" (Ph.D. diss., University of Pennsylvania, 1992).

16. See, for example, Stan Sesser, "Logging the rain forest," *New Yorker*, May 27, 1991, 42. For an account of the relationship between new architectural technologies and the fate of American forests, see Steve Moore, "Feller-bunchers, grapple-skidders, chippers, and Martin Heidegger in the Great North Woods," *Center: Architecture and Design in America* 10 (1997): 92–105.

17. Personal observations and interviews in Ukraine, July 1990.

18. Information from David Week.

19. Edward Shils, *Tradition* (Chicago: University of Chicago Press, 1981), is an excellent account of the idea of tradition. See also T.S. Eliot, " Tradition and the Individual Talent," in T. S. Eliot, *Selected Essays 1917–1932* (New York: Harcourt, Brace and Company, 1932), 3–11.

20. See, for example, Martin Pawley, "A precedent for the Prince," *Architectural Review* 187, no. 1115 (Jan. 1990): 80–82, a particularly pernicious example of this view.

21. This meaning was applied to the question of development in Third World cultures, which have often maintained a large number of vernacular buildings, in an article by Janet Abu-Lughod, "Disappearing dichotomies: First World—Third World; Traditional—Modern," *Traditional Dwellings and Settlements Review* 3, no. 2 (Spring 1992): 7–12. In this article, Abu-Lughod introduces the concept of "traditioning," as an active verb, in much the same way that John Turner introduced the idea of "housing" as a verb, in his *Freedom to Build* (New York: Macmillan, 1972) and *Housing by People* (London: Marion Boyars, 1976).

22. William Morris, "The worker's share of art," *Commonweal* (Apr. 1885), quoted in Asa Briggs, ed., *William Morris: Selected Writings and Designs* (Harmondsworth: Penguin, 1962), 140–41.

23. In opposition to this view, it may be argued that the production of some of the most enduring works of architecture, from the Pyramids of Giza on down, has depended on many people who were slaves or otherwise not acting according to the socialist ideals of William Morris. But in the same way that we are cautioned to look at history accurately with respect to the means and conditions of production, we should also recognize that an Egyptian stonecutter 4,500 years ago, or a medieval stonecutter 800 years ago, likely lived in a psychological world that was very different from our own. This might have been a world in which the economic conditions of work that we would now consider to be unacceptable were not incompatible with spiritual fulfillment in carrying out the work itself.

Chapter 1

1. Richard Critchfield, *Villages* (Garden City, N.Y.: Anchor Books, 1983), vii.

2. Clifford Geertz, "Thick description: Toward an interpretive theory of culture," in *The Interpretation of Cultures* (New York: Basic Books, 1973), 3–30.

3. This view is expressed by Critchfield (*Villages*, 341–46). Critchfield cites the anthropologist Robert Redfield, *Peasant Society and Culture* (Chicago: University of Chicago Press, 1956).

4. Roxana Waterson, *The Living House: An Anthropology of Architecture in South-east Asia* (Singapore: Oxford University Press, 1990), 101–3.

5. Peter Nabokov and Robert Easton, *Native American Architecture* (New York: Oxford University Press, 1989).

6. Christine Hugh-Jones, *From the Milk River: Spatial and Temporal Processes in Northwest Amazonia* (Cambridge: Cambridge University Press, 1979), 43.

7. A very good introduction to this material is found in Paul Oliver, *Dwellings: The House across the World* (Austin: University of Texas Press, 1987), and an encyclopedic treatment, covering hundreds of different cultures, is Oliver's *Encyclopedia of Vernacular Architecture of the World* (Cambridge: Cambridge University Press, 1997).

8. See, for example, Edward Allen, *Stone Shelters* (Cambridge: MIT Press, 1969), 80–81.

9. Waterson, *The Living House*.

10. Torvald Faegre, *Tents: Architecture of the Nomads* (Garden City, N.Y.: Anchor Books, 1979), 9–59.

11. Matthew Johnson, *Housing Culture: Traditional Architecture in an English Landscape* (Washington: Smithsonian Institution Press, 1993), 55–56.

12. Edward A. Gargan, "Village life in India is invaded by big city tastes," *New York Times*, Apr. 16, 1992, 3.

13. Critchfield, *Villages*, 225–34.

14. "It makes you think of Cobbett's 'Great Wen' and the anarchic evils of early industrialisation. . . . And yet to see it in these terms is already to fall into a sentimental and peculiarly British trap—that of thinking of industry and its concomitant urban growth as something inherently bad." Gillian Tindall, *City of Gold: The Biography of Bombay* (New Delhi: Penguin, 1992), 3.

15. This does not necessarily imply a depopulation of the countryside. In India the countryside can support only so many people, even within an agricultural system that is still highly labor-intensive.

16. The material in this section comes from personal observations, conversations in India with Tom Kerr in July and Aug. 1995, and from Meera Bapat, "Shanty town and city: The case of Poona," *Progress in Planning* 15, part 3 (1981).

17. Tom Kerr's phrase.

Chapter 2

1. Many of these buildings are described in John Schofield, *Medieval London Houses* (New Haven: Yale University Press, 1994), a book based on both archaeological and documentary evidence of the City.

2. These lists are from John Harvey, *Medieval Craftsmen* (London: Batsford, 1975).

3. L. F. Salzman, *Building in England down to 1540* (Oxford: Oxford University Press, 1952), 294.

4. Harvey, *Medieval Craftsmen*, 36. In London, it was not until the second half of the eighteenth century that the post of district surveyor, an official clearly acting on behalf of the government, was established.

5. H. Thomas Johnson, "Cathedral building and the medieval economy," *Explorations in Entrepreneurial History*, 2d ser., 4, no. 3 (Spring–Summer 1967): 191–210.

6. Of course, not all building workers were property owners, but the rough proportion, based on records of property ownership, might be valid. Among the 426 property owners, 24 were in clerical/legal occupations, 90 in cloth and wool, 19 in clothing, 56 in leather, and 88 in food, and 75 were merchants. Data is from

Derek Keene, *Survey of Medieval Winchester i, part I* (Oxford: Oxford University Press, 1985), 352–65.

7. Harvey, *Medieval Craftsmen*, 20–22.

8. See, for example, Ronald Brunskill, *An Illustrated Handbook of Vernacular Architecture* (London: Faber and Faber, 1978), 199.

9. The word *designed* is in quotation marks because even that activity was not the same as it is today.

10. John Harvey, *The Gothic World* (New York: Harper & Row, 1969), 32.

11. Ibid. It is these masons whom Harvey and other writers consider architects—and indeed they were, if architecture is the conception of a building or part of a building before it is built, and involves not only the ability to repeat something by rote but also the ability to create something new. But they were still so intimately involved with the building's construction that they cannot be considered architects in today's sense of the word.

12. Harvey, *Medieval Craftsmen*, 127.

13. John James, *The Contractors of Chartres* (Dooralong, Australia: Mandorla, 1979) and *Chartres: The Masons Who Built a Legend* (London: Routledge & Kegan Paul, 1982).

14. Douglas Knoop and G. P. Jones, "The first three years of the building of Vale Royal Abbey, 1278–1280: A study in operative masonry," *Trans. Quatuor Coronati Lodge* 44 (1931): 4.

15. See, for example, Gianluigi Maffei, *La Casa Fiorentina nella Storia della Citta* (Venezia: Marsilio Editore, 1990), for a comprehensive account, including many drawings of Florentine houses and house complexes.

16. Richard Goldthwaite, "The Florentine palace as domestic architecture," *American Historical Review* 77 (1972): 977–1012.

17. Maffei, La Casa Fiorentina.

18. Goldthwaite, *The Building of Renaissance Florence*, 13–14, 19.

19. Ibid, 399.

20. William E. Wallace, *Michelangelo at San Lorenzo: The Genius as Entrepreneur* (Cambridge: Cambridge University Press, 1994), 152.

21. Goldthwaite, *The Building of Renaissance Florence*, 252–66.

22. Samuel Cohn Jr., *The Laboring Classes in Renaissance Florence* (New York: Academic Press, 1980), 66–71.

23. This is described in detail by Richard Goldthwaite in "The building of the Strozzi Palace: The construction industry in Renaissance Florence," in William M. Bowsky, ed., *Studies in Medieval and Renaissance History*, vol. 10 (Lincoln: University of Nebraska Press, 1973), [97]–194. See also Goldthwaite's *The Building of Renaissance Florence*.

24. Goldthwaite, "The building of the Strozzi Palace."

25. Wallace, *Michelangelo at San Lorenzo*, 140.

26. Ibid., 141.

27. Goldthwaite, *The Building of Renaissance Florence*, 221–22.

28. Ibid., 368.

29. Wallace, *Michelangelo at San Lorenzo*, 41.

30. James S. Ackerman, "Architectural practice in the Italian Renaissance," *Journal of the Society of Architectural Historians* 13, no. 3 (Oct. 1954), 3–11.

31. Wallace, *Michelangelo at San Lorenzo*, 89.

32. Ibid., 124.

33. Ibid., 137.

34. See, for example, Donald Olsen, *Town Planning in London: The Eighteenth and Nineteenth Centuries* (New Haven: Yale University Press, 1964); John Summerson, *Georgian London* (Harmondsworth: Penguin, 1962).

35. This system is described for towns outside London in C. W. Chalklin, *The Provincial Towns of Georgian England*.

36. Construction processes are described in detail in Ayres, *Building the Georgian City*.

37. In 1900 there were 8,266 garment manufacturing establishments, out of a total of 39,776 manufacturing establishments in total, employing 90,950 workers, out of a total of 462,763 workers. These census figures are reported in Kenneth T. Jackson, ed., *The Encyclopedia of New York City* (New Haven and New York: Yale University Press and the New-York Historical Society, 1995), 359–60.

38. But even brick firing was becoming more mechanized; the nineteenth century saw a number of important inventions that led to greater and more consistent production.

39. The archives of the McKim Mead and White firm in the New-York Historical Society contain the correspondence files relating to the construction of the Metropolitan Club. Background information on the building may be found in Paul Porzelt, *The Metropolitan Club of New York* (New York: Rizzoli, 1982), and in Leland Roth, *McKim Mead and White Architects* (New York: Harper & Row, 1983).

40. This information about 64 Oliver Street comes from the contract books of John Snook in the archives of the New-York Historical Society.

41. Jacob Riis, *How the Other Half Lives* (New York: Dover, 1971).

Chapter 3

1. Data in table is from an article by Robert Murray and Kermit Baker, "Architecture market outlook: Two crystal balls," *Architectural Record* 184, no. 6 (June 1996): 37, concerning a report by the Economics Department, Construction Information Group, McGraw-Hill Information Services Company.

2. This is more true in the United States than in Europe, where more office buildings are custom designed for particular tenants.

3. For a detailed description of the process of office building development, see John R. White, ed., *The Office Building: From Concept to Investment Reality* (Chicago and Washington: Counselors of Real Estate [American Society of Real Estate Counselors], the Appraisal Institute and the Society of Industrial and Office Realtors Educational Fund, 1993). For a historical account of the development of skyscrapers in New York and Chicago, see Carol Willis, *Form Follows Finance: Skyscrapers and Skylines in New York and Chicago* (New York: Princeton Architectural Press, 1995).

4. See, for example, Peter Hellman, "The fine art of assemblage," *Real Estate Review* 4, no. 2 (Summer 1974): 101–8.

5. Competitions are relatively rare in the United States, but they are normal practice in some countries in Europe, where virtually every project of any public importance is the subject of a competition; in these countries, architecture firms expect to spend a certain amount of their time and resources on uncompensated competitions that they are likely not to win. This system allows young and innovative firms to be "on the playing field" along with everyone else and for new ideas to be considered equally.

6. Conversations with Rob Thallon, University of Oregon, Feb. 1998.

7. Conversation with Rob Thallon, Feb. 11, 1998.

8. National Association of Home Builders, *1997 Housing Facts, Figures, and Trends*.

9. Robert Gutman, *The Design of American Housing: A Reappraisal of the Architect's Role* (New York: Publishing Center for Cultural Resources, 1985), 38–39.

10. Wendy Moonan, "Who needs an architect?," *Architectural Record* (Nov. 1997): 117. The figures are from the National Association of Home Builders.

11. Gutman, *The Design of American Housing*, 9.

12. The stock-plan businesses are described in ibid.

13. Katherine Cole Stevenson and H. Ward Jandl, *Houses by Mail: A Guide to Houses from Sears, Roebuck and Company* (Washington: Preservation Press, 1986).

14. Donald Albrecht, ed., *World War II and the American Dream: How Wartime Building Changed a Nation* (Washington and Cambridge: National Building Museum and MIT Press, 1995). This work is an exhibition catalog from the National Building Museum, Washington.

15. Richard Bender, *A Crack in the Rear-View Mirror: A View of Industrialized Building* (New York: Van Nostrand Reinhold, 1973), 110–16.

16. U.S. Department of Commerce, Bureau of the Census, 1995.

17. Manufactured Housing Institute statistics.

Chapter 4

1. For a thorough account of this process, see Cassandra Adams, "Japan's Ise Shrine and its thirteen-hundred-year-old recontruction tradition," *Journal of Architectural Education* 52 no. 1 (Sept. 1998): 49–60.

2. Michael Jeremy and M. E. Robinson, *Ceremony and Symbolism in the Japanese Home* (Honolulu: University of Hawaii Press, 1989), 141–42.

3. Ismet Khambatta, "The meaning of residence in traditional Hindu society," in Jean-Paul Bourdier and Nezar Alsayyad, eds., *Dwellings, Settlements, and Tradition* (Berkeley: International Association for the Study of Traditional Environments, 1989), 262.

4. Waterson, *Living House*, 122.

5. This was the case, for example, with many medieval European cities.

6. This is described in some detail in Goldthwaite, *The Building of Renaissance Florence*. See also Goldthwaite's "The building of the Strozzi Palace."

7. Nikolaus Pevsner, *The Englishness of English Art* (London: Architectural Press, 1956), 83–84.

8. Christian Norberg-Schulz, *Nightlands* (Cambridge: MIT Press, 1996), 36.

9. Juni-chiro Tanizaki, *In Praise of Shadows* (New Haven, Conn.: Leete's Island Books, 1977), 17–18.

10. Coaldrake, *The Way of the Carpenter*, 5.

11. This is described by Michael Dennis for the French *hôtel* in *Court and Garden* (Cambridge: MIT Press, 1986); for the colonial Virginia house by Henry Glassie in *Folk Housing in Middle Virginia*; for the city of Edinburgh by Peter Reed in "Form and context: A study of Georgian Edinburgh," in Thomas Markus, ed., *Order in Space and Society: Architectural Form and Its Context in the Scottish Enlightenment* (Edinburgh: Mainstream Publishing, 1982).

12. This is described for various institutional buildings like schools, prisons, and hospitals by Thomas Markus, in *Buildings and Power* (London: Routledge, 1993), in which Markus uses the "space syntax" techniques of Bill Hillier to demonstrate these changes. See also Bill Hillier and Julienne Hanson, *The Social Logic of Space* (Cambridge: Cambridge University Press, 1984), and Bill Hillier, *Space Is the Machine* (Cambridge: Cambridge University Press, 1996).

13. Stanford White did it another way: he belonged to many exclusive clubs in New York, whose members included the city's "movers and shakers." Some see McKim Mead and White as the prototype for the modern architecture firm.

14. An article by Edwin H. Silverman, "Architecture is a business!," *Pencil Points* 20 (Dec. 1939): 780–90, suggests that it was necessary, up until the first decades of this century, to teach architects how to run a business.

15. Andrew Abbott, *The System of Professions* (Chicago: University of Chicago Press, 1988), 11.

16. The table is based on data in Harold L. Wilensky, "The professionalization of everyone?," *American Journal of Sociology* 70, no. 2 (Sept. 1964): 143.

17. Gutman, *The Design of American Housing*, 15–20.

18. W. D. Peckham, "Chichester city deeds," *Sussex Archaeological Collections* 89 (1950).

19. Ibid.

20. The relation between these understandings and cultural notions of privacy is described by Diane Shaw in "The construction of the private in medieval London," *Journal of Medieval and Early Modern Studies* 26, no. 3 (Fall 1996): 447–66.

21. *First Report of the Commissioners Appointed to Consider the Subject of Weights and Measures, House of Commons, 7 July 1819*. Volume 11 of Commissioners' Reports, Appendix B, Abstract of the Statutes Relating to Weights and Measures.

22. See, for example, Theodore M. Porter, *Trust in Numbers: The Pursuit of Objectivity in Science and Public Life* (Princeton: Princeton University Press, 1995), 21–29.

23. See E. P. Thompson, "Time, work-discipline, and industrial capitalism."

24. F. M. L. Thompson, *Chartered Surveyors: The Growth of a Profession* (London: Routledge & Kegan Paul, 1968), 9–10. Thompson writes that the idea of private ownership in general had a more significant effect than enclosure alone, that "the concept of landed property as a bundle of assorted rights over different bits of territory gave way to the idea that property lay in definable pieces of soil, that every field ought to belong to someone, an idea that cried aloud for commitment to paper."

25. See, for example, Yi-Fu Tuan, *Topophilia: A Study of Environmental Perception, Attitudes, and Values* (Englewood Cliffs, N.J.: Prentice-Hall, 1974), 30–44.

Chapter 5

1. Lon R. Shelby, "The education of mediaeval English master masons," *Mediaeval Studies* 32 (1970): 22.

2. Joseph Moxon, *Mechanick Exercises or the Doctrine of Handy-Works* (London, 1703; reprint, Morristown, N.J.: Astragal Press, 1989), 117.

3. Apprentice relationships in American architecture are described in Roxanne Williamson, *American Architects and the Mechanics of Fame* (Austin: University of Texas Press, 1991).

4. There is a large body of research dealing with the economic aspects of apprenticeship and its decline. See, for example, T. K. Derry, "The repeal of the apprenticeship clauses of the statute of apprentices," *Economic History Review* 3, no. 1 (Jan. 1931): 67.

5. Knoop and Jones, "The first three years of the building of Vale Royal Abbey," 25.

6. For descriptions of the education and apprenticeship of medieval master masons see Shelby, "The education of medieval English master masons," 1–26; and Douglas Knoop and G. P. Jones, "Masons and apprenticeship in mediaeval England," *Economic History Review* 3 (1931–32): 346–66.

7. Harvey, *Medieval Craftsmen*, 49.

8. George Sturt, *The Wheelwright's Shop* (Cambridge: Cambridge University Press, 1923), 130–31.

9. In Gerry Williams, ed., *Apprenticeship in Craft* (Goffstown, N.H.: Daniel Clark Books, 1981), 40.

10. John Harvey, *The Medieval Architect* (New York: St. Martin's Press, 1972), 99.

11. Jerome Bruner, *Toward a Theory of Instruction* (New York: W. W. Norton, 1968), 124.

12. E. W. Cooney, "The origins of the Victorian master builders," *Economic History Review*, 2d ser., 8, no. 2 (Dec. 1955): 167–76.

13. F. M. L. Thompson, *Chartered Surveyors*, 19–38.

14. "Masters and men in Manchester," *The Builder* 23, no. 1189 (Nov. 18, 1865): 821. Many other issues of *The Builder*, published in London during the last half of the century, also contain accounts of such disputes.

15. Richard Goy, *Venetian Vernacular Architecture* (Cambridge: Cambridge University Press, 1989), 114.

16. This story is told in Olsen, *Town Planning in London*.

17. Cubitt's life and work is described in Hermione Hobhouse, *Thomas Cubitt: Master Builder* (New York: Universe Books, 1971).

18. Herbert J. G. Bab, "The evolution of the British building society," *Economic History Review* 9 (1938–39): 56–63.

19. Marc A. Weiss, *The Rise of the Community Builders: The American Real Estate Industry and Urban Land Planning* (New York: Columbia University Press, 1987).

20. See, for example, Sam Bass Warner, *Streetcar Suburbs: The Process of Growth in Boston, 1870–1900* (Cambridge: Harvard University Press, 1962), for a description of the early role of highly capitalized transportation systems in land development.

21. Weiss, *The Rise of the Community Builders*, 69.

22. Ibid., 65.

23. In the introduction to his edited book *The Architect: Chapters in the History of the Profession* (New York: Oxford University Press, 1977), Spiro Kostof called architecture "the world's second oldest profession."

24. RIBA SMK 2, manuscript collection of the British Architectural Library, Royal Institute of British Architects.

25. The firm's correspondence files are contained in the archives of the New-York Historical Society.

26. For examples of articles in the first half of the twentieth century describing the necessarily businesslike nature of architectural practice, see Silverman, "Architecture is a business!," and D. Everett Waid, "The business side of an architect's office," *The Brickbuilder* 22, no. 8 (1913): 179–81, 197–200.

27. See, for example, Dana Cuff, *Architects: The Story of Practice* (Cambridge: MIT Press, 1991); Judith Blau, *Architects and Firms: A Sociological Perspective on Architectural Practice* (Cambridge: MIT Press, 1984); and Magali Sarfatti Larson, *Behind the Postmodern Facade: Architectural Change in Late-Twentieth-Century America* (Berkeley: University of California Press, 1993), for good accounts of the details of the contemporary architectural profession.

28. For a description of these arrangements, see Dana Cuff, "Divisive tactics: Design-production practices in architecture," *Journal of Architectural Education* 45, no. 4 (July 1992): 204–12.

29. See, for example, Andrea Oppenheimer Dean, "Listening to contractors," *Architectural Record*, Feb. 1998, 54–57.

30. Bruner, *Toward a Theory of Instruction*, 151–52.

31. This story is told for one city in Jeffrey A. Cohen, "Building a discipline: Early institutional settings for architectural education in Philadelphia," *Journal of the Society of Architectural Historians* 53, no. 2 (June 1994): 139–83.

32. A detailed description of the operation of the Ecole des Beaux-Arts is in Jean Paul Carlhian, "The Ecole des Beaux-Arts: Modes and manners," *Journal of Architectural Education* 33, no. 2 (Nov. 1979): 7–17. The system is placed in the context of the history of architectural education, and compared to the Arts and Crafts movement, in Mark Crinson and Jules Lubbock, *Architecture—Art or Profession?: Three Hundred Years of Architectural Education in Britain* (Manchester: Manchester University Press, 1994), 76–85. It is placed in the context of architectural

ideas in David Brain, "Discipline and style," *Theory and Society* 18, no. 6 (Nov. 1989): 807–68.

33. Michael J. Crosbie, "The schools: How they're failing the profession (and what we can do about it)," *Progressive Architecture* 76, no. 9 (Sept. 1995): 47–51, 94, 96. See also Peter Buchanan, "What is wrong with architectural education? Almost everything," *Architectural Review* 185, no. 1109 (July 1989): 24–26.

34. Louise Rogers, "The power of persuasion," *Journal of The Royal Institute of British Architects* 100, no. 8 (Aug. 1993): 12–13.

35. In many cases such "design-build" arrangements are business arrangements that allow for more efficiency but do not necessarily result in better quality of building. For a discussion of these arrangements see Nancy B. Solomon, "Design/build ventures," *Architecture*, Sept. 1991, 107–12.

36. R. Sprunt, "Building knowledge and building law," *Journal of Architectural Research* 4, no. 3 (Dec. 1975).

Chapter 6

1. Edward A. Chappell, "Acculturation in the Shenandoah Valley: Rhenish houses of the Massanuten Settlement," *Proceedings of the American Philosophical Society* 124, no. 1 (Feb. 1980): 55–89, reprinted in Dell Upton and John Michael Vlach, eds., *Common Places: Readings in American Vernacular Architecture* (Athens: University of Georgia Press, 1986), 27–57.

2. Christopher Martin, "Skeleton of settlement: Ukrainian folk building in western North Dakota," in Thomas Carter and Bernard L. Herman, eds., *Perspectives in Vernacular Architecture III* (Columbia: University of Missouri Press, 1989), 86–98.

3. Michael Meinecke, *Patterns of Stylistic Change in Islamic Architecture: Local Traditions versus Migrating Artists* (New York: New York University Press, 1996), 89–116.

4. Anthony D. King, *The Bungalow: The Production of a Global Culture* (London: Routledge & Kegan Paul, 1984).

5. This phenomenon is analyzed in the context of economic globalization in Manuel Castells, *The Rise of the Network Society* (Oxford: Blackwell, 1996), 417.

6. Harvey, *The Medieval Architect*, 105.

7. Names of the craftsmen for the house are from Dan Cruickshank and Neil Burton, *Life in the Georgian City* (London: Viking, 1990); names of craftsmen for the church are from E. G. W. Bill, comp., *The Queen Anne Churches: A Catalogue of the Papers in Lambeth Palace Library of the Commission for Building Fifty New Churches in London and Westminster, 1711–1759* (London: Church of England, 1979).

8. F. H. W. Sheppard, ed., *Survey of London*, vol. 27: *Spitalfields and Mile End New Town* (London: Athlone Press, 1957).

9. These plans are taken from Jacques Revault, *Palais et Demeures de Tunis (XVI et XVII siècles)* (Paris: Éditions du Centre National de la Recherche Scientifique, 1967).

10. Ron Walkey, "A lesson in continuity: The legacy of the builders guild in northern Greece" (Research report, University of British Columbia School of Architecture, 1987).

11. In Palladio's time, the word *villa* meant not only the rural residence but the entire agricultural complex that might have been associated with the residence. The quotes from the *Four Books of Architecture* are taken from the Dover edition of 1965, which "is an unabridged and unaltered reproduction of the work first published by Issac Ware in 1738" (New York: Dover Publications, 1965).

12. Myra Nan Rosenfeld, *Sebastiano Serlio on Domestic Architecture: Different Dwellings from the Meanest Hovel to the Most Ornate Palace* (London and Cambridge: Architectural History Foundation and MIT Press), 1978.

13. Rosenfeld writes, "There are many interrelationships between both rural and urban building types. The typology of Serlio's houses confirms recent suggestions that the Renaissance villa and town house were composites and variations of many different types. One can observe in Renaissance depictions of cities how often rural building types were adapted to the city, as in the manors found on the Giudecca in Jacopo da Barbari's map of Venice or the town houses outside the walls of Feurs in Auvergne." Ibid., 50.

14. Ibid., 69.

15. Denis Cosgrove, *The Palladian Landscape: Geographical Change and Its Cultural Representations in Sixteenth-Century Italy* (University Park: Pennsylvania State University Press, 1993).

16. Margaret Symonds, *Days Spent on a Doge's Farm* (London: T. Fisher Unwin, 1893), 57.

17. The fifteenth and sixteenth centuries saw the Ottoman conquest of Constantinople and the beginning colonization of the Americas.

18. Claudia Lazzaro, "Rustic country house to refined farmhouse: The evolution and migration of an architectural form," *Journal of the Society of Architectural Historians* 44 (Dec. 1985): 346–67.

19. See, for example, Vincent Scully, *American Architecture and Urbanism* (New York: Praeger, 1969), 100–105.

20. Paul Clifford Larson, "H. H. Richardson goes west: The rise and fall of an eastern star," in Paul Clifford Larson and Susan M. Brown, eds., *The Spirit of H. H. Richardson on the Midland Prairies: Regional Transformations of an Architectural Style* (Ames: Iowa State University Press, 1988).

21. John C. Hudson, "The midland prairies: Natural resources and urban settlement," in Paul Clifford Larson and Susan M. Brown, eds., *The Spirit of H. H. Richardson on the Midland Prairies*.

22. Myra Dickman Orth, "The influence of the 'American Romanesque' in Australia," *Journal of the Society of Architectural Historians* 34, no. 1 (Mar. 1975): 3–18.

23. James Johnson Sweeney and Josep Lluis Sert, *Antoni Gaudi* (New York: Praeger, 1960), 55.

24. Le Corbusier, *The Journey to the East*, edited and annotated by Ivan Zaknic (Cambridge: MIT Press, 1987), 60–62.

25. See, for example, Harris Sobin, "The role of regional vernacular traditions in the genesis of Le Corbusier's brise-soleil sun-shading techniques," in Nezar Alsayyad, ed., *Architects and the Reinterpretation of Tradition*, Traditional Dwellings and Settlements Working Paper Series, vol. 74 (Berkeley: Center for Environmental Design Research, University of California at Berkeley, 1994), 43–71.

26. Richard Murphy, *Carlo Scarpa and the Castelvecchio* (London: Butterworth, 1990).

27. Anthony Quiney, *House and Home: A History of the Small English House* (London: British Broadcasting Corporation, 1986), 43–49.

28. Richard Plunz, *A History of Housing in New York City* (New York: Columbia University Press, 1990), 11–15.

29. "The majority of arguments against it could be sifted down to opposition on account of some selfish interest of the opponent. The speculative builder accustomed to small rooms, narrow courts and dark halls, found that a larger lot with a smaller percentage of building and more generous lay-out of rooms would be required, and he was frightened. An operator who purchased plots to divide into lots of certain size to be laid out on the old lines, feared that

he would not have purchasers, or would have to divide his property to a disadvantage." Elisha Harris Janes, "The development and financing of apartment houses in New York-I," *The Brickbuilder* 17 (Dec. 1908): 278.

30. See, for example, Marsha Ritzdorf, "Zoning barriers to residential innovation," *Journal of Planning Education and Research* 4, no. 3 (Apr. 1995): 177–84, and Peter Maass, "How to make housing affordable: Let people subdivide their homes," *U.S. News and World Report*, Dec. 30, 1996, 51–52.

31. William W. Clark and Robert Mark, "The first flying buttresses: A new reconstruction of the nave of Notre-Dame de Paris," *Art Bulletin* 66, no. 1 (Mar. 1984): 47–65.

32. Stefan Muthesius, *The English Terraced House* (New Haven: Yale University Press, 1982), 101–42.

33. There is a large literature on the cost of regulation and the resultant difficulty of housing innovation, for example, in the present institutional climate.

34. Clare Cooper Marcus, *House as a Mirror of Self: Exploring the Deeper Meaning of Home* (Berkeley: Conari Press, 1985), 280.

35. P. Bourdieu, "The Berber house," in Mary Douglas, ed., *Rules and Meanings: The Anthropology of Everyday Knowledge* (Harmondsworth: Penguin, 1977), 98–110.

36. Mark Girouard, *Life in the English Country House* (New Haven: Yale University Press, 1978).

37. High profit margins on convenience store items also help offset low margins on gasoline. See R. Lee Sullivan, "Exxonsafeway," *Forbes*, Mar. 11, 1996, 106; and Agis Salpukas, "Fill it up? Send a fax? Have a taco?," *New York Times*, national edition, Dec. 27, 1993, C1.

38. "Upscaled and up to date: Upgrading food courts boosts sales 20–25%," *Chain Store Age Executive*, Nov. 1989, 76. A consultant who developed a new color palette for a large national restaurant chain told me that because the new palette was slightly disquieting, the number of parties per table during a typical lunch hour increased from two to three. People would get up and leave, but not knowing why, and so they would come back. See also Margaret Crawford, "The world in a shopping mall," in Michael Sorkin, ed., *Variations on a Theme Park: The New American City and the End of Public Space* (New York: Hill and Wang, 1992), 3–30; and Carole Rifkind, "America's fantasy urbanism: the waxing of the mall and the waning of civility," in Katharine Washburn and John Thorton, eds., *Dumbing Down: Essays on the Strip-Mining of American Culture* (New York: W. W. Norton, 1996), 261–269.

Chapter 7

1. The annual gross domestic product for the United States was estimated at $5,544 billion in Sept. 1995, and the value of new building construction at about $463 billion, indicating that building construction represents about 8 percent of the gross domestic product. Source is data from the U.S. Bureau of the Census.

2. For an elaboration, by a philospher, of this idea as applied to public spaces, see Elizabeth Anderson, "Consumer sovereignty or citizen disenfranchisement? The question of economic value in relation to public spaces," *Center: Architecture and Design in America* 10 (1997): 26–39.

3. Of course, such investment may increase the value of taxable property near it, even if the investment is done on property that is not itself on the tax rolls. Haussmann's boulevards in Paris resulted in large increases in value and taxes for the new buildings built along them. These increases partly—but not completely—paid for the cost of the improvements until the municipality

stopped authorizing loans for public improvements at the outbreak of war with Prussia in 1870. See David H. Pinkney, *Napoleon III and the Rebuilding of Paris* (Princeton: Princeton University Press, 1958), 180–209.

4. The social effect of that restoration has been questioned, however. See Sharon Zukin, "Landscapes of economic value," *Center: Architecture and Design in America* 10 (1997): 141.

5. Lecture by Eric Schmidt at the University of Oregon, Nov. 1992.

6. Douglas Martin, "Concrete deserts bloom as Parks Dept. thinks small," *New York Times*, Web edition, Mar. 4, 1998.

7. This point is made by Christopher Alexander in Alexander, Murray Silverstein, and Sara Ishikawa, *The Oregon Experiment* (New York: Oxford University Press, 1985), and in Alexander, Hajo Neis, Artemis Anninou, and Ingrid King, *A New Theory of Urban Design* (New York: Oxford University Press, 1987).

8. This principle was applied in a project for the redevelopment of an American urban neighborhood and is described in Christopher Alexander and Howard Davis, *Rebuilding the Inner City: The North Omaha Plan* (Berkeley: Center for Environmental Structure, 1981).

9. Christopher Alexander, Gary Black, and Miyoko Tsutsui, *The Mary Rose Museum* (New York: Oxford University Press, 1995), 89.

10. Goldthwaite, *The Building of Renaissance Florence*, 151.

11. See, for example, C. W. Chalklin, *The Provincial Towns of Georgian England.*

12. Ibid., 241.

13. Ibid., 240.

14. Clarke, *Building Capitalism*, 129.

15. A standard book on mortgage finance is William B. Brueggeman and Leo D. Stone, *Real Estate Finance* (Homewood: Richard D. Irwin, 1981).

16. Alec Clifton-Taylor, *The Pattern of English Building* (London: Faber, 1972), 386.

17. R. Machin, *The Building Accounts of Mapperton Rectory, 1699–1703* (Dorset Record Society, Publication no. 8, 1983).

18. Cruickshank and Burton, *Life in the Georgian City*, 217.

19. Ibid., 232.

20. See Hobhouse, *Thomas Cubitt*, 276–78.

21. Pamela Simpson has dealt with the development of several industrialized building products in articles in the *Perspectives in Vernacular Architecture* series. These include "Cheap, quick, and easy: The early history of rockfaced concrete block building," in *Perspectives in Vernacular Architecture III* (Columbia: University of Missouri Press, 1989), 108–18; "Cheap, quick, and easy, part II: Pressed metal ceilings, 1880–1930," in Elizabeth Collins Cromley and Carter L. Hudgins, eds., *Gender, Class, and Shelter: Perspectives in Vernacular Architecture V* (Knoxville: University of Tennessee Press, 1995), 152–63; and an upcoming article on linoleum.

22. Green, "The birth of the American paint industry."

23. Carl Lounsbury, "The wild melody of steam: The mechanization of the manufacture of building materials, 1850–1890," in Bishir et al., *Architects and Builders in North Carolina.*

24. See, for example, Robert P. Guter and Janet W. Foster, *Building by the Book: Pattern Book Architecture in New Jersey* (New Brunswick, N.J.: Rutgers University Press, 1992), 158–59.

25. Goldthwaite, *The Building of Renaissance Florence*, 51.

26. See, for example, Lounsbury, "The wild melody of steam," 193–239.

27. Immigrants were resisted in the trades, however, and sometimes formed their own unions. See Colin J. Davis, "Building trades," in Jackson, *The Encyclopedia of New York City*, 167.

28. Jock Ferguson, "The sultans of cement," *The Nation*, Aug. 3/10, 1992, 130–32.

29. Sesser, "Logging the rain forest," 42.

Chapter 8

1. This contract is taken from Salzman, *Building in England down to 1540*, 560.

2. Contract between Thomas Steane and Joseph Titcombe. RIBA Documents Collection TiJ/1/1/1.

3. Contract and specification for building No. 10, St. James's Square, London, 1734–36. RIBA Documents Collection HeW 1/1/2.

4. Contract for construction of the Union Club (now Canada House), Cockspur Street. RIBA Documents Collection SMK 2.

5. Lease from the Duke of Bedford to Margaret Griffith, 31/32 King Street, 1706. Greater London Record Office, Covent Garden leases.

6. Contract and specification for building No. 10, St. James's Square, London, 1734–36. RIBA Documents Collection HeW 1/1/2.

7. Contract for construction of the Essex Serpent. Greater London Record Office, Covent Garden leases: E/BER/CG/ES/5/22.

8. Contract between Thomas Steane and Joseph Titcombe. RIBA Documents Collection TiJ/1/1/1.

9. Agreement with William Long, abutting on Covent Garden market. Greater London Record Office, Covent Garden leases: CG/L206/2.

10. Contract for construction of the Essex Serpent. Greater London Record Office, Covent Garden leases: E/BER/CG/ES/5/22.

11. Agreement with Thomas Phillips for premises in Bow Street, west side. Greater London Record Office, Covent Garden leases: CG/L/206/10a.

12. Contract with Robert Willson, Fore Street, 1770. RIBA Documents Collection WiR/1/1/1.

13. Catherine W. Bishir, "Good and sufficient language for building," in Thomas Carter and Bernard L. Herman, eds., *Perspectives in Vernacular Architecture IV* (Columbia and London: University of Missouri Press for the Vernacular Architecture Forum, 1991), 44–52.

14. Lease for 36 King Street, Covent Garden. Greater London Record Office, Covent Garden leases: E/BER/259/3.

15. Contract and specification for building No. 10, St. James's Square, London, 1734–36. RIBA Documents Collection HeW 1/1/2. This is also described in F. H. W. Sheppard, ed., *Survey of London, The Parish of St. James Westminster: Part One, South of Piccadilly* (London, 1960), 122.

16. Contract for construction of the Essex Serpent. Greater London Record Office, Covent Garden leases: E/BER/CG/ES/5/22.

17. Specification of Works for 36 Maiden Lane, Covent Garden. Greater London Record Office, E/BER/CG/ES/4/43.

18. Quoted in Thomas W. Waterman, *A Practical Treatise on the Law Relating to the Specific Performance of Contracts* (New York: Baker, Voorhis & Co., 1881).

19. *Mosely v. Virgin*, 1796. 3 Ves. Jun. 183.

20. Contract and specification for building No. 10, St. James's Square, London, 1734–36. RIBA Documents Collection HeW 1/1/2.

21. This contract is quoted in James Deetz, *In Small Things Forgotten: An Archaeology of Early American Life* (1977; reprint, New York: Anchor Books, 1996), 135–37.

22. Contract between Thomas Steane and Joseph Titcombe. RIBA Documents Collection TiJ/1/1/1.

23. Lease from the Duke of Bedford to Margaret Griffith, 31/32 King Street, 1706. Greater London Record Office, Covent Garden leases.

24. Lease for 36 King Street, Covent Garden. Greater London Record Office, Covent Garden leases: E/BER/259/3.

25. Contract for construction of the Essex Serpent. Greater London Record Office, Covent Garden leases: E/BER/CG/ES/5/22.

26. Saunders was an architect who acted as surveyor to the County of Middlesex, authored several papers on architectural history, and designed projects in Birmingham, London, and Oxford, including work at the Sheldonian Theatre, the Bodleian Library, and the British Museum. See Howard Colvin, *A Biographical Dictionary of British Architects, 1660–1840* (New Haven: Yale University Press, 1995).

27. Report from the Commissioners of Inquiry into the Office of Works, 194. Parliamentary Reports, 1812.

28. RIBA Documents Collection.

29. Letter of Robert Goelet to unidentified party, May 22, [1891]. New-York Historical Society archives.

30. The complete records for the construction of the Metropolitan Club, which were in the possession of McKim Mead and White, are now in the archives of the New-York Historical Society, New York City, and I examined them in 1996.

31. Hobhouse, *Thomas Cubitt*, 212.

32. Ibid., 352.

33. The idea of decentralized control in complex organizations is becoming more the norm, and many companies are now looking to innovative examples.

Chapter 9

1. "For a custom taketh beginning and groweth to perfection in this manner. When a reasonable Act once done is found to be good, and beneficial to the People, and agreeable to their nature and disposition, then do they use it and practise it again and again, and so by often iteration and multiplication of the Act, it becomes a Custom; and being continued without interruption time out of mind, it obtaineth the force of a Law." Carter, in *Lex Custumaria* (1696), quoted by E. P. Thompson, *Customs in Common* (New York: New Press, 1991), 97.

2. This settlement is described in A. L. M. T. Nijst et al., *Living on the Edge of the Sahara: A Study of Traditional Forms of Habitation and Types of Settlement in Morocco* (The Hague: Government Publications Office, 1973).

3. These sorts of simulations, involving sequences of generative rules, have been carried out in various housing projects undertaken by the Center for Environmental Structure, including projects in Venezuela, Colombia, and Israel. Some of them are described in Book 3 of Christopher Alexander's *The Nature of Order*. The detailed rules of Islamic cities derived from the Koran are presented in Besim Hakim, *Arabic-Islamic Cities* (London: KPI Limited, 1986); and the idea of a generative sequence in the Islamic city is mentioned in Jamel Akbar, *Crisis in the Built Environment: The Case of the Muslim City* (Singapore: Concept Media, 1988). But neither of these books attempts a conjecture of the actual detailed steps of a development sequence in an Islamic city.

4. This doctrine is described in Howard Davis, "The future of ancient lights," *Journal of Architectural and Planning Research* 6, no. 2 (Summer 1989): 132–53.

5. One of the people making this argument was an architect named Delissa Joseph, who argued bitterly against this law, arguing at one point that he had

been forced to practice for forty years "in the continuous glare of ancient lights." Delissa Joseph, "Building heights and ancient lights," *Journal of the Royal Institute of British Architects* 30, no. 15 (June 16, 1923): 477–88. The buildings that Delissa Joseph designed, however, show another impact of this law. The buildings are very precisely shaped, in order to meet the intention of the law, and no more: there is no need, for example, for the whole building to be made low, or for a setback to exist in a place where it will not be useful to preserve a neighbor's light.

6. *Ough v. King* (1967), 1 W.L.R. 1550.

7. Ibid.

8. *Lawrence v. Horton* (1890), 59 L.J. Ch. 440.

9. *Parker v. Foote*, 19 Wend. 309.

10. Bryan Anstey, "Man's ancient right to light," *Journal of the Royal Institution of Chartered Surveyors* 34, part 4 (Oct. 1954): 254.

11. *City of Euclid v. Ambler Realty Co.*, 272 U.S. 365 (1926).

12. Eugene Code, chapter 9, "Land use."

13. Richard Lai, *Law in Urban Design and Planning: The Invisible Web* (New York: Van Nostrand Reinhold, 1988), 85.

14. California Code.

15. Lai, *Law in Urban Design and Planning*, 90.

16. Ibid., 87.

17. For an excellent discussion of zoning from the perspective of an architect who has extensively researched zoning's role in urban design, see Michael Kwartler, "Legislating aesthetics," in Charles M. Haar and Jerold S. Kayden, eds., *Zoning and the American Dream* (Chicago: American Planning Association, 1989), 187–220.

18. See, for example, Susan S. Fainstein, *The City Builders: Property, Politics and Planning in London and New York* (Oxford: Blackwell, 1994), 49.

19. *Southern Burlington County NAACP vs. Township of Mt. Laurel* (92 N.J. 158, 456 A.2d 390), 1983.

20. See, for example, C. C. Knowles and P. H. Pitt, *A History of Building Regulation in London, 1189–1972* (London: Architectural Press, 1972), or Summerson, Georgian London.

21. A good discussion of pattern books and their relationship to builders and architects—in America—is Dell Upton, "Pattern books and professionalism: Aspects of the transformation of domestic architecture in America," *Winterthur Portfolio* 19, no. 2–3 (Autumn 1984): 107–50.

22. Joseph D. McGoldrick, Seymour Graubard, and Raymond J. Horowitz, *Building Regulation in New York City: A Study in Administrative Law and Procedure* (New York: Commonwealth Fund, 1944), 40.

23. See Sara Wermeil, "The role of the fire insurance industry in advancing structural fire protection in nineteenth century America," Center for the History of Business, Technology, and Society, Research Seminar Paper no. 35, Hagley Museum and Library, Wilmington, Delaware, 1996; and Gary Stanton, "'Alarmed by the cry of fire': How fire changed Fredericksburg, Virginia," in Carter L. Hudgins and Elizabeth Collins Cromley, eds., *Shaping Communities: Perspectives in Vernacular Architecture VI* (Knoxville: University of Tennessee Press, 1997), 122–34.

24. Building officials have a journal called *Building Official and Code Administrator*, which provides an overview of modern building regulation.

25. Elliott O. Stephenson, "The silent and inviting trap," *Building Official and Code Administrator*, Nov./Dec. 1988, 29.

26. A discussion by a lawyer of the perniciousness of bureaucratic rules is

Philip Howard, *The Death of Common Sense: How Law Is Suffocating America* (New York: Random House, 1994).

Chapter 10

1. This point is also made by Christopher Alexander in *The Nature of Order*.

2. Clark and Mark, "The first flying buttresses," 53. See also "Gothic structural experimentation," *Scientific American*, Nov. 1984, 176–85, by the same authors.

3. Catherine Bishir, "Jacob Holt, an American Builder," *Winterthur Portfolio* 16, no. 1 (Spring 1981): 1–31, reprinted in Upton and Vlach, *Common Places*.

4. Paraskevi Bozineki-Didonis, *Greek Traditional Architecture: Crete* (Athens: Melissa, 1985), 61.

5. See, for example, Harvey, *Medieval Craftsmen*, 147, and Schofield, *Medieval London Houses*, 141.

6. Schofield, *Medieval London Houses*, 142–43.

7. The changes in framing technique that occurred partly because of decreased availability of large timbers is described, for rural houses in Kent, in David Martin, "The decline of traditional methods of timber framing in South-East England," in Neil Burton, ed., *Georgian Vernacular: Papers Given at a Georgian Group Symposium 28 October 1995* (London: Georgian Group, 1996), 27–33. These changes included the elimination of the widened jowl at the top of posts that had accommodated joints for both the tie beam and the wall plate. Martin describes this change and others as part of a "debased" system of framing that replaced traditional techniques and that eventually led to stud walling.

8. Knowles and Pitt, *The History of Building Regulation in London*, 18.

9. Salzman, *Building in England down to 1540*.

10. David Yeomans, *The Architect and the Carpenter* (London: RIBA Heinz Gallery, 1992), 41.

11. Moxon, *Mechanick Exercises or the Doctrine of Handy-Works*, 118.

12. See Glassie, *Folk Housing in Middle Virginia*, and Matthew Johnson, *Housing Culture*.

13. For an account of how such traditional practices persisted in the country even into the twentieth century, see Walter Rose, *The Village Carpenter* (Cambridge: Cambridge University Press, 1937).

14. David Yeomans, *The Trussed Roof* (Aldershot: Scolar Press, 1992), 32–33.

15. Ibid., 34.

16. I transcribed these excerpts from correspondence in the McKim Mead and White archives at the New-York Historical Society.

17. Thomas J. Suhrbuhr, "The economic transformation of carpentry in late-nineteenth-century Chicago," *Illinois Historical Journal* 81 (Summer 1988): 109–24.

18. A classic article on the subject is Walker Field, "A reexamination into the invention of the balloon frame," *Journal of the Society of Architectural Historians* 2 (1942): 3–29.

19. Martin, "The decline of traditional methods of timber framing in South-East England."

20. This point is made by Yeomans, *The Trussed Roof*, 91, in discussing the increasing role of architects in providing technical details for roofs. Yeomans writes, "This evidence of a growing control by the architect over such technical matters was not necessary because of ignorance on the part of the carpenters but because of the growing complexity of buildings. This can be seen in Barry's drawings for his London clubs which provide examples of structures that could

not be left to the carpenter. Even church designs were becoming more complex and required their architects to give some attention to the details of their structures. The Inwood's, St Pancras Church or Edward Jenkins's design sketches for an unidentified church are examples of such attention to technical details. Moreover, before engineering became a recognized profession some architects were providing the services of a structural engineer, like the Smirkes in their re-roofing work at York Minster, and so were deeply involved in the design of structures."

21. Joseph Rykwert, *The Idea of a Town* (Cambridge: MIT Press, 1988), 41–49.

Part III

1. Le Corbusier, *Towards a New Architecture* (New York: Praeger, 1960), 210.

Chapter 11

1. Alexander, *The Timeless Way of Building*, lays out the theory behind this aspect of Alexander's work.

2. This project was carried out by Christopher Alexander acting as principal architect and Hajo Neis acting as executive architect. It is described in Christopher Alexander and Hajo Neis, *Battle: The History of a Crucial Clash between World System A and World System B*, unpublished manuscript.

3. Described in Christopher Alexander, Howard Davis, Julio Martinez, and Don Corner, *The Production of Houses* (New York: Oxford University Press, 1985).

4. Described in Alexander, Black, and Tsutsui, *The Mary Rose Museum*, 86–100. This includes full sample contracts.

5. Ibid., 90.

6. Ibid., 89.

7. Conversation with Peter Clegg, March 1997. For an example of such an arrangement with building cladding, see "Creative team work," *Architects' Journal* 190, no. 8–9 (Aug. 23–30, 1989): 46–47.

8. This section is based on conversations with Seishi Unuma and Hajo Neis; Dana Buntrock, "Collaborative production: Building opportunities in Japan," *Journal of Architectural Education* 50, no. 4 (May 1997): 219–29; and Kenneth Frampton and Kunio Kudo, *Japanese Building Practice from Ancient Times to the Meiji Period* (New York: Van Nostrand Reinhold, 1997).

9. The first sentence of Article 1 of the standard construction contract in Japan reads, "The Owner and the Contractor shall perform this Contract sincerely through cooperation, good faith, and equality." "General Conditions of Construction Contract," revised Sept. 1981.

10. Conversation with Seishi Unuma, Feb. 1997.

11. Buntrock, "Collaborative production," 222–24.

12. Ibid., 226.

13. Hajo Neis, "Details of feeling in design and construction: Twelve years of living and working in Japan," manuscript (1998).

14. Ibid.

15. A general discussion of the use of computers in construction is Thomas Bock, "CAD—so what?," in Richard Junge, ed., *CAAD Futures 1997: Proceedings of the Seventh International Conference on Computer Aided Architectural Design Futures held in Munich, Germany, 4–6 August 1997* (Dordrecht: Kluwer Academic Publishers, 1997), 15–44.

16. Malcolm McCullough, *Abstracting Craft: The Practiced Digital Hand* (Cambridge: MIT Press, 1996), 52.

17. Ibid., 53.

18. On the work of El-Wakil, see Mohammad Al-Asad, "The mosques of Abdelwahed El-Wakil, *Mimar* 12, no. 42 (March 1992): 34–39; and Chris Abel, "Work of El-Wakil," *Architectural Review* 180, no. 1077 (Nov. 1986): 52–60.

19. Stanley Abercrombie, "Stepping stones," *Historic Preservation* 44, no. 5 (Sept./Oct. 1992): 36.

20. Annette LeCuyer, "Building Bilbao," *Architectural Review* 202, no. 1210 (Dec. 1997): 43.

21. Catherine Slessor, "Atlantic star," *Architectural Review* 202, no. 1210 (Dec. 1997): 34.

22. See, for example, Kevin Matthews, Stephen Duff, and Donald Corner, "A model for integrated spatial and structural design of buildings," conference paper, *CAADRIA 98: The Third Conference on Computer Aided Architectural Design Research in Asia*, Osaka, Japan, Apr. 22–24, 1998.

23. See also Ziva Friedman, ed., "Model making: A model of practice," *Progressive Architecture*, May 1995, 78–83.

24. Ziva Friedman, ed., "Process: Shakespeare on the Thames," *Progressive Architecture*, May 1995, 96–103.

25. Data is from Tom Jones, William Pettus, and Michael Pyatok, *Good Neighbors: Affordable Family Housing* (New York: McGraw-Hill, 1997), 90–91.

26. N. John Habraken, *Variations: The Systematic Design of Supports* (Cambridge: Laboratory of Architecture and Planning at MIT, 1976).

27. Avi Friedman, "Residential modification of narrow front affordable Grow Homes in Montreal, Canada," *Open House International* 21, no. 2 (1996): 4–17.

28. The details of the system are described in a report by Avi Friedman, David Krawitz, Jasmin S. Frechette, Cyrus Bilimoria, and Doug Raphael, *The Next Home* (Montreal: Canadian Mortgage and Housing Corporation and McGill University School of Architecture, 1996).

29. Friedman, "Residential modification of narrow front affordable Grow Homes," 4–17.

30. These projects are by the Center for Environmental Structure, Berkeley, Calif.

Chapter 12

1. Francis Duffy, "Architecture and practice: Future directions," text of speech at Africa 2000 Conference, Cape Town, South Africa, Apr. 1995, *Architectural Review* 198, no. 1182 (Aug. 1995): 83.

2. This voice included the formation, about 1970, of the Environmental Design Research Association, which promotes research on relationships between the built environment and human activity and pushes for changes in the profession that take this research into account.

3. Duffy, "Architecture and practice," 82.

4. For specialized buildings and custom houses, the percentage of construction cost taken as fee may be higher. In general the percentage goes down as the size goes up and/or the complexity of the building goes down.

5. Ikujiro Nonaka, "The knowledge-creating company," *Harvard Business Review*, Nov./Dec. 1991, 96–104.

6. For theoretical and historical descriptions of the gradual emergence of modern institutional buildings, see Markus, *Buildings and Power*.

7. David Week, *The Culture of Work* (Canberra: Royal Australian Institute of Architects, forthcoming).

8. See, for example, Clare Cooper Marcus and Marni Barnes, *Gardens in Healthcare Facilities: Uses, Therapeutic Benefits, and Design Recommendations* (Martinez, Calif.: Center for Health Design, 1995).

9. This attitude is beginning to be supported in the corporate world. See, for example, Nichole M. Christian, "Not your father's Chrysler: At new headquarters, parking still a headache but culture improves," *Wall Street Journal*, Oct. 29, 1997, B16.

10. Charles, Prince of Wales, speech at "Build a Better Britain" exhibition, London, Apr. 1989, quoted in Andreas C. Papadakis, ed., *Prince Charles and the Architectural Debate, Architectural Design*, profile 79 (London: Academy Group Ltd., 1989), 32.

11. Roger Scruton, "Vernacular architecture," in *The Classical Vernacular: Architectural Principles in an Age of Nihilism* (New York: St. Martin's Press, 1994), 25.

12. Leon Krier, *Architecture and Urban Design*, 1967–1992 (London: Academy Editions, 1992), 111.

13. See Deborah Meier, *The Power of Their Ideas: Lessons for America from a Small School in Harlem* (Boston: Beacon Press, 1995), and various articles of Meier's in *The Nation*, for which she is education editor. Buildings to serve these ideas were explored in an architectural competition sponsored by the Architectural League of New York, and the designs were published in Architectural League of New York, *New Schools for New York* (New York: Princeton Architectural Press, 1992).

14. James Steele, "The cosmic connection" (interview with Rasem Badran), *World Architecture* 44 (Mar. 1996): 52.

15. Publications about this work include Peter Katz, *The New Urbanism: Toward an Architecture of Community* (New York: McGraw Hill, 1994).

16. Jørn Orum-Nielsen, *Dwelling—At Home, in Community, on Earth: The Significance of Tradition in Contemporary Housing* (Copenhagen: Danish Architectural Press, 1996), 79.

17. This project (and much other responsible housing work) is described in Jones, Pettus, and Pyatok, *Good Neighbors*, 208–9.

18. Meem's work, however, raises the question of what is really "vernacular" or "indigenous." His work was part of a general movement beginning at the turn of the century to restore to New Mexico architecture a "Hispanic" character. This issue is dealt with in Chris Wilson, *The Myth of Santa Fe* (Albuquerque: University of New Mexico Press, 1997).

19. Geoffrey Bawa, "Statement by the architect," in Brian Brace Taylor, *Geoffrey Bawa* (Singapore: Concept Media, 1986), 16.

20. David Williams, "An indigenous architecture," *Southwest Review* 14 (1928–29): 67–68.

21. Kenneth Frampton, "Ten points on an architecture of regionalism: A provisional polemic," *Center: A Journal for Architecture in America* 3 (1987): 20–27.

22. Tony Hiss, *The Experience of Place* (New York: Knopf, 1990).

23. Sassen has pointed out, for example, that the stock market crash in 1987, which sent instantaneous financial waves all around the world, also affected many Dominican immigrants, then living in Washington Heights in northern Manhattan, who were working as menial laborers on Wall Street. Lecture at IASTE conference, Berkeley, Calif., Dec. 1996.

24. See Andrew Gruft, "Seabird Island community school," *Canadian Architect* 37, no. 1 (Jan. 1992): 14–23; and Donald Canty, "Aerodynamic school," *Progressive Architecture* 73, no. 5 (May 1992): 142–47.

25. Canty, "Aerodynamic school," 142–47.

26. Rory Spence, "Community spirit," *Architectural Review* 189, no. 1136 (Oct. 1991): 56–60.

27. Conversation with Greg Burgess, Feb. 1998.

28. Dan Underwood, "Snake charmer," *Architectural Review* 200, no. 1197 (Nov. 1996): 46–51.

29. Barrie Evans, "Theatre in the frame," *Architects' Journal*, Feb. 15, 1996, 35–44, and Alan Powers, "Back in the frame," *Perspectives in Architecture*, Feb./Mar. 1998, 52–55.

30. Dean Hawkes and William Bordass, "Building study: Feilden Clegg Architects' building 16 for the BRE," *RIBA Profile*, Apr. 1997.

31. Lecture by Peter Clegg at the University of Oregon Department of Architecture, Feb. 2, 1998.

32. "The notions of subjective and objective have been completely reversed. Objective means the non-controversial aspect of things, their unquestioned impression, the facade made up of classified data, that is, the subjective; and they call subjective anything which breaches that facade, engages the specific experience of a matter, casts off all ready-made judgements and substitutes relatedness to the object for the majority consensus of those who do not even look at it, let alone think about it—that is, the objective. . . . Anyone who, drawing on the strength of his precise reaction to a work of art, has ever subjected himself in earnest to its discipline, to its immanent formal law, the compulsion of its structure, will find that objections to the merely subjective quality of his experience vanish like a pitiful illusion: and every step that he takes, by virtue of his highly subjective innervation, towards the heart of the matter, has incomparably greater force than the comprehensive and fully backed-up analyses of such things as 'style', whose claims to scientific status are made at the expense of such experience. This is doubly true in the era of positivism and the culture industry, where objectivity is calculated by the subjects managing it. In face of this, reason has retreated entirely behind a windowless wall of idiosyncracies, which the holders of power arbitrarily reproach with arbitrariness, since they want subjects impotent, for fear of the objectivity that is preserved in these subjects alone." Theodor Adorno, *Minima Moralia* (Frankfurt, 1951; reprint, London: Verso, 1997), 69–70.

Chapter 13

1. This point was eloquently made by John Turner in *Housing by People*, 54–72.

2. See Arthur Bonner, *Averting the Apocalypse: Social Movements in India Today* (Durham, N.C.: Duke University Press, 1990), 25–32.

3. This project is described in Howard Davis, David Week, and Paul Moses, "The village meets the city," in *Architecture + Design* (New Delhi), Apr.–May 1993, and in Howard Davis, "Learning from Vellore," *Arcade* (Seattle), Mar.–Apr. 1993.

4. The obvious contradiction contained in this approach—that *any* kind of knowledge coming from "the outside" represents a form of cultural imperialism—will perhaps always be there. But it is tempered by the understanding that the relationship between two cultures may be a mutual exchange, which may help to liberate and empower the community as well as people from outside.

5. Rory Spence, "Grass roots tech," *Architectural Review* 181, no. 1085 (July 1987): 58–63.

6. Ken Costigan, "Sustaining architectural traditions in Papua New Guinea," conference paper, *Traditions and Modernity: Contemporary Architecture in Southeast Asia and Beyond*, Jakarta, Dec. 9–11, 1996.

7. Jay Walljasper, "What works? Denmark!," *The Nation* 266, no. 3 (Jan. 26, 1998): 22–24.

8. See, for example, Paul Lewis, "Small loans may be key to helping Third World," *New York Times*, Jan. 26, 1997, sec. 1, p. 5.

9. J. Linn Allen, "Pride, investment help South Shore fuel its resurgence," *Chicago Tribune*, May 30, 1993.

10. John K. Bullard, "There's no specialization like home," *Utne Reader*, Jan./Feb. 1993, 99, excerpted from *Places: A Quarterly Journal of Environmental Design* (Fall 1991).

11. Peter Wislocki, "A model practice," *Architects' Journal* 193, no. 6 (Feb. 6, 1991): 28–31, and conversation with Brook Muller, Jan. 1998.

12. Michael J. Crosbie, "Putting design back in design/build," *Progressive Architecture* 76, no. 12 (Dec. 1995): 54–61.

13. American Consulting Engineers Council and the American Institute of Architects, "A project partnering guide for design professionals" (1993).

14. See, for example, Thomas Fisher, "Three models for the future of practice," in William S. Saunders, ed., *Reflections on Architectural Practices in the Nineties* (New York: Princeton Architectural Press, 1996), 36–43.

15. For a discussion of research supporting such ideas, see Colin Clipson, "Contradictions and challenges in managing design," *Journal of Architectural Education* 45, no. 4 (July 1992): 218–24.

16. Lecture by Peter Clegg at the University of Oregon Department of Architecture, Feb. 2, 1998.

17. For a collection of writings by one of the principals of DEGW (and a former president of the RIBA), see Francis Duffy, *The Changing Workplace* (London: Phaidon, 1992).

18. See, for example, Michael Frank, "Homework," Planning, June 1993, 16; and Rae Anderson, "Integrating residence and work in building codes in Canada," *Open House International* 21, no. 2 (1996): 41–48.

19. Ned Warnick, "The role and effect of design regulation in Portland, Oregon" (M.A. thesis, University of Oregon, 1995).

20. Kwartler, "Legislating aesthetics," 214–15.

21. Susan Freiden and Richard Winters, "Performance zoning helps city comeback," *American City and County* 112, no. 6 (June 1997): 70.

22. Jerry Frug, "The geography of community," *Stanford Law Review* 48 (May 1996): 1077. This is an excellent commentary on contemporary issues in urban planning.

23. John J. Costonis, *Icons and Aliens: Law, Aesthetics, and Environmental Change* (Urbana: University of Illinois Press, 1989), 102.

24. Virginia Kent Dorris, " Single international building code to simplicity the code process," *Architectural Record* 186, no. 10 (Oct. 1998): 173.

25. Crosbie, "The schools," 47–51.

26. John Ellis, "Realism and relevance in the Bay Area," *Architectural Review* 185, no. 1109 (July 1989): 34–37.

27. A series of articles in *Architecture* magazine has focused on the programs of different architecture schools. See, for example, "Classical education," followed by descriptions of the schools at Notre Dame and Miami, *Architecture*, Nov. 1994, 117–21.

28. Robert Gutman, "Two discourses in architectural education," *Practices* (Center for the Study of Practice in Architecture), issue 3/4 (Spring 1995): 11–19.

29. Such connections are called for in Ernest Boyer and Lee D. Mitgang, *Building Community: A New Future for Architecture Education and Practice*, a major

study published in 1996, commissioned by the Carnegie Commission for the Advancement of Teaching.

30. The literature contains a few exceptions to this, such as Kostof's *The Architect*. But the changing role of the architect is not dealt with in most courses on architectural history, and courses in professional practice, that are required for schools' accreditation, do not deal with the issue from a historical point of view, either.

31. See Mark Alden Branch, "Building to learn," *Progressive Architecture*, Mar. 1994, 56–59.

32. Rory Spence, "Constructive education," *Architectural Review* 185, no. 1109 (July 1989): 27–33.

33. "Mockbee's mission," *Architecture* 86, no. 1 (Jan. 1997): 49–51.

34. Abercrombie, "Stepping stones."

Conclusion

1. See, for example, Ricardo Semmler, *Maverick* (New York: Warner Books, 1993), for an account of the radical and successful decentralization of control in a Brazilian company. The Japanese case is described in Castells, *The Rise of the Network Society*, 159.

2. Howard, *The Death of Common Sense*.

3. Meier, *The Power of Their Ideas,* and many articles in *The Nation*.

4. Michael H. Shuman, "Going local," *The Nation* 267, no. 11 (Oct. 12, 1998): 11–15.

5. See Karl Popper, *The Poverty of Historicism* (Boston: Beacon Press, 1957), for a discussion of "piecemeal social engineering" as an alternative to large-scale, monolithic social planning.

BIBLIOGRAPHY

Unpublished Sources

Agreement with Thomas Phillips for premises in Bow Street, west side. Greater London Record Office, Covent Garden leases: CG/L/206/10a.

Agreement with William Long, abutting on Covent Garden market. Greater London Record Office, Covent Garden leases: CG/L206/2.

Contract and specification for building No. 10, St. James's Square, London, 1734–36. RIBA Documents Collection HeW 1/1/2. This is also described in F. H. W. Sheppard, ed., *Survey of London, The Parish of St. James Westminster: Part One, South of Piccadilly.* London, 1960.

Contract between Thomas Steane and Joseph Titcombe. RIBA Documents Collection TiJ/1/1/1.

Contract for construction of the Essex Serpent. Greater London Record Office, Covent Garden leases: E/BER/CG/ES/5/22.

Contract for construction of the Union Club (now Canada House), Cockspur Street. RIBA Documents Collection SMK 2.

Contract with Robert Willson, Fore Street, 1770. RIBA Documents Collection WiR/1/1/1.

Costigan, Ken. "The patterns of structure in the Trobriand Islands." M.Arch. thesis, University of California, Berkeley, 1995.

———. "Sustaining architectural traditions in Papua New Guinea." Conference paper, "Traditions and Modernity: Contemporary Architecture in Southeast Asia and Beyond," Jakarta, Dec. 9–11, 1996.

Goelet, Robert. Letter to unidentified party, May 22, [1891]. New-York Histori-
    cal Society archives.

Green, Teresa Osterman. "The birth of the American paint industry." M.A. the-
    sis, University of Delaware, 1965.

Harms, Martin. "1770, 1870, 1970: Craft, the machine, and human transaction in
    the technology of three Philadelphia buildings." Ph.D. diss., University of
    Pennsylvania, 1992.

Horridge, Frederick. "The problem of apprenticeship in the six basic building
    trades." Ph.D. dissertation, University of California, Berkeley, 1926.

Lease for 36 King Street, Covent Garden. Greater London Record Office,
    Covent Garden leases: E/BER/259/3.

Lease from the Duke of Bedford to Margaret Griffith, 31/32 King Street, 1706.
    Greater London Record Office, Covent Garden leases.

Neis, Hajo. "Details of feeling in design and construction: Twelve years of living
    and working in Japan." Unpublished manuscript, 1998.

RIBA SMK 2, manuscript collection of the British Architectural Library, Royal
    Institute of British Architects.

Records for the construction of the Metropolitan Club, McKim, Mead and
    White, in the archives of the New-York Historical Society, New York City.

Sassen, Saskia. Lecture at IASTE conference, Berkeley, December 1996.

Snook, John. Contract books, archives of the New-York Historical Society.

Specification of Works for 36 Maiden Lane, Covent Garden. Greater London
    Record Office, E/BER/CG/ES/4/43.

U.S. Department of Commerce, Bureau of the Census, 1995.

Walkey, Ron. "A lesson in continuity: The legacy of the builders guild in north-
    ern Greece." Research report, University of British Columbia School of
    Architecture, 1987.

Warnick, Ned. "The role and effect of design regulation in Portland, Oregon."
    M.A. thesis, University of Oregon, 1995.

Wermeil, Sara. "The role of the fire insurance industry in advancing structural
    fire protection in nineteenth-century America." Center for the History of
    Business, Technology, and Society, Research Seminar Paper no. 35, Hagley
    Museum and Library, Wilmington, Delaware, 1996.

Published Sources

Abbott, Andrew. *The System of Professions*. Chicago: University of Chicago Press,
    1988.

Abel, Chris. "Work of El-Wakil." *Architectural Review* 180, no. 1077 (Nov. 1986):
    52–60.

Abercrombie, Stanley. "Stepping stones." *Historic Preservation* 44, no. 5
    (Sept./Oct. 1992): 28–36, 88.

Abu-Lughod, Janet. "Disappearing dichotomies: First World—Third World;
    Traditional—Modern." *Traditional Dwellings and Settlements Review* 3, no. 2
    (Spring 1992): 7–12.

Ackerman, James S. "Architectural practice in the Italian Renaissance." *Journal of
    the Society of Architectural Historians* 13, no. 3 (Oct. 1954): 3–11.

Adorno, Theodor. *Minima Moralia*. Frankfurt, 1951; reprint, London: Verso,
    1997.

Akbar, Jamel. *Crisis in the Built Environment: The Case of the Muslim City*. Singapore:
    Concept Media, 1988.

Al-Asad, Mohammad. "The mosques of Abdel Wahed El-Wakil." *Mimar* 12, no.
    42 (March 1992): 34–39.

Albrecht, Donald, ed. *World War II and the American Dream: How Wartime Building Changed a Nation*. Washington and Cambridge: National Building Museum and MIT Press, 1995.

Alexander, Christopher. *The Mary Rose Museum*. New York: Oxford University Press, 1995.

————. *The Nature of Order*. New York: Oxford University Press, forthcoming.

————. *The Timeless Way of Building*. New York: Oxford University Press, 1979.

Alexander, Christopher, Gary Black, and Miyoko Tsutsui. *The Mary Rose Museum*. New York: Oxford University Press, 1995.

Alexander, Christopher, and Howard Davis. *Rebuilding the Inner City: The North Omaha Plan*. Berkeley: Center for Environmental Structure, 1981.

Alexander, Christopher, with Howard Davis, Julio Martinez, and Don Corner. *The Production of Houses*. New York: Oxford University Press, 1985.

Alexander, Christopher, Hajo Neis, Artemis Anninou, and Ingrid King. *A New Theory of Urban Design*. New York: Oxford University Press, 1987.

Alexander, Christopher, and Hajo Neis. *Battle: The History of a Crucial Clash between World System A and World System B*. Unpublished manuscript.

Alexander, Christopher, Murray Silverstein, and Sara Ishikawa. *The Oregon Experiment*. New York: Oxford University Press, 1985.

Allen, Edward. *Stone Shelters*. Cambridge: MIT Press, 1969.

Allen, J. Linn. "Pride, investment help South Shore fuel its resurgence." *Chicago Tribune*, May 30, 1993.

American Consulting Engineers Council and the American Institute of Architects. "A project partnering guide for design professionals." 1993.

Anderson, Rae. "Integrating residence and work in building codes in Canada." *Open House International* 21, no. 2 (1996): 41–48.

Anderson, Elizabeth. "Consumer sovereignty or citizen disenfranchisement? The question of economic value in relation to public spaces." *Center: Architecture and Desgin in America* 10 (1997): 26–39.

Angel, Shlomo. "Seventeen reasons why the squatter problem can't be solved." *Ekistics* no. 242 (Jan. 1976): 20–26.

Anstey, Bryan. "Man's ancient right to light." *Journal of the Royal Institution of Chartered Surveyors* 34, part 4 (Oct. 1954): 254.

————. "Rights of light." *Chartered Surveyor* (1961): 544–51.

Architectural League of New York. *New Schools for New York*. New York: Princeton Architectural Press, 1992.

Aspinall, J. "The evolution of urban tenure systems in 19th century cities." Birmingham: Centre for Urban and Regional Studies, University of Birmingham, 1978.

Ayres, James. *Building the Georgian City*. New Haven: Yale University Press, 1998.

Bab, Herbert J. G. "The evolution of the British building society." Economic History Review 9 (1938–39): 56–63.

Baer, William C. "The shadow market in housing." *Scientific American* 255, no. 5 (Nov. 1986).

Bannister, Turpin C. "Bogardus Revisited. Part I: The Iron Fronts." *Journal of the Society of Architectural Historians* 15, no. 4 (Dec. 1956): 12–22.

————. "Bogardus Revisited. Part II: The Iron Towers." *Journal of the Society of Architectural Historians* 16, no. 1 (March 1957): 11–19.

Bapat, Meera. "Shanty town and city: The case of Poona." *Progress in Planning* 15, part 3 (1981).

Basalla, George. *The Evolution of Technology*. Cambridge: Cambridge University Press, 1988.

Bawa, Geoffrey. "Statement by the architect." In Brian Brace Taylor, *Geoffrey Bawa*, 16. Singapore: Concept Media, 1986.

Belser, Karl. "The making of slurban America." *Cry California* 5, no. 4 (Fall 1970): 1–21.

Bender, Richard. *A Crack in the Rear-View Mirror: A View of Industrialized Building*. New York: Van Nostrand Reinhold, 1973.

Benjamin, Walter. "The work of art in the age of mechanical reproduction." In Hannah Arendt, ed., *Illuminations*, 217–51. New York: Schocken Books, 1969.

Bill, E. G. W., comp. *The Queen Anne Churches: A Catalogue of the Papers in Lambeth Palace Library of the Commission for Building Fifty New Churches in London and Westminster, 1711–1759*. London: Church of England, 1979.

Bishir, Catherine W. "Good and sufficient language for building." In Thomas Carter and Bernard L. Herman, eds., *Perspectives in Vernacular Architecture IV*, 44–52. Columbia and London: University of Missouri Press for the Vernacular Architecture Forum, 1991.

———. "Jacob Holt, an American builder." Winterthur Portfolio 16, no. 1 (Spring 1981): 1–31. Reprinted in Dell Upton and John Michael Vlach, eds., *Common Places: Readings in American Vernacular Architecture*. Athens: University of Georgia Press, 1986.

Bishir, Catherine, Charlotte V. Brown, Carl R. Lounsbury, and Ernest H. Wood III. *Architects and Builders in North Carolina*. Chapel Hill: University of North Carolina Press, 1990.

Black, R. Gary, and Stephen Duff. "A model for teaching structures: Finite element analysis in architectural education." *Journal of Architectural Education* 48, no. 1 (Sept. 1994): 38–55.

Blake, Peter. *God's Own Junkyard*. New York: Holt Rinehart & Winston, 1964.

Blau, Judith. *Architects and Firms: A Sociological Perspective on Architectural Practice*. Cambridge: MIT Press, 1984.

BOCA. "The BOCA code change process." *Building Official and Code Administrator* 24, no. 5 (Sept./Oct. 1990): 43–46.

Bock, Thomas. "CAD—so what?," in Richard Junge, ed., *CAAD Futures 1997: Proceedings of the 7th International Conference on Computer Aided Architectural Design Futures held in Munich, Germany, 4–6 August 1997*, 15–44. Dordrecht: Kluwer Academic Publishers, 1997.

Bonine, Michael E. "The morphogenesis of Iranian cities." *Annals of the Association of American Geographers* 69 (1979): 208–24.

Bonner, Arthur. *Averting the Apocalypse: Social Movements in India Today*. Durham, N.C.: Duke University Press, 1990.

Bourdieu, P. "The Berber house." In Mary Douglas, ed., Rules and Meanings: *The Anthropology of Everyday Knowledge*, 98–110. Harmondsworth: Penguin, 1977.

Boyd, D. Knickerbocker. "Standardization of Building Codes: Effect of Wall Thicknesses on Cost and Plans of Small Houses." *Architecture and Building* 53, no. 10 (Oct. 1921): 77–78.

Boyd, John Taylor, Jr. "The New York Zoning Resolution and its influence upon design." *Architectural Record* 48, no. 3 (1920): 193–218.

Boyer, Ernest, and Lee D. Mitgang. *Building Community: A New Future for Architecture Education and Practice*. New York: Carnegie Commission for the Advancement of Teaching, 1996.

Boyer, M. Christine. *Manhattan Manners: Architecture and Style, 1850–1900*. New York: Rizzoli, 1985.

Bozineki-Didonis, Paraskevi. *Greek Traditional Architecture: Crete*. Athens: Melissa, 1985.

Brain, David. "Discipline and style: The Ecole des Beaux Arts and the social production of an American architecture." *Theory and Society* 18 (1989): 807–68.

Branch, Mark Alden. "Building to learn." *Progressive Architecture* 75, no. 3 (Mar. 1994): 56–59.

Brand, Stewart. *How Buildings Learn*. New York: Viking, 1994.

Briggs, Martin. *The Architect in History*. Oxford: Clarendon Press, 1927.

British Parliament. "Report from the Commissioners of Inquiry into the Office of Works." Parliamentary Reports, 1812.

Brolin, Brent. *The Failure of Modern Architecture*. New York: Van Nostrand Reinhold, 1976.

Brown, Frank E. "Continuity and change in the urban house: Developments in domestic space organisation in seventeenth-century London." *Comparative Studies in Society and History* 28, no. 1 (Jan. 1986).

Brownell, Charles E. "Latrobe, his craftsmen, and the Corinthian order of the Hall of Representatives," in Ian M. G. Quimby, ed., *The Craftsman in Early America*, 247–72. New York: W. W. Norton, 1984.

Brueggeman, William B., and Leo D. Stone. *Real Estate Finance*. Homewood: Richard D. Irwin, 1981.

Bruner, Jerome. *Toward a Theory of Instruction*. New York: W. W. Norton, 1968.

Brunschwig. "Urbanisme medieval et droit musulman." *Revue des etudes islamiques* 16 (1947).

Brunskill, Ronald. *An Illustrated Handbook of Vernacular Architecture*. London: Faber and Faber, 1978.

Buchanan, Peter. "What is wrong with architectural education? Almost everything." *Architectural Review* 185, no. 1109 (July 1989): 24–26.

Bullard, John K. "There's no specialization like home." *Utne Reader*, Jan./Feb. 1993, 99, excerpted from *Places: A Quarterly Journal of Environmental Design* (Fall 1991).

Bunting, Bainbridge. *John Gaw Meem: Southwestern Architect*. Albuquerque: University of New Mexico Press, 1983.

Buntrock, Dana. "Collaborative production: Building opportunities in Japan." *Journal of Architectural Education* 50, no. 4 (May 1997): 219–29.

Burns, Howard. *The Portico and the Farmyard: Andrea Palladio, 1508–1580*. London: Arts Council of Great Britain and Centro Internazionale di Studi de Architettura, 1975.

California Code. "Chapter 4: Zoning Regulations." 1980.

Camille, Michael. "Prophets, canons and promising monsters." *Art Bulletin* 78, no. 2 (June 1996).

Camille, Michael, et al. "Rethinking the canon: A range of critical perspectives." *Art Bulletin* 78, no. 2 (June 1996): 198–217.

Canty, Donald. "Aerodynamic school." *Progressive Architecture* 73, no. 5 (May 1992): 142–47.

Carlhian, Jean Paul. "The Ecole des Beaux-Arts: Modes and manners." *Journal of Architectural Education* 33, no. 2 (Nov. 1979): 7–17.

Carter, Brian, ed. *Patkau Architects: Selected Projects, 1983–1993*. Halifax: TUNS Press, 1994.

Castells, Manuel. *The Rise of the Network Society*. Oxford: Blackwell, 1996.

Castellano, Aldo. *La Casa Rurale in Italia*. Milano: Edizioni Electa, 1986.

Chalklin, C. W. *The Provincial Towns of Georgian England: A Study of the Building Process, 1740–1820*. Montreal: McGill-Queens University Press, 1974.

Chambers, Thomas, and George Tattersall. *The Laws Relating to Buildings, Comprising the Metropolitan Buildings Act; Fixtures; Insurance against Fire; Action on Builders' Bills; Dilapidations; and a Copious Glossary of Technical Terms*. London: Lumley, 1844.

Chappell, Edward A. "Acculturation in the Shenandoah Valley: Rhenish houses of the Massanuten Settlement." *Proceedings of the American Philosophical Society* 124, no. 1 (Feb. 1980): 55–89, reprinted in Dell Upton and John Michael Vlach, eds., *Common Places: Readings in American Vernacular Architecture*, 27–57 (Athens: University of Georgia Press, 1986).

Charles, Prince of Wales. Speech at "Build a Better Britain" exhibition, London, Apr. 1989, quoted in Andreas C. Papadakis, ed., *Prince Charles and the Architectural Debate*, Profile 79 of *Architectural Design*. London: Academy Group Ltd., 1989.

———. *A Vision of Britain*. New York: Doubleday, 1989.

Chiaramonte, Louis. *Craftsman-Client Contracts: Interpersonal Relations in a New-foundland Fishing Community*. Vol. 10. St. John's: Institute of Social and Economic Research, Memorial University of Newfoundland, 1970.

Christian, Nichole M. "Not your father's Chrysler: At new headquarters, parking still a headache but culture improves." *Wall Street Journal*, Oct. 29, 1997, B16.

Clark, William W. "Spatial innovations in the chevet of Saint-Germain-des-Pres." *Journal of the Society of Architectural Historians* 38 (1979): 348–65.

Clark, William W., and Robert Mark. "The first flying buttresses: A new reconstruction of the nave of Notre-Dame de Paris." *Art Bulletin* 66, no. 1 (Mar. 1984): 47–65.

———. "Gothic structural experimentation." *Scientific American*, Nov. 1984, 176–85.

Clarke, Linda. *Building Capitalism: Historical Change and the Labour Process in the Production of the Built Environment*. London: Routledge, 1992.

"Classical education." *Architecture*, Nov. 1994, 117–21.

Clifton-Taylor, Alec. *The Pattern of English Building*. London: Faber, 1972.

Clipson, Colin. "Contradictions and challenges in managing design." *Journal of Architectural Education* 45, no. 4 (July 1992): 218–24.

Coaldrake, William. *The Way of the Carpenter: Tools and Japanese Architecture*. New York and Tokyo: Weatherhill, 1990.

Cohen, Jeffrey A. "Building a discipline: Early institutional settings for architectural education in Philadelphia." *Journal of the Society of Architectural Historians* 53, no. 2 (June 1994): 139–83.

Cohn, Samuel, Jr. *The Laboring Classes in Renaissance Florence*. New York: Academic Press, 1980.

Colean, Miles L. "Can the architect capture the small house?" *AIA Journal* 1 (Feb. 1944): 51–54.

Collins, George. "The transfer of thin masonry vaulting from Spain to America." *Journal of the Society of Architectural Historians* 3 (Oct. 1968): 176–201.

Collins, Peter. "The eighteenth century origins of our system of full-time architectural schooling." *Journal of Architectural Education* 33, no. 2 (Nov. 1979): 2–6.

Colvin, Howard. *A Biographical Dictionary of British Architects, 1660–1840*. New Haven: Yale University Press, 1995.

Comer, John. *New York City Building Control, 1800–1941*. New York: Columbia University Press, 1942.

Cooney, E. W. "The organisation of building in England in the 19th century." *Architectural Research and Teaching* 1, no. 2 (Nov. 1970).

———. "The origins of the Victorian master builders." *Economic History Review*, 2d ser., 8, no. 2 (Dec. 1955): 167–76.

Cosgrove, Denis. *The Palladian Landscape: Geographical Change and Its Cultural Representations in Sixteenth-Century Italy*. University Park: Pennsylvania State University Press, 1993.

Costonis, John J. *Icons and Aliens: Law, Aesthetics, and Environmental Change.* Urbana: University of Illinois Press, 1989.

Coulton, J. J. *Ancient Greek Architects at Work: Problems of Structure and Design.* Ithaca: Cornell University Press, 1977.

Crawford, Margaret. "The world in a shopping mall." In Michael Sorkin, ed. *Variations on a Theme Park: The New American City and the End of Public Space.* New York: Hill and Wang, 1992, 3–30.

"Creative team work." *Architects' Journal* 190, no. 8–9 (Aug. 23–30, 1989): 46–47.

Crinson, Mark, and Jules Lubbock. *Architecture—Art or Profession?: Three Hundred Years of Architectural Education in Britain.* Manchester: Manchester University Press, 1994.

Critchfield, Richard. *Villages.* Garden City, N.Y.: Anchor Books, 1983.

Cromley, Elizabeth. "The development of American apartment houses from the Civil War to the Depression. Introduction: Boston, Chicago, New York, and Washington: Housing context for the first apartment house development." *Architectura: Zeitschrift für Geschichte der Baukunst* 21, no. (1991): 47–52.

———. "New York, Paris, and the French flat." *Architectura: Zeitschrift für Geschichte der Baukunst* 21, no. 1 (1991): 53–67.

Crook, J. Mordaunt. "The pre-Victorian architect: Professionalism and patronage." *Architectural History* (UK) 12 (1969): 62–80.

Crosbie, Michael J. "Putting design back in design/build." *Progressive Architecture* 76, no. 12 (Dec. 1995): 54–61.

———. "The schools: How they're failing the profession (and what we can do about it)." *Progressive Architecture* 76, no. 9 (Sept. 1995): 47–51, 94, 96.

Cruickshank, Dan, and Neil Burton. *Life in the Georgian City.* London: Viking, 1990.

Cruickshank, Dan, and Peter Wyld. *London: The Art of Georgian Building.* London: Architectural Press, 1975.

Crummy, Philip. "The system of measurement used in town planning from the ninth to the thirteenth centuries." *Anglo-Saxon Studies in Archaeological History I. BAR British Series* 72 (1979): 149–64.

Cuff, Dana. *Architects: The Story of Practice.* Cambridge: MIT Press, 1991.

———. "Divisive tactics: Design-production practices in architecture." *Journal of Architectural Education* 45, no. 4 (July 1992): 204–12.

Curtis, William. "Towards an authentic regionalism." *MIMAR* 19 (1986).

Dacquisto, David J. "Why BOCA should reverse the residential '7–11' stair requirement." *Building Official and Code Administrator Magazine* 26, no. 4 (July/Aug. 1992): 24–25, 27–28.

Dacquisto, David J., and Jake Pauls. "The '7–11' stair story." *Building Official and Code Administrator Magazine* 19, no. 3 (May/June 1985): 26–35.

Dalton, Dolores Ann. "San Francisco's residential rezoning: Architectural controls in central city neighborhoods." *University of San Francisco Law Review* 13 (Summer 1979).

Davis, Colin J. "Building trades." In Kenneth T. Jackson, ed., *The Encyclopedia of New York City*, 167. New Haven and New York: Yale University Press and New-York Historical Society, 1996.

Davis, Howard. "The future of ancient lights." *Journal of Architectural and Planning Research* 6, no. 2 (Summer 1989): 132–53.

———. "Learning from Vellore." *Arcade* (Seattle) (Mar.–Apr. 1993).

Davis, Howard, David Week, and Paul Moses. "The village meets the city." *Architecture + Design* (New Delhi) (Apr.–May 1993).

Dean, Andrea Oppenheimer. "Listening to contractors." *Architectural Record* (Feb. 1998): 54–57.

Deetz, James. *In Small Things Forgotten: An Archaeology of Early American Life*. 1977. Reprint, New York: Anchor Books, 1996.

Dennis, Michael. *Court and Garden*. Cambridge: MIT Press, 1986.

Derry, T. K. "The repeal of the apprenticeship clauses of the statute of apprentices." *Economic History Review* 3, no. 1 (Jan. 1931): 67.

Domer, Dennis. "The old and new of vernacular architecture—a review essay." *Journal of Architectural Education* 42, no. 4 (1989): 45–56.

Dorris, Virginia Kent. "Single international building code to simplify the code process." *Architectural Record* 186 no. 10 (Oct. 1998): 172–73.

Dostoglu, Sibel B. "Lincoln Cathedral versus the bicycle shed." *Journal of Architectural Education* 36, no. 4 (Summer 1983): 10–15.

Duffy, Francis. "Architecture and practice: Future directions." Text of speech at Africa 2000 Conference, Cape Town, South Africa, Apr. 1995, reprinted in *Architectural Review* 198, no. 1182 (Aug. 1995): 81–83.

———. *The Changing Workplace*. London: Phaidon, 1992.

Dunlap, David W. "Lawyers who mold the shape of a city." *New York Times*, Feb. 25, 1996, sec. 9, p. 1.

Eliot, T. S. "Tradition and the individual talent." In T. S. Eliot, *Selected Essays 1917–1932*. New York: Harcourt, Brace and Company, 1932.

Ellickson, Robert C. *Order without Law: How Neighbors Settle Disputes*. Cambridge: Harvard University Press, 1991.

Ellis, John. "Realism and relevance in the Bay Area." *Architectural Review* 185, no. 1109 (July 1989): 34–37.

Erlande-Brandenburg, Alain. *The Cathedral: The Social and Architectural Dynamics of Construction*. Ed. Robin Middleton, Joseph Rykwert, and David Watkin. Trans. Martin Thom. Cambridge: Cambridge University Press, 1994.

Erlich, Mark. *With Our Hands: The Story of Carpenters in Massachusetts*. Philadelphia: Temple University Press, 1986.

Eugene, City of. Chapter 9, "Land use," in *Code of City of Eugene*.

Evans, Barrie. "Theatre in the frame." *Architects' Journal*, Feb. 15, 1996, 35–44.

Faegre, Torvald. *Tents: Architecture of the Nomads*. Garden City, N.Y.: Anchor Books, 1979.

Fainstein, Susan S. *The City Builders: Property, Politics and Planning in London and New York*. Oxford: Blackwell, 1994.

Fathy, Hassan. *Housing for the Poor*. Chicago: University of Chicago Press, 1973.

Ferguson, Jock. "The sultans of cement." *The Nation*, Aug. 3/10, 1992, 130–32.

Ferguson, R. S. "Building regulations: Problems of tradition and knowledge." *Journal of Architectural Research* 4, no. 2 (Aug. 1975).

Field, Walker. "A reexamination into the invention of the balloon frame." *Journal of the Society of Architectural Historians* 2 (1942): 3–29.

Fisher, Thomas. "Three models for the future of practice." In William S. Saunders, ed., *Reflections on Architectural Practices in the Nineties*, 36–43. New York: Princeton Architectural Press, 1996.

Fitchen, John. *The Construction of Gothic Cathedrals*. Chicago: University of Chicago Press, 1961.

Forster, Kurt. "Back to the farm: Vernacular architecture and the development of the Renaissance villa." *Architectura: Zeitschrift für Geschichte der Architektur* 1 (1974).

Frampton, Kenneth. "Ten points on an architecture of regionalism: A provisional polemic." *Center: A Journal for Architecture in America* 3 (1987): 20–27.

Frampton, Kenneth, and Kunio Kudo. *Japanese Building Practice from Ancient Times to the Meiji Period*. New York: Van Nostrand Reinhold, 1997.

Frank, Michael. "Homework." *Planning* (June 1993): 16.

Frankl, Paul. "The secret of the medieval masons." *Art Bulletin* 27 (1945): 46–60.

Frantz, Douglas. *From the Ground Up: The Business of Building in the Age of Money.* Berkeley: University of California Press, 1991.

Freiden, Susan, and Richard Winters. "Performance zoning helps city come-back." *American City and County* 112, no. 6 (June 1997): 70.

Friedman, Avi. "Residential modification of narrow front affordable Grow Homes in Montreal, Canada." *Open House International* 21, no. 2 (1996): 4–17.

Friedman, Avi, David Krawitz, Jasmin S. Frechette, Cyrus Bilimoria, and Doug Raphael. *The Next Home.* Montreal: Canadian Mortgage and Housing Corporation and the McGill University School of Architecture, 1996.

Friedman, Ziva, ed. "Model making: A model of practice." *Progressive Architecture* 76, no. 5 (May 1995): 78–83.

————. "Process: Shakespeare on the Thames." *Progressive Architecture* 76, no. 5 (May 1995): 96–103.

Frothingham, A. "The architect in history." *Architectural Record* 23 (Feb. 1908): 81–96; 24 (Nov. 1908): 321–38; 25 (Mar. 1909): 179–92; 25 (Apr. 1909): 281–303; 26 (July 1909): 55–59; 26 (Aug. 1909): 140–52.

Frug, Jerry. "The geography of community." *Stanford Law Review* 48 (May 1996): 1047–1108.

Gardner, S. "The influence of castle building on ecclesiastical architecture in the Paris region, 1130–1150." In K. Reyerson and F. Powe, eds., *The Medieval Castle, Romance and Reality*, Medieval Studies at Minnesota, no. 1, pp. 97–123. Minneapolis: University of Minnesota, 1984.

Gargan, Edward A. "Village life in India is invaded by big city tastes." *New York Times*, Apr. 16, 1992, 3.

Geertz, Clifford. "Thick description: Toward an interpretive theory of culture." In *The Interpretation of Cultures*, 3–30. New York: Basic Books, 1973.

George, Mary Carolyn Hollers. *O'Neil Ford, Architect.* College Station: Texas A&M University Press, 1992.

Girouard, Mark. *Life in the English Country House.* New Haven: Yale University Press, 1978.

Glassie, Henry. "Eighteenth-century cultural process in Delaware Valley folk building." *Winterthur Portfolio* 7 (1972): 29–57.

————. *Folk Housing in Middle Virginia: A Structural Analysis of Historic Artifacts.* Knoxville: University of Tennessee Press, 1975.

————. "The variation of concepts within tradition: Barn-building in Otsego County, New York." *Geoscience and Man* 5 (1974).

Goldthwaite, Richard. *The Building of Renaissance Florence.* Baltimore: Johns Hopkins University Press, 1980.

————. "The building of the Strozzi Palace: The construction industry in Renaissance Florence." In William M. Bowsky, ed., *Studies in Medieval and Renaissance History*, vol. 10. Lincoln: University of Nebraska Press, 1973.

————. "The Florentine palace as domestic architecture." *American Historical Review* 77 (1972): 977–1012.

Goy, Richard. *Venetian Vernacular Architecture.* Cambridge: Cambridge University Press, 1989.

Gruft, Andrew. "Seabird Island community school." *Canadian Architect* 37, no. 1 (Jan. 1992): 14–23.

Guter, Robert, and Janet W. Foster. *Building by the Book: Pattern Book Architecture in New Jersey.* New Brunswick, N.J.: Rutgers University Press, 1992.

Gutman, Robert. *The Design of American Housing: A Reappraisal of the Architect's Role.* New York: Publishing Center for Cultural Resources, 1985.

———. "Two discourses in architectural education." *Practices* (Center for the Study of Practice in Architecture) 3/4 (Spring 1995): 11–19.

Haar, Charles M., and Jerold S. Kayden, eds. *Zoning and the American Dream*. Chicago: American Planning Association, 1989.

Habraken, N. John. *Variations: The Systematic Design of Supports*. Cambridge: Laboratory of Architecture and Planning at MIT, 1976.

———. *The Structure of the Ordinary*. Cambridge: MIT Press, 1998.

Hakim, Besim. *Arabic-Islamic Cities*. London: KPI Limited, 1986.

Harper, Douglas. *Working Knowledge: Skill and Community in a Small Shop*. Chicago: University of Chicago Press, 1987.

Harvey, John. *The Gothic World*. New York: Harper & Row, 1969.

———. *The Medieval Architect*. New York: St. Martin's, 1972.

———. *Medieval Craftsmen*. London: Batsford, 1975.

Hawkes, Dean, and William Bordass. "Building study: Feilden Clegg Architects' building 16 for the BRE." *RIBA Profile*, Apr. 1997.

Hellman, Peter. "The fine art of assemblage." *Real Estate Review* 4, no. 2 (Summer 1974): 101–8.

Hillier, Bill, and Julienne Hanson. *The Social Logic of Space*. Cambridge: Cambridge University Press, 1984.

Hillier, Bill. *Space Is the Machine*. Cambridge: Cambridge University Press, 1996.

Hiss, Tony. *The Experience of Place*. New York: Knopf, 1990.

Hobhouse, Hermione. *Thomas Cubitt: Master Builder*. New York: Universe Books, 1971.

Hodgson, Fred T. *Cyclopedia of the Building Trades*. 6 vols. Chicago: American Building Trades School, 1907.

Horn, Walter. "On the origins of the medieval bay system." *Journal of the Society of Architectural Historians* 17, no. 2 (Summer 1958): 2–23.

House of Commons, Great Britain. *First Report of the Commissioners Appointed to Consider the Subject of Weights and Measures, House of Commons, 7 July 1819*. Vol. 11 of Commissioners' Reports, Appendix B, Abstract of the Statutes Relating to Weights and Measures.

Howard, Philip. *The Death of Common Sense: How Law Is Suffocating America*. New York: Random House, 1994.

Hubka, Thomas C. "The American ranch house: Traditional design method in modern popular culture." *Traditional Dwellings and Settlements Review* 7, no. 1 (1995): 33–39.

Hudson, John C. "The midland prairies: Natural resources and urban settlement." In Paul Clifford Larson and Susan M. Brown, eds. *The Spirit of H. H. Richardson on the Midland Prairies: Regional Transformations of an Architectural Style*. Ames: Iowa State University Press, 1988.

Hugh-Jones, Christine. *From the Milk River: Spatial and Temporal Processes in Northwest Amazonia*. Cambridge: Cambridge University Press, 1979.

Huxtable, Ada Louise. "New York's zoning law is out of bounds." *New York Times*, Dec. 14, 1980, II 41.

Ikujiro, Nonaka. "The knowledge-creating company." *Harvard Business Review*, Nov./Dec. 1991, 96–104.

Jackson, Kenneth, ed. *The Encyclopedia of New York City*. New Haven and New York: Yale University Press and the New-York Historical Society, 1995.

Jacobs, Jane. *The Death and Life of Great American Cities*. New York: Random House, 1961.

James, John. *Chartres: The Masons Who Built a Legend*. London: Routledge & Kegan Paul, 1982.

———. *The Contractors of Chartres*. Dooralong, Australia: Mandorla, 1979.

————. "Evidence for flying buttresses before 1180." *Journal of the Society of Architectural Historians* 51, no. 3 (Sept. 1992): 261–87.

————. "An investigation into the uneven distribution of early Gothic churches in the Paris basin, 1140–1240." *Art Bulletin* 66, no. 1 (1984): 15–46.

Janes, Elisha Harris. "The development and financing of apartment houses in New York-I." *The Brickbuilder* 17 (Dec. 1908): 276–78.

Jenkins, Frank. *Architect and Patron: A Survey of Professional Relations and Practice in England from the Sixteenth Century to the Present Day.* London: Oxford University Press, 1961.

Jeremy, Michael, and M. E. Robinson. *Ceremony and Symbolism in the Japanese Home.* Honolulu: University of Hawaii Press, 1989.

Johnson, H. Thomas. "Cathedral building and the medieval economy." *Explorations in Entrepreneurial History*, 2d ser., 4, no. 3 (Spring–Summer 1967): 191–210.

Johnson, Matthew. *Housing Culture: Traditional Architecture in an English Landscape.* Washington: Smithsonian Institution Press, 1993.

Jones, Tom, William Pettus, and Michael Pyatok. *Good Neighbors: Affordable Family Housing.* New York: McGraw-Hill, 1997.

Joseph, Delissa. "Building heights and ancient lights." *Journal of the Royal Institute of British Architects* 30, no. 15 (June 16, 1923): 477–88.

Katz, Peter. *The New Urbanism: Toward an Architecture of Community.* New York: McGraw-Hill, 1994.

Kay, Jane Holtz. "Ticky-tacky big boxes." *The Nation* 264, no. 1 (Jan. 6, 1997): 6–7.

Kaye, Barrington. "Early Architectural Societies and the Foundation of the RIBA." *RIBA Journal* 62 (Oct. 1955): 497–99.

————. "Professional Conduct in the Eighteenth and Nineteenth Centuries." *RIBA Journal* 63 (July 1956): 377–80.

Keene, Derek. *Survey of Medieval Winchester i, part I.* Oxford: Oxford University Press, 1985.

Keller, Charles, and Janet Keller. *Cognition and Tool Use: The Blacksmith at Work.* Cambridge: Cambridge University Press, 1996.

Khambatta, Ismet. "The meaning of residence in traditional Hindu society." In Jean-Paul Bourdier and Nezar Alsayyad, eds., *Dwellings, Settlements and Tradition*, 257–73. Berkeley: International Association for the Study of Traditional Environments, 1989.

King, Anthony D. *The Bungalow: The Production of a Global Culture.* London: Routledge & Kegan Paul, 1984.

Kingsford, Peter Wilfred. *Builders and Building Workers.* London: Arnold, 1973.

Kniffen, Fred. "Folk housing: Key to diffusion." *Annals of the Association of American Geographers* 55, no. 4 (Dec. 1965).

————. "Louisiana house types." *Annals of the Association of American Geographers* 26, no. 4 (Dec. 1936): 179–93.

Knoop, Douglas, and G. Jones. "The decline of the mason-architect in England." *Journal of the Royal Institute of British Architects*, Sept. 11, 1937.

————. "The first three years of the building of Vale Royal Abbey, 1278–1280: A study in operative masonry." *Trans. Quatuor Coronati Lodge* 44 (1931).

————. *The London Mason in the Seventeenth Century.* Manchester: Manchester University Press and the Quatuor Coronati Lodge, no. 2076.

————. "Masons and apprenticeship in mediaeval England." *Economic History Review* 3 (1931–32): 346–66.

————. "The rise of the mason contractor." *Journal of the Royal Institute of British Architects*, Oct. 17, 1936.

————. "The sixteenth century mason." *Ars Quatuor Coronatorum* 50, no. 3 (1937): 3–20.

Knowles, C. C., and H. Pitt. *The History of Building Regulation in London, 1189–1972*. London: Architectural Press, 1972.

Kostof, Spiro. *The Architect: Chapters in the History of the Profession*. New York: Oxford University Press, 1977.

Kouwenhoven. *The Columbia Historical Portrait of New York*. New York: Harper and Row, 1953.

Krauss, Henry. *Gold Was the Mortar: The Economics of Cathedral Building*. London: Routledge & Kegan Paul, 1979.

Krier, Leon. *Architecture and Urban Design, 1967–1992*. London: Academy Editions, 1992.

Kroll, Lucien. *An Architecture of Complexity*. Cambridge: MIT Press, 1987.

Kubelik, Martin. "Palladio's villas in the tradition of the Veneto farm." *Assemblage* 1 (Oct. 1986): 90–115.

Kunstler, James. *The Geography of Nowhere*. New York: Simon & Schuster, 1993.

————. *Home from Nowhere*. New York: Simon & Schuster, 1996.

Kwartler, Michael. "Legislating aesthetics." In Charles M. Haar and Jerold S. Kayden, eds., *Zoning and the American Dream*, 187–220. Chicago: American Planning Association, 1989.

Lai, Richard. *Law in Urban Design and Planning: The Invisible Web*. New York: Van Nostrand Reinhold, 1988.

Landau, Sarah Bradford. "The Row Houses of New York's West Side." *Journal of the Society of Architectural Historians* 34, no. 1 (Mar. 1975): 19–36.

Larson, Magali Sarfatti. *Behind the Postmodern Facade: Architectural Change in Late-Twentieth-Century America*. Berkeley: University of California Press, 1993.

Larson, Paul Clifford. "H. H. Richardson goes west: The rise and fall of an eastern star." In *The Spirit of H. H. Richardson on the Midland Prairies: Regional Transformations of an Architectural Style*. Ames: Iowa State University Press, 1988.

Lazzaro, Claudia. "Rustic country house to refined farmhouse: The evolution and migration of an architectural form." *Journal of the Society of Architectural Historians* 44 (Dec. 1985): 346–67.

Le Corbusier. *The Journey to the East*. Edited and annotated by Ivan Zaknic. Cambridge: MIT Press, 1987.

————. *Towards a New Architecture*. New York: Praeger, 1960.

LeCuyer, Annette. "Building Bilbao." *Architectural Review* 202, no. 1210 (Dec. 1997): 43–45.

Lewis, Paul. "Small loans may be key to helping Third World." *New York Times*, Jan. 26, 1997, sec. 1, p. 5.

Lindeman, Bruce. "Anatomy of land speculation." *Journal of the American Institute of Planners* 42, no. 2 (Apr. 1976): 142–52.

Lockwood, Charles. *Bricks and Brownstone: The New York Row House, 1783–1929*. New York: Abbeville Press, 1972.

Lounsbury, Carl. "The wild melody of steam: The mechanization of the manufacture of building materials, 1850–1890." In Catherine Bishir et al., *Architects and Builders in North Carolina: A History of the Practice of Building*. Chapel Hill: University of North Carolina Press, 1990.

Maass, Peter. "How to make housing affordable: Let people subdivide their homes." *U.S. News and World Report*, Dec. 30, 1996, 51–52.

Machin, R. *The Building Accounts of Mapperton Rectory, 1699–1703*. Dorset Record Society, Publication no. 8, 1983.

Maffei, Gianluigi. *La Casa Fiorentina nella Storia della Citta*. Venezia: Marsilio Editore, 1990.

Marcus, Clare Cooper. *House as a Mirror of Self: Exploring the Deeper Meaning of Home*. Berkeley: Conari Press, 1985.

Marcus, Clare Cooper, and Marni Barnes. *Gardens in Healthcare Facilities: Uses, Therapeutic Benefits, and Design Recommendations*. Martinez, Calif.: Center for Health Design, 1995.

Markus, Thomas. *Buildings and Power*. London: Routledge, 1993.

Martin, Christopher. "Skeleton of settlement: Ukrainian folk building in western North Dakota." In Thomas Carter and Bernard L. Herman, eds., *Perspectives in Vernacular Architecture III*, 86–98. Columbia: University of Missouri Press, 1989.

Martin, David. "The decline of traditional methods of timber framing in South-East England." In Neil Burton, ed., *Georgian Vernacular: Papers Given at a Georgian Group Symposium, 28 October 1995*, 27–33. London: Georgian Group, 1996.

Martin, Douglas. "Concrete deserts bloom as Parks Dept. thinks small." *New York Times*, Web edition, Mar. 4, 1998.

"Masters and men in Manchester." *The Builder* 23, no. 1189 (Nov. 18, 1865): 821.

Matthews, Kevin, Stephen Duff, and Donald Corner. "A model for integrated spatial and structural design of buildings." Conference paper, "CAADRIA 98: The Third Conference on Computer Aided Architectural Design Research in Asia," Osaka, Japan, Apr. 22–24, 1998.

Mayer, Martin. *The Builders: Houses, Peoples, Neighborhoods, Governments, Money*. New York: Norton, 1978.

McCullough, Malcolm. *Abstracting Craft: The Practiced Digital Hand*. Cambridge: MIT Press, 1996.

McDougal, Luther L., III. "Performance standards: A viable alternative to Euclidean zoning?" *Tulane Law Review* 47, no. 2 (Feb. 1973): 255–83.

McGoldrick, Joseph D., Seymour Graubard, and Raymond J. Horowitz. *Building Regulation in New York City: A Study in Administrative Law and Procedure*. New York: Commonwealth Fund, 1944.

McNeill, William H. "Diffusion in history." In Peter J. Hugill and D. Bruce Dickson, eds., *The Transfer and Transformation of Ideas and Material Culture*, 77–78. College Station: Texas A&M University Press, 1988.

Meier, Deborah. *The Power of Their Ideas: Lessons for America from a Small School in Harlem*. Boston: Beacon Press, 1995.

Meinecke, Michael. *Patterns of Stylistic Change in Islamic Architecture: Local Traditions versus Migrating Artists*. New York: New York University Press, 1996.

Michelson, William. "Most people don't want what architects want." *Trans-action* 5, no. 8 (July–Aug. 1968): 37–43.

"Mockbee's mission." *Architecture* 86, no. 1 (Jan. 1997): 49–51.

Moneo, Rafael "On typology." *Oppositions* 13 (Summer 1978).

Moonan, Wendy. "Who needs an architect?" *Architectural Record* (Nov. 1997): 117.

Moore, Steven A. "Feller–bunchers, grapple-skidders, chippers, and Martin Heidegger in the Great North Woods." *Center: Architecture and Design in America* 10 (1997).

Morley, Jane. "Building themes in construction history: Recent work by the Delaware Valley group." *Construction History* 3 (1987).

Morris, William. "The worker's share of art." Commonweal, Apr. 1885, quoted in Asa Briggs, ed., *William Morris: Selected Writings and Designs*, 140–41. Harmondsworth: Penguin, 1962.

Moudon, Anne Vernez. *Built for Change: Neighborhood Architecture in San Francisco*. Cambridge: MIT Press, 1986.

Moxon, Joseph. *Mechanick Exercises or the Doctrine of Handy-Works*. London, 1703. Reprint, Morristown, N.J.: Astragal Press, 1989.

Mulfinger, Dale. *The Architecture of Edwin Lundie*. St. Paul: Minnesota Historical Society Press, 1995.

Murphy, Richard. *Carlo Scarpa and the Castelvecchio*. London: Butterworth, 1990.

Murray, Robert, and Kermit Baker. "Architecture market outlook: Two crystal balls." *Architectural Record* 184, no. 6 (June 1996): 36–39.

Muthesius, Stefan. *The English Terraced House*. New Haven: Yale University Press, 1982.

Nabokov, Peter, and Robert Easton. *Native American Architecture*. New York: Oxford University Press, 1989.

National Association of Home Builders. *1997 Housing Facts, Figures, and Trends*.

Nijst, A. L. M. T., et al. *Living on the Edge of the Sahara: A Study of Traditional Forms of Habitation and Types of Settlement in Morocco*. The Hague: Government Printing Office, 1973.

Nonaka, Ikujiro. "The knowledge-creating company." *Harvard Business Review*, Nov./Dec. 1991, 96–104.

Nonaka, Ikujiro, and Hirotaka Takeuchi. *The Knowledge-Creating Company: How Japanese Companies Created the Dynamics of Innovation*. New York: Oxford University Press, 1994.

Norberg-Hodge, Helena. "Break up the monoculture: Why the drive to create a homogenized world must inevitably fail." *The Nation*, July 15/22, 1996.

Norberg-Schulz, Christian. *Nightlands*. Cambridge: MIT Press, 1996.

Oliver, Paul. Dwellings: *The House across the World*. Austin: University of Texas Press, 1987.

———, ed. *Encyclopedia of Vernacular Architecture of the World*. Cambridge: Cambridge University Press, 1997.

Olsen, Donald. *Town Planning in London: The Eighteenth and Nineteenth Centuries*. New Haven: Yale University Press, 1964.

Orth, Myra Dickman. "The influence of the 'American Romanesque' in Australia." *Journal of the Society of Architectural Historians* 34, no. 1 (Mar. 1975): 3–18.

Orum-Nielsen, Jørn. *Dwelling—At Home, in Community, on Earth: The Significance of Tradition in Contemporary Housing*. Copenhagen: Danish Architectural Press, 1996.

Palladio, Andrea. *The Four Books of Architecture*. New York: Dover Publications, 1965.

Parks, Janet, and Alan G. Neumann. *The Old World Builds the New: The Guastavino Company and the Technology of the Catalan Vault, 1885–1962*. New York: Avery Architectural and Fine Arts Library and the Miriam and Ira D. Wallach Art Gallery, 1996.

Pawley, Martin. "A precedent for the Prince." *Architectural Review* 187, no. 1115 (Jan. 1990): 80–82.

Peckham, W. D. "Chichester city deeds." *Sussex Archaeological Collections* 89 (1950).

Pevsner, Nikolaus. *The Englishness of English Art*. London: Architectural Press, 1956.

———. *An Outline of European Architecture*. Harmondsworth: Penguin, 1963.

Pinkney, David H. *Napoleon III and the Rebuilding of Paris*. Princeton: Princeton University Press, 1958.

Plunz, Richard. *A History of Housing in New York City*. New York: Columbia University Press, 1990.

Polanyi, Michael. *Personal Knowledge*. Chicago: University of Chicago Press, 1962.

Popper, Karl. *The Poverty of Historicism*. Boston: Beacon Press, 1957.

Port, M. H. "The office of works and contracts in early-nineteenth-century England." *Economic History Review*, 2d ser., 20 (1967).

Porter, Theodore M. *Trust in Numbers: The Pursuit of Objectivity in Science and Public Life*. Princeton: Princeton University Press, 1995.

Porzelt, Paul. *The Metropolitan Club of New York*. New York: Rizzoli, 1982.

Powers, Alan. "Back in the frame." *Perspectives in Architecture*, Feb./Mar. 1998, 52–55.

Pyatok, Michael. "Neighborhood development in a democratic city: Toward a 'real' urbanism." *Arcade* 15, no. 2 (Winter 1996): 6–8, 45.

Quiney, Anthony. *House and Home: A History of the Small English House*. London: British Broadcasting Corporation, 1986.

Redfield, Robert. *Peasant Society and Culture*. Chicago: University of Chicago Press, 1956.

Reed, Peter. "Form and context: A study of Georgian Edinburgh." In Thomas Markus, ed., *Order in Space and Society: Architectural Form and Its Context in the Scottish Enlightenment*. Edinburgh: Mainstream Publishing, 1982.

Real Estate Record and Builder's Guide. *A History of Real Estate, Building, and Architecture in New York City, 1868–1893*. New York, 1894.

Revault, Jacques. *Palais et Demeures de Tunis (XVI et XVII siècles)*. Paris: Éditions du Centre National de la Recherche Scientifique, 1967.

Rifkind, Carole, "America's Fantasy urbanism: the waxing of the mall and the waning of civility." In Katherine Washburn and John Thornton, eds., *Dumbing Down: Essays on the Strip-Mining of American Culture*. New York: W. W. Norton, 1996, 261–69.

Riis, Jacob. *How the Other Half Lives*. New York: Dover, 1971.

Ritzdorf, Marsha. "Zoning barriers to residential innovation." *Journal of Planning Education and Research* 4, no. 3 (Apr. 1995): 177–84.

Rogers, Louise, "The power of persuasion." *Journal of the Royal Institute of British Architects* 100, no. 8 (Aug. 1993): 12–13.

Rose, Walter. *The Village Carpenter*. Cambridge: Cambridge University Press, 1937.

Rosenfeld, Myra Nan. *Sebastiano Serlio on Domestic Architecture: Different Dwellings from the Meanest Hovel to the Most Ornate Palace*. London and Cambridge: Architectural History Foundation and MIT Press, 1978.

Rossi, Aldo. *The Architecture of the City*. Cambridge: MIT Press, 1984.

Rossi, Aldo, Eraldo Consolascio, and Max Bosshard. *La Construzione del Territorio: Uno Studio sul Canton Ticino*. Milano: Cooperative Libraria Universitaria del Politecnico, 1986.

Roth, Leland. *McKim Mead and White, Architects*. New York: Harper & Row, 1983.

Roulac, Stephen E. "Anatomy of a land deal." *Real Estate Review* 4, no. 4 (Winter 1975): 93–96.

Rybczynski, Witold, Avi Friedman, and Susan Ross. *The Grow Home*. Montreal: Affordable Homes Program, School of Architecture, McGill University, 1990.

Rykwert, Joseph. *The Idea of a Town*. Cambridge: MIT Press, 1988.

———. "On the oral transmission of architectural theory." *AA Files* 6 (May 1984): 14–27.

Saalman, Howard. "Designing the Pazzi chapel: The problem of metrical analysis." *Architectura: Zeitschrift für Geschichte der Baukunst* 9, no. 1 (1979): 1–5.

Salpukas, Agis. "Fill it up? Send a fax? Have a taco?" *New York Times*, national edition, Dec. 27, 1993, C1.

Salzman, L. F. *Building in England down to 1540*. Oxford: Oxford University Press, 1952.

San Francisco, City and County of. *City Planning Code*. 1979.

Santelli, Serge. *Medinas: Traditional Architecture of Tunisia*. Tunis: Dar Ashraf Editions, 1992.

Saunders, William S., ed., *Reflections on Architectural Practices in the Nineties*. New York: Princeton Architectural Press, 1996.

Schofield, John. *Medieval London Houses*. New Haven: Yale University Press, 1994.

Scruton, Roger. "Vernacular architecture." In *The Classical Vernacular: Architectural Principles in an Age of Nihilism*. New York: St. Martin's Press, 1994.

Scully, Vincent. *American Architecture and Urbanism*. New York: Praeger, 1969.

Semmler, Ricardo. *Maverick*. New York: Warner Books, 1993.

Sesser, Stan. "Logging the rain forest." *New Yorker*, May 27, 1991, 42.

Shaw, Diane. "The construction of the private in medieval London." *Journal of Medieval and Early Modern Studies* 26, no. 3 (Fall 1996): 447–66.

Shelby, L. "The contractors of Chartres." *Gesta* 20 (1980): 173–78.

Shelby, Lon R. "The education of medieval English master masons." *Mediaeval Studies* 32 (1970): 1–26.

———. "The 'secret' of the medieval masons." In B. Hall and D. West, eds., *On Pre-Modern Technology and Science*, 201–19. Malibu, 1976.

Sheppard, F. H. W., ed. *Survey of London: The Parish of St. James Westminster: Part One, South of Piccadilly*. London, 1960.

———. *Survey of London*, vol. 27: *Spitalfields and Mile End New Town*. London: Athlone Press, 1957.

Shils, Edward. *Tradition*. Chicago: University of Chicago Press, 1981.

Shuman, Michael H. "Going local: devolution for progressives." *The Nation* 267, no. 11 (Oct. 12, 1998): 11–15.

Silverman, Edwin H. "Architecture is a business!" *Pencil Points* 20 (Dec. 1939): 780–90.

Simpson, Pamela. "Cheap, quick, and easy: The early history of rockfaced concrete block building." In *Perspectives in Vernacular Architecture III*, 108–18. Columbia: University of Missouri Press, 1989.

———. "Cheap, quick, and easy, part II: Pressed metal ceilings, 1880–1930," in Elizabeth Collins Cromley and Carter L. Hudgins, eds., *Gender, Class, and Shelter: Perspectives in Vernacular Architecture V*, 152–63. Knoxville: University of Tennessee Press, 1995.

Slater, T. R. "The analysis of burgage patterns in medieval towns." *Area* 13, no. 3 (1981): 211–16.

Slessor, Catherine. "Atlantic star." *Architectural Review* 202, no. 1210 (Dec. 1997): 30–42.

Sobin, Harris. "The role of regional vernacular traditions in the genesis of Le Corbusier's brise-soleil sun-shading techniques." In Nezar Alsayyad, ed., *Architects and the Reinterpretation of Tradition*, 43–71, vol. 74 of the series "Traditional Dwellings and Settlements Working Papers." Berkeley: Center for Environmental Design Research, University of California at Berkeley.

Solomon, Nancy B. "Design/build ventures." *Architecture*, Sept. 1991, 107–12.

Speidel, Manfred, ed. *Team ZOO Buildings and Projects, 1971–1990*. New York: Rizzoli, 1991.

Spence, Rory. "Community spirit." *Architectural Review* 189, no. 1136 (Oct. 1991): 56–60.

———. "Constructive education." *Architectural Review* 185, no. 1109 (July 1989): 27–33.

————. "Grass roots tech." *Architectural Review* 181, no. 1085 (July 1987): 58–63.

Sprunt, R. "Building knowledge and building law." *Journal of Architectural Research* 4, no. 3 (Dec. 1975): 10–16.

Stanton, Gary. "'Alarmed by the cry of fire': How fire changed Fredericksburg, Virginia." In Carter L. Hudgins and Elizabeth Collins Cromley, eds., *Shaping Communities: Perspectives in Vernacular Architecture VI*, 122–34. Knoxville: University of Tennessee Press, 1997.

Steele, James. "The cosmic connection." *World Architecture* 44 (Mar. 1996): 52.

Stephenson, Elliott O. "The silent and inviting trap." *Building Official and Code Administrator* (Nov./Dec. 1988): 29.

Stern, Robert A. M., Gregory Gilmartin, and John Massengale. *New York 1900: Metropolitan Architecture and Urbanism, 1890–1915*. New York: Rizzoli, 1983.

Stevenson, Katherine Cole, and H. Ward Jandl. *Houses by Mail: A Guide to Houses from Sears, Roebuck and Company*. Washington: Preservation Press, 1986.

Sturges, Will. "Design and Construction at the University of Oregon." *Friends of Kebyar* 14, no. 60 (Sept. 1995–June 1996).

Sturt, George. *The Wheelwright's Shop*. Cambridge: Cambridge University Press, 1923.

Suhrbuhr, Thomas J. "The economic transformation of carpentry in late-nineteenth-century Chicago." *Illinois Historical Journal* 81 (Summer 1988): 109–24.

Sullivan, R. Lee. "Exxonsafeway." *Forbes*, Mar. 11, 1996, 106.

Summerson, John. "Charting the Victorian building world." In *The Unromantic Castle and Other Essays*. London: Thames and Hudson, 1990.

————. *Georgian London*. Harmondsworth: Penguin, 1962.

————. "The London building world of the 1860s." In *The Unromantic Castle and Other Essays*. London: Thames and Hudson, 1990.

Sweeney, James Johnson, and Josep Lluis Sert. *Antoni Gaudi*. New York: Praeger, 1960.

Symonds, Margaret. *Days Spent on a Doge's Farm*. London: T. Fisher Unwin, 1893.

Tanizaki, Juni-chiro. *In Praise of Shadows*. New Haven, Conn.: Leete's Island Books, 1977.

Tate, W. E. *The Enclosure Movement*. New York: Walker, 1967.

Taylor, Brian Brace. *Geoffrey Bawa*. Singapore: Concept Media, 1986.

Thompson, E. *Customs in Common*. New York: New Press, 1991.

————. "Time, work-discipline, and industrial capitalism." *Past and Present* 38 (Dec. 1967): 56–97.

Thompson, F. M. L. *Chartered Surveyors: The Growth of a Profession*. London: Routledge & Kegan Paul, 1968.

Tindall, Gillian. *City of Gold: The Biography of Bombay*. New Delhi: Penguin, 1992.

Tuan, Yi-Fu. *Topophilia: A Study of Environmental Perception, Attitudes, and Values*. (Englewood Cliffs, N.J.: Prentice-Hall, 1974).

Turner, John. *Freedom to Build*. New York: Macmillan, 1972.

————. *Housing by People*. London: Marion Boyars, 1976.

Underwood, Dan. "Snake charmer." *Architectural Review* 200, no. 1197 (Nov. 1996): 46–51.

"Upscaled and up to date: Upgrading food courts boosts sales 20%–25%." *Chain Store Age Executive*, Nov. 1989, 76.

Upton, Dell. "Outside the academy: A century of vernacular architecture studies, 1890–1990." *Studies in the History of Art* 35 (1990): 199–213.

————. "Pattern books and professionalism: Aspects of the transformation of domestic architecture in America." *Winterthur Portfolio* 19, no. 2–3 (Autumn 1984): 107–50.

Upton, Dell, and John Michael Vlach, eds. *Common Places: Readings in American Vernacular Architecture*. Athens: University of Georgia Press, 1986.

Ventre, Francis T. "Regulation: A realization of social ethics." *VIA* 10 (1990): 51–61.

Waid, D. Everett. "The business side of an architect's office." *The Brickbuilder* 22, no. 8 (1913): 179–81, 197–200.

Wallace, William E. *Michelangelo at San Lorenzo: The Genius as Entrepreneur*. Cambridge: Cambridge University Press, 1994.

Walljasper, Jay. "What works? Denmark!" *The Nation* 266, no. 3 (Jan. 26, 1998): 22–24.

Warner, Sam Bass. *Streetcar Suburbs: The Process of Growth in Boston, 1870–1900*. Cambridge: Harvard University Press, 1962.

Waterman, Thomas W. *A Practical Treatise on the Law Relating to the Specific Performance of Contracts*. New York: Baker, Voorhis & Co., 1881.

Waterson, Roxana. *The Living House: An Anthropology of Architecture in Southeast Asia*. Singapore: Oxford University Press, 1990.

Week, David. *The Culture of Work*. Forthcoming.

Weiss, Marc A. *The Rise of the Community Builders: The American Real Estate Industry and Urban Land Planning*. New York: Columbia University Press, 1987.

White, John R., ed., *The Office Building: From Concept to Investment Reality*. Chicago and Washington: Counselors of Real Estate (American Society of Real Estate Counselors), the Appraisal Institute, and the Society of Industrial and Office Realtors Educational Fund, 1993.

Wilensky, Harold L. "The professionalization of everyone?" *American Journal of Sociology* 70, no. 2 (Sept. 1964): 143.

Williams, David. "An indigenous architecture." *Southwest Review* 14 (1928/29): 67–68.

Williams, Gerry, ed. *Apprenticeship in Craft*. Goffstown, N.H.: Daniel Clark Books, 1981.

Williamson, Roxanne. *American Architects and the Mechanics of Fame*. Austin: University of Texas Press, 1991.

Willis, Carol. *Form Follows Finance: Skyscrapers and Skylines in New York and Chicago*. New York: Princeton Architectural Press, 1995.

Wilson, Chris. *The Myth of Santa Fe*. Albuquerque: University of New Mexico Press, 1997.

Wislocki, Peter. "A model practice." *Architects' Journal* 193, no. 6 (Feb. 6, 1991): 28–31.

Yeomans, David. *The Architect and the Carpenter*. London: RIBA Heinz Gallery, 1992.

———. *The Trussed Roof*. Aldershot: Scolar Press, 1992.

Zeldin, Theodore. *An Intimate History of Humanity*. London: Minerva, 1994.

Zukin, Sharon. "Landscapes of economic value." *Center: Architecture and Design in America* 10 (1997): 134–45.

CREDITS

Figure 6.13. Howard Davis

Figure 6.14. Drawn by John Paull

Figure 6.15. Howard Davis

Figure 6.16. Map drawn by John Paull

Figure 6.17. Drawn by John Paull after Palladio, *The Four Books of Architecture*

Figure 6.18. Drawn by John Paull after *La Casa Rurale in Italia*

Figure 6.19. Jenny Young

Figure 6.20. Jenny Young

Figure 6.21. Courtesy of Paul Larson

Figure 6.22. Howard Davis

Figure 6.23. Howard Davis

Figure 6.24. Howard Davis

Figure 6.25. Howard Davis

Figure 6.26. Howard Davis

Figure 6.27. From *House and Home* (1986), © Anthony Quiney

Figure 6.28. Howard Davis

Figure 6.29. Howard Davis

Figure 6.30. Drawn by John Paull after Plunz, *A History of Housing in New York City*

Figure 6.31. Howard Davis

Figure 6.32. Howard Davis

Figure 6.33. Eugene Atget. *Rue du Jour*, c. 1925. Albumen print, 8 5/8 x 6 13/16". The Museum of Modern Art, New York. Abbott-Levy Collection. Partial gift of Shirly C. Burden. Photograph © 1998 The Museum of Modern Art, New York.

Figure 7.1. Eugene Atget. *Place du Tertre*, 1922. Albumen-silver print, 7 x 9 3/8" (18 x 24 cm). The Museum of Modern Art, New York. Abbott-Levy Collection. Partial gift of Shirley C. Burden. Print by Chicago Albumen Works, 1981. Copy print © 1998 The Museum of Modern Art, New York.

Figure 7.2. Howard Davis

Figure 7.3. Drawn by Anup Janardhanan and Howard Davis

Figure 7.4. Howard Davis

Figure 7.5. Peter Wyld

Figure 7.6. Unknown. From *The Book of Trades and Useful Arts* (London, 1821). "The Bricklayer" (opp. p. 45). Engraving. Page: 6 15/16 x 3 7/8 in (17.6 x 9.8 cm). Spine: 7 x 1 1/4 in (17/8 c 3/2 cm.). Yale Center for British Art, Paul Mellon Collection. T47 B73 1821

Figure 7.7. Unknown. From *The Book of Trades and Useful Arts* (London,

1821). "The Brick Maker" (opp. p. 49). Engraving. Page: 6 15/16 x 3 7/8 in (17.6 x 9.8 cm). Spine: 7 x 1 1/4 in (17/8 c 3/2 cm.). Yale Center for British Art, Paul Mellon Collection. T47 B73 1821

Figure 7.8. Unknown. From *The Book of Trades and Useful Arts* (London, 1821). "The Carpenter" (opp. p. 70). Engraving. Page: 6 15/16 x 3 7/8 in (17.6 x 9.8 cm). Spine: 7 x 1 1/4 in (17/8 c 3/2 cm.). Yale Center for British Art, Paul Mellon Collection. T47 B73 1821

Figure 7.9. Unknown. From *The Book of Trades and Useful Arts* (London, 1821). "The Plumbers" (opp. p. 256). Engraving. Page: 6 7/16 x 3 7/8 in (16.4 x 9.8 cm). Spine: 7 x 1 1/4 in (17/8 c 3/2 cm.). Yale Center for British Art, Paul Mellon Collection. T47 B73 1821

Figure 7.10. Unknown. From *The Book of Trades and Useful Arts* (London, 1821). "The Sawyer" (opp. p. 282). Engraving. Page: 6 15/16 x 3 7/8 in (17.6 x 9.8 cm). Spine: 7 x 1 1/4 in (17/8 c 3/2 cm.). Yale Center for British Art, Paul Mellon Collection. T47 B73 1821

Figure 7.11. Unknown. From *The Book of Trades and Useful Arts* (London, 1821). "The Stone Mason" (opp. p. 316). Engraving. Page: 6 15/16 x 3 7/8 in (17.6 x 9.8 cm). Spine: 7 x 1 1/4 in (17/8 c 3/2 cm.). Yale Center for British Art, Paul Mellon Collection. T47 B73 1821

Figure 7.12. Diderot's *Encyclopedia*

Figure 7.13. U.S. Gypsum/David Joel

Figure 7.14. Howard Davis

Figure 7.15. Diderot's *Encyclopedia*

Figure 7.16. Pilkington plc

Figure 7.17. Real Estate Record and Guide, January 7, 1893. Avery Architectural and Fine Arts Library, Columbia University in the City of New York

Figure 7.18. © Alvin Comiter

Figure 7.19. Donald B. Corner

Figure 7.20. Peter A. Keyes

Figure 8.1. Drawn by Anup Janardhanan after Brunskill, *Illustrated Handbook of Vernacular Architecture*

Figure 8.2. British Architectural Library, RIBA, London

Figure 8.3. London Metropolitan Archives. By kind permission of the Marquess of Tavistock and the Trustees of the Bedford Estates

Figure 8.4. British Architectural Library, RIBA, London

Figure 8.5. Howard Davis

Figure 8.6. Howard Davis

Figure 8.7. Howard Davis

Figure 8.8. Howard Davis

Figure 8.9. London Metropolitan Archives. By kind permission of the Marquess of Tavistock and the Trustees of the Bedford Estates

Figure 8.10. Howard Davis

Figure 8.11. *Building News*, May 26, 1876.

Figure 8.12. Howard Davis

Figure 8.13. © Collection of The New-York Historical Society

Figure 8.14. Drawn by John Paull

Figure 8.15. Drawn by Anup Janard-hanan

Figure 9.1. Drawn by John Paul after Santelli, *Medinas*

Figure 9.2. Drawn by Kevin Sauser and Anup Janardhanan

Figure 9.3. Howard Davis

Figure 9.4. Howard Davis

Figure 9.5. Howard Davis

Figure 9.6. Drawn by Peter DeMaria

Figure 9.7. Drawn by Peter DeMaria

Figure 9.8. Howard Davis

Figure 9.9. Howard Davis

Figure 9.10. Donald B. Corner

Figure 10.1. Eugene Atget. *Chatenay, rue Sainte-Catherine*, 1901. Albumen silver print, 7 x 9 3/8" (18 x 24 cm). The Museum of Modern Art, New York. Abbott-Levy Collection. Partial gift of Shirley C. Burden. Photograph © 1998 The Museum of Modern Art, New York.

Figure 10.2. Howard Davis

Figure 10.3. Stephen Duff

Figure 10.4. Stephen Duff

Figure 10.5. Stephen Duff

Figure 10.6. From Moxon, *Mechanick Exercises*

Figure 10.7. From Diderot's *Encyclopedia*

Figure 10.8. From Moxon, *Mechanick Exercises*

Figure 10.9. © Alvin Comiter

Figure 10.10. Courtesy of Philip Dole

Figure 10.11. Courtesy of Philip Dole

Figure 10.12. From *Masonry Carpentry Joinery*, International Library of Technology series beginning 1899

Figure 10.13. Howard Davis

Figure 10.14. Donald B. Corner

Figure 10.15. Christie Coffin

Figure 10.16. Christie Coffin

Figure 10.17. Howard Davis

Figure 10.18. National Gallery, London

Figure 11.1. Hajo Neis

Figure 11.2. Hajo Neis

Figure 11.3. Hajo Neis

Figure 11.4. Hajo Neis

Figure 11.5. Howard Davis

Figure 11.6. Howard Davis

Figure 11.7. Howard Davis

Figure 11.8. Hajo Neis

Figure 11.9. Hajo Neis

Figure 11.10. Hajo Neis

Figure 11.11. Hajo Neis

Figure 11.12. Hajo Neis

Figure 11.13. Howard Davis

Figure 11.14. Howard Davis

Figure 11.15. Howard Davis

Figure 11.16. Howard Davis

Figure 11.17. Avi Friedman/Affordable Homes Program, McGill University

Figure 11.18. Avi Friedman/Affordable Homes Program, McGill University

Figure 11.19. Center for Environmental Structure

Figure 11.20. Center for Environmental Structure

Figure 12.1. Greg Burgess

Figure 12.2. Greg Burgess

Figure 12.3. Rasem Badran

Figure 12.4. Rasem Badran

Figure 12.5. Rasem Badran

Figure 12.5a. Rasem Badran

Figure 12.6. Howard Davis

Figure 12.7. Peter A. Keyes

Figure 12.8. Drawn by John Paull after plans in Orum-Nielsen, *Dwelling*

Figure 12.9. Peter A. Keyes

Figure 12.10. Peter A. Keyes

Figure 12.11. Howard Davis

Figure 12.12. Howard Davis

Figure 12.13. Patkau Architects

Figure 12.14. Patkau Architects

Figure 12.15. Bill Gilland

Figure 12.16. Bill Gilland

Figure 12.17. Greg Burgess

Figure 12.18. Howard Davis

Figure 12.19. Howard Davis

Figure 12.20. Greg Burgess

INDEX

Numbers in *italics* indicate pages with illustrations.

construction
architect-client-builder relationship, 198–99
dispersion of control in,
195–200
construction loans, contemporary, 165
construction management, 252–53
construction organization
Japanese, 253–54
in Renaissance Florence, 53
construction practice, innovative,
310–13
construction work, U.S.
developers, 69–72, 74–77
volume, 68
contracts by measure, 183
contracts in gross, 183
control of money in building
in contemporary building culture, 165
eighteenth-century England, 164
Renaissance Florence, 164
convenience store/gas station, 155,
156
Copenhagen, 307, *307*, *308*
Corippo, *28*, *29*
Corner, Donald, *81*
Correa, Charles, 284
cosmic order, representation of, in
villages, 29
Costigan, Ken, 303, 306
courtyard buildings, Middle East
cities, 135–39
courtyard houses, Tunis, 137–39, *138*,
139
Covent Garden, theater, *163*
craft, and apprenticeship, 108–12
craftsmanship
careful work and typological
invention, 222
characteristics, 219
discretion and human judgment,
220–22
feedback in, 219, 238
as modern process, 245
urban, 235–238
Creek Native American ground, *31*
Critchfield, Richard, 37
Crosbie, Michael, 125
cross-fertilization of rules and types,
132
cruck building, *36*
Cruickshank, Dan, 171
Cubitt, Thomas, 115, *117*, 172–73, 197
cultural sustainability, 15–16
customary practice and law, 341 n. 1

Dallas, *94*
DEGW, 313
Delft, *7*
Denmark
contemporary houses, 281–82
Copenhagen, 307, *307*, *308*
traditional houses, 281–82
Denning, Thomas, 134
design review, 313–14
design-build, 336 n. 35
in architecture schools, 316–18,
316
developers, 69–71, 74–77, 114–18
Dickinson v. Harbottle, 209
diffusion of building types, 132–50
discretion, and craftsmanship, 220–22
distribution of value in built environment, 160–65
Duany, Andres, 314
Duff, Stephen, *317*, 318
Duffy, Francis, 270, 313
Dunn, Thomas, 133

Ecole des Beaux Arts, 123–24
Edgar's Farm, *225*
Edinburgh, New Town of, 99
Egypt, New Gourna, 323–24
Eishin School, 246–49, *247*, *248*, *249*,
253, 259, 276
El-Wakil, Abdelwahed, 259
Eldem, Sedad, 19, 284
Ellis, Thomas, 134
enclosure, of common fields, 104–5
England, building process
building societies, 115
eighteenth-century, control of
money for building, 164
fifteenth-century farmhouse,
value added in construction,
166–72
See also London
England, buildings and places
Abbotsbury, Dorset, *261*
Bath, *14*
Bengough's House, Bristol, *291*
cruck building, Lacock, *36*
early farmhouses, 150–51
Great Coxwell barn, *225*
nucleated agricultural village,
33–37, *35*
Sherbourne Abbey, *96*
Stowmarket, Edgar's Farm, *225*
Thurlaston, *35*
Woolpit, St. Mary's Church,
226
See also London